About Island Press

Island Press is the only nonprofit organization in the United States whose principal purpose is the publication of books on environmental issues and natural resource management. We provide solutions-oriented information to professionals, public officials, business and community leaders, and concerned citizens who are shaping responses to environmental problems.

In 1994, Island Press celebrated its tenth anniversary as the leading provider of timely and practical books that take a multidisciplinary approach to critical environmental concerns. Our growing list of titles reflects our commitment to bringing the best of an expanding body of literature to the environmental community throughout North America and the world.

Support for Island Press is provided by Apple Computer, Inc., The Bullitt Foundation, The Geraldine R. Dodge Foundation, The Energy Foundation, The Ford Foundation, The W. Alton Jones Foundation, The Lyndhurst Foundation, The John D. and Catherine T. MacArthur Foundation, The Andrew W. Mellon Foundation, The Joyce Mertz-Gilmore Foundation, The National Fish and Wildlife Foundation, The Pew Charitable Trusts, The Pew Global Stewardship Initiative, The Philanthropic Collaborative, Inc., and individual donors.

About The Global Development And Environment Institute

The Global Development And Environment Institute (G-DAE) was founded in 1993 to combine research and curricular development activities of two ongoing programs at Tufts University: the Program for the Study of Sustainable Change and Development in the School of Arts and Sciences, and the International Environment and Resource Policy Program at the Fletcher School of Law and Diplomacy. The combination creates a center of expertise in economics, policy, science, and technology.

G-DAE works toward understanding actual and possible past and future trajectories of economic development, emphasizing the relation between social and economic well-being on the one hand and ecological health on the other. It develops an improved theoretic understanding of economic systems as they are embedded in the physical contexts of history, politics, ethics, culture, institutions, and human motivations and goals. Finally, it assists the public and private sectors of nations at different stages of development to develop policies that promote sustainability. G-DAE pursues its goals through research, publication projects, curriculum development, networking, and policy work.

HUMAN
WELL-BEING
AND
ECONOMIC
GOALS

FRONTIER ISSUES IN ECONOMIC THOUGHT
VOLUME 3
NEVA R. GOODWIN, SERIES EDITOR

Titles published by Island Press
in the Frontier Issues in Economic Thought series include:

R. Krishnan, J. M Harris, and N. R. Goodwin (eds.),
A Survey of Ecological Economics, 1995

N. R. Goodwin, F. Ackerman, and D. Kiron (eds.),
The Consumer Society, 1997

Upcoming volumes
in the Frontier Issues in Economic Thought series address:

The Changing Nature of Work
Inequality and Market Power
Sustainable Development

HUMAN WELL-BEING AND ECONOMIC GOALS

Edited by
Frank Ackerman,
David Kiron,
Neva R. Goodwin,
Jonathan M. Harris,
and Kevin Gallagher

The Global Development
And Environment Institute
Tufts University

ISLAND PRESS

Washington, D.C. ■ Covelo, California

Library of Congress Cataloging-in-Publication Data

Human well-being and economic goals / edited by Frank Ackerman . . . [et al.].
    p. cm.
  "A research and publication project of the Program for the Study of Sustainable Change and Development, The Global Development And Environment Institute, Tufts University."
  Includes bibliographical references and index.
  ISBN 1-55963-560-6 (cloth). — ISBN 1-55963-561-4 (paper)
  1. Neoclassical school of economics. 2. Economic man. 3. Values.
4. Utility theory. 5. Welfare economics. I. Ackerman, Frank.
II. Program for the Study of Sustainable Change and Development
(Tufts University. Global Development And Environment Institute)
HB98.2.H85 1997
330.15'7—dc21   97-36687
                                                       CIP

To Amartya K. Sen,
with appreciation for the fresh thinking
and the breadth he has brought to economics

Note to the Reader

In general, the summaries presented here do not repeat material from the original articles verbatim. In a few instances it has seemed appropriate to include in the summaries direct quotations from the original text ranging from a phrase to a few sentences. Where this has been done, the page reference to the original article is given in square brackets. The complete citation for the article always appears at the beginning of the summary. References to other books or articles appear in endnotes following each summary.

Contents

PART I
Interdisciplinary Perspectives on Well-Being

Contents   xi

PART V
Economics and the Good, I: Individuals

PART VI
Economics and the Good, II: Community

PART VII
Economics and the Good, III: Society

PART VIII
National Development: From Basic Needs to the Welfare State

PART IX
Critiques of National Income Accounting and GNP

PART X
Alternatives to Gross National Product: A Critical Survey

Authors of Original Articles

George Akerlof Dept. of Economics, University of California, Berkeley, California

Elizabeth Anderson Dept. of Philosophy, University of Michigan, Ann Arbor, Michigan

Kenneth Arrow Dept. of Economics, Stanford University, Stanford, California

Nahid Aslanbeigui Dept. of Economics and Finance, Monmouth University, West Long Branch, New Jersey

Nicholas Barr Dept. of Economics, London School of Economics and Political Science, London, United Kingdom

Nancy Birdsall Vice President of Inter-American Development Bank, World Bank, Washington, DC

R. D. Collison Black Dept. of Economics, Queen's University of Belfast, Belfast, Ireland

Fred Block Dept. of Sociology, University of California, Davis, California

John Bonner Dept. of Economics,University of Leicester, Leicester, United Kingdom

Daniel Bromley Dept. of Agricultural and Applied Economics, University of Wisconsin, Madison, Wisconsin

John Broome Dept. of Moral Philosophy, University of St. Andrews, Fife, United Kingdom

James T. Campen Dept. of Economics, University of Massachusetts, Boston, Massachusetts

Ann Chadeau Dept. de Administrations, Institute Université de Technologie, Paris, France

James S. Coleman (deceased)

Robert Cooter Dept. of Law, University of California, Berkeley, California

David A. Crocker Institute for Philosophy and Public Policy, University of Maryland, College Park, Maryland

Partha Dasgupta Dept. of Economics, St. John's College, Cambridge, Cambridgeshire, United Kingdom

Robert Eisner Dept. of Economics, Northwestern University, Evanston, Illinois

Gøsta Esping-Andersen Facoltia ai Sociologia, University of Trento, Trento, Italy

Marc Fleurbaey Dept. de Economie, Université de Cergy Pontoise, France

Robert H. Frank Dept. of Economics, Cornell University, Ithaca, New York

Bruno S. Frey Institute for Empirical Economic Research, University of Zurich, Zurich, Switzerland

Robert S. Goldfarb Dept. of Sociology, George Washington University, Washington, DC

Ian Gough Dept. of Social Administration, The University of Manchester, Greater Manchester, United Kingdom

Robin Hahnel Dept. of Economics, American University, Washington, DC

Peter J. Hammond Dept. of Economics, Stanford University, Stanford, California

W. Michael Hanemann Dept. of Agricultural and Resource Economics, University of California, Berkeley, California

Jr. C. Harsanyi Dept. of Economics, Haas School of Business, University of California, Berkeley, California

Daniel M. Hausman Dept. of Philosophy, University of Wisconsin, Madison, Wisconsin

Hazel Henderson St. Augustine, Florida

Albert O. Hirschman School of Social Science, Institute for Advanced Studies, Princeton University, Princeton, New Jersey

Richard B. Howarth Dept. of Environmental Science, University of California, Santa Cruz, California

E. K. Hunt Dept. of Economics, University of Utah, Salt Lake City, Utah

Peter Jackson Dept. of Economics, University of Leicester, Leicester, United Kingdom

Naila Kabeer Institute for Development Studies, University of Sussex, Brighton, United Kingdom

Shelly Kagan Dept. of Philosophy, Yale University, New Haven, Connecticut

Daniel Kahneman Dept. of Psychology, Princeton University, Princeton, New Jersey

Robert Kuttner The American Prospect, Cambridge, Massachusetts

Simon Kuznets (deceased)

Will Kymlicka Dept. of Philosophy, University of Ottawa, Ottawa, Canada

Robert E. Lane Dept. of Political Science, Yale University, New Haven, Connecticut

Carrie A. Meyer Dept. of Economics, George Mason University, Fairfax, Virginia

Ezra J. Mishan Professor Emeritus, London School of Economics and Political Science, London, United Kingdom

David G. Myers Dept. of Psychology, Hope College, Holland, Michigan

Richard B. Norgaard Energy and Resources Group, University of California, Berkeley, California

Martha Nussbaum School of Law, University of Chicago, Chicago, Illinois

Rod O'Donnell School of Economics and Financial Studies, Macquarie University, Australia

John O'Neill Dept. of Philosophy, Furness College, Lancaster University, Bailrigg, Lancaster, United Kingdom

Prasanta K. Pattanaik Dept. of Economics, University of California, Riverside, California

Henry M. Peskin Edgevale Associates, Inc., Nellysford, Virginia

Robert Putnam John F. Kennedy School of Government, Harvard University, Cambridge, Massachusetts

John Rawls Dept. of Philosophy, Harvard University, Cambridge, Massachusetts

Joan Robinson (deceased)

John E. Roemer Dept. of Economics, University of California, Davis, California

Mark Sagoff Institute for Philosophy and Public Policy, School of Public Affairs, University of Maryland, College Park, Maryland

John Salter Dept. of Economics, School of Economic Studies, The University of Manchester, Greater Manchester, United Kingdom

Thomas Scanlon Dept. of Philosphy, Harvard University, Cambridge, Massachusetts

Tibor Scitovsky Professor Emeritus of Economics, Stanford University, Stanford, California

Jerome M. Segal Institute for Philosophy and Public Policy, School of Public Affairs, University of Maryland, College Park, Maryland

Andrew Sterling Energy Group, Science Policy Research Unit, University of Sussex, Falmer, Brighton, United Kingdom

Joseph E.Stiglitz Chairman of the Council of Economic Advisors, Office of the President of the United States

Paul Streeten Professor Emeritus of Economics, Boston University, Boston, Massachusetts

Robert Sugden Dept. of Economics and Social Studies, University of East Anglia, Norwich/Norfolk, United Kingdom

Timothy Tilton Dept. of Political Science, University of Indiana, Bloomington, Indiana

Peter Travers Dept. of Social Sciences, School of Social Administration and Social Work, Flinders University, Adelaide, Australia

Hal R. Varian Dean, School of Information Management and Systems, University of California, Berkeley, California

A. Vatn Dept. of Economics, Agricultural University of Norway, Norway

Michael Walzer Institute for Advanced Study, Princeton, New Jersey

Marilyn J. Waring Dept. of Social Policy and Social Work, Massey University, Palmerson North, Auckland, New Zealand

John Oliver Wilson Bank of America, San Francisco, California

Foreword

All human activities aim to satisfy our needs and desires, and since many of those activities are economic, they are of great interest to economists. But economic activities and economic theory do not span the full range of our wants and desires—a fact to which most present-day economists pay for too little attention. As our economic models have grown more rigorous and elegant, we have grown ever more forgetful of the fact that the wants economic activity satisfies are not the only motivating source of human activity.

Economists have not always been so single-minded. Two hundred years ago, economics and psychology were branches of philosophy and shared common insights into human desires and behavior. The classical economists of the 19th century were quite close to those origins and often had complex understandings of human nature. John Stuart Mill and Karl Marx were two important if very different examples. In the 20th century, Alfred Marshall pointed out, and criticized fellow economists for not noticing, that human activity not only aims to produce goods and services that satisfy wants but is also pursued for its own sake, mentioning literature, science, and travel as examples; and Keynes added businessmen's "animal spirits" as their spontaneous urge to take the bother and risk of innovating action. A. C. Pigou was yet another economist to stress that economic welfare is just a subset of human welfare, the only one that can be brought in relation with the measuring rod of money.

Those important reminders of the limits of economic motivation by earlier generations of economists were all but forgotten by my generation of the profession. Increasingly overwhelmed by the elegance of the mathematical formulation of economic theory, many of us were easily tempted to overlook the gap between that beautiful theory and the much more complex and imperfect reality. Instead of analyzing human needs and activities we tended to rely exclusively on revealed preference—people's desire for services and material goods as revealed by their actions in the marketplace. The theoretical structure erected on that narrow foundation left out many sources, aspects, and problems of human welfare, yet the way economics taught gave the impression that we learned all that mattered, because all important sources of satisfaction went through markets and competitive markets were the best means for harmonizing desires and availabilities.

My first problem with economic theory when I learned it in London during the great depression of the 1930s was its inability to explain and deal with unemployment; yet we students often watched labor demonstrations that protested the almost 20 percent rate of unemployment of that time.

My second concern in those days was how to relate economic institutions, activities, and policies to human welfare. Thirty years later, when our economy reached unprecedented and uninterrupted prosperity, with negligible homelessness, low unemployment, and ever-rising incomes, I came upon yet a third problem economists ignored but ought to have been aware of—the insufficiency of money and what it can buy for providing a full, interesting, and enjoyable life.

I tried to deal with all three but especially the last two, and I am glad that their importance, too long neglected, is at last getting increasingly recognized, as shown by the first two volumes in this valuable and provocative series on Frontier Issues in Economic Thought. The editors of the series and I appear to be traveling in opposite directions in time, in that they have moved from my later to my earlier topics of research. My latest work deals with the implications of human psychology for economics. That and many related subjects of consumer behavior, motivation, and the process of consumption are addressed in *The Consumer Society*, the predecessor to this volume.

My early work dealt with problems of welfare economics, the place of economic welfare in human welfare, and with whether an economic change can be said to alter society's well-being in the same direction, and, if so, when and in what limited sense. The results of that work were frustratingly limited; but that in itself was an important result. One response to the difficult dilemmas of welfare economics has been to narrow the inquiry to mechanically applying cost-benefit analysis to matters of public policy. A better response is to broaden the inquiry to encompass related philosophical questions about the purpose of economic activity and the context within which it should be evaluated. I very much hope that the new explorations at the frontiers of economics and philosophy introduced in this volume will close and restore the connection between the two disciplines that existed some two hundred years ago, at the dawn of modern economics.

I want to congratulate Tufts University's Global Development And Environment Institute for managing to review and assemble so diverse a body of literature in such a compact and accessible form. The unique format of mid-length summaries (longer than abstracts, shorter than the full texts) of all the relevant articles should enable readers interested in exploring the frontiers of economics to cover that no-man's land easily and provide serious students of the field with a quick overview to help them seek out the most helpful originals in areas of their particular interest. I look forward with curiosity and interest to future volumes in this series.

Tibor Scitovsky
Stanford University

Acknowledgments

The editors of *Human Well-Being and Economic Goals* received essential assistance in research and writing from many colleagues at the Global Development And Environment Institute (G-DAE). Nandana Mewada, Payal Sampat, and Doug Schuster were graduate students in various parts of Tufts University while they worked closely with us to carry out the enormous research task that lies behind this book. In the work of summarizing articles we were assisted by Carolyn Logan, Cathy Crumbley, Maria Ibarraran, and Doug Schuster. Nandana, Payal, and Carolyn (the latter is also a Tufts graduate student) have been integral members of the Frontier team for several years; we recognize that it is a good thing for them to graduate, but we will miss them.

Another Tufts graduate student, Carol Chouchani, has served most ably as copy editor on this volume. Undergraduates Shea O'Neill and Stacie Bowman have been first-rate library assistants. G-DAE associate Elizabeth Kline, who works on community sustainability, gave us valuable assistance with the literature on indicators and community-related issues. The Institute's Program Coordinator, Laura Goss, has efficiently and with good humor managed much of the bureaucratic detail that is required in fielding such a large team. Our Publications Coordinator, Leigh Stoecker, has been a gracious and helpful liaison with the publisher and with a number of other interested groups and individuals outside Tufts.

An individual who made an extraordinary contribution to the project is Richard W. England, Chair of the University of New Hampshire Economics Department. During the 1996 spring semester Richard was a research associate at G-DAE; the results of his labors are most concentrated in Part X, but his ideas and comments aided us throughout the book.

We have been fortunate to be able to draw on a rich pool of intellectual interest and talent in many parts of Tufts University. Seymour Bellin, a sociologist in the Program on Community Health, has been a warm friend to the Frontier series and to all associated with it. Others who advised us at various points include: Steve Block in the Fletcher School of Law and Diplomacy; Norman Daniels in the Philosophy Department; Sheldon Krimsky in the Department of Urban and Environmental Policy; and Rajaram Krishnan in the Economics Department.

This project has been made possible, in ways that it would not have been even a few years ago, by the progress of information technology. However it is only because of the flexibility and good spirit of our friends at the Inter-Library Loan Office at Tufts' Tisch Library that we have been able to fully benefit from this technological progress. We are grateful for their taking our incessant requests as an interesting challenge.

At an early stage in the work on *Human Well-Being and Economic Goals* we contacted individuals who could guide us in the formulation of an initial bibliography for review and consideration. We were extremely fortunate in receiving expert and often lengthy suggestions from Ed Diener, James Griffin, Marina Karides, Kathleen Langley, Alisdair McIntyre, Mike Meyer, Steve Nathanson, and Amartya Sen.

Midway in the bibliographical search, several members of The Feminist Economic Network (an e-mail discussion group) helped us to add to the list of women commentators on the subjects in this book. At a later stage we sent a semi-final bibliography out for review and were greatly aided by comments and suggestions by Elizabeth Anderson, Samuel Bowles, David Crocker, Cheryl Doss, Robert Lane, Bruce Mazlish, Sabine O'Hara, Mark Sagoff, Gale Summerfield, and Richard Wilk.

Our list of helpful conversations and communications must inevitably fall short of the reality, and we ask pardon from those whose names should have been included here but are not. We can at least mention that a significant number of valuable exchanges of ideas and papers occurred at two excellent conferences in 1996: "Economics, Values, and Organization," which was coordinated at Yale University by Louis Putterman and Avner Ben-Ner, and the "Enjoyment and Suffering Conference" at the Woodrow Wilson School of Public and International Affairs at Princeton University, which was organized by Ed Diener, Daniel Kahneman, and Norbert Schwarz.

Any amount of intellectual potential would go for naught without two final requisites: a good publisher and funding to cover salaries and other project costs. At Island Press we have benefited from and enjoyed working with Stacye White and Todd Baldwin. The funding that has made the undertaking possible has come from the Marilyn Simpson trust, the Bauman, Island, and Ford Foundations. We are exceedingly grateful for their understanding and enthusiasm for the mission of the Global Development And Environment Institute in general and the Frontier series in particular.

Volume Introduction

by Neva R. Goodwin

[A]n economic system is not only an institutional device for satisfying existing wants and needs but a way of creating and fashioning wants in the future. How men work together now to satisfy their present desires affects the desires they will have later on, the kind of persons they will be. These matters are, of course, perfectly obvious and have always been recognized. They were stressed by economics as different as Marshall and Marx. Since economic arrangements have these effects, and indeed must do so, the choice of these institutions involves some view of human good and of the design of institutions to realize it. This choice must, therefore, be made on moral and political as well as on economic grounds. Consideration of efficiency are but one basis of decisions and often relatively minor at that.

—John Rawls[1]

The Questions We Address

This book, the third volume in the Frontier Issues in Economic Thought series is designed to provide ready access to those writings about human well-being that are most relevant to economic realities and economic theory. The writings summarized here have been selected to shed light on the question:

What conceptions of human well-being are used—and what conceptions should be used—as a guide to the design and maintenance of economic systems and institutions?

The intention of the book is to assist in a reexamination of the implicit and explicit goals of economic theory, policy, and action.

What are these goals? They are not easy to discover: the mainstream of the economics profession has not encouraged—and may even be hostile to—a broad exploration of economic goals and their relationship to human well-being. The casual reader of economics textbooks or other expositions might be excused for concluding that efficiency is the primary goal and value for economists; but if that observation is stated, it will quickly be refuted by the contention that efficiency can never be a final goal—it is only a means to other ends.

What other ends? The most thoughtful answers are likely to cite human well-being as the ultimate goal of the activities studied and aided by all the social sciences. However, human well-being is a hard thing to define and to measure, and so the discourse of economics often slips into the easy alternative of holding up some measure of material wealth—its level and/or its growth—as final goals. When the discussion is brought to this point, few would defend material wealth as a fully adequate proxy for human well-being. However, it has been difficult to bring to prominence, within the economics profession, the issues that are raised if we inquire: What if in some circumstances the intermediate, economic goals of growth and wealth do not lead to—even lead us away from—our final goals? How should we then change our economic behavior, and the economic theory that explains and supports that behavior?

In recent years, a spate of writings on these issues has emerged building on work from older traditions of considering "the good society." There is also growing interest in questions of valuation—e.g., debates over treating nonmarket values as externalities, as well as attempts to evaluate the negative value of pollution and the positive value of the contributions of health and safety regulations to human life and health. And there is a lively public and (to some degree) academic debate over indicators that might be used as alternatives to GNP (gross national product) and GDP (gross domestic product).

This renewal of interest in the deeper meaning of economic success is encouraging, but it has not yet become ingrained in the profession. Meanwhile, it sometimes appears that even where Western, capitalist economies have succeeded in achieving the intermediate goals of increasing material wealth, they have done so at the expense of the underlying human values. Development policy, as it evolved since the second World War, has generally been geared to the achievement of a rather narrow set of goals that almost exclusively focus on the macroeconomic issues of growth of productive capacity along with growth in the output of marketed goods and services. In a 1930 essay, John Maynard Keynes anticipated the many-fold increases in labor productivity that have actually occurred, and assumed that the resultant prosperity would solve "the economic problem."[2] In fact, among a large fraction of the human population—at least as many as the 1.6 billion who were on the planet at the start of the century—global wealth has not translated into the elimination of health-injuring poverty or soul-numbing drudgery. Indeed, rapid GDP growth is sometimes accompanied by increasing inequality and misery, while the environmental impacts of growth threaten reversals in the future—which will, again, fall most heavily on the poor. In rich countries inequalities have recently been widening, and even individuals at the upper end of the consumption pyramid do not seem to be achieving the happiness, self-respect, or serenity that some might cite as the purpose of material progress. Capitalism has emerged as the world's triumphant economic system, but, as success comes tantalizingly in sight, there is an uneasy concern that something has gone wrong.

The hypothesis behind this book is that an important piece of what has gone wrong is to be found in the way we define and justify the economic goals we pursue, and that an essential part of the solution must be found in a reexamination of economic goals—starting with the definitions current within the economics profession. That hypothesis will be investigated in the articles summarized in this volume and in the essays that introduce each part.

The "Frontier" Perspective

The comments made above reflect a position that should be spelled out, because it is basic to the selection of articles that go into each book in this series, as well as the way we have selected the topics for our six projected books.

The Frontier Issues in Economic Thought series by definition does not deeply explore positions that are centrally held in the core of the economic discipline. This is because the starting point for selection of our Frontier topics is the observation that there are subjects that should, because of their human importance, be central to a science, such as economics, that describes and prescribes a significant range of human activities. However, among these humanly-crucial topics are some that are not given core attention.

Among the important topics that have been marginalized in this way are the six that have, so far, been selected for this series. They are:

Vol. 1: *A Survey of Ecological Economics* (published 1996)
Vol. 2: *The Consumer Society* (published 1997)
Vol. 3: *Human Well-Being and Economic Goals* (this volume)
Vol. 4: *The Changing Nature of Work*
Vol. 5: *Inequality and Market Power*
Vol. 6: *Fully Sustainable Development*

The fact that the Frontier series has been designed to give a new emphasis to relatively neglected issues makes this, by definition, a somewhat unusual endeavor. Having chosen topics that lie outside of the mainstream, we have found (not surprisingly) that those who have thought much about our topics also tend to reject certain of the standard neoclassical positions. We do not know whether this rejection is the result of such thoughtfulness or whether the direction of causation runs the other way. Perhaps a predisposition not to believe in the standard worldview causes people to ask further questions about the relationships in question.

An insistence on recognizing the crucial role of values in economics turns out to be a common characteristic among all six volumes. Values serve as motivators and guides for economic behavior and as bases for setting economic goals and for judging the success of economic policies. The idea that economic policies can be judged purely "positively" according to their contribution to efficiency merely pushes the normative issue back a step, for the choice of efficiency as a desideratum and the definition of efficiency are, again, value-laden. A leading reason for economists' reluctance to recognize this is methodological: values are hard to define, identify, and analyze in a way that fits with what is thought of as "scientific."

More generally, the core of economics has increasingly been filled with topics that are amenable to the methods and techniques that are popular in the field (i.e., those whose exercise is welcomed by the editors of leading economics journals and can assist young academic economists to promotion and tenure). Topics that are not amenable to the type of abstract modeling that has been favored in recent decades have been pushed to the margins of the field. But if it appears unscientific to abandon the most sophisticated available methods of analysis, it is even more so to ignore, for methodological convenience, crucial aspects of the content of one's discipline.

It was interesting to discover in researching Volume 1, *A Survey of Ecological Economics,* that the young discipline of ecological economics is relatively bold in exploring value issues, even though the topic it most obviously adds to standard economics—the natural world—can, at least sometimes, be studied as a set of value-free objects. One fact with value-laden implications that emerged from Volume 1 had to do with long versus short views of time. As firms, individuals, or other economic actors adopt a longer time perspective, the likelihood grows that private interests will converge with the public interest in social and ecological health and well-being. (To give an example: a farmer acting on informed concern for the future will avoid excessive chemical application, thereby preserving soil fertility and reducing downstream run-off.) It is especially important to build this fact, and its implications, into the core of economic theory.

To derive a subtler point that emerged from Volume 1 and led toward Volume 2, *The Consumer Society,* try the following test. Ask an environmentalist to enter into a thought experiment in which technological breakthroughs make possible, with no environmental harm, the use of virtually unlimited amounts of energy and materials. Then ask, Are you content to have society continue on its present high-consumption path? A common answer, No, will indicate something about the underlying reason for many people to participate in the environmental movement: it establishes a value system expressive of the feeling suggested earlier—that something has gone sour in the pursuit of what had been thought of as "progress." Scenarios of a continued pursuit of material consumption as society's highest goal are unappealing to many, even under imaginary circumstances where all the environmental problems are solved. A focus on environmental problems sometimes serves as the practical expression of a deeper malaise.

Volume 2, *The Consumer Society,* zeroed in on the evidence that, after the satisfaction of basic needs has been achieved, a generalized increase in consumption (the covert or open goal of most current economic discourse) adds little or nothing to human well-being.[3] The exception is when it is declared to do so by definition, as when an article begins with some variant of the too-common statement, "since utility is unobservable, we will use consumption as a proxy for utility." This finding left us with the question: if consumption is not the definition of utility, or well-being, that economists should use, what is?

So we come to the present book. Working on it has been extraordinarily exciting and challenging—even more challenging than the first two volumes, because the subject is less defined. In all of the Frontier books, one of the benefits to the reader is the fact that the selection of articles to summarize has been made on the basis of an unusually extensive literature search. The range over which we had to search in the first two books was at least relatively circumscribed. "Ecological Economics" is a new field with its own journal and a relatively small number of other outlets where much of the work in the area is appearing. "The Consumer Society" was a somewhat more amorphous topic, but still not so vast as "Human Well-Being and Economic Goals." Thus, both of the first two books were able to aim at comprehensiveness. While financial and human resources have limited us to surveying the literature that is printed in English and accessible in the United States, within this (regrettable) limitation we felt that we were making our selection out of a nearly complete set. We knew where to draw the limits of the topics, and we extended our search out to those limits.

Work on the present topic has required constant decision making, not only on the question, Which of these articles covering topic X will be most useful to Frontier readers? We have also faced, even more so than with the other volumes, the questions, Should topic X be represented at all?, and if so, with what emphasis? Our ability to make these decisions was aided by extensive correspondences with a number of colleagues in a wide variety of disciplines. Yet we cannot pretend to be comprehensive, for virtually every discipline in the social sciences or the humanities has a full literature on some aspect of our topic. At the same time, the topic of Volume 3 has in recent years probably received even less attention as a defined subject than any of our other Frontier topics. Thus, even more than in the other volumes, we must offer selectivity as our strength.

Since *Human Well-Being and Economic Goals* ranges so widely over other disciplines, it is perhaps necessary to offer one further disclaimer. It is not the purpose of the editors to colonize other disciplines or to expand the influence of economics. Instead, we hope to facilitate communication in many directions, across many boundaries. From the economics perspective, there is much to be learned, and this discipline stands to be enriched by shifting emphasis onto some areas that are now relatively neglected, even when these are subjects on which it is not fruitful to use the standard neoclassical tools and assumptions.

The Organization of This Volume

Much of the effort involved in producing this volume went into the process of selection and organization of material into the ten parts of this book.

Part I presents a sampling of introductions to the themes and perspectives that appear in contemporary discussion of economic well-being.

Because we are especially interested in the issue of how well-being should be understood for economic purposes, an obvious focus for this book is the relationship between "utility," as conceived in economics, and the broader human concepts of "well-being" or "welfare." Economists have been addressing these topics for at least 200 years. The discussion of utility, utilitarianism, and the "invisible hand" that continued through the 19th century is the subject of Part II.

The 19th century closed with the appearance of a new, seemingly more scientific and successful paradigm, namely neoclassical economic theory. More recent developments in welfare economics, social choice theory, and other approaches to well-being appear in Part III. The 20th century is closing on a note of dissension and disappointment of many earlier hopes for a theory of welfare, together with selected promising new insights.

Despite difficulties and complexities in the theory of welfare economics, there has been a steady growth in applications of the theory to practical problems, in the form of cost-benefit analyses and valuation of environmental and other externalities. Part IV takes up these issues by focusing on the question of which nonmarket values can be made commensurate with the "measuring rod of money" and how society can take seriously those values that are not easily quantifiable.

Philosophers and economists are popularly supposed to take very different views of the world—a supposition that is by no means without basis. However, in recent years a number of bridges have been thrown over the gap between the two disciplines. In Parts V, VI, and VII, we have collected work by authors from both sides of the chasm (as well as from several other disciplines), starting, on the philosophers' side, from the attempt to define what is "the good," or "a good life;" on the economists' side, from ideas of utility and the attempt to give it nontautological meaning via such notions as preference, efficiency, or freedom of choice.

We have sorted these bridging works into three levels. Part V presents efforts to deal with difficulties that have arisen in attempts to use information about individual preferences as a proxy for information about the individual good. Here the emphasis is on critiques of utility theory, along with some efforts to revise it into something more subtle and more comprehensive.

Another criticism of utility theory has stressed the fact that individuals, even in their economic roles, are not solitary Robinson Crusoes, but are generally best understood as participants in a network of social relationships. In Part VI we review work that emphasizes these linkages, especially with regard to ethical norms and citizenship. The point is made that economic efficiency, as well as other aspects of the quality of our lives, depends critically upon these linkages. We are asked to consider whether our approach to economic life, and the theory behind it, is actually corrosive of such social bonds.

Part VII moves to a more macro view of these issues by bringing into focus the social issues of justice, the objectives of egalitarianism, and the conflicts that arise, in the arenas of freedom and justice, between the rights of individuals and the health of society.

Another macro view is provided in Part VIII, where the question, What are the goals of economic activity? is featured in a consideration of the economic development of nations. This is looked at from two directions: one, the concept of development as applied to the third world; the other, reflections on the European style welfare state. Both approaches provide opportunities to consider the relationship between human well-being and the goals espoused by economic policy makers and by the political figures they advise.

For more than half a century the dominant measure of economic well-being on the macro level has been either GNP or GDP. These measures have recently come under sustained attack from a number of directions. This issue is central to the issue of how to bring economists, philosophers, sociologists, political commentators, and activists to a workable, common understanding of well-being—so much so that Part IX is devoted to critiques of existing methods (such as GNP/GDP) for evaluating the contribution of economic activity to human well-being, while Part X consists of a single essay that summarizes and compares eight different approaches to assessing the economic success of a nation.

In this volume of the Frontier series we have departed from our usual approach in two places. One is in the way we have dealt with alternatives to GNP. As just noted, Part X is not a collection of summaries, but, instead, a single essay providing an overview of the issues involved in devising and using something like a GDP figure. The other major departure is in our treatment of the work of the economist Amartya Sen (and, to some extent, that of the philosopher Martha Nussbaum, with whom much of Sen's use of the Aristotelian approach was developed).

Sen has written a very large number of articles that have built on one another and developed, over time, the still-evolving conception of capabilities and human functioning. As he prefers not to have his articles appear in summary form, it is fortunate that there exist several articles (one by Robert Sugden is summarized in Part VII; two more, by David Crocker, are summarized in Part VIII) that, together, cover about 15 of the critical papers in this corpus. By developing unusually long summaries of these secondary sources and writing a review essay of our own (for Part V), we have been able to cover this important topic much more effectively than would have been possible with summaries devoted to single articles.

Conclusion

The need for assistance from beyond the borders of economics is evident in the questions that have motivated the Frontier series. These embrace and extend the question cited initially as the starting point for the present book. Over all, the series asks:

- What is the purpose of the study of economics?
- Whom is economics intended to serve?
- What should be its subject matter?

These are clearly normative questions in that the answers given will depend on the values held. The group of economists and others who have worked on the Frontier series propose, as a starting point, the following answers (each of which requires further definition):

- Economics is studied to achieve a better understanding of that part of human behavior that is associated with the production, distribution, and consumption of goods and services. This, however, is only an intermediate goal.
- The deeper purpose for wishing to achieve such understanding is to help ensure that economic behavior contributes to general human well-being.
- The content of economic studies should include all subjects that bear on economic behavior, or on the interrelation of such behavior with issues of importance for human well-being.

For those who ask such questions, and who answer them as above, it is evident that the field of economics is not only of interest or concern to economists. Economic behavior affects how people interact with the natural world, impacts on a wide variety of human relationships, and creates the conditions within which some people feel successful and others are seen as failures. Of course, economic activity also performs the more obvious functions of producing needed and wanted (as well as unneeded and unwanted) goods and services; creating the jobs through which people may earn the income with which to buy these goods and services; and, through various mechanisms, distributing what has been produced. All of these functions are of great and immediate concern to virtually all people. Not all of them are equally well-represented within mainstream economics. The Frontier series aims to help correct this emphasis.

Notes

1 . John Rawls, *A Theory of Justice* (Cambridge: Harvard University Press, 1971), 259–260.

2. John Maynard Keynes, "Economic Possibilities for Our Grandchildren," *Essays in Persuasion* (New York: Norton, 1963). Summarized in *The Consumer Society*, eds. Neva R. Goodwin, Frank Ackerman, and David Kiron, Volume 2 of this series, *Frontier Issues in Economic Thought* (Washington, DC: Island Press, 1997), 343–345.

3. See the discussion and footnotes 8 through 11 in the Overview Essay for Part I. See also the Overview Essay and summaries in Part V.

PART I

Interdisciplinary Perspectives on Well-Being

Overview Essay

by Neva R. Goodwin

As an overview and introduction to the topics of the whole book, Part I will give examples of an ongoing dialogue between philosophy and economics in which the former poses the "big questions"—What is the good life? What is happiness? What is well-being?—while economics, even in its most philosophical mode, rarely goes beyond the narrower question: What is economic well-being (or material prosperity, or a good standard of living)? The purpose of this overview essay is to present this dialogue in such a way that the reader can make a solid start on our larger project: to explore the notion of well-being and its relationship to economic concepts and concerns.

The essay will begin with two fairly abstract sections. The first will present three different ways in which one might understand how economic growth relates to human well-being. The second section will indicate how the term economic growth is being used here, while providing some definitions for that concept and for human well-being.

With these frameworks in mind, the next section will raise a topic that will recur throughout this book: the issues of measurements and indicators. How much do we actually know—in a "scientific" manner—about well-being? The answer is that there has been real progress in this area of study. Some conclusions will be cited, going beyond the works summarized here. The final section will emphasize what philosophy has to contribute to the question of how economics should define its concerns.

Abstractions Rendered Visually: Three Worldviews

As a starting point for thinking about the interface between the philosophical and economic questions cited above it will be useful to consider some schematic frameworks for our subjects.

Figure 1 and the two figures to follow may be understood as depicting three

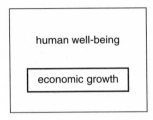

Figure 1. All Economic Growth Contributes
to Well-Being.

different worldviews. In Figure 1, economic growth is seen as a subset of human well-being; the larger set also contains and depends on other things than economic growth. However, the diagram implies that wherever economic growth occurs it will always contribute to human well-being. This position may be associated with major personalities in the history of economic thought, such as Alfred Marshall, who said that economics "examines that part of individual and social action which is most closely connected with the attainment and with the use of *the material requisites of well-being.*"[1] Marshall would evidently have accepted Figure 1, assuming a relatively broad definition of human well-being, or social welfare, as a framework for the economic welfare that depends on economic growth.

Figure 1 represents the core of what is now the standard neoclassical economic model, which defines its goal in terms of utility maximization achieved through optimal resource allocation, depending on free exchange in which rational, selfish individuals trade in a competitive market.

The neoclassical approach was sharpened by the concept of "revealed preferences," a concept that grew out of a perhaps too-ready conclusion that utility is scientifically unobservable. (See the Overview Essays to Parts III and V for more on revealed preferences.) The fallback (carrying positivism to its logical extreme) was to say that all we can scientifically know about people is their actions. *Purchasing behavior* is the "preference revealing" type of action that economists choose to emphasize (thereby significantly overrepresenting consumers at the expense of workers). "Utility," "satisfaction," and "happiness" are thus identified with the purchase of marketed goods and services.

The revealed preference model does not logically have to be interpreted this way, though it is often used to generate an especially restricted worldview where human well-being entirely depends on economic activity. Worse yet, the only aspect of economic activity that is expected to contribute to human well-being is the satisfaction of *consumer* wants and preferences. This model gives no regard to the experience of human beings in their other economic roles as producers, regulators, merchandisers, etc. (let alone other human roles, such as citizens, parents, and so on).

Jerome Segal, in the first paper summarized in this section, proposes the term *instrumental consumptionism* for the view that assumes that the overwhelmingly dominant aspect of economic growth is increased consumption. An example of a weak version of instrumental consumptionism may be found in the second paper summarized in Part I. The author, Tibor Scitovsky, notes that it is impossible to aggregate individual, subjective preferences into a global or social preference if we are dealing with "*the entire range* of human needs and desires."[2] However, he identifies a large subset ("the greater part of that range") that "comprises all the needs and desires that consumer goods and services can satisfy"—that is, "the goods and services that are separable and saleable piecemeal to individuals though consumer markets."

For reasons that were explained in the Volume Introduction, the summaries in this book represent relatively few proponents of the dominant Figure 1 worldview. The position of the editors of this book, and that of many of the writers summarized in this volume, is better to be found in Figures 2 and/or 3.

As in Figure 1, we can find in Figures 2 and 3 the assumption that economic growth is a smaller set than human well-being. However, here the two concepts are portrayed as *overlapping* sets: not only are some parts of human well-being untouched by economic growth, there are also some parts of economic growth that lie outside of—i.e., do not contribute to—human well-being.

The difference between them is that in Figure 2 all aspects of economic growth that lie outside of the larger set are neutral in their effect on human well-being. Figure 3 depicts a different belief. Here the picture is complicated

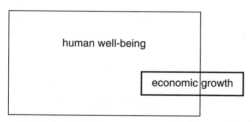

Figure 2. Some Economic Growth is Neutral with Respect to Well-Being.

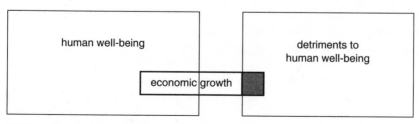

Figure 3. Some Economic Growth May Detract from Well-Being.

with the inclusion of another set, of "detriments to human well-being." This is relevant to Figure 3 because the worldview depicted here conceives of some aspects of economic growth as lying within the "detriments" set; aspects of economic growth (in the shaded area) not only do not contribute to, but actually detract from the more general human well-being.

When economic growth causes pollution, this would be an aspect of economic growth that lies in the shaded area. Other examples might include an increase in selfishness or a breakdown in community when the value of acquiring wealth is elevated above many other human values; or the destruction of indigenous communities through resource exploitation by global corporations; or the legal sale of tobacco and other health-harming products.

Some criminal activities will also turn up in the shaded area. Many of them do contribute to economic growth—consider the billions of dollars that flow on the black markets for illegal drugs and weapons—but they are illegal because society considers them harmful to human well-being. Laws can change: gambling or lotteries may be legal at one time, then become illegal, and then again be legalized. We could subdivide the shaded area into "legal" and "illegal" portions; then we may find some economic activities associated with gambling or drug use moving over the dividing line between legal and illegal, while still staying in the shaded area.

Definitions and Lists (and More Questions)

The topic of this book is the relationship between human well-being and economic goals. The three figures shown so far have dwelt on economic growth as a way of leading into economic goals. As we consider what can be learned from these renderings we will need some definitions.

As a start, let us say that by "economic goals" we mean the goals of economic policy, and the goals assumed in economic theory. Now, with the three figures in mind, we can ask: (1) Should economic goals be limited to the achievement of economic growth?, and (2) Are there aspects of economic growth that should not be included within our economic goals?

More definitions are still required. Drawing on our earlier quotations from Marshall and Scitovsky we may approach "economic growth" by saying that it consists of an increase in the production, for exchange in a market, of the goods and services for which there is effective demand. This, then, is the activity—this increase in production for market exchange—about which we are asking: (1) Is this a sufficient goal for economic policy and theory?, and (2) Is it possible, or likely, that such an increase will sometimes detract from human welfare?

If the last answer is Yes, we might then add another question: (3) How should economic theory and/or policy adapt to such a possibility? That is an extremely important issue, which will only be touched on in a few places here. (This question was also raised in Frontier Volume 2, *The Consumer Society*.)

To complete our definitions we still need to address the broader issue of what we mean by "human well-being." "Social well-being" or "social welfare"[3] are topics that, for a while at least, received a good deal of attention in the economics literature. If we could find good definitions for these terms we might be able to use or revise them for our present purposes. Unfortunately such an effort only illustrates the difficulties attending our present search. These difficulties are laid out in the *MIT Dictionary of Economics* entry on "Social Welfare," which it defines as "The well-being of the society or community at large." The entry continues as follows:

> In defining social welfare we face two sets of problems. The first problem concerns the "social" aspect. In general, social welfare is seen as some aggregation of the welfare of individual members of society—this raises the question of how the aggregation is to be achieved. The second problem relates to the concept of "welfare." I. M. D. Little has argued that "welfare" is an ethical concept since to define something as contributing to welfare is to make a value judgment about whether that thing is good or bad. Alternatively it has been argued that welfare should be equated with the satisfaction of individual preferences and regarded as a "technical" term. On the whole, Little's argument is more widely accepted and definitions of social welfare are usually regarded as value judgments.[4]

The technical approach to social welfare that is de-emphasized here is, presumably, revealed preferences. The choice is presented fairly starkly: either conclude that purchasing behavior is all that matters (because it is all that we can know) about social welfare; or else give up on any attempt at science and conclude that broad definitions of welfare must be left to the realm of value judgments.

Fortunately, there is more that can be said. Some thinkers have approached a definition of human well-being by composing lists of the elements that go into it. Two such will be cited here.[5] Robert Lane, a political scientist who has written extensively on this topic, states that the maxims for a social science should be "subjective well-being" and "human development," where the first of these can be divided into the components of "happiness" and "satisfaction with life as a whole," while the second is composed of "cognitive complexity," "self-attribution," and "self-esteem." His treatment of these subjects in the book *The Market Experience* contains much that is interesting and thought-provoking, but is more suggestive than incisive in defining these terms.[6]

Another take is found in the article by John Oliver Wilson summarized in this section. In a helpful distillation he, like Lane, identifies two "social goals"—individual happiness and economic justice—and then lays out the "social values" of which each is composed. He also lists the "socioeconomic outputs" required to achieve these social values, thus[7]:

Social goods	Social values	Socioeconomic outputs
Individual happiness	• Sustenance • Quality of life • Participation	• Basic economic essentials • Economic security • Equal opportunities • Respect, acknowledgment
Economic justice	• Equity • Fairness • Human rights	• Commutative justice • Productive justice • Distributive justice

These samples from the writings of Lane and Wilson raise the interesting and basic issue of the distinction between final and intermediate ends and also the question of whether there can/should be more than one final end.[8] It is, indeed, when welfare is looked at only as a final end (or a set of final ends) that Little's conclusion seems inescapable: this must be a matter of value judgment (combined, some might say, with personality). That is because the choice of final goals cannot be derived from anything else; after the fact it may be supported by arguments, but each person (implicitly or explicitly) makes his or her choice on essentially intuitive grounds, as the answer to the question, What matters?

An example of an answer to that question is that *needs* matter—either exclusively or at least a great deal more than *wants*. The paper by Ian Gough that is summarized in this section proposes a theory worked out in relation to such a final goal. His comparison of outcomes with needs illustrates another important way of assessing well-being (as opposed, for example, to comparing satisfactions with desires). Gough's discussion of categories of needs is useful and serves him as the basis for a "taxonomy of economic institutions" in which he makes a comparison between markets and two alternatives: Soviet-style planning and "community."

If we disagree with someone's opinion as to "what matters"—such as Gough's final goal definition: "successful and, if possible, critical participation in one's social form of life"[9]—there is virtually no basis on which to argue the issue. (Agreement is least likely when there is a strongly-held difference on the issue of whether to look for single or multiple goals.) In fact, however, many thinkers in the Western tradition find that their sets of final goals overlap to a considerable degree.

Once one has selected the final goal(s) and has accepted some system of relationship between means and ends, the choice of intermediate goals is more amenable to scientific debate. If there is also agreement on a methodological approach (such as the basic principles of Western science, with its concepts of evidence and its logical system of cause and effect), then there are rational grounds for discussing whether our behavior, policies, or philosophical approach are consistent with the final goal(s) we have accepted. For example, one could discuss with Gough whether he has appropriately selected *physical health* and *autonomy* as "the universal prerequisites" for his version of need satisfaction.

From Definitions to Measurements and Indicators

The Segal summary usefully points out that the issues discussed here have a long history. Segal sees the modern views on the connection between economic goals and human well-being as having started with Mandeville's *The Fable of the Bees: or, Private Vices, Publick Benefits* (published in 1714). This modern worldview is one that overlooks the difference between intermediate and final goals. It might seem obvious that economic growth is only desirable if it leads to other, final goals. Segal, however, observes a modern cultural orientation that has come to depend on economic indicators (e.g., of growth, or unemployment) as a society's final measure of success.

Advances in survey research over the last 50 years have contributed to the growing field of "quality of life" and "subjective well-being" studies. This work suggests that we can gain a good deal of scientific knowledge about the comparative well-being of large groups of people, with more certainty than attaches to efforts to measure and compare utility in single individuals. This may prove to be an important direction for those who seek an alternative to the assumptions of the revealed preference approach, with their strong support for a consumerist mentality. We have already noted that the paper by Scitovsky is one that seems to accept much of the standard economic emphasis on consumption as a major element in human well-being. However, Scitovsky's is one of the many voices that will be heard in this book, protesting that such indicators as GNP/GDP are inadequate to reveal the kinds and amounts of human well-being that are actually received from consumption.

If GNP and GDP do not adequately reflect the human benefits of consumption, they are even less appropriate as measures for the totality of well-being, including the important components of well-being (noted also by Scitovsky) that are not achieved through markets. This observation has led a number of people to seek other ways of assessing well-being. The growing literature on assessments of well-being is only lightly sampled here, with a chapter from a book by Peter Travers and Sue Richardson that analyzes the components and the meaning of material well-being in Australia. (See also the Myers and Diener summary in Part V.) Rather than repeat what is to be found in the summaries, it may be useful to add some additional observations.

As a very brief overview, let us start with data that indicate that there is a modest (by no means consistent) correlation at a given time—but not over time—between national affluence and reported levels of subjective well-being.[10] Ed Diener and Eunkook Suh comment on this:

> The causal factors relating wealth to well-being, however, are not yet understood. The wealth of nations strongly correlates with human rights, equality between people, a cooler climate, the fulfillment of basic biological needs, and individualism. Because of the high intercorrelations between these predictor variables and wealth, their separate effects on SWB [subjective well-being] have not yet been isolated. Another variable that correlates with higher subjective well-being in nations is political stability and a related variable, interpersonal trust.

> Individualism is a cultural variable that correlates across nations with both higher reported subjective well-being and also with higher suicide rates. . . . Individualists believe that happiness is more important than do collectivists, who emphasize other values such as "respect."[11]

The correlation remarked here between SWB and national (political, cultural, etc.) characteristics may have a role to play in explaining a seeming paradox: while, at a given moment in time, well-being seems higher in most richer nations than in most poorer ones, we do not observe a similar correlation as nations progress from moderately well-off to very well-off.

In spite of still-to-be-resolved inconsistencies, and keeping in mind the other explanations offered by Diener and Suh, still the *national* correlations between wealth and SWB seem strong enough to support the common moral sense that the people in very poor nations would be better off if their country could raise its level of economic activity. What may be in question is the nature of that economic activity—whether, for example, the best way to raise general, human well-being is to follow the economic development path of the industrialized nations. (This is a topic that will be taken up further in Part VIII.)

Moving from the variance among nations to the variance in subjective well-being among individuals, we find the topic complicated by a growing consensus among SWB researchers that a large part of that variance can be accounted for by genetic factors. Of the remainder, it is thought that another significant fraction can be traced to early childhood experiences,[12] with the rest being accounted for by elements such as "marriage, employment, occupational status, leisure, and the 'competencies' of health and social skills."[13] Lane's conclusion is that

> The sources of satisfaction that do not go through the market are substantial and generally make greater contributions to well-being than do those that do

go through the market. Of those that may be said to be market-related, *the important ones relate to the labor market much more than to the consumer market.*[14]

What policy implications come out of this line of research? One specific one may be noted: the major influence of early childhood experience on later abilities to derive well-being from a variety of life circumstances reinforces the belief that the quality of childhood experience should be a major source of public concern. This is not a new conclusion, having also been based on common sense and common morality.

More generally, economic growth—past a certain point—does not appear to be nearly so important a contributor to well-being as has often been assumed. One theoretical implication is that economic theory needs to shift its focus from maximizing the satisfaction of consumer wants to considering the ways in which economic activity affects the rest of human life, starting with the work experience and the broader implications and meanings of work.[15] However, if markets are not the basis for most of human well-being, this does not impel any of the authors represented here to suggest that market systems should or could be abandoned. Rather, some authors (such as Lane and Elizabeth Anderson) propose ways of restricting the influence of markets. In addition to attempting to limit the ways in which economic growth detracts from human well-being, Anderson also stresses the importance of preserving alternatives, such as nonprofit employment.

Some Philosophical Conclusions on Economic Goals

The writing by O'Neil summarized here comes from a book that in the opening paragraph asks, "Should a book on *environmental* philosophy begin with questions about *human* well-being?"[16] Referring to environmental economists and some of the early exponents of the neoclassical school, O'Neil notes that

Economics, for these thinkers, *is* concerned with human well-being, and that stance is not substantially changed when environmental issues are raised. Well-being is characterized in terms of the satisfaction of wants or preferences—the stronger the preference satisfied, the greater the well-being. The strength of the preference is captured in terms of the price a person would pay at the margin for its satisfaction. . . . [A] basic theorem of neo-classical economics is that "ideal" markets are an efficient mechanism for satisfying preferences. "Ideal" markets are not, however, found in reality—and cost-benefit analysis is introduced as a way of rectifying the "failures" that result from the departure of real markets from their "ideal" conditions. Cost-benefit analysis still, however, begins with human well-being understood in terms of the satisfaction of prefer-

ences, the strength of which is expressed in terms of willingness to pay: it aims
to maximize well-being thus understood.[17]

This statement summarizes nicely some salient aspects of the critique of neoclassical economics that is implicit and explicit in many places in this book.

Having found the neoclassical approach too narrow, O'Neil considers and rejects the alternative provided by deep ecology. His third, favored option is an
application of Aristotelian philosophy. The "objective goods" that he cites as
the desiderata in this approach include "friends, the contemplation of what is
beautiful and wonderful, the development of one's capacities, the ability to
shape one's own life."[18]

We will find that the Aristotelian approach also comes to the fore in a number of other writings represented in this book. (See, e.g., the summaries of
Crocker, Part VIII, and Sugden and Nussbaum, Part VII; also the review essay
of Sen's work in Part V and the summary of Segal in this section.) Aristotle's
view of human goodness is both interesting and relevant to contemporary concerns, in that it allows us to focus on a collection of desiderata that are usefully
grouped together as final goals, but that have been imprisoned in separate categories in other thinking on goal definition.

The uninitiated may be confused by the fine divisions in contemporary philosophy, between ethical theories that are outcome-based (consequentialist)
versus those that are rights-based (contractualist); and between principles of
justice that focus on end-states (consequentialist and contractualist) versus
those that are procedural (libertarian, à la Nozick). The Aristotelian focus on
activities is not only concerned with the results of activities, such as achievements or states of being; if it were, Aristotle could be classified as a pure consequentialist. He regarded activities as valuable, so that they could be called ends
in themselves; but they are not only ends in themselves. Modern Aristotelians,
such as philosopher Martha Nussbaum and economist Amartya Sen, have
stressed the conclusions concerning basic needs that emerge when we consider
what is necessary to enable people to engage in the kinds of activities that sum
up to a good life. Sen has argued that the capability to live well—to carry out
the activities that, over time, constitute a good life—should be a more fundamental value for economics than the satisfaction of preferences. Such an emphasis on capabilities has the virtue of directing attention to the social, environmental, and political circumstances that give people a fair chance to devise and
pursue good ends.

Thus, a major achievement of Sen's and Nussbaum's work is a goal definition
that can accommodate simultaneously two types of values that are, in fact, iter-
ative and inextricably intertwined. These are, on the one hand, process values
(i.e., capabilities) and, on the other hand, outcome values, including both basic
needs satisfaction to support capabilities, as well as the "good ends" (such as re-

lationships, self-actualization, etc.), which are defined and pursued by a person whose capabilities are adequately supported. This way of thinking embraces, within the category of final goals, both capabilities and the results of capabilities and also the social and other support necessary to allow all people to develop and use their capabilities.

The result is a very broad conception of well-being. Will this prove to be useful for economists? Or should they remain bound to some narrower, economic concept, such as material prosperity or GDP? Many current efforts to improve the measurements (such as GDP) that we use to try to assess our situation recognize that economic decisions are being based on the wrong things: we rely on what we can measure rather than on what really matters to us. Some would say that this is the best that economics can do. If so, the appropriate conclusion might be that economics should play a much smaller role than it now does, e.g., in setting national policies. If economics is not able to expand its conception of well-being as a goal, there is a danger of another type of expansionism (à la Gary Becker) claiming to be able to understand everything of importance, because the discipline has shrunk down its definition of "everything of importance" to fit the narrow compass of what its tools can handle.

It is a similar issue that is addressed, in a slightly different form, when Hausman and McPherson ask whether morality matters to economic analysis. They cite the caricatured view of the economist as, in essence, a value-free "tool" who supplies technical assistance to others (policy makers, ethicists) who are responsible for the values. Their probing questions—What is the moral basis of a concern with efficiency? Is it really less controversial than the moral commitments that lie behind notions of equity?[19]—remind us of how difficult it is, after all, for economists to be only economists—without also being human beings who are, almost inevitably, involved in value judgments.

For too long the goals of economics have been given short shrift, if not left out of consideration altogether. Two assumptions have relieved economists of the obvious necessity to consider the final goals implicit in the theory and its application. One is the assumption that people know and act in their own best interest; the other, that the aggregated result of individuals pursuing their best interest will be a social optimum. (See the Overview Essays for Parts III and V for more discussion of these assumptions.)

One issue here is especially sticky, raising concerns about paternalism along with uncomfortable questions about the political/economic process that inevitably gives more weight to some people's values than to others (whether the elite gain their power through money, education, or other sources of influence). To question whether people know what is good for them always raises a sense of uneasiness, for it brings to mind the thought, If I am not assumed to know what is good for me, is there someone else who can claim to know better? Those who conclude that each person is probably, on average, the *best* judge of what is good for him/her still tend to leave aside the question of whether that means that most people are *very good* at judging what will contribute to their own well-being.

In spite of the problems with this topic, the previous Frontier volume, *The Consumer Society,* contained a number of writings suggesting that, at least in the area of consumer behavior, there is a need to protect people from making choices that will be bad for them, either as individuals or as members of society (see also the Joan Robinson summary in this volume, Part II). This issue is fairly obvious when we think about children, whose opinions are yet to be molded. Responsible parents prefer to take a hand in that molding, rather than passively leaving all value education to market forces. Paternalistic behavior is also generally acceptable when the subjects are the mentally ill or people (such as addicts) who are presumed not fully responsible for their values and preferences. What is less obvious as an issue for all citizens is that there are powerful economic actors who are vigorously committed to shaping preferences, and the values that lie in back of preferences, in order to maximize the consumption desires of the public.

Paternalism and elitism are the words used to protest against individual or government efforts to influence values. There are no equally emotive terms commonly applied to commercial efforts to do this; yet these ubiquitous and effective efforts have long since eliminated the option of preserving a neutral field of values. The choice is either to accept the commercial values that dominate the media in industrialized economies or to find ways of publicly promoting a competing set of values and preferences.

A few economists have questioned whether consumers, unaided, should be assumed to be the best judges of their own welfare. Tibor Scitovsky and Alfred Marshall have stressed the need for various kinds of education to help people achieve more developed tastes. Karl Marx talked about false consciousness. John Kenneth Galbraith more concretely observed that tastes and preferences may be manipulated by advertising and other aspects of the cultural environment that are designed by those who have something to sell. Robert Frank (summarized in Part VI) points out ways in which competition in a "winner take all" society wastes economically valuable resources while reducing well-being. Thorsten Veblen, James Duesenbury, and Fred Hirsch have contributed to the view that competitive consumerism creates an upwards spiral of dissatisfaction, in which everyone strives for a position on "top" that, by definition, can only be attained by a very few.[20]

Environmentalists see such competition through consumption as contributing to a "tragedy of the commons" type of outcome, when individual decisions do not take into account the combined effect of multiple similar decisions (e.g., my use of a car or a lawn-mower makes a negligible contribution to global climate change, but use of these devices by everyone in North America has an impact that cannot be ignored). These are joined by a growing communitarian movement that mistrusts the linkages between local communities and global powers and feels that one of the most pernicious of such links is the globalizing consumer culture. Behind many of these positions we may sometimes discern an anti-materialistic view based on spiritual or religious convictions, including Puritanism, some Eastern beliefs, etc.

What goal is economics designed to serve? That is the basic question of this book. In recent years the available answers have been "efficiency and the maximization of consumer satisfaction." Many thinkers have concluded that a course set by these standards will often fail to lead toward human well-being—and may, in some cases, lead in the wrong direction. The rest of the book will examine a variety of arguments that examine the basic question and attempt to work toward more constructive answers.

Notes

1. Alfred Marshall, *Principles of Economics: An Introductory Volume* (originally published 1920) 8th ed. (Philadelphia: Porcupine Press, 1982), 1; italics added.

2. Tibor Scitovsky, 93; italics in the original. The next quotation is from *Ibid.*, 93–94.

A strong version of instrumental consumptionism would include the belief that greater consumption *inevitably* increases well-being. Other parts of Scitovsky's work make it clear that, even if Scitovsky believes that "the greater part" of the range of human needs and desires can be satisfied by consumer goods and services, he also would subscribe to the implication of our Figure 3: that there are some ways of satisfying consumer needs and desires that, in fact, reduce overall human well-being.

3. Note that we are following a common practice of assuming that welfare and well-being mean the same thing, except in cases where pains are taken to give a very particular definition to one term or the other.

4. David Pearce, ed. *The MIT Dictionary of Economics* (Cambridge, MA: MIT Press, 1994), 400.

5. The reader might also want to look at the list contained in the summary of the article by Martha Nussbaum in Part VII.

6. Robert Lane, *The Market Experience* (New York: Cambridge University Press, 1991).

7. Table from "Figure 14.1: Social Goods, Social Values, and Socioeconomic Outputs" in John Oliver Wilson, 237.

8. The decision to adopt a plurality of final goals as is done by Lane and Wilson, or a single one (such as "utility maximization" or "the glorification of God"), seems to be a function, in part at least, of personality. One thinks of the ecstatic delight of the young John Stuart Mill, when he recognized how utilitarianism could serve to sum up various goals into a single, final end. The principle of utility, he said (in his autobiography)

> fell exactly into its place as the keystone which held together the detached and
> fragmentary component parts of my knowledge and beliefs. It gave unity to my

> conception of things. I now had opinions; a creed, a doctrine, a philosophy; in
> one among the best senses of the word, a religion.

John Stuart Mill, *Autobiography* (New York: The Liberal Arts Press, Inc., reprinted 1957), 44.

9. Ian Gough, 28.

10. See David G. Myers, *The Pursuit of Happiness: Who is Happy—and Why* (New York: Morrow, 1992).

11. Ed Diener and Eunkook Suh, "National Differences in Subjective Well-Being" (October 1, 1996) (manuscript draft), 1–2.

12. See Diener et al. forthcoming from Sage Publications.

13. Michael Argyle, "Causes and Correlates of Happiness," presented at the "Enjoyment and Suffering Conference," Princeton University, November 1–3, 1996; in manuscript, 38.

14. Lane, 477; italics added.

15. This will be subject of the next volume in the Frontier series. The negative effects of economic growth on environmental aspects of human well-being were discussed in Volume 1, *A Survey of Ecological Economics*.

16. O'Neil, 1.

17. Ibid., 1–2.

18. Ibid., 3.

19. Hausman and McPherson, 675.

20. The viewpoints cited in this paragraph have been summarized or discussed in *The Consumer Society,* eds. Neva R. Goodwin, Frank Ackerman, and David Kiron (Washington, DC: Island Press, 1997); Volume 2 of this series.

Summary of

Alternative Conceptions of the Economic Realm

by Jerome M. Segal

[Published in *Morality, Rationality, and Efficiency:*
New Perspectives on Socio-Economics, ed. Richard M. Coughlin
(Armonk, New York: M. E. Sharpe, Inc., 1991), 287–306.]

[W]hat is at issue is really a vast cultural orientation, how an entire society, not
a mere limited body of professionals, thinks about economic life. [288]

To be reasonably grounded, economic action must be placed within the greater
context of human existence and an understanding of the nature of man and of
the good life. However, at least since the 18th century, Western society has
tended to ignore these "big questions" in its economic decision making, sus-
pending all belief in a greater purpose or meaning to human existence and treating economic activity as a separate, scientific sphere to be managed by "experts." In effect, "(w)e bracket our deepest concerns and carry on with
economic life as though they were irrelevant. And this is irrational." [287–288]
This paper reviews the intellectual history of perceptions of the economic realm
and its relation to the rest of life, beginning with Aristotle and concluding with
Mandeville, who introduced much of this modern orientation.

Overview

History affords us a variety of alternative ways of understanding the economic
realm. For example, Aristotle's position may be called *noble enablism* (human
well-being emerges from what we do and what we become, not from what we
have). The medieval position was *extratemporal instrumentalism* (behavior
within the economic realm must be governed by anticipation of extratemporal
rewards and punishments, to be meted out by God), while Calvin took a position of *extratemporal dramatism* ("Economic behavior does not cause extratemporal rewards but manifests one's character within that drama." [304]).
The Renaissance perspective was *scientific and aesthetic progressivism* (the goal is
general human progress, especially in the aesthetic and scientific realms; economic achievements are to be judged against this standard).

One strand in Marx may be called *mass enablism* ("the economic realm is a
necessary evil to be passed through historically so that most of mankind can live
outside that realm" [ibid.]), while another strand was *human transactionism*
(an economy is judged according to its ability to create meaningful, transfor-
mative roles for people).

Other possible perspectives include *instrumental consumptionism* (the belief that greater consumption increases well-being), *international supremacism* (the purpose of the economy is maintaining the state's international position), and *economic liberalism* ("good" is whatever people think it is, and the function of the economy is to enable as many people as possible to pursue what they think is good). This paper will sketch out the process through which we arrived where we are, in a culture that is largely governed by instrumental consumptionism and international supremacism, but also paying lip service to economic liberalism.

Aristotle's View of the Economic Realm

In contrast to some of the "confused" doctrines of his day that associated human happiness with pleasure and amusement, Aristotle argued that happiness is not a kind of experience, but a kind of life. Specifically, it is a kind of life that involves expending effort in the pursuit of excellence and virtue. In his view, "the good life is one in which a person most fully, and at the highest level of excellence, fulfills his deepest nature." [289] Such a way of life is not a means to other ends—including feelings and sensations—but an end in itself.

Within this framework, economic activity is only indirectly necessary to the good life; there are strict limits to the value of economic activity. Aristotle contrasted "goods of the soul" such as fortitude and wisdom, for which greater amounts produce greater utility, with "external goods" such as wealth and power, which are only beneficial in limited amounts. He essentially made the first statement of the principle of diminishing marginal utility, taking the especially radical view that the marginal utility of excessive amounts of external goods declines not just to zero, but actually becomes negative. This theory can thus be translated into an argument for limiting growth, which can be harmful to human well-being beyond a certain point.

Aristotle also distinguished between two forms of the "art of acquisition." The first, "natural" form of this art is concerned with management of the household and acquisition of the resources needed by the household (e.g., through fishing, farming, and herding). The second form is based on retail trade and reflects an "unnatural" concern with obtaining ever higher levels of income. Here human personality and capacities are separated from their proper function of pursuing virtue and become distorted as they are placed entirely in the service of earning money. It is not, however, particular economic activities that Aristotle criticized here, so much as the outlook and form of life. For Aristotle it was essential that economic life not be treated as a separate realm, but that it be rooted in a larger understanding of human fulfillment and the good life.

Aristotle believed that there are naturally higher and lower classes of humans, and that slavery for the lower classes is just and for the good of all. He thus accepted mass poverty as a natural condition, and never concerned himself with the issue of generating sustained economic growth to provide for the development of the poorer segments of society. It was only in the 18th century that the claims of the masses to higher levels of human development found expression. In the 19th century Marx synthesized this mass perspective with Aristotle's view of the place of economics in human life, giving rise to a powerful new vision of the place of economic growth within the story of human development.

The Economic Thought of the Reformation

During the Middle Ages, economic interests were subordinated to a concern with salvation. Economic activity was fully subjected to the rules of morality that bound all individual conduct, and efforts to increase material wealth above a basic level were condemned. However, this attitude eventually broke down, not as a result of theoretical challenges, but due to the onslaught of sustained economic growth.

Reformation thinking emerged in the 16th century as a reaction against this collapse, but within this reaction there were two very different attitudes toward economics. Luther's goal was the restoration of medieval principles uncorrupted by the commercial spirit. Calvin, on the other hand, accepted commercialism, but sought to restrain it with a moral creed; the work ethic developed on the grounds that work was a means for expressing virtue, not for achieving consumption. The economic realm then became the place where an individual's very identity—and thus his fate—were revealed; "Puritans produced not in order to consume, but in order to *be*." [297] While Calvin's creed certainly does not imply a complete reversal of virtues and vices, it does reflect a major shift in emphasis among the virtues. In contrast to the medieval period, sloth is now a more serious a sin than covetousness.

Mandeville and the Fable of the Bees

Early in the 18th century, Bernard Mandeville published a poem entitled *The Fable of the Bees: or, Private Vices, Publick Benefits,* which presents a view of the economic realm that reflects a dramatic break with the past. He begins by promoting the radical thesis that vice is economically beneficial. Analyzing consumption, for example, "he looks at what lies behind the demand curve, and finds vice and folly, vanity and envy and the fashion industry! Yet he embraces it all," [299] because it produces the benefits of jobs, higher income, and the material comforts of life—in particular, for the poor.

More importantly, Mandeville goes a step further by separating economic life from more transcendent human concerns. Assuming a violent and competitive international arena, he argues that a prosperous and powerful economy is the most important goal. Any behavior is acceptable in pursuit of this end, regardless of whether it violates religious or moral ideals; traditional virtues such as frugality and honesty are even condemned as likely to get in the way of achieving the economic aim. Mandeville is "thoroughly divorced from the religious world view that characterized both the Reformation and the medieval world." [301] "(H)e simply is not seized by the project of our becoming very different than we are . . . all that matters is simply that we be better off." [301] Mandeville's poem provides a remarkably good portrayal of the present orientation toward economic life, which is so different from those that preceded it.

The Modern View of the Economic Realm

Today we evaluate economies in terms of three main indicators—the unemployment rate, the growth rate, and the inflation rate—but these are means to other ends, not ends in themselves. Low unemployment is valued both for its distributional effects and because it indicates that productive resources are being fully utilized to raise income levels. Growth also leads to higher levels of income. Income is of interest because of its presumed contribution to well-being; the modern economic conception of well-being equates it with utility, which is in turn a function of the level of consumption, and hence of income. This way of thinking reflects both economists' understandings and the cultural orientation of our entire society, but there is nothing inevitable about it; even in the West it has only been influential for the last 200 years, while the history of economic thought extends back at least three millennia.

Summary of

The Meaning, Nature, and Source of Value in Economics

by Tibor Scitovsky

<mark>[Published in *The Origin of Values*, eds. Michael Hechter, Lynn Nadel, and Richard E. Michod (New York: Aldine de Gruyter, 1993), 93–105.]</mark>

Economists are interested in the subjective values associated with the sources of individual satisfaction because of their concern with the economy's ability to allocate resources and coordinate production and distribution so as to create the greatest benefit to society. For many needs and desires, competitive markets are a relatively good means for determining and responding to individual preferences. There are, however, limits to this solution, because not all sources of satisfaction go through markets, and markets may fail in other ways as well. National product and income estimates as measured by market transactions are therefore incomplete and inadequate measures of overall welfare. Correcting for this by estimating values uncounted by the market can help, although this is often difficult, and at times virtually impossible.

Strengths and Weaknesses of Competitive Markets

In order for an economy to "create the greatest benefit at the least cost as *those benefits and costs are evaluated by the people who experience them*," [93] it is necessary to aggregate individual preferences into global preferences. There is no completely objective unit of measure for doing this, but competitive markets can use money (the best available measure of subjective value) to perform this aggregation—not for the entire range of needs and desires, but for that large subset that can be satisfied by consumer goods and services. The theoretical advantages of market economies derive from the fact that there is a market-clearing price for each good; this further implies that, for a given good, each purchaser attributes the same money valuation (which is the price) to the last unit purchased of that good; and thus prices function as "signals that enable a perfectly competitive economy to utilize and allocate resources and productive methods in best conformity to consumers' preferences."[1]

When it comes to evaluating overall levels of satisfaction, however, competitive markets are seriously limited by a number of market failures. First, markets can only measure values attached to needs or desires that are satisfied within them, but many important economic goods and services, as well as costs or pains, do not reach people via markets. In addition, market prices only adequately reflect subjective valuations in situations of perfect competition, yet in reality most markets are imperfect. Consumer preferences can also be unreliable or undesirable and may need to be overridden or corrected. Finally, production and consumption can have positive or negative side effects, or externalities, that are not measured by markets, but that may have significant impact on overall levels of well-being.

Each of these problems is considered in more detail below.

Collective and Merit Goods

Collective or public goods are equally available to everyone, but may be valued differently by different people. Some of these public goods are created by the asymmetric situation in which consumers compete with one another according to the ideal competitive model, while sellers often do not. When there is insufficient competition to force the latter to lower prices to the marginal cost of production, we find such forms of nonprice competition as provision of customer services, agreeable shopping conditions, and aesthetically agreeable displays. The buyers' response (e.g., preferring to shop in pleasanter, even if more expensive, surroundings) suggests that the buyers' marginal valuations can still be deduced from the market price; but the sellers' marginal valuations are overstated in these less than fully competitive situations.

"More important, more valuable, and much more numerous than the privately provided collective services just discussed are those provided by government and paid for out of taxes." [96] Here, the difficulty is to determine the appropriate nature and quantity to be supplied. In theory, public participation in the political process should yield some indication of their valuation of these goods, but this approach is tenuous. An alternative is to aggregate individual statements of willingness to pay for a good, but this too is impracticable, not least because of the incentives for people to mis-state their levels of preference depending on how they think the information is going to be used. No adequate solution to this dilemma is yet available.

Income distribution is a special kind of collective good because preferences for it are based on moral judgments, which are "bound to be much more nearly uniform than . . . judgments of personal gratifications and their sources." [97] Most people value some degree of equity, though not complete equality, since work incentives and opportunities to pursue superior economic status are also sources of satisfaction. Societies usually resolve these opposing impulses by pursuing equality of *opportunity,* and by promoting greater equity by raising people at the low end of the income scale above the poverty line, while leaving the rest alone.

The value of certain goods may not be sufficiently recognized by everyone, so it may be necessary to override markets and actively encourage their consumption. Consumption of these "merit goods" can be promoted through compulsion (e.g., mandatory contributions for social security and unemployment insurance), subsidization (e.g., for the arts), or free provision (e.g., health care in some countries). Another type of merit goods that also requires market intervention includes goods or services, such as hospitals, that are valued even by those who do not use them. We might use the term "demerit goods" for harmful products (such as narcotics) where the user pays another cost for consumption, in addition to the purchase price. Informed opinion favors discouraging at least some of the market activities related to these demerit goods.

Economies and Diseconomies

Many goods and services can have side effects on third parties that are known as external economies or diseconomies. The benefits and costs of these externalities do not pass through the market, and so are not reflected in market prices. Health services and education generate external economies, while pollution and environmental degradation produce external diseconomies. The ideal way to correct for them is to supplement market prices, for example by imposing taxes or fines on producers equal to the cost of the diseconomy; however, estimating these costs can be difficult or even impossible, and enforcement is also problematic.

Work is a particularly important realm in which many nonmonetary side effects are experienced, both positive and negative. However, both the positive effects of challenging and responsible work and negative impacts, such as the tendency of technical progress to render work more monotonous and less satisfying, are often overlooked. Undervaluing worker satisfaction results in excessive emphasis on financial incentives. Both Keynes and Schumpeter also warned against "exaggerating the role of profit as the motive force of investment and growth." [100]

Scarcity Values

As economies grow due to technical progress or expansion of the labor force, uneven changes in the balance of supply and demand are resolved by price changes. For goods or resources such as land that have fixed or decreasing supply, prices will always increase. Even more problematic is the case of fixed resources that are also collective goods, such as the atmosphere, beautiful settings, and fresh water supplies; these have no market price, so rising prices cannot motivate conservation or adaptation. There is a danger that, without the warning of an increasing scarcity price, the response will be degradation of the resource rather than decreased use. For such goods, "their husbanding . . . cannot be left to the market but must be undertaken collectively, by the state." [102] Like external diseconomies, however, monetizing and internalizing scarcity costs—the theoretically correct solution to this problem—are difficult to impose in practice.

Welfare and Growth

Since price is taken by economists as a measure of the value attributed to goods by consumers, it is not surprising that they use the sum of the value of all market transactions—national product or national income—as an indicator of both the economy's performance and public welfare. However, while these may be good indexes of economic performance, their use as measures of welfare is much more problematic. One reason for this is that the satisfaction derived from a good is related not just to price but to quantity and quality as well.

Another is that, when we increase the national product, we may incur some costs that are not measurable. Expanding output by means of increasing labor input has obvious implications for worker well-being; national product should therefore be expressed *per annual work hours,* but this is seldom done. In the short run, increased production can also be driven by allowing capital equipment and infrastructure to deteriorate, as the Reagan administration did, but this exaggerates the impression of economic prosperity while leading to long-term problems. The unmeasurable costs of economic activity such as decreasing equity of income distribution and negative environmental impacts must also be considered. For all of these reasons, indexes of national income or national product cannot be considered adequate measures of human welfare.

Note

1. Editor's note: It is important to be clear that the value on which all consumers agree—that is, the price they are all willing to pay for the marginal unit consumed—does not imply identical subjective values for those marginal purchases, because money itself may be expected to have a very different subjective value to different people, depending on how much money they have, what their needs are, etc. The allocation according to preferences cited here is, in fact, allocation according to *effective* demand.

Summary of

Human Values and Economic Behavior: A Model of Moral Economy

by John Oliver Wilson

[Published in *Socio-Economics: Toward a New Synthesis,*
ed. Amitai Etzioni (New York: M. E. Sharpe, 1991), 233–263.]

Positions taken in the debate about the relationship between human values and economic behavior range from a denial that the two are connected, to the assertion that human values must be the very source of the legitimacy of the economic system. Although economics involves many choices about the use and distribution of scarce resources that profoundly impact human life, most economists resort to the equivocal position that economics should be treated as a value-free "science." This response is, however, inadequate, and economists must better integrate concepts of human value and economic behavior. This paper presents a moral model of economic behavior that attempts to do this, expressed in terms of seven basic postulates.

Conventional Economic Models

The view that human values and ethical considerations are on a different plane from economic issues of production and distribution is deeply embedded in conventional models of economic behavior, especially the dominant neoclassical model. This model is portrayed as a purely positive model of behavior, independent of any normative considerations. It argues that the source of human motivations is rational, self-interest maximization; no nonself-interested goals—altruism for example—need be taken into consideration. The model does not provide any means for assessing social achievement to make comparisons among economic systems. It cannot be counted on to indicate a quality distinction between a system of great inequality with many destitute members and a system of relative equality.

The social-welfare model of economic behavior provides an alternative that does at least incorporate some normative considerations. It allows economists to make judgments when comparing different economic systems by using a social-welfare function, which, in theory, should be determined by a political process, and so should reflect the values of society, especially with respect to the desired distribution of income. However, the social-welfare approach is severely hampered by the difficulty of making interpersonal comparisons of utility. This difficulty has thrown economists back on Pareto optimality as the only criterion available for judging economic systems. This approach also continues to rely on the assumption that maximization of self-interest is the main motivation for economic behavior so situations of extreme inequality may still be judged no worse than situations of general equality.

The Moral Model: Seven Postulates

Another model that better integrates human values and economic behavior is the "moral model." It can be expressed in terms of seven basic postulates. The first states that:

> In an economic system, individuals confront a range of alternative socioeconomic actions, and in making a choice among these actions an individual will act upon a particular set of moral values. [237]

There are several approaches to understanding how these moral values affect individual choice, such as a simple dichotimization between an individual's "ethical preferences" and his or her "subjective preferences," or Amartya Sen's more complex system of "meta-rankings" of whole ranges of preferences. In either case, though, the important contrast with neoclassical theory is that the moral model portrays choices that are shaped by a preference function based on moral values, not simply on self-interest maximization. One alternative can therefore be said to be better than another, not simply *preferred* to it.

The second postulate states that:

> Any set of moral values that satisfies the conditions of legitimacy consists of social values, and these values function to integrate individual self-interests into an economic system. [239]

If each individual is left alone to determine what constitutes moral behavior, then there is no way to study the relation between economic behavior and human values. But identifying a common, legitimate set of social values that links these two realms presents problems. Universal, absolute values can only be revealed through metaphysics or religion, not rational analysis. The most promising alternative approach involves identifying the commonalities among various conceptions of justice and morality and identifying the conditions that all must satisfy. This reveals that moral values must in all cases serve as: (1) *social values* that shape interpersonal relationships and the social externalities involved; (2) *shared values* that represent what all individuals in an economic system regard worthy of achievement; and (3) *integrative values* that integrate individual self-interest into the larger economic system.

The third postulate states that:

> Associated with the social values of an economic system are appropriate sets of social goods that characterize how a particular economic system chooses to realize its social values. The dominant social goods are individual happiness and economic justice. [241]

In contrast to either utilitarian or subjective, individualist views of happiness, the objective view implied here asserts that the happiness of each individual is connected to that of all others in society. The desired socioeconomic outputs associated with this social good must be chosen by society; they can range from provision for basic economic needs, to meeting communal needs for fair distribution, human development needs for individual freedom, love and belonging, and self-fulfillment needs for enjoyment and a sense of completeness. This definition of valued outputs implies value judgments by society about the nature of acceptable behavior in pursuit of individual happiness.

With regard to economic justice, traditionally only distributional justice has captured the (insufficient) attention of social-welfare economists, who have focused on the trade-offs between economic efficiency and equality. However, the definition of the socioeconomic outputs associated with economic justice as a social good should also include indicators of commutative justice (equivalence of exchange) and of productive justice, i.e., the ability of all individuals to participate in the economic system to fulfill their basic needs. The particular outputs desired in association with each of these concepts of justice must also be socially determined, based in part on their effects on individual happiness, since these two social goods are interdependent.

In fact, the fourth postulate states that:

> The social goods of an economic system are interdependent. Given such interdependency, an economic system must determine how one social value and its associated goods will be traded off against other social values and associated goods. [246]

Neoclassical models generally assume absolute independence of all economic behavior, but in reality there are various types, and varying degrees, of interdependence. Socioeconomic externalities caused by production and consumption involve the lowest degree of interdependence and are in fact dealt with—as anomalies—in the neoclassical model. The interdependence of social goods, as well as communal interdependence—the idea that happiness and justice for individuals cannot be defined or understood apart from the rest of society—represent progressively higher degrees of interdependence. While these two forms of interdependence also pervade economic systems, the extent to which they are actually recognized, and the approaches taken to resolve the trade-off issues that arise, will depend on a society's dominant ideology.

The fifth postulate therefore states that:

> How an economic system integrates its values into rules of economic behavior, distributes the rewards from participation in the economy, and solves the trade-off problem between interdependent social values and associated socioeconomic outputs is determined by the primary ideology that prevails in the economic society. The two dominant ideologies are individualism and totality. [249]

The ideology of individualism is based on three major concepts: (1) individual autonomy; (2) individual dignity, or the belief that all individuals are equal and exist as ends in themselves, and that the purpose of society is to advance individual welfare; and (3) the right and duty of individuals to pursue self-development. Likewise, the ideology of totality, which sees the universe as an organism composed of interdependent parts, is based on the concepts of: (1) absolute emptiness, or the belief that individuals do not have a true reality independent of others; (2) mutual identity, or the belief that parts can only be defined in relation to the whole of which they are a part; and (3) universal intercausality, which denies linear flows of cause and effect by arguing that all entities are both causes and effects of the totality. These ideologies are far more influential in shaping economic systems than political ideologies, such as capitalism or socialism.

Finally, the sixth and seventh postulates state the dominant characteristics of economic behavior in economic systems based on the ideologies of individualism and totality respectively. Those based on individualism will institutionalize:

> . . . the *autonomous* individual as the primary unit within the economic system; *optimization* behavior regarding the role of the individual within the economic system; and *conflict generation-resolution* as the essential nature of interaction between individuals and institutions within the economic system. [252] [emphasis added]

Systems based on the ideology of totality will instead institutionalize *interdependent* individuals, *satisficing* behavior,[1] and *consensus formation*. Of course, no economic system is a pure model of either ideology. The range of possible economic systems reflects each of these ideologies to varying degrees, but in all cases the choice of system determines the nature of prevailing economic behavior and of moral choice.

Note

1. Conduct aimed at achieving satifactory aspiration levels of the objectives of decision making and which may not therefore involve maximizing profits.

Summary of

Material Well-Being and Human Well-Being

by Peter Travers and Sue Richardson

[Chapter 4 in *Living Decently: Material Well-Being in Australia* (Oxford and New York: Oxford University Press, 1993), 117–156.]

This chapter is devoted to evaluating the relationship between material well-being and the rest of life—i.e., *human* well-being. The concept of material well-being is only an abstraction, and it only covers one aspect of human life; we must be careful not to misuse it, or place more importance on it than is warranted. In fact, only weak relations can be discerned between measures of material well-being and three other aspects of life: happiness, health, and social participation. This is good news, since dominance of all life by one type of good (wealth) or one type of distribution system (the market) would be unjust and undesirable.

Material Well-Being and Happiness

The "fallacy of misplaced concreteness" is the mistake involved "whenever thinkers forget the degree of abstraction involved in thought and draw unwarranted conclusions about concrete actuality."[1] One such fallacy occurs when we put too much weight on the meaning of an abstraction such as material well-being and conclude that richness in this respect implies richness in all aspects of life, or even that no other aspects of life are important. Turning a useful abstraction that is meant to serve particular analytical purposes into a defining reality in this way leads to misinterpretations and poor decision making, especially with respect to social welfare policy. It is therefore necessary to carefully evaluate the actual relationship between the concept of material well-being and other aspects of human well-being.

Few people, economists included, would actually argue that material well-being can be directly equated with happiness. But economists do argue that because material well-being expands options and so contributes to human well-being, it can adequately serve as a proxy indicator of individual and national welfare. However, although evidence suggests that the association between subjective evaluations of happiness and wealth is positive, the relationship appears to be quite weak; within a given country, "rich people invariably declare themselves to be happy more often than do poor people, but not by a large margin." [119] Comparisons between countries show an even less certain relation; cross-country studies have found that levels of happiness in poor countries are not much different from those in their wealthier counterparts.

In the debate about the explanations for these low correlations, some discard subjective indicators altogether, but among those who believe that subjective measures are essential, there are two schools of thought. The first treats subjective assessments of well-being as a reflection of the gap between an individual's situation and his or her aspirations and argues that aspirations are adjusted to conform to reality. The second school focuses on an individual's sense of relative superiority, arguing that the perception that one is doing better than average adds to subjective well-being. In either case, "some kind of adaptive mechanism seems to be at play whereby people come to terms with their situation." [125]

So what does contribute to happiness? Surveys in Australia indicate that the main causes of unhappiness include health problems, lack of friendship or a spouse, lack of social support and community connections, and financial difficulties. Markets are not irrelevant to happiness, but they cannot meet all of these needs. For one thing, trying to convert all of these needs and experiences into marketable goods would radically transform their very nature, perhaps destroying their capacity to create happiness; "friendships" provided by markets would be a much different thing from what we now know. Markets also have difficulty delivering positional or scarce goods, since making them available to everyone can destroy their quality and value. Finally, markets make a virtue of competition and are hostile to cooperation and a sense of community, but these latter attitudes are important sources of well-being in their own right. Thus, at times there may actually be trade-offs between material wealth and overall human well-being.

Material Well-Being and Health

Material well-being and health also appear to be related, if weakly, but the correct interpretation of this relationship is not clear. Australian data, for example, demonstrate a clear inverse relation between occupational prestige and mortality, although this relation is not evident for all causes of death. Self-assessed levels of health also improve with material well-being. But approaches to defining and measuring health are complex and contested. Self-assessment is influenced by cultural factors, and criteria such as the use of health services may reflect common social practices or access more than need. Approaches that focus on characteristics such as pain or functional capacity are also highly relativistic. In the end, blunt instruments such as mortality and life expectancy may be the best available indicators.

The Black Report, published by the British Department of Health and Social Security in 1980, related class differences to health and found that the gaps were growing, generating a great deal of debate. The report was based on *achieved class*—i.e., class based on *current* occupation, not class at birth—during a period of high social mobility, so it was not clear whether health had determined class, or the opposite. It also provoked debate about materialist versus lifestyle explanations of health inequalities. Materialists focus on how differences in access to consumption goods and services can affect health, i.e., they focus on what income can buy. This view can, however, be extended to include entire ways of life associated with a given status, in which case it is not entirely distinct from the lifestyle explanation, which emphasizes the ability of individuals to influence their own health through behavior and consumption choices. However, this materialist-lifestyle distinction is actually misleading and not very productive.

Research on poor countries with exceptionally low mortality relative to per capita income levels—in particular, Sri Lanka, Costa Rica, and Kerala in South India—is more revealing. The determinants of this low mortality appear to include high inputs into universally accessible health and education services, egalitarian food distribution, a high degree of autonomy for women, and open political systems that respond to popular demands—conditions that seem to arise out of certain shared cultural and social patterns. Many of these factors do require substantial public investment of scarce resources, so material well-being *on a national scale* is clearly important, but the experiences of these countries clearly demonstrate that social attitudes and political will can have enormous impact as well, "delinking" an individual's health and material well-being from his or her income. Thus, "the issue is not so much one of materialist versus lifestyle factors, but rather one of the interaction between cultural and material inputs into health, and of the social circumstances that make an egalitarian distribution of these inputs possible." [142]

Material Well-Being and Social Participation

Active participation in community life is a highly valued component of human well-being; some pre-modern welfare systems focused more on securing access for all to community participation than on providing for material needs so as to ensure that wealth did not dominate social activity. In the modern era, some analysts argue that poverty is closely tied to social deprivation, but the evidence does not bear this out. Australian data suggest that, as in the cases of happiness and health, the relationship between wealth and social participation—based on an aggregate sample of twelve activity indicators—is positive, but small; nor does there appear to be any threshold income below which social exclusion occurs. Moreover, when these activities are divided into subgroups related to social support, friendship, sports activities, and "yuppie" activities (theater- and movie-going, eating out, and taking holidays), all categories except the last show statistically significant but *extremely weak* correlations to wealth. The correlation between the more cash-dependent yuppie activities and full income is somewhat stronger.

It is also necessary to ask, however, whether individuals with low incomes are more likely than others to suffer from *multiple social deprivations* (i.e., scoring in the lowest 20 percent in more than one of the activity categories) even if the overall incidence is low. It appears that low income is somewhat associated with experiencing multiple deprivations, but again, the relation is relatively weak. However, when recast in terms of the likelihood of experiencing multiple problems, the data show that even though only a small proportion of the lowest income group does experience this, these individuals are still five times more likely to suffer multiple social deprivations than those at the top of the income scale.

The results are quite similar when considering the likelihood that individuals will suffer problems in more than one of the categories of happiness, health, and social participation. Relatively few actually experience multiple problems, but the poorest are eleven times more likely than the wealthy to suffer this fate. On the whole, however, it does not appear that the distribution of human well-being mirrors that for material well-being. Walzer has defined as unjust a society where the distribution of nonmaterial goods is determined by the distribution of material resources; even if the distribution of wealth, participation, etc. is relatively egalitarian, the intrinsic meaning of friendship, political activity, etc. is perverted if these things can be bought. It is thus a welcome finding that money does not dominate the other spheres of human well-being examined here. This finding should have major implications for public policy.

Note

1. Herman Daly and John B. Cobb, Jr., *For the Common Good: Redirecting the Economy Toward Community, the Environment, and a Sustainable Future* (Boston: Beacon Press, 1989), 36; cited by Traverse and Richardson 117–118.

Summary of

The Joyless Market Economy

by Robert E. Lane

[Paper delivered to the *Conference on Economics, Values, and Organization,* Yale University, New Haven, Connecticut, April 19–21, 1996.]

Levels of both general happiness and satisfaction with various aspects of our lives have been declining in the U.S. for at least a quarter century, and perhaps much longer. This reflects the declining power of money—the one source of happiness that the market can provide—to make people happy. In fact, the true sources of happiness, especially people and relationships, are ignored or treated as mere externalities by the market, with little concern for whether market activity enhances or inhibits them. Examination of the labor market provides especially clear evidence of the ability of markets to actually inhibit, rather than facilitate, utility maximization.

Indicators and Causes of Declining Well-Being

The National Opinion Research Center has been asking people whether they are very happy, pretty happy, or not too happy in annual national surveys since 1972. Underlying the year-to-year variations, there appears to be a gradual decline in "very happy" responses. This increasing unhappiness affects the young with particular force. Satisfaction with marriages, work, finances, and communities of residence all move in the same direction. The strongest correlation is between overall happiness and marital satisfaction, supporting the argument that people and relationships are the most important sources of happiness. The direction of causality is not clear, but evidence suggests that it runs in both ways (i.e., greater happiness is both a cause and an effect of increased marital satisfaction), and that exogenous factors such as personality predispositions are also important.

The rising incidence of major depression in rapidly modernizing and already advanced economies provides additional evidence of this disturbing trend. People born after 1955 are three times as likely to suffer from major depression at least once in their lives as people born earlier; in rapidly developing countries, each successive generation is likely to be more depressed than the last. It is not clear whether these trends reflect mere historical blips in levels of happiness, or represent a more serious fundamental change in people's ability to attain high levels of well-being.

Several studies have evaluated correlations between particular features of people's lives and their overall level of happiness, which can tell us whether or not the main sources of happiness pass through the market. These studies find high correlations between happiness and indexes of efficacy (self-esteem, the ability to handle problems), family life, financial security, and leisure. Studies of the causes of depression show that while market-based factors such as housing and jobs are important, family problems seem to be of central concern. Thus, the role of the market is still uncertain; markets can be volatile and cause hardship, but they also relieve poverty, yet poverty does not appear to be an important source of depression in poor societies.

Money and Well-Being

The economistic fallacy is the belief that, even when one is beyond the poverty line, higher levels of income still contribute to increasing well-being. In reality, most evidence from advanced countries suggests that above the poverty line this relationship holds only weakly at best; the rich are no happier than the merely comfortable. However, many economists ignore evidence of the declining marginal utility of money and perpetuate the assumption that markets do in fact satisfy human wants.

Comparisons of subjective evaluations of well-being between rich and poor countries make this effect especially clear. While rich societies are on average somewhat happier than poor ones—the *affluence effect*—the differences between them are not systematic, and there are significant differences among the rich countries themselves. It may be that the increased stresses that result from growth counterbalance the benefits of increasing income. However, many people in wealthy countries seem to be trapped on a "hedonic treadmill" in always believing that just one more increase in income will be enough to make them happy. Rather than focusing on maximizing growth, seeking an optimal mix of economic growth and creation of other valued goods might be a more effective means of increasing well-being.

Happiness and Labor Market Externalities

Workers have less control over how labor markets affect them than they have over the impacts of consumption markets (because skills are less fungible than cash, they may face monopsony among employers, and exit is a costly option), so it is worth focusing our attention here. Labor markets are also important determinants of several sources of happiness, including employment itself, work enjoyment, and job security—all factors that are treated as labor market externalities by economists.

One reason for economists' undervaluation of the psychic importance of work is its appearance on firms' ledgers as an accounting cost, whereas efforts to increase happiness through "better" consumer products appear in ledgers as profits from increased sales. In effect, firms treat work as "a disutility for which income and consumption are the compensating utilities." [14] This ignores the fact that work and mastery of skills can be important sources of happiness. Enjoyment and security of work are also treated as externalities because worker satisfaction has little effect on productivity, and because, contrary to Adam Smith's prediction, wage scales have not developed so as to compensate workers for unpleasant aspects of their work.

Looking in more detail at some of these labor market externalities, we must first dispute Juliet Schor's claim that increasing work stress and time demands are a leading cause of unhappiness. Both overworked and underworked people tend to be very unhappy, but there are at least twice as many of the latter. In fact, unemployment appears to be one of the most painful experiences associated with the labor market, yet it too is treated as an externality. However, unemployment fluctuates, and its trends do not parallel those of the rising tide of dissatisfaction, so while it contributes to unhappiness, it is not the source of the observed secular increases.

Too much attention is often focused on *levels* of income, while income *security* is usually undervalued. In fact, security may be the most important aspect of income to many people; some studies indicate that financial security is the most important determinant of general life satisfaction. There can be little doubt that job insecurity has been increasing for Americans, although this trend is perhaps too recent to account for long-term trends in unhappiness. However, as with unemployment, the market does not deal well with issues of job security.

Work satisfaction may in part come from pay, especially for job *seekers*, but fair treatment, independence, and reduction of repetitive tasks in favor of challenging work are even more important. The greater job satisfaction of elites may derive more from the psychic advantages of their work than the added income they receive. But again, these important factors are ignored by the market. People are not compensated for especially unpleasant tasks, nor do they lose pay if they are doing work that they enjoy.

Satisfaction with the level of one's income is a more important determinant of subjective well-being than the absolute level. In the case of friends, however, having them and deriving satisfaction from them are much more closely connected. This suggests that increasing everyone's income may have little impact on overall levels of happiness, while increasing the friendliness of society might have a substantial effect. Fortunately, while satisfaction with financial status has decreased in the last 25 years, satisfaction with friendships has not. For obvious reasons, friendship is not treated as a market commodity.

While some evidence indicates that satisfaction with family life has remained relatively stable in recent decades, levels of divorce and marital strain have been rising. Unhappy marriages may be a product of the indirect effects of the labor market on family life; increasing time demands, unemployment, and decreasing work satisfaction and/or security are, not surprisingly, closely related to marital satisfaction. In the eyes of employers these familial costs are just externalities, but they are destructive, and may increase real costs of labor in the future. Treating the stresses on family life caused by labor markets as mere externalities leads to the disintegration of family life, and hence to increasing unhappiness and depression.

A Historical Turning Point?

While subjective well-being increases on the way up the economic ladder to modernity, once societies "arrive," their levels of happiness plateau briefly and then begin to turn downward as values and expectations change. Subjective well-being follows a curvilinear path: "where the affluence effect meets the economistic fallacy, there is a downturn in felicity." [29] Optimism is necessary to avoid depression, but optimism has been declining with economic development. Thus, the notion that economic development is the root of progress is seriously flawed, and utility in its traditional neoclassical sense is not an acceptable standard of happiness. Our primary sources of satisfaction are not measured in the market, so it is not surprising that subjective well-being and GDP growth are not closely linked once basic needs have been met.

Economic progress and development of human capital are cumulative, but in the case of happiness, perhaps people constantly adapt to changing circumstances and make the present the new standard of evaluation. However, to explain the fact that happiness is not just constant but actually declining, we must consider the effects of our institutions, especially the market, on the sources of our happiness. Economic functions are not ends in themselves; they are only valuable in so far as they bring men peace in their hearts and in their relationships. But "the offerings of the market no longer satisfy, not because the payoff is not large enough but because it is made in the wrong currency." [32]

Summary of

Economic Institutions and the
Satisfaction of Human Needs

by Ian Gough

[Published in *Journal of Economic Issues* vol. 28 (March 1994), 25–66.]

Economists have often doubted that there are any objective human needs, or have believed that all needs are historically relative. This paper argues that there are, in general terms, universal human needs and suggests that different economic systems can be evaluated in terms of their ability to satisfy those needs.

Need Satisfaction as a Measure of Welfare Outcomes

"All persons have an objective interest in avoiding serious *harm* that in turn prevents them from pursuing their vision of the good, whatever that is." [28] Human needs consist, at least, of the universal preconditions for pursuit of one's vision of the good, i.e., physical health and autonomy of agency. Autonomy requires mental health, cognitive skills, and opportunities for participation in social activity. More specific "intermediate needs," such as food, housing, health care, education, etc., are valuable because they contribute to physical health and autonomy.

There are both procedural and material preconditions for enhancement of need satisfaction by economic institutions. Procedurally, need satisfaction is increased by rational identification of needs, availability and use of practical knowledge, and democratic resolution of disagreements. Materially, need satisfaction depends on the production, distribution, and appropriate use (e.g., in household consumption processes) of goods and services relevant to human needs. These criteria can be used to evaluate different economic systems.

Many writers have distinguished three modes of economic organization— market, state, and community. The first two are familiar and can be represented by the theoretical model of a free market economy and by Soviet-style central planning, respectively. The third is less familiar and is not the dominant mode of organization anywhere in the modern world. However, it has been described in such diverse sources as utopian socialist and anarchist writings, the libertarian vision of voluntary communities, and the new school of "democratic communitarianism." Common to these varied approaches is the assumption that economic coordination takes place in decentralized, democratic negotiation and is facilitated by the feelings of solidarity, loyalty, and reciprocity within the community.

No real-world economy can rely solely on markets, central planning, or communitarian cooperation. Some mixture of different systems of coordination is inevitable in practice. Nonetheless, it is useful to contrast the three ideal types in terms of their influence on the satisfaction of needs.

Free Markets and Central Planning

Does the free market provide the procedural preconditions for need satisfaction? Rational identification of needs is often obfuscated by market activity. The market responds to wants and desires, no matter how urgent or trivial, so long as they are backed by money. Indeed, the market may even generate additional wants endogenously, leading farther away from the identification of real needs. The market fares better in terms of availability and use of practical knowledge, allowing the application of the dispersed knowledge of millions of actors; however, the sheer number of commodities produced in market societies may overwhelm consumers, leading to poorly informed decision making. Finally, democratic resolution of conflict is furthered in some cases by decentralized market processes; yet the market also distorts the political process, in cases where involvement of the state is essential.

The claims of market capitalism are stronger, but still problematical, in the area of material preconditions of need satisfaction. The standard model of a market economy suggests that it excels at increasing production and innovation. Critics have countered that unregulated markets have tendencies toward monopoly, are unable to supply public goods, lead to a self-defeating production of positional goods, and satisfy wants only in commodified forms. "Laissez-faire capitalism may be an efficient system for satisfying *certain* wants by means of *commodities,* but that is all." [38]

The distribution of goods and services resulting from unregulated markets cannot provide entitlements to basic needs for all, even in rich societies. Household and family relationships, within which consumption largely occurs, are in part eroded by market society; in part, however, gendered inequalities within households are perpetuated by markets, affecting the levels and distribution of need satisfactions.

Soviet-style state planning and control of the economy fail on most of the procedural requirements for needs satisfaction. Rational identification of needs occurs only to the extent that central planners can correctly define society's needs, as in wartime or other emergencies. Under normal, peacetime conditions the planning apparatus is likely to misstate or distort actual needs. Application of practical knowledge is severely limited; democratic resolution of conflicts is virtually unknown.

In terms of material preconditions for need satisfaction, state socialism has several advantages over capitalism in principle. Production for basic needs can receive priority; entitlements and egalitarian distribution can be ensured; household relationships and the status of women can be transformed by supportive social policies. In practice, central planning has encountered growing problems of coordination as development proceeds, failing to produce the goods people want or to provide incentives for improvement in production. Egalitarian distribution is limited by special privileges for the elite and by shortages and queues, which add to the burdens of the persistent, gendered division of household labor.

In short, both a pure market economy and a pure command economy suffer from procedural and material drawbacks as institutional settings for the satisfaction of needs.

Community and Communitarianism

Utopian visions have defined the communal economy as a society of absences: one without markets, money, the state, hierarchy, inequality, and scarcity. Such visions have often been rejected as unrealistic or ill-conceived. Yet there has also been a renewed interest in communitarian alternatives in recent years. The great advantage of a communitarian economy would be a procedural one: by allowing dialogue and direct democracy, it would facilitate learning about needs and how to meet them. Application of experiential knowledge and democratic resolution of conflicts would be the norm. In an environment of trust, reciprocity, and moral obligation, "collective needs can be asserted over individual wants as the dominant goal of a communitarian economy." [43]

On the other hand, there are fundamental procedural problems with communitarianism. Intense communities may become coercive in their agreement on values, undermining the autonomy of individual members. If membership is voluntary, "misfits" and outsiders may not be accepted by any community, necessitating some form of state intervention or provision for their needs. Solidaristic communities in general run the risk of becoming parochial in their view of insiders versus outsiders.

In terms of material preconditions for the satisfaction of human needs, the communitarian alternative has barely been developed. Coordination within communities is difficult enough, and coordination between communities is still more intractable (unless it reverts to market or state planning mechanisms). Likewise, the problem of distribution within communities and the persistence of issues of household labor and gender inequality are often overlooked by communitarian writers. A realistic communitarianism must integrate the benefits of community with a continuing role for the market and the state.

Summary

The three systems may be summarized by describing their ideas of human needs:

> Free market capitalism essentially equates needs with wants, an equation that is logically flawed and morally untenable. State socialism by contrast operates with an idea of universal and objective need but equates this with the views of the party and state functionaries. Need is identified with one particular form of codified knowledge, which reflects constellations of power incompatible with the pursuit of truth. Communitarian models interpret need as those interests defined by particular cultural groups or communities. They thus make relative the idea of universal human need and denude it of an evaluative or moral role. None of the three systems embody a notion of human need that is universal and objective, yet open-ended and cumulative. (45–46)

The article goes on to advocate a form of mixed economy combining elements of market, planning, and negotiated coordination as the best feasible economic framework for improving need satisfaction.

Summary of

The Ethical Limitations of the Market

by Elizabeth Anderson

[Published in *Value in Ethics and Economics* (Cambridge, MA and London: Harvard University Press, 1993), 141–167.]

Why not put everything up for sale? One answer is that we value goods in many ways that cannot be expressed in markets. This paper argues that a liberal commitment to freedom and autonomy that acknowledges a plurality of values justifies more stringent ethical limits on the market than previously recognized by liberal theory.

Pluralism and Freedom

Pluralism about values says that goods are properly valued in fundamentally different ways: for example, some goods are most properly respected, others merely used. To be able to value goods in different ways people must produce, exchange, or enjoy goods in different social spheres governed by distinct social norms and ideals. The market is just one social sphere that enables us to value goods as private, exclusive use-values but not to value them in other ways; people need to place goods in nonmarket social settings.

These facts imply that to enjoy freedom and autonomy, people must place limits on markets. If the market governed the production and circulation of all goods, people would lose freedom by losing opportunities to value goods in nonmarket ways. For example, libertarian proposals to "divide (privatize) the commons" eliminate the public spaces of civil society that are needed for citizens to enjoy the shared goods of civic interaction on terms of equality and open access. If the market wholly governed the way people treat goods embodied in the person, such as freedom of action, people would lose autonomy when they sold these goods. The liberal concern to protect autonomy thus requires that we make some goods embodied in the person inalienable through the market.

Liberal pluralism requires limits on the market, not its elimination. But the limits can be drawn only if market settings are distinguished from other institutional settings within civil society. These settings can be differentiated by identifying the norms, goods, and values distinctive of each, along the lines described in Michael Walzer's *Spheres of Justice* (see summary in Part VII).

Markets and Economic Goods

Market relations are structured by norms with five characteristic features that express attitudes concerning use and embody the ideal of economic freedom, i.e., greater choice. Market norms are *impersonal* in that each party to a transaction views the other as an instrument to one's own ends. *Egoism* governs those market relations in which parties to a transaction are presumed to take care of their own. Economic goods are *exclusive* since their benefits go only to the purchaser, and individual wants are determined without consideration of others' interests. As a *want-regarding* institution, the market responds only to effective demand and pays no attention to the reasons why people may want a good. It overlooks the distinctions between urgent need and intense desire between *a priori* desire and *a posteriori* satisfaction. Consumers influence provision and exchange primarily through *exit* not *voice*. They have no voice in the design of products, except through willingness to pay.

A pure economic good is governed by the five market norms, and its value is realized through use. Other goods are only partially commodified and belong to nonmarket spheres of life, such as civil society, personal life, and politics.

Civil Society and the Market

Civil society includes markets as well as many other institutions, including profitmaking firms and nonprofit organizations, such as schools, labor unions, professional associations, and political parties. Given his/her concern for freedom, which clearly allows for the sale of professional products and services, the liberal pluralist is faced with the challenge of articulating the proper relation of the market to these other institutions.

The profit and nonprofit institutions of civil society establish internal norms of excellence regarding conduct and achievement. Professionals such as doctors, lawyers, academics, athletes, and artists pursue standards of excellence that are set by their respective institutions. Adherence to these norms may be costly in terms of foregone opportunities to make money; e.g., good doctors will not perform medically unwarranted but profitable services. "Sphere differentiation should not be confused with complete sphere segregation." [147] There are obvious advantages to the availability of a market sphere through which artists, doctors, etc. can sell their services rather than relying on the patronage of the wealthy or of the state. However, if market norms are allowed to overwhelm institutional norms, we face the dangers of greed, diminished autonomy, artistic pandering to popular taste, and worse. One remedy is to maintain employment opportunities in both profit and nonprofit institutions.

Some have argued that only market norms should govern the sale of professional services—that whoever pays for a good may refuse to pay for any goods that fail to meet his/her preferred specifications. This argument has been used to defend government censorship of the arts: it assumes that the state is a customer who can exit projects that do not satisfy its preferences. This market approach to government funding ignores the fact that for certain projects the state is very unlike a customer—one of its most important aims is to expand the range of significant opportunities open to its citizens, not to satisfy the majority's preferences. Government sponsored art, even distasteful art, offers to minority views opportunities for expression that may be foreclosed in market settings.

Personal Relations and the Market

Market intrusion within the personal sphere tends to disrupt the pursuit of its distinctive ideals: intimacy and commitment. Transactions involving goods proper to the personal sphere are ideally regulated by gift exchange norms rather than market norms. Consumers may exit market exchanges without penalty, but the refusal of an appropriate gift is an insult. Unlike market transactions, which involve the exchange of distinct, impersonal goods, gift exchange affirms the bonds between donor and recipient and aims at realizing a shared good. Also, reciprocity in gift exchange may occur over the long term, while delays in market exchanges are grounds for legal action.

It can be demonstrated that freedom and autonomy are supported when gift exchange norms, rather than market norms, govern human sexuality and conduct within marriages. If this is right, liberal pluralism offers reasons against the legalization of prostitution and extreme efforts to fix the terms of exchange in marriages, e.g., through elaborate contracts.

Political Goods and the Market

Political goods can be secured only through a form of democratic provision that is governed by three types of political norms. First, nonexclusive political norms imply that everyone has access to political goods, not just those who pay. Next, political goods should be distributed according to public principles that are responsive to needs rather than to unexamined wants. Finally, political goods emphasize voice (rather than exit). These norms embody the two ideals of social democracy: fraternity and democratic freedom. Provision of political goods through the market mechanism undermines these ideals by diminishing our capacity to value and realize ourselves as fraternal democratic citizens.

Limitations of Market Ideologies

Market ideologies, such as libertarianism and welfare economics, claim that most expansions of markets represent gains in freedom and welfare. Against this, the liberal pluralist argues that these gains appear to follow only if freedom and welfare are defined in the same limited terms to which the market responds. Market ideologies are blind to a more robust, adequate conception of freedom and welfare.

This blindness stems from three errors in value theory. The first error is to define freedom as a matter of expressing one's preferences without having to consider others' values. But the freedom to value things as shared goods requires responsiveness to others' values. The second error is the assumption of individualism: that individual autonomy is given prior to market transactions and is preserved in them. This ignores the fact that autonomy can be undermined by social relations of domination created by markets in goods embodied in the person. The third error is the assumption that freedom is expressed only in the use of exclusively owned goods. This ignores the freedoms we can only enjoy through collective action.

We are not free to pursue the shared goods of deepest significance to human life within the terms of libertarian freedom alone. The personal and political spheres offer different ideals of freedom. In genuinely committed and intimate relationships we are free to reveal ourselves to others, without having our self-disclosure become the object of another's manipulations in egoistic market-oriented bargaining. In democratic societies we are free to participate in collective decisions that affect everyone. This is the freedom to be included, rather than to exclude others. When exit is impossible, when decisions concern shared goods, or when freedom can be effectively exercised by all only in public spaces of free and equal association, democratic freedom supersedes market freedom. (165–166)

Conclusion

According to liberal pluralism, the value of freedom can be realized only if the market does not dominate all social settings. "The realization of some forms of freedom, autonomy, and welfare demands that certain goods be produced, exchanged, and enjoyed outside of market relations or in accordance with non-market norms." [166] This requires a deeper understanding of the ways we value goods, the social relations within which we enjoy them, and the ideals these relations are supposed to embody.

> The difficult task for modern societies is to reap the advantages of the market while keeping its activities confined to the goods proper to it. [167]

Summary of

Human Well-Being and the Natural World
and
Nature, Intrinsic Value, and Human Well-Being
by John O'Neill

[Chapters 1 and 2 in *Ecology, Policy, and Politics: Human Well-Being and the Natural World* (London: Routledge, 1993), 1–25.]

Much of the recent debate about the environment has centered on the extent to which human well-being should factor into environmental concerns. Two approaches have dominated the response, one based on a traditional market-oriented evaluation of well-being, and a second that denies the validity of well-being as the basis of decision making and instead insists on recognition of the *intrinsic* value of nonhuman entities. However, showing that natural entities have intrinsic values does not, in itself, entail any obligation on the part of humans, but at the same time, intrinsic value is not necessarily incompatible with a concern for human well-being. Both of these approaches should be rejected in favor of an Aristotelian conception of well-being based on the objective goods that a person may possess.

The Standard Responses

The neoclassical response to environmental concerns argues that they can be adequately accommodated by incorporation into existing decision-making procedures via the standard economic tools on which they are grounded, especially cost-benefit analysis. Within this paradigm, economic assessment is based on human well-being, interpreted in terms of the satisfaction of wants and willingness to pay (market prices). The market is seen as the best institutional framework for maximizing well-being and cost-benefit analysis as the best tool for evaluation, particularly when markets do not function perfectly. Environmental values can be priced and incorporated into this framework, but human well-being remains the focus of analysis.

Proponents of the "deep green" or "deep ecological" approach, on the other hand, argue that anthropocentric efforts to incorporate environmental concerns into methods of analysis based on human well-being are inadequate. Neoclassical methods, and the ideology of science and industrial society in general, can only value the nonhuman world in terms of its instrumental value for enhancing human well-being. This does not give proper due to the nonhuman world or to the interests of future generations. The starting point must instead be an "environmental ethic" grounded in a belief in the intrinsic value of nonhuman entities.

Both of these responses can be rejected. Cost-benefit analysis is fundamentally flawed. It is difficult to incorporate the interests of entities (such as yet-unborn humans) that are unable to articulate their preferences, and a preference-based interpretation of well-being is too narrow. These are neither arbitrary nor easily remedied mistakes of market systems. Rather, "different institutions carry with them different definitions of well-being," [7] and the market system itself institutionally fosters this self-understanding and a conception of well-being defined in terms of endless acquisition of material goods. The "deep" responses, meanwhile, are flawed in their assumption that a concern for human well-being is inherently incompatible both with recognition of the intrinsic value of nonhuman entities and with concern for future generations.

An alternative Aristotelian conception characterizes well-being not in the welfare economist's terms of preference satisfaction, but rather in terms of access to certain objective goods, such as friends, the ability to develop one's own capacities and shape one's life, or the opportunity to contemplate what is beautiful. This objectivist conception of human well-being, which is systematically undermined by the market, suggests that "the gap between well-being and ideals is narrower than is usually assumed, and more specifically, it reveals that the capacity to appreciate environmental goods is a component of human well-being." [5] This view is thus entirely compatible with a concern for the good of nonhumans and future generations.

Definitions of Intrinsic Value and Their Conflation

Deep ecologists hold that an understanding of the intrinsic value of nonhuman entities is the proper centerpiece of an environmental ethic, but the term "intrinsic value" has several interpretations, and conflation of these interpretations confuses many of the arguments about environmental issues. One common use of the term is as a synonym for *noninstrumental value,* i.e., to describe objects that are valued as ends in themselves rather than as means to other ends. A second use is in reference to the *intrinsic properties* of an object, properties that exist independently of their relation to other objects. Finally, intrinsic value can also be employed as a synonym for *objective value,* or the value of an object that exists independently of valuers.

The first and third of these definitions are often interchanged, confusing claims about the *sources* of value and claims regarding the *objects* of value. It is often assumed that if valuation is subjectivist (evaluations by humans are the only source of value) rather than objectivist (value is independent of human evaluation), then nonhuman entities can only be granted instrumental value. This is false; it conflates the source of value with its object. In fact, there is no reason why a *subjective* human evaluator cannot value nonhuman entities as ends in themselves or future states as much as present ones. There is nothing in the subjectivist approach that dictates the content of what is valued. Nor does objectivist valuation imply that the nonhuman world does have noninstrumental value. "It does not follow from the claim that values do not have their source in humans that they do not have humans as their sole ultimate object." [13]

Problems also arise from conflating the first and second meanings. Many environmental characteristics that are valued in practice, such as rarity and diversity, are clearly relational, so they are not intrinsic values in the second sense of the term. The mistake arises when this is taken to imply that these characteristics cannot have intrinsic value in any of the other senses either (e.g., in the sense of noninstrumental valuation) and that they therefore have no place in an environmental ethic. In fact, "We might value an object in virtue of its relational properties, for example its rarity, without thereby seeing it as having only instrumental value for human satisfactions." [14] Moreover, an entity such as wilderness "might have value in virtue of its relation with human beings without thereby being of only instrumental value for humans." [15]

Objective Value and the Natural World

An objectivist evaluation of value contends that evaluative properties are real properties of objects that they hold independently of valuation by evaluating agents. In the weak interpretation of this view, evaluative properties are simply properties that exist *in the absence of* such agents, while in the strong interpretation, these properties can be identified *without reference to* an evaluating agent.

One popular defense of an environmental ethic has been to establish the objectivity of evaluative properties or values by drawing an analogy between these and secondary qualities (e.g., color). Under the weak interpretation (but not the strong one), secondary qualities persist in the absence of observers and so are real properties of objects; by analogy, the same is said to be true for evaluative properties. However, this analogy is weak, and in any case the approach does not really get to the core of the debate about the nature of values.

It is more useful to show that objective values exist in the strong sense. Evaluative utterances about the natural world—phrases such as "x is good for the greenfly" (or "x helps the greenfly to flourish")—help to demonstrate this. Such phrases show that things that are capable of flourishing or being injured have their own goods independent of human interests and attitudes; these evaluative properties are therefore real properties in the strong sense. It can also be shown that the class of entities that can be said to have such goods includes not only individual living creatures, but collective entities as well.

Intrinsic Value and Human Well-Being

The next step in defending an environmental ethic is usually to argue that the very existence of goods that are independent of human interests or observations implies that they are worthy of moral consideration. However, this assumption is incorrect.

> It is possible to talk in an objective sense of what constitutes the goods of entities, without making any claims that these ought to be realized. . . . One can recognize that something has its own goods, and quite consistently be morally indifferent to these goods or believe one has a moral duty to inhibit their development. . . . There is a logical gap between facts and oughts. [22–23]

The goods of the HIV virus provide one such example.

The failure of this argument raises problems in the discussion of environmental ethics, since showing the existence of objective goods is not in itself sufficient grounds on which to argue that nonhuman entities are legitimate objects of moral concern. One means of bridging this gap is a quasi-utilitarian objectivist approach that invokes a moral duty to maximize the amount of objective good in the world. This approach fails, however, for a number of reasons, especially in its inability to account for the fact that some goods are not ethically desirable or acceptable, such as those that provide for the flourishing of sadists, viruses, or dictatorships.

The more productive alternative is an Aristotelian bridge. Human beings, as well as other types of entities, possess two types of goods—goods that are *constitutive* of our flourishing, and goods that are *instrumental* to our flourishing. The Aristotelian ethic argues that we should promote flourishing of many other living things not because they are instrumental to our own flourishing, but because they are constitutive of our flourishing. This is more than a narrow anthropocentric ethic, because it does in fact value components of the natural world *for their own sake,* not merely as a means to serve our own interests. However, arguing that "care for the natural world is constitutive of a flourishing human life" [24] does not finish our work. This claim still needs a detailed defense, a defense that should begin with the appeal that a good human life requires a broad, not a narrow, spectrum of goods.

Summary of

Taking Ethics Seriously: Economics and Contemporary Moral Philosophy
by Daniel M. Hausman and Michael S. McPherson

[Published in *Journal of Economic Literature* 31 (June 1993): 671–731.]

To be a good person, one must take ethics seriously. But can the same be said about being a good *economist*? Does morality matter to economic analysis? [671]

This article provides an extensive review and bibliography of recent work by economists and moral philosophers that borders the two disciplines.

Why Should Economists Be Interested in Moral Questions?
"The simple picture of the economist who provides value-free technical information to the decision maker is at best a useful caricature." [672] Real-world

policy decisions are almost never formulated as well-defined, purely technical problems, as the caricature implies.

Economists should care about moral questions for at least four reasons. First, the moral positions of economic agents, as well as of economic theory, can influence economic behavior; a description of the economy that overlooks the importance of social norms, commitments, and altruistic motivations is positively flawed and normatively biased. Second, standard welfare economics rests on a number of controversial moral principles, including the comparison of alternatives exclusively in terms of outcomes (rather than processes) and the identification of the social good with the satisfaction of individual preferences. Third, public policy is universally discussed in terms of moral concepts such as needs, fairness, and individual dignity; economics needs to be relevant to that discourse. Finally, positive and normative elements are inseparable even in academic economics as it exists today.

Morality and Rationality

The homo economicus of contemporary economics is 'homo rationalis.' . . . But the view of rationality economists endorse—utility theory—may not even be compatible with moral behavior, and it does not provide a rich enough picture of individual choice to permit one to discuss the character, causes and consequences of moral behavior. [688]

Is economic rationality incompatible with moral behavior? The answer depends on what is being maximized by the "rational" individual. Amartya Sen distinguishes between three types of motivations: self-interest, sympathy with others, and duty or commitment to moral principles. If economic rationality is restricted to maximization of self-interest, or even self-interest plus sympathetic concerns, then morality may appear irrational. However, if rationality more broadly means acting on reasons that seem to be good ones, then actions based on moral commitments can be as rational as any others. Recent analyses of labor markets and worker motivation provide good examples of the importance of moral principles in economic modeling. Contracts between workers and employers are notoriously hard to enforce on both sides. The existence of trust and fairness, as well as cultural norms regarding cooperation and work effort, is essential to the smooth functioning of the labor process.

Evaluating Economic Arrangements

Moral evaluations of economic policies and outcomes are an inescapable part of the discussion and application of economics. In such evaluations, all plausible moral views assign an important place to individual well-being, which is often identified, by economists, with the satisfaction of preferences. This economic approach is questionable because preferences are difficult to measure; they may be based on false beliefs or unusually expensive tastes; they may be idiosyncratic or socially controversial; or they may reflect adaptation to unfair circumstances.

To avoid these and other problems, some theorists have proposed alternative conceptions of well-being. In addition, the evaluation of economic processes and outcomes must involve more than well-being; questions of rights and liberties are also important. "Negative" liberties, or freedoms from interference, are often justified on instrumental grounds: leaving individuals free to make their own choices is both individually and socially beneficial. Many would also view freedom, self-determination, or autonomy as intrinsically valuable, regardless of the utility of their outcomes. In terms of ethical theory, there is a distinction between consequentialist views, in which only outcomes matter, and nonconsequentialist views that attach importance to the processes as well as to the results of social interactions.

A related debate concerns the question of which is the more important aspect of equality: equality of welfare (outcomes) or of resources? Principles of justice provide a final dimension for economic evaluation. For example, many people believe that hard or dangerous work should be rewarded, that wages should not be race or gender dependent, and so on. Yet, although these principles are of great importance in practical politics, their theoretical elaboration and defense is difficult; they have accordingly received comparatively less attention than other issues discussed here.

Four Bases for Overall Moral Judgments

There are at least four possible bases for a moral assessment of economic institutions. First is the criterion of efficiency (or Pareto optimality) that has been traditionally favored by economists. This approach is severely limited as it does not apply to the many economic events that involve losers as well as winners. Cost-benefit analysis is a controversial extension of efficiency considerations to such cases.

A second perspective, libertarianism, typically links the fundamental virtue of liberty to a rights-based view of justice. Philosophical libertarians, such as Robert Nozick, are committed to the primacy of "natural rights" independent of any consequences for human welfare; others, such as Friedrich Hayek, argue for libertarian policies on the grounds that many social goals are best advanced by minimizing the role of government.

Third, utilitarianism and consequentialism were resurrected and transformed in the 1980s, in the works of such diverse authors as Richard Brandt, John Broome, John Harsanyi, Amartya Sen, and others. None of these thinkers accept the neoclassical economists' view of utility as an index of satisfaction of *actual* preferences; some use modified or restricted categories, such as "rational" or "well-informed" preferences. Other authors have developed consequentialist theories that are nonutilitarian, wherein the good consequences to be maximized include more than individual happiness or preference satisfaction. "If philosophers can specify a well-defined and clearly measurable good to be achieved, then the welfare economist can step in and discuss how best to achieve it." [706] One example might be a carefully defined notion of human needs.

Fourth, "contractualist" approaches assume that an acceptable moral view for a society should reflect some form of agreement among members of that society. One approach, developed independently by William Vickrey, Harsanyi, and Rawls, begins by asking what moral principles rational agents would agree to if they did not yet know what roles they would play in society. For Vickrey and Harsanyi this leads to utilitarianism: not knowing who you will be, you will prefer to maximize average utility for society as a whole. Rawls assumes differently that people in the "original position," behind a "veil of ignorance" about who they will become, would first choose to safeguard everyone's basic liberties, and then would try to promote the interests of those who are least well off, so as to guard against the possibility of being a member of that disadvantaged group. Different assumptions about the nature and the prevalence of self-interest, in moral, political, and economic settings, result in different theoretical and practical applications of contractualism.

These examples of the areas in which economists and moral philosophers have consciously overlapped in recent years are useful to remind us that "[v]ery little in ethics is completely uncontroversial, and very little can be said about economics that relies on only uncontroversial moral premises." [712] At the same time, "[a]n economics that is engaged actively and self-critically with the moral aspects of its subject matter cannot help but be more interesting, more illuminating, and ultimately more useful than one that tries not to be." [723]

PART II

Utility and Welfare I: The History of Economic Thought

Overview Essay

by Frank Ackerman

Those who succeed in penetrating the mathematical armor cannot fail to notice the narrowness at the heart of modern economics. Contemporary theory takes for granted a one-dimensional understanding of human goals, restricted to the maximization of the satisfaction of existing, unchanging desires for ever more private consumption. Where does this conceptual narrowness come from? Why is a broader understanding of human motivation excluded from economics? In pursuit of an answer, this section and the next explore the historical origins of the modern economic treatment of welfare, values, and well-being.

The discipline was not always so single-minded. One of the great 19th-century economists, John Stuart Mill, could write:

> Except on matters of mere details, there are perhaps no practical questions . . . which admit of being decided on economical premises alone.[1]

Mill, of course, was not speaking of the need for advanced mathematical knowledge, but rather of the need for historical, social, and, above all, ethical perspectives on economic problems. Leading economists from Adam Smith to Mill to Alfred Marshall (the period covered in this section) were also philosophers; Smith and Marshall both received their first teaching positions in moral philosophy. Yet it is their more technical work, those aspects of their writings that could be formalized in models, that have become part of the ongoing development of the discipline of economics. On the moral and philosophical side, there have been periodic changes in intellectual fashion, but no evidence of cumulative advances.

Amartya Sen has suggested that economics has two different origins, one in ethics and the other in concerns more closely related to engineering.[2] He traces the ethical questions about economics back to Aristotle and the engineering concerns to another author of the same era: Kautilya, an advisor to the Indian emperor in the 4th century B.C. There is, however, nothing approaching a continuous debate on either of these perspectives over the ensuing 2,500 year span. For the purposes of this essay it will be sufficient to start with the background of Adam Smith and the genesis of modern economics.

Founding Fathers: Smith and Bentham

For Smith, as for many early economists, ethical and "engineering" issues were intertwined. He is famous for his analytical work, such as his description of the efficiency of the division of labor and the operation of the competitive market. In this area, he built on the earlier work of William Petty, as well as the French physiocrats, while adding new insights with a clarity and comprehensiveness that made *The Wealth of Nations* a classic.

Smith's ethical writings, while less famous today, occupied a substantial part of his career. The "invisible hand" metaphor for the harmonious mechanism of a competitive market first appeared in the earlier and more philosophical of his two major works, *The Theory of Moral Sentiments*. A number of authors have examined the relationship between Smith's ethics and economics, including John Salter in the first article summarized here. For the background to Smith's philosophy, it is also useful to consult the article by Istvan Hont and Michael Ignatieff, which is cited (and criticized) by Salter.

Smith learned philosophy from members of the comparatively new school of utilitarianism, which was emerging as an alternative to the earlier "natural law" perspective. Utilitarians held that the moral course of action was that which promoted the greatest happiness of the greatest number of people. This stood in contrast to the older moral tradition that there were natural laws, derived from divine revelation, logic, or understanding of human nature, that defined the right way to act and live. Vocabulary and concepts derived from both schools can be found in Smith's writings.

The natural law tradition and its ambiguous implications for private property and markets reflect the contradictory opinions of Thomas Aquinas, whose 13th-century writings framed the terms of medieval philosophical debate. Aquinas argued that even though God's estate on earth was originally given to humanity in common, individual possession was a rational addition to natural law, since it provided incentives to care for property and work hard to improve it. However, in cases of famine or other urgent necessity, property rights could be overruled by the original claim of all to share in the community of goods.

As capitalist relationships became more and more the norm in western Europe in the 17th and 18th centuries, natural law theorists tended to resolve the contradiction in Aquinas's views in favor of property rights. A succession of authors, of whom John Locke is the best known, secularized the account of natural law that supported private property and made the emergency claims of the poor on society increasingly limited and exceptional. These philosophical developments paralleled events in the marketplace: in both England and France, ancient laws limiting the price of grain and ensuring provision for the poor were increasingly ignored in good years, but were still occasionally invoked when harvests were bad.

Adam Smith's contribution to this debate was to maintain that property rights should be favored in all cases, and that government should not place restraints on the market, even to provide low-priced grain to the poor when harvests failed. What was the ethical justification for this seemingly heartless stance? Hont and Ignatieff cite passages from Smith's earlier work in which he optimistically claimed that the prosperity resulting from the division of labor in a competitive market will provide for the poor more effectively and reliably than any government intervention.

Salter rejects this argument and finds a break between Smith's younger, more optimistic philosophical writings and his mature economic analysis in *The Wealth of Nations*. The latter work still expressed the hope that in the long run, and in most particular situations, the market will provide adequate subsistence for all—but the hope is no longer a certainty. Meanwhile, property rights have become absolute and are not constrained by anyone else's claim to subsistence. In the worst case, according to Salter's reading of *The Wealth of Nations*, Smith's ideal market would be quite harsh to the poor.

Worst cases, however, do not loom large in Smith's upbeat presentation. The reputation of classical economics as the "dismal science" came only later from other authors. Another decidedly nondismal voice, heard just after Smith, was that of Jeremy Bentham. While Smith, like a number of authors discussed later, could be described as an economist who also wrote philosophy, Bentham was a philosopher who also wrote economics. Bentham did not invent utilitarianism, but he became its most influential proponent by developing and popularizing its implications in some detail.

As described in the chapter by John Bonner summarized here, Bentham relied on a psychological theory of hedonism that would be dismissed as simplistic today (or even, as Thorstein Veblen noted, a century ago). Behavior is said to be motivated by pleasure or pain; an individual's net satisfaction, or pleasure minus pain, is a quantifiable entity called "utility." All the same, Bentham's notion of utility had a number of subtleties that were not always preserved by economists who followed him. Self-interest, for Bentham, included charity, sympathy, and respect for social conventions, motivations that are banished in many later, formalized models of utility maximization. His proposed "calculus" of pleasure and pain involved consideration of several elements of each sensation, such as intensity, duration of feeling, certainty or uncertainty, the probability of being followed by a similar or opposite sensation, and the number of people affected.

Bentham developed numerous proposals for specific economic reforms; few succeeded in his day, as Bonner points out, though some were adopted in later years.[3] A liberal reformer by political inclination, Bentham's philosophy expressed an egalitarian individualism: each individual's happiness is counted equally, and each is the best judge of his/her own satisfaction. Utilitarianism was, however, inconsistent with other contemporary philosophical expressions of individualism and equality. Both the Declaration of Independence of the American Revolution and the Declaration of the Rights of Man of the French Revolution received a contemptuous dismissal from Bentham, since both documents spoke about natural rights, not just about happiness.

Bonner notes that Bentham offered little guidance on how to go about measuring and adding up individual utilities to determine whether the greatest happiness had been in fact achieved. This was no accidental oversight; there was no practical method of empirical measurement of utility. Thus it was convenient for utilitarians that laissez-faire economics predicted social harmony in the marketplace; the two theories went hand in invisible hand.[4] With an economic theory showing that everyone's happiness is maximized by competition, moral philosophers could avoid the impossible task of measuring and adding utilities.

Mid-Century Changes: Mill, Bastiat, and Marx

Utilitarianism went on to play a central role in the development of neoclassical economic theory, which will be discussed in the next section. But its acceptance by economists in the course of 19th century was uneven. Classical economics, with its labor theory of value, had little need of Bentham's utility concept. According to R. D. Collison Black, intellectual interest in utilitarianism was receding by mid-century and was only revived by the publication of John Stuart Mill's *Utilitarianism* in 1863.

Mill, however, was a decidedly unorthodox utilitarian; by strict Benthamite standards he could be described as "a reformer who claimed to be a utilitarian," in the words of the first E. K. Hunt chapter summarized here. Mill's utilitarianism included the notion that there was a hierarchy of qualitatively different types of pleasure, allowing for a more complex picture of human motivation. Moving away from Bentham's pure individualism, Mill recognized the importance of social influences on individual attitudes, and hence concluded that individuals were not always the best judges of their own interests.[5] Similarly, Mill defended classical economics, private property, and the free market, except when they failed to work well. Unlike Adam Smith, Mill believed that the government should offer public assistance to the poorest members of society and should in general work toward a more equitable distribution of income.

A type of intellectual schizophrenia seen in Mill recurs among leading liberal economists of later generations, such as Marshall, Pigou, and Keynes. Two rival orientations coexist within the same person; Sen's two origins of economics have achieved only a truce, not a permanent reconciliation. Mill the ethical visionary contemplated the complexity of human nature and looked forward to an ideal, cooperative society of the future, after immediate economic problems have been solved and human character has been ennobled. Meanwhile, Mill the economic engineer examined the operation of the competitive, capitalist economy of his day, explaining it to others and seeking to improve its efficiency. Mill offered an agenda of reforms, aimed at amelioration of the most painful and inequitable effects of the market, as an attempt to bridge the gap—but his reforms are by no means logically necessary consequences of his economic analysis.

Two other approaches from the same period offer very different reconciliations of ethical ideals and economic reality. Frederick Bastiat, the author that Hunt contrasts with Mill, set out to demonstrate that capitalism, despite its inequalities, was indeed the ideal form of economic organization. The key to Bastiat's approach was the rejection of the labor theory of value, still generally accepted by economists at the time, in favor of a formally parallel treatment of the productive effort and contribution of workers, capitalists, and landlords. Though little remembered today, Bastiat was cited by Jevons as one of the important influences on his development of neoclassical economics.

The second approach was to accept the critique of existing inequality and injustice and to demand that economic reality be transformed along more ethical lines. In the hands of Karl Marx this became the basis for a sweeping theory of history and society and a call to political action whose impact on the world exceeded, until recently, that of other economic theories. If prevailing economic institutions are fundamentally oppressive, why not overthrow them? If labor is the source of value, why don't those who labor also control the uses of the value they create? These ideas soon spread widely enough that they could no longer be ignored, even by economists who totally disagreed with them.

With Marx, as with Adam Smith, a longstanding debate has questioned whether his earlier writings are connected to or disjoint from his later economic analyses. Hunt's article on the subject, summarized here, argues for a close connection, viewing Marx's later economic theories as answers to his earlier philosophical questions. Capitalist production, for Marx, represents the alienated social potential of human existence; money is the reification of abstract labor time, a fetishized symbol that allows private appropriation of the social product. Analysis of the failures of the capitalist economy is the foundation for understanding what could and should be created in its place. Practical politics aside, the subtleties of Marx's social thought far surpassed those of other economists and raised a number of themes taken up by 20th-century sociology.

The Neoclassicals and Their Critics

Meanwhile, the new school of neoclassical economics was emerging. In the early 1870s, quite similar ideas were independently developed by Jevons, Menger, Walras, and probably by Marshall as well (though he did not publish his work until later). By the 1890s the neoclassicals had come to dominate British economics; their descendants continue to define economic theory today. The key to the new approach was the notion of declining marginal utility. This explained Adam Smith's famous paradox of water and diamonds: water is essential for life, yet its price is little or nothing compared to inessential but expensive diamonds. The explanation was that, despite the vastly greater total utility of water, so much of it is consumed that the last unit has little marginal utility. Diamonds have little utility in total, but so few are purchased that an additional one still has substantial value on the margin.

The neoclassical approach thus originally rested on the assumptions that there is a single, quantifiable thing called utility, and that people seek to maximize it. Joan Robinson, in the essay summarized here, described utility as a metaphysical and circular concept; evidence for the existence and extent of utility came only from the market phenomena it was supposed to explain. The mathematics offered a soothing symmetry of sacrifice: as with Bastiat, all factors of production, not just labor, experienced disutility from participation in the production process and were rewarded accordingly.

The rapid rise of the neoclassical school, sometimes described as the "marginal revolution," remains a bit of a historical puzzle. Mark Blaug, in his detailed history of economic thought, identifies no less than six economists who had proposed the idea of marginal utility between 1834 and 1855 (Lloyd, Longfield, Senior, Dupuit, Gossen, and Jennings), as well as others, such as Cournot and Bastiat, who had previously developed important aspects of what later became neoclassical economics.[6] Moreover, he claims that the reaction to Marxism is unlikely to have motivated work done in the 1860s or early 1870s, since Marxist ideas first gained widespread acceptance in the 1880s. The search for an alternative to Marx may have hastened the adoption of neoclassical theory, but came too late to explain its origins. What, then, did the intellectual revolution of the 1870s consist of?

From the beginning, an increase in mathematical complexity was one of the defining characteristics of the neoclassical school. (The exception was Menger, whose claim to be a founder of neoclassical economics has always been somewhat debatable.) Marshall maintained a nonmathematical prose exposition in the text and wrote of the dangers he foresaw in excessive use of "long chains of deductive reasoning"; nonetheless, he developed the mathematics in his extensive notes and appendices. Others made the mathematics even more central to their exposition.

Economists have long been influenced by, and sought to emulate, the mathematical rigor and success of natural sciences, as is detailed in an intricate history by Philip Mirowski.[7] John Stuart Mill maintained that the methods of research in economics should be identical to those in astronomy, perhaps the most prestigious science of the early 19th century. Rapid development of new mathematical models in physics led to a number of successes in the 1860s;

Jevons and Walras quite explicitly set out to adapt the same approaches in economics. Marshall, offering his usual subtle qualifications, advocated biological analogies as more appropriate, but went on to state that since biology was more complex than physics, mechanical analogies must play a relatively large role in the foundations of economics.

Together with the new mathematical techniques came a change in the scope of economic problems being analyzed. The classical economics of earlier years, like 20th-century macroeconomics and development economics, focused on the process of economic growth; in contrast, neoclassical theory tended to assume fixed resources and analyzed the constrained maximization problem of obtaining the greatest possible profit, or utility, from the given starting point. One of Joan Robinson's important theoretical contributions is relevant to this issue: there is a potential circularity in using capital as a factor of production in an explanation of prices, since the quantity of capital does not exist independent of prices. The mathematically symmetrical treatment of the payment of capital and labor thus becomes all the more problematical, as Robinson's essay explains.

Marshall is again the exception on this point, making a provocative distinction between short-run analyses with fixed resources and long-run analyses where growth may occur (his treatment of the latter encounters a different objection from Robinson). The extent of the differences between Marshall and other early neoclassical authors, which is addressed in the article on Jevons and Marshall by R. D. Collison Black, is one of the intriguing questions in the history of economics that is summarized here.

Jevons represents a relatively pure case of the engineering origins of economics. His studies in the sciences had a major impact on his economic theories. He strongly preferred Bentham and Bastiat to Mill's amended, nuanced utilitarianism, let alone other currents in philosophy. Old-fashioned calculation of pleasure and pain was enough of a theory of human behavior and motivation for Jevons; he did much to promote Bentham's reputation as the philosophical forefather of neoclassical economics. Black offers only a slight modification of the traditional picture, suggesting that in the case of Jevons, mathematical advances were coupled with regression in social and philosophical understanding. One of the major new ideas of the day, the theory of evolution, had some influence on Jevons and other early neoclassicals. But aside from Marshall's speculations about biological analogies, the principal message that economists received from the work of Darwin and Spencer was the facile idea that market competition represents a natural process of "survival of the fittest."

Marshall is different but is not simply the opposite of Jevons. Rather, Marshall resembles Mill in presenting separable ethical and economic arguments; the connection between the two modes of discourse is personal, not logical. Marshall admired Mill and much preferred his modified utilitarianism to Bentham's original. Like Mill, Marshall saw a hierarchy of higher and lower human motivations and advocated measures that were intended to help people move up the ethical ladder. The efficiency of the free market was desirable because it usually promoted admirable character traits; extremes of poverty should be alleviated because of their damaging effects on character. The result is not a synthesis of ethics and efficiency so much as a process of picking personal favorites: Marshall favored protective legislation limiting factory work by women and children, for example, but opposed minimum wage laws.

A sympathetic account of Marshall's social thought by John Whitaker, who advocates the incorporation of a broader moral vision in modern economics, concludes that Marshall was very much a product of his times:

> With all [the Victorian era's] virtues, he shared to the full the defects of his age—its tendency to moralize and a certain parochialism and narrowness of vision. . . . [I]t is hard to absolve him entirely of charges of a certain naivety and unrealism as to human nature which limits the permanent value of his vision on social issues.[8]

Black, likewise, suggests that the way in which Marshall presented his ethical judgments—in difficult, overly qualified language, divorced from his formal economics—made it possible for later economists to use his ample technical contributions while ignoring his philosophy.

Further discussion of Marshall's approach to economics and its contrast to later neoclassical developments will appear in the next section. For now, it should be recalled that the neoclassical school, while quickly rising to prominence in the late 19th century, was not without its critics. The principal opposition came not from the dwindling ranks of classical economists, but from advocates of a more historical, institutional, and empirical approach to the field. In Germany, an especially bitter methodological controversy left the historical school dominant until the 1920s. In the United States, one of the most important critics of neoclassical theory, Thorstein Veblen, also advocated a more historical and institutional approach to the subject.

As indicated in the last summary in this section, by E. K. Hunt, Veblen approached economics from a philosophical perspective quite distinct from the utilitarianism of the neoclassical theorists. As with Marx, the stance of an outsider allowed Veblen the freedom to incorporate a more sophisticated theory of human nature and needs, while analyzing economic institutions in detail. Veblen's sarcastic dismissals of the fiction of utility maximization remain more readable and relevant than most hundred-year-old economics tracts. He saw human behavior, instead, as governed by two sets of instincts, the creative and the exploitive, expressed in ever-changing institutional contexts. The points of commonality with Marx are extensive: Veblen saw the institution of private property as a historically specific event that led to inequality and subjugation; business ownership constantly threatens to thwart the creative, cooperative potential of workers; government is dominated by the capitalist class, dedicated to preserving property rights and fond of promoting patriotism and imperialism for ideological as well as financial reasons.

Less obvious, but also important, are the distinctions between Veblen and Marx. Veblen never attempted anything comparable to Marx's quantitative theories of wages, profits, prices, and investment, nor did he explore crises and depressions in the same detail. In fact, Veblen's description of indefinitely expandable consumerism almost appears to deny the possibility of long-term insufficiencies in aggregate demand. On the other hand, Veblen had a better understanding of consumerism, patriotism, and gender inequalities than Marx; the analysis of the power of consumerism and patriotism may have led him to more pessimistic political conclusions.

Although Veblen, again like Marx, has more influence on sociology than on economics today, this was not always the case. Kenneth Arrow, describing his graduate school days at Columbia University in 1940–42, has said that neoclassical theory in general was far from dominant, while the work of Veblen was a prominent part of the curriculum.[9]

Such days are long gone in mainstream economics at the end of the 20th century. The further transformations of economists' treatment of utility and welfare are the subject of the next section.

Notes

1. From the preface to his *Principles of Political Economy*, as quoted in Everett J. Burtt, Jr., *Social Perspectives in the History of Economic Theory* (New York: St. Martin's Press, 1972), 106.

2. Amartya Sen, *On Ethics and Economics* (New York: Basil Blackwell, 1987).

3. For an older account that views Bentham's contributions to practical politics and economic theory in a more positive light than Bonner, see Jacob Viner, "Bentham and J. S. Mill: The Utilitarian Background," *American Economic Review* 39 (March 1949), 360–382.

4. Gunnar Myrdal, *The Political Element in the Development of Economic Theory* (New Brunswick, NJ: Transaction Publishers, 1990; and Cambridge, MA: Harvard University Press, 1954), Chapter 2.

5. On the endogeneity of preferences in Mill's framework and its potential importance for economic theory, see Michael S. McPherson, "Mill's Moral Theory and the Problem of Preference Change," *Ethics* 92 (January 1982), 252–273.

6. Mark Blaug, *Economic Theory in Retrospect*, 4th edition (New York: Cambridge University Press, 1985), Chapter 8.

7. Philip Mirowski, *More Heat Than Light: Economics as Social Physics, Physics as Nature's Economics* (New York: Cambridge University Press, 1989), Chapter 5.

8. John Whitaker, "Some Neglected Aspects of Alfred Marshall's Economic and Social Thought," *History of Political Economy* 9 (1977), 161–197; quote from 196–197.

9. Kenneth Arrow, "Thorstein Veblen as an Economic Theorist," in *Essays in Economics: The John Commons Memorial Lectures*, ed. Michael Szenberg (Boulder, CO: Westview Press, 1986), 47–56.

Summary of

Adam Smith on Justice and Distribution in Commercial Societies

by John Salter

[Published in *Scottish Journal of Political Economy* 41 (1994), 299–313.]

For many years, scholars have debated the relationship between Adam Smith's concept of justice and issues of distribution. Some argue that income inequality and the needs of the poor are treated by Smith as questions of justice. In contrast, this paper argues that matters of distribution play no part in Smith's theory of justice. Rather, Smith restricts the scope of economic justice to respect for existing property rights.

Smith's Definition of Justice

Smith based his narrow legal definition of justice on the views of 17th-century natural law theorists such as Locke, but broke from them in many respects. Smith adopted Grotius's view that justice means abstaining from taking what belongs to another. This approach led Smith to develop a theory that focused on commutative, rather than distributive justice. Commutative justice concerns injury to a person, his estate, or his reputation; distributive justice involves inequality and the subsistence needs of the poor. In accordance with natural law theorists, Smith associated perfect rights (things one is entitled to receive) with commutative justice and imperfect rights (things one should receive, but that cannot be compelled) with distributive justice. Violations of perfect rights, such as theft, are punishable, whereas violations of imperfect rights, such as ignoring a beggar's right to charity, are not.

For Smith, breaches of justice—violations of perfect rights—were more serious threats to the viability of society than failures of beneficence—violations of imperfect rights. He reserved the notion of injustice to those acts that cause injury, rather than those harms that result from indifference; in his view it is the former that tend to destroy the fabric of society.

Smith's distinction between justice and beneficence is grounded in natural sentiments. Justice stems from a natural sense of resentment that a hypothetical impartial spectator would feel when an injury takes place. By definition, the spectator is able to sympathize with the actors in a situation; if this sympathy gives rise to resentment, then a right has been violated.

Two Alternative Views: A Critique

Two recent analyses, relating Smith's concept of justice to distributional questions, are both problematical. J. T. Young argues that Smith could have analyzed the concept of natural price within the framework of commutative justice.[1] In this view, the impartial spectator is used to decide whether income distributions that flow from labor and property are just. According to Smith, the right of property owners to be paid for the use of their property rests on the fact that an impartial spectator would agree that they possess the property and could reasonably expect to continue to use it. Young extends this point to claim that the impartial spectator would approve of fair economic returns for time and effort expended, thus coming close to traditional notions of a just price. This approach links the social constructs in Smith's major earlier work, *The Theory of Moral Sentiments*, with the economic analysis of *Wealth of Nations*.

Young's view confuses the fundamental distinction that Smith makes between perfect and imperfect rights. Smith argues that rights can only be assigned to those things that are possessed. Private property may confer rights to *seek* financial reward, but this in no way implies that property owners have an enforceable right to *receive* this reward. Similarly, the object of the impartial spectator's sympathy is the property owner's expectation of continued possession, not the expectation of a natural rate of reward for a given expenditure of labor, time, and pain. Failure to obtain a natural rate of reward is a loss, not an injury. For Smith, only injury falls within the scope of commutative justice.

The second analysis, by I. Hont and M. Ignatieff, views the *Wealth of Nations* as a detailed answer to the paradox of commercial societies: despite extreme inequality, modern commercial societies are better at satisfying the basic needs of the poor than were earlier, more equal societies.[2] Smith's answer, according to Hont and Ignatieff, was that the productivity of the modern division of labor and the workings of the invisible hand mechanism combined to guarantee the subsistence of the poor as an unintended consequence of the self-interest of the rich. Market-based distribution of resources was morally legitimate, therefore, because it provided an adequate minimum for all.

While this is an impressive attempt to relate Smith's central economic themes to his concern for justice, it is unsuccessful in two respects. First, a careful reading of Smith's analysis of the determination of wages makes it clear that he never argued that commercial society would automatically provide subsistence for all. The level of wages is contingent on the rate of accumulation of capital, the rate of population growth, and other factors. Scattered passages of optimism about the market providing for everyone, found in some of Smith's earlier writings, are not carried into the *Wealth of Nations*. Second, Smith's justification for property rights does not derive from the imperative of self-preservation. Thus the right of the poor to survival is not, in his theory, a constraint on the right of private appropriation.

Smith on Property Rights

Smith wrote at a time when the views of natural law theorists were very influential. Some of these theorists held that acts of private appropriation are only just if they do not violate humanity's general right to subsistence. The justice of the original acquisition of property was central to their views of property rights. In opposition to this tradition, Smith argued that property rights emerge only after possession is established; he defines possession of property as the expectation of continued use. Those who are accustomed to possessing and using property have a right to own it because an impartial spectator would share their resentment if it were taken away. (This does not mean that the impartial spectator applies a pre-existing set of moral standards to make judgments. Rather, the spontaneous reaction of the impartial spectator is itself the standard.)

The existing distribution of property requires legitimation in other moral theories, where people are assumed to possess original rights over resources, or rights to subsistence and survival. By omitting any such rights from his theory, Smith avoided this problem of legitimation and narrowed his conception of justice. While he cared about the poor and hoped that the market would provide for them, he did not establish this as a right that should be enforceable on society.

> The *Wealth of Nations* shows that Smith was unprepared to make unrealistic claims about the ability of commercial societies to satisfy the needs of the poor. The contrast with the optimistic stance of the invisible hand passage of the *Theory of Moral Sentiments*, where Smith claims that the needs of the poor will be taken care of in *all* societies, is clear enough. His reflections on the extreme inequality and oppression in commercial societies show that he is taking a more realistic view of the benefits of progress and how they are distributed. [312]

The invisible hand of the market can always balance the supply and demand of labor, but the process is often a painful one. There is no happily resolved paradox of commercial society that would soften the blow of this message.

Notes

1. J. T. Young, "The Impartial Spectator and Natural Jurisprudence: An Interpretation of Adam Smith's Theory of the Natural Price," *History of Political Economy* 18 (1986); cited by Salter, 300.

2. I. Hont and M. Ignatieff, "Needs and Justice in the Wealth of Nations: An Introductory Essay," in *Wealth and Virtue: The Shaping of Political Economy in the Scottish Enlightenment*, eds. I. Hont and M. Ignatieff (Cambridge, MA: Cambridge University Press, 1983); cited by Salter, 300.

Summary of

Jeremy Bentham

by John Bonner

[Published in *Economic Efficiency and Social Justice: The Development of Utilitarian Ideas in Economics from Bentham to Edgeworth* (Aldershot, Hants, England, and Brookfield, VT: Edward Elgar, 1995), 17–46.]

The concept of utility was first developed in detail by Jeremy Bentham (1748–1832), the father of utilitarianism. Although never highly regarded as an economist, Bentham strongly influenced the early development of normative economics and was a key figure in the transition from classical to neoclassical economics. Bentham's theory of psychological hedonism, which analyzed all behavior in terms of the pursuit of pleasure and avoidance of pain, and his systematic application of the "greatest happiness" principle to ethics and political economy set the stage for the marginalist revolution. This paper describes Bentham's contributions to the field of economics.

Benthamite Utilitarianism

As a secular student of rationalism, Bentham shared the view of many of his contemporaries that the established Christian views on private and public conduct must be replaced with a new ethical code based on reason and self-interest. With his "discovery" of the principle of utility, i.e., that society should seek the greatest happiness for the greatest number, he founded the "philosophic radicals" or utilitarians, a school of applied philosophy. Often credited with inventing the principle of utility, Bentham was aware of earlier discussions of the same idea and never claimed to be its inventor.

In addition to the principle of utility, the major tenets of Bentham's utilitarianism include the following: all individual behavior is motivated by pain and pleasure; there are no qualitative distinctions to be made among pleasures or among pains; individual happiness must include the happiness of others; and to ensure universal happiness, government regulation is a necessary evil—Smith's "invisible hand" cannot do the job alone. Bentham discusses utility sometimes as if it were a state of mind, related to feeling pleasure or pain, but at other times as if it were a metaphysical property of objects that produces pleasure or pain.

A basic component of Bentham's psychological theory is that personal well-being depends on the well-being of others. Self-interest requires obedience to social conventions and laws, positive acts of charity, negative acts of refraining from harming others, as well as attracting the approval of others. Character traits such as prudence, probity, and beneficence play a significant role in the cultivation of utility. Citizens must have a reasonable expectation that the law will protect them. Thus utility becomes a multi-dimensional function of economic, political, social, and personal factors.

Bentham's Economics

Bentham considered himself an economist, but his contemporaries among classical economists did not. Later economists derided his contributions to economic theory; John Maynard Keynes went so far as to claim that Bentham was no economist at all. This image is understandable if inaccurate: most of his writings on economics appeared posthumously; there is scant evidence that he understood the importance of the debates between Ricardo and Malthus on the subjects of value, distribution, and growth; he used terms like "property," "wealth," and "income" interchangeably; and he once said that his little treatise, *Manual of Political Economy*, was to Adam Smith's *Wealth of Nations* as a book on art is to a book on anatomy or physiology.

Nevertheless, Bentham first achieved fame in economics with the 1787 pamphlet, *In Defence of Usury*, and went on to write other pamphlets and articles on a variety of economic themes. Most of his work focused on improving the effectiveness of monetary and fiscal policy, while other writings took on easing the national debt and imposing inheritance taxes. He fenced with Smith on whether to impose legal limits on interest rates, made pioneering attempts to use the few available statistical measures of economic performance, and gave a new twist to the issue of the role of banks in the determination of money supply.

Despite the fact that none of his policy cures were adopted in his lifetime, his systematic application of the principle of utility became the source for both the subjective utility theory of value and welfare economics. Bentham's value theory, which reduces all motivations to the pursuit of pleasure and avoidance of pain, consists of a much more complex analysis than commonly acknowledged. His theory introduces intensity, duration, certainty or uncertainty, and nearness and remoteness as factors that influence the value of pains and pleasure. He recognizes that losses are felt more keenly than gains and that individuals may differ in their capacities to convert income or wealth into utility.

Welfare Economics

Almost all of the early neoclassical economists who elaborated Bentham's theory of value were indifferent to Bentham on policy. Only Jevons saw the necessary connection between Bentham's value theory and the "greatest happiness principle" of utility.

Bentham certainly felt that the two were strongly linked. In his view, all political and economic policy should be assessed on the basis of its effects on human feelings. He discussed the trade-offs between efficiency, equality, and happiness; wrote extensively on the scope of markets and the role of government; and discussed issues related to measurement and aggregation.

Like the Physiocrats and Adam Smith, Bentham claimed that individuals are the best judges of their own welfare. No higher authority is needed to dictate what is in a person's best interests. In his later writings, he allowed more exceptions to the rule of minimizing government interference, recognizing that individuals sometimes either lack the inclination, the power, or the knowledge to increase their own welfare or do not have access to markets that could increase their welfare. In fact, his *Constitutional Code* prescribes quite a large role for government and recommends hospitals and work houses for the poor, insurance against unemployment and ill-health, education for the children of the poor, and a public health system.

Bentham believed that a society's happiness will increase as inequality is reduced. He used "equality" in two senses: equal treatment for all individuals before the law (no one's happiness or utility counts more than anyone else's) and equal distribution of income and wealth (but not so much as to reduce incentives). Bentham favored gradual redistribution through taxation. Threats to security should be weighed against gains in aggregate happiness. Although exceptional circumstances may occasionally justify sacrificing the few for the many, Bentham emphasized that net happiness generally requires adherence to the disappointment-preventing principle: the minority should not suffer a destruction of their expectations of future abundance.

Aggregation and Measurement

In principle, a Benthamite measure of society's well-being can be obtained by adding up the happiness or utilities of its citizenry. However, Bentham offers little guidance on how to accomplish this feat. It is difficult to assess policies to redistribute wealth given that happiness cannot be measured; individuals may vary in their ability to enjoy income or wealth, and the same increment of wealth will bring more utility to poorer individuals. Bentham comes close to making interpersonal comparisons of utility, but does not fully pursue the logic of summing utilities. He advocates using wealth as a proxy for happiness, but also recognizes the ambiguous relationship between the two. More wealth brings more happiness, but it is not clear by how much.

Conclusion

Clearly Bentham incorporated an embryonic notion of diminishing marginal utility in his analysis of political economy. However, his application did not flourish until it was taken up by W. S. Jevons in the 1870s. Bentham was neither the originator of the concept of utility, nor its most articulate proponent. Yet his utilitarian school of philosophy laid the foundation on which contemporary welfare economics is built.

Summary of

Pure versus Eclectic Utilitarianism: The Writings of Bastiat and Mill

by E. K. Hunt

[Published in *History of Economic Thought: A Critical Perspective* (Belmont, CA: Wadsworth Publishing Company, 1979), 154–179.]

In the early 19th century, conservatives had to confront the growing challenge posed by the rise of socialist ideas and the expanding influence of the labor theory of value. As this article explains, the leading utilitarians of the day offered two different responses, leading to two distinct schools of economic thought. One response, by Frederick Bastiat, was to defend the utilitarian foundation of laissez-faire capitalism and to deny the need for an alternative theory of value. The other response, by John Stuart Mill, was to integrate the labor theory of value with an eclectic, reformist utilitarianism. Bastiat's route established a foundation for the later Austrian and Chicago schools, while Mill's alternative paved the way for Marshallian neoclassical economics.

Bastiat's Utilitarian Defense of Laissez-Faire

Between 1820 and 1850, working class movements flourished in England and France, often raising the increasingly influential socialist critique that capitalism creates inequality and class conflict. In his *Economic Harmonies* (1848), Bastiat sets out to demonstrate on utilitarian grounds that open, competitive markets operate in the best interests of all classes. His argument for harmony combined the "scientific" law that self-interest motivates all behavior with the assumption that exchange would not take place unless it was beneficial for all participants. Unlike Adam Smith, who devoted only a few dozen pages of his thousand-page *Wealth of Nations* to exchange, Bastiat's analysis of political economy focused exclusively on market exchange. According to Bastiat, "exchange is political economy." [157]

The focus on exchange led Bastiat to confront Smith's water/diamond paradox: Why does a scarce but useless commodity have a higher price than a plentiful, but essential commodity? Bastiat's answer makes a distinction between two types of utility. Utility purchased with effort, as from diamonds, differs from that obtained without effort, as from water. Bastiat's revised principle of utility maximization asserts that individuals seek to increase satisfaction in relation to effort.

Bastiat's distinction between productive and natural utility served as the basis of his theory of value and as a justification for the private ownership of capital. Productive or onerous utility meant a type of painful service that capitalists, landowners, and laborers underwent for production to take place. Laborers performed painful work, capitalists endured the pain of owning money and accumulating interest, yet postponing consumption, while landowners suffered the use of their land by others. Once the contributions of laborers, capitalists, and landowners are all viewed as types of productive service, then it is easy to conclude that the value of a product is identical with the value of the services required to produce it. Thus, there is no need for a labor theory of value: the utility of service becomes the source of all value.

It remained for Bastiat to justify private ownership and explain why capitalists and landlords are entitled to their profits. Bastiat's class bias is clearly evident in his defense of the sacredness of existing property rights. His natural law defense of private property implies that "[p]roperty does not exist because there are laws," but rather that "laws exist because there is property." [161] God's will is the source of property, so human law should be directed to its protection or security. Consequently, the main role of government is to protect property and provide security. He goes on to reassure landowners that rents are just compensation for services rendered and received by them and assumes without argument that landlords charge for preparing the land, working on it, enclosing it, draining it, and improving it.

In defense of profits on capital, Bastiat again appeals to the pain suffered by capitalists. However, he astonishingly fails to compare (accurately) the privations and sacrifice endured by capitalists, which derive entirely from postponing consumption and spending, with the disproportionate pains suffered by the laboring poor is astonishing.

> Bastiat never even considered the socialists' belief that an ordinary working man earned in wages just enough (and sometimes less) for his family's subsistence; that there was utterly no possibility for him to save the millions necessary to become a capitalist from his meager paycheck; that in actual fact the origins of most capitalists' fortunes were deceit, treachery, fraud, coercion, and bribery; and that once capitalism was established, after a generation or two, the origin of most capitalists' fortunes was inheritance. [162]

In fact, Bastiat goes on to defend inheritance from those who would tax it, arguing that history and God are on the side of landowners.

In sum, Bastiat's argument for the universal harmony of all classes in a free market economy comes down to a simple defense of free exchange and protection of the sanctity of property. All social ills would be cured if everyone were left free to pursue their interests.

Mill's Defense of a Mixed Economy

John Stuart Mill differed from Bastiat and other utilitarians in many crucial respects. Against Bastiat, Mill believed that private property was a human convention, not sacrosanct; and that subsistence needs as well as exchange should be the focus of political economy. Against "pure" utilitarianism, he rejected two of Bentham's most fundamental tenets: that all motives can be reduced to self-interest and that each individual is the best judge of his or her own welfare. Perhaps most famously, Mill defended the possibility that pleasures differ in quality. Mill's approach is a significant alternative to the conception of utility proposed by Bentham. It theoretically permits interpersonal comparisons of utility, on the basis of whatever principle is used to rank different pleasures. His eclectic vision is so distinctive it hardly warrants the name "utilitarian."

Although he described himself as a disciple of both Bentham and Ricardo, Mill differed with both of his "masters." He rejected Ricardo's labor theory of value, which holds that the value of commodities depends on the quantity of labor needed for its production. Instead, Mill followed Smith in arguing that production costs (the sum of the price of the services of land, labor, and capital) eventually determine market prices. Unlike Ricardo, Mill viewed profit as arising from exchange rather than from production. Profit was the remuneration through exchange for abstinence, risk, and exertion. According to Mill, labor is the most important but not exclusive determinant of value.

Unlike Bastiat, Mill believed that gross inequalities in wealth and income were not only morally unacceptable, but would ultimately be abolished. Property claims, many of which had arisen from violence and conquest, were far from sacrosanct. Concentration of wealth and nearly all the means of production in the hands of a small capitalist class created a "tiny, parasitic class, living in luxury, whose income had no necessary connection to productive activity." [173] Despite the fact that Mill was deeply troubled by the capitalism of his day and preferred an ideal communist or socialist society to his own, he was not a consistent advocate of socialism in practice. Although he favored small-scale cooperatives, he believed that socialism could only triumph after people's characters have been elevated in a far distant future. Until that happens, political economy must be primarily concerned

> with the conditions of existence and progress belonging to a society founded on private property and individual competition; and that the object to be principally aimed at, in the present stage of human improvement, is not the subversion of the system of individual property, but the improvement of it, and the full participation of every member of the community in its benefits. [175]

Although Mill insisted that the government should, as a general practice, avoid regulating markets, he also believed that state intervention was necessary in three areas. First, he argued that everyone does not always know what is in his or her best interests. According to Mill, this is especially true of the poor. His corrective was for the government to develop the character, habits, and judgments of the poor through a program of national education and to eliminate poverty for one generation through money and land transfers. He also supported the Poor Law of 1834, which provided meager subsistence for those unwilling or unable to work on the grounds that public assistance was only desirable "if, while available to everybody, it leaves to everyone a strong motive to do without if he can. . . ."[1] [177] Second, Mill advocated an inheritance tax on the grounds that the lucky few to be born into wealth neither earn nor deserve to inherit the profits of their fathers. Finally, he argued that the state should limit the development and expansion of monopolies, which he recognized as harmful to societal well-being.

Utilitarianism, particularly when elaborated into a theory of value and exchange, tends to provide intellectual support for laissez-faire capitalism, as with Bastiat. Mill, however, was a reformer who claimed to be a utilitarian. His support for an extensive program for reform reflects his optimistic view of human nature and its perfectability, not a rigorous deduction from his variant of utilitarianism.

Note

1. John Stuart Mill, *Principles of Political Economy* (New York: Augustus M. Kelley, 1965), 968.

Summary of

Philosophy and Economics in the Writings of Karl Marx

by E. K. Hunt

[Published in *Marx, Schumpeter, and Keynes*, eds. Suzanne W. Helburn and David F. Bramhall (Armonk, NY: M. E. Sharpe, 1986), 95–120.]

Discussion of the thought of Karl Marx frequently distinguishes between his earlier philosophical and humanistic writings and his later economic, political, and historical analyses. This article argues that Marx's early and later works are closely connected, and suggests that his economic theories can be viewed as elaborated answers to questions posed in his initial philosophical writings.

Human Essence and Existence

Marx's philosophy was influenced by Ludwig Feuerbach's critique of religion. According to Feuerbach, human beings created religion by mentally projecting their human essence into the heavens, turning it into a deity that was separate from, and more important than, their actual existence. Marx generalized this concept of religious alienation into a theory of generalized human alienation in a capitalist society: in economics and politics, as well as in religion, human existence was ruled by alienated forms of human essence. Marx's interpretation of essence was similar to Aristotle's, referring to the inherent developmental potential of every human being, whether or not that potential is realized: the essence of every acorn is a mighty oak tree, whether or not any particular acorn becomes a tree.

The essence of the human species, for Marx, is that each individual is the unity of the particular and the general. Individuals, while unique, also contain a generality or "species-being," meaning both that we are social beings and that we can understand our material existence and act upon that understanding (the two meanings are closely connected, since our understandings and actions are inherently social processes). Through work, humanity creates itself by socially transforming nature; the products of work become the objectification of the human-species being. Yet in capitalism, as in earlier societies, production is not controlled by the producers. Consequently, human existence has always contradicted its essence.

Value Production as Alienated Sociality

Production in a capitalist society is only indirectly social. Many earlier modes of production, in contrast, were directly social, with visible personal (though often unequal) relationships between producers and consumers. In a capitalist market, producers and consumers frequently do not know or care about each other's identities; they are only interested in the value of the product and the act of exchanging it for other values. Through such market exchanges, people are trading the products of their individual and collective labor. The value of products therefore must, in an abstract sense, rest on the amount of social labor required for their production. This is the core of Marx's labor theory of value, which should be understood as a definition of "value" rather than as an empirical proposition subject to proof or disproof. The merits of the labor theory of value depend on the usefulness of the insights it yields about the nature of capitalism.

Value, Marx insisted, is generally not understood by either capitalists or workers. (Prices derive from values, but in a complex manner that adds to the difficulty of understanding the process.) Rather, everyone experiences the fetishism of commodities, in which superficial market relationships between things take the place of underlying social relationships between people. Commodities simultaneously have use values, reflecting their material characteristics, and exchange values, abstractly reflecting the social system within which they are produced and sold.

Money and Alienation

The drastically unequal facts of human material existence in a capitalist society are unconnected to the frequent political and religious affirmations of our abstractly equal human essence as voters, "children of God," etc. Likewise, material inequality appears disconnected from the economic essence of undifferentiated abstract labor that we all possess. One aspect of humanity's economic essence does, however, have a real but alienated existence in capitalism—money, the universal equivalent that represents the commonality of values of all commodities. Marx referred to money as the "reification of universal labor time," and summed up his *1844 Manuscripts*, one of his early philosophical works, with the statement, "Money is the alienated ability of mankind." [Hunt, 108] An individual's relationships and capabilities, in an unalienated society, would be developed by acquiring or enhancing specific personal characteristics; in capitalism, the same objectives are met by the accumulation and use of money.

Statements about the contradictory nature of money can be found throughout Marx's earliest and latest works, illustrating the impossibility of separating his philosophical and economic theories.

> . . . the contradictory nature of money is manifested in its two fundamentally different roles: First, as a mere thing it serves merely as a symbol to be used and controlled by men. Second, as the real, physical embodiment of man's species powers it has full control over men. [110]

Three of Marx's major concerns—the labor theory of value, the concept of commodity fetishism, and the analysis of alienation—merge in his treatment of the nature of money. Discussing the inadequacy of the classical economists' labor theory of value, Marx argued that they failed to understand the difference between the abstract, universal meaning of value and the historically specific forms of exchange value embodied in commodities and money:

> We consequently find that economists, who are thoroughly agreed as to labor-time being the measure of the magnitude of value, have the most strange and contradictory ideas of money, the perfected form of the general equivalent. [Marx, *Capital*, Volume I, cited in Hunt, 112]

Only in a money economy could labor itself become a commodity with an exchange value, a development that was one of the defining characteristics of capitalism for Marx.

The contradictory nature of money is at the heart of Marx's theory of economic crises. Just as human beings are essentially a unity of particularity and generality, so, too, are the estranged forms of human essence, such as money. On the one hand, money is in general the representative of all value, as emphasized today by Keynesian theories; on the other hand, money is in particular simply one commodity among many, as emphasized by the Chicago school and other adherents of the quantity theory of money.

Neither view grasps the full, contradictory reality of money, and neither offers an adequate understanding of crises. The Keynesian approach leads to unwarranted faith in the government's ability to eliminate crises through fiscal and monetary policy, while the Chicago school and its predecessors are incapable of comprehending any cause of economic crisis except government interference with the money supply and the market. For Marx, both views of money are valid and are parts of a single contradictory reality; the fact that money must simultaneously play such divergent roles, with no necessary coordination, is what creates the ever-present potential for crisis. Marx discussed several possible immediate causes of crises (it is a common mistake to misread him as offering a specific, mechanical breakdown theory) and argued that the contradictory nature of commodities and money is the heart of every crisis of capitalism, "no matter what its cause." [*Capital*, Volume I, cited in Hunt, 119]

Conclusion

Marx's views on the class structure of capitalism, on the labor theory of value, on money, on capital, and on crises are all involved in his intellectual working out of Feuerbach's far more limited insight, that in contemporary society religion is a human creation that in turn inhumanly controls its creators. Marx sought to show that religion merely reflected a more fundamental process—a process whereby in capitalism human beings produce objects that come to control them. In general, we may conclude that in his crisis theory, as well as his theories of value, money, and capital, Marx was finishing the task that he set for himself in his youth—the task of understanding the social and economic foundations of that peculiar form of human alienation and estrangement whereby the products of human creation appear to take on a life of their own and come to dominate and degrade their creators. [119–120]

Summary of

The Neoclassics: Utility

by Joan Robinson

[Published in *Economic Philosophy* (Garden City, NY: Doubleday, 1964), 48–74.]

Neoclassical economics, unlike the classical school that preceded it, relies on the concept of utility for its theory of value and behavior. This selection examines the meaning of utility to the founders of neoclassical economics and presents (and criticizes) the ways in which the early theorists dealt with some of the internal contradictions in their approach. [Note: the author's discussion of free trade policy has been omitted from this summary.]

Neoclassical Metaphysics

Utility is a metaphysical and circular concept: "*utility* is the quality in commodities that makes individuals want to buy them, and the fact that individuals want to buy commodities shows that they have *utility*." [48] Still, it appears to be a quantitative magnitude, allowing discussion of total and marginal utility— as Alfred Marshall and W. Stanley Jevons independently concluded. Although Marshall surrounded the discussion with many qualifications, he argued that the law of "satiable wants," or of diminishing marginal utility of additional units of any good, was a fundamental tendency of human nature.

The problem of reliance on a metaphysical concept remains, even when utility is replaced by "revealed preference"; the newer formulation still carries the implication that it is a good thing to satisfy revealed preferences. Yet drug addicts should be cured, and children should go to school; value judgments must inevitably be made about which preferences should be satisfied.

Moreover, there is a contradiction in the notion that behavior reveals preferences, as Marshall acknowledged. If we make two observations of a person's choices of different bundles of goods, they will occur at different times; we must assume that there has been no change in preferences between the two observations. Consumption of some goods, however, changes the consumer's preference for more of the same. Listening to good music increases the taste for it—as does drinking too much liquor. So observation of choices at two points in time may not provide information about a single set of underlying preferences.

The Vanishing Egalitarianism of Utility Theory

The ideological content of utility theory was curiously double-edged. As Wicksell pointed out, it was an egalitarian perspective, valuing the satisfactions enjoyed by the working class as much as those of anyone else; in this it differed from classical economics, which had focused on accumulation of capital as the principal measure of success. Marshall observed that diminishing marginal utility applied to money as well as individual goods, an observation that can be used to justify unions, progressive taxation, and the welfare state.

On the other hand, the point of utility theory was to justify laisser-faire, allowing everyone to maximize individual utility by spending their income as they see fit—and allowing competitive businesses to maximize profit, which also maximizes consumer satisfaction. Egotistical individual action leads to the social good, an idea that originated with Adam Smith, but was carried to extremes by the neoclassical economists.

Not all of the neoclassical pioneers accepted the full laisser-faire political program; Walras and, more tentatively, Marshall in his younger days had socialist leanings, while Wicksell and Pigou also expressed doubts about the virtue of unfettered competition. On a theoretical level, though, the problem remained of reconciliation between the redistributive implications of utility theory and the conservative implications of laisser-faire.

"The method by which the egalitarian element in the doctrine was sterilized was mainly by slipping from *utility* to physical output as the object to be maximized." [56] Marshall in his later years, recanting his early socialist tendencies, emphasized the idea that growth of material output promotes human well-being. Connected with this was the argument that only the rich save, so inequality is necessary for capital accumulation.

The other way of evading the egalitarian side of utility theory was to explicitly separate growth from distribution, asserting that the latter could be handled by an appropriate set of taxes and subsidies. No one takes the taxes and subsidies seriously, nor explores the effects they would have on work incentives—but the problems of growth can now be handled as isolated logical questions, apparently free of ethical judgments.

> All the same, even economists are human beings, and cannot divest themselves of human habits of thought. Their system is saturated with moral feeling. Those within it, who have grown used to breathing its balmy air, have lost the power to smell it. [59]

Profits and Morality

Classical economics, with its labor theory of value, made it easy to discuss exploitation. Neoclassical theory changed this by placing capital and labor on the same moral level. Workers are rewarded for their labor; what are capitalists rewarded for? The answer is "waiting," i.e., agreeing to defer consumption and allowing their resources to be used in production. This view was elaborated in two distinct versions.

To Walras, Jevons, the Austrian school, Wicksell, and perhaps Robbins, it seemed natural to assume that the supply of all factors of production is fixed. All economic actors then seek to deploy their resources where they earn the greatest returns; the conceptual distinction between work and property has disappeared.

> Setting the whole thing out in algebra is a great help. The symmetrical relations between x and y seem smooth and amiable, entirely free from the associ-

ations of acrimony which are apt to be suggested by the relations between "capital and labour." [61]

Marshall, on the other hand, assumed that factor supplies were not fixed; each factor had a rate of return that was required to bring an increased supply into use. Workers had to be rewarded to do more work; capitalists had to be rewarded to do more waiting. Yet each approach failed to provide an adequate explanation of capital markets and profits.

The first view cannot explain the existence of an aggregate rate of profit or rate of interest. The fixed factors of production include particular machines and inventories of goods, not abstract capital; equilibrium should imply a different rental price for the use of each type of machine. Only if capitalists are mysteriously free to change one type of machine into another can there be an equalized rate of profit throughout the economy.

Marshall's view, while avoiding this problem, fails to distinguish between the stock of existing capital and the rate of investment (i.e., the change in the existing stock). It appears that a particular rate of profit should be required to keep a given stock of capital in use, not to induce a specified rate of new investment. And it is not clear what sacrifice is involved in waiting to consume an already-existing stock of capital. Pigou addressed these problems through analysis of the hypothetical stationary state of the future, where accumulation has ceased; this makes the equations work nicely, at the cost of a loss of connection to reality.

The Seductions of Mathematics

The introduction of utility into economics allowed the rapid advance of mathematical models, as both Jevons and Edgworth were pleased to observe. By emphasizing the quantitative nature of utility, Edgworth was in danger of offering mathematical proof of radically egalitarian conclusions—a fate that he avoided by suggesting that people have immeasurable differences in their capacity for happiness. Thus the utilitarian unit of happiness is ultimately the same kind of unobservable mirage as Marx's abstract labor.

Despite its mathematical sophistication, the neoclassical scheme was rather barren of results. Clapham, in a satire of the field in the 1920s, described economists who spent their lives abstractly discussing industries with increasing, constant, and diminishing returns, but never identified any existing industry as belonging in any of these categories. One reason for this sterility was that "the questions being discussed were of no practical importance. The policy recommended was laisser-faire, and there was no need to describe in any detail how to do nothing." [73] If Pigou's taxes had been taken seriously, empirical research would have been required to implement them—but as Clapham noted, this did not occur.

Another reason for the lack of results was that the mathematics of equilibrium led the field away from testable hypotheses, since the world so clearly is
not in equilibrium. "The soothing harmonies of equilibrium supported laisser-
faire ideology and the elaboration of the argument kept us all too busy to have
any time for dangerous thoughts." [74]

Summary of

Jevons, Marshall, and the Utilitarian Tradition

by R. D. Collison Black

[Published in *Scottish Journal of Political Economy* 37 (February 1990), 5–17.]

Utilitarian philosophy was an important influence on the development of neoclassical economics in the late 19th century. Two of the pioneers of the neoclassical school, W. Stanley Jevons and Alfred Marshall, had differing understandings of utilitarianism; this was one of the factors leading to their distinct
approaches to economics. This article reviews and revises the conventional understanding of the differences between Jevons and Marshall, in relation to utilitarianism and other intellectual currents of their time.

Utilitarianism at Mid-Century

By the middle of the 19th century, some aspects of utilitarianism were widely
accepted in English social and economic thought. While many classical economists did not consider themselves Benthamites, the use of the "greatest happiness" principle for judging economic policy was no longer controversial. Still,
it was not yet evident that utilitarianism would become central to future developments in economics. Other intellectual trends, such as the theory of evolution, historical methods of inquiry, and philosophical idealism appeared to be
rising in importance. Interest in utilitarianism revived with the publication of
John Stuart Mill's treatise on the subject in 1863; Mill presented a substantial
reworking of utilitarian moral philosophy, differing from Bentham in several
respects.

Against this background, Jevons and Marshall developed their new theories,
each drawing in their own way on the utilitarian tradition. The conventional interpretation of their differences is that Jevons was a thoroughgoing Benthamite, whereas Marshall was hardly a utilitarian at all. This simple, clear-cut
view is incomplete, but not entirely wrong.

Jevons versus Marshall: The Standard Interpretation

Jevons's best-known works, in both economic theory and policy, are directly and explicitly based on Bentham's theories. Jevons encountered Bentham's utilitarianism in his early religious and philosophical education. Although he read a variety of other philosophers, they had less influence on him; he dismissed Kant, for example, as "full of wordy nonsense." Jevons opposed Mill's reinterpretation of utilitarianism, objecting to Mill's assumption that some kinds of pleasure are intrinsically more desirable and more valuable than others. Reliance on Bentham's unidimensional net sum of pleasure and pain allowed Jevons to introduce the mathematical model of constrained maximization into economics. Despite the obvious problems of measurement of utility, Bentham's approach seemed to provide an adequate theoretical basis for addressing practical policy debates.

Marshall, according to John Maynard Keynes, was "at the opposite pole from Jevons" in his philosophical orientation. Although he never explicitly departed from utilitarian approaches to economics, Marshall made an extensive study of other philosophical traditions. He went to Germany to read Kant in the original and was also influenced by Hegel. Marshall's first Cambridge appointment was to a lectureship in moral science, not economics. Trained in mathematics as well as philosophy, he seems to have been reluctant to draw too heavily on either discipline in the development of his economic theories.

Both Jevons and Marshall were convinced of the importance of measurement for the development of economic analysis, but they drew different conclusions about the problems that arose. Jevons granted that measurement of pleasure and pain was nearly impossible, but went on to construct a theory based on hypothetical measurements of utility and disutility. Marshall insisted that motives for economic activity must be indirectly measurable in terms of money and retained the notion of utility maximization as the key to demand theory, but objected to basing economics on so crude a foundation as hedonistic psychology. Human nature, in his view, involved more complex motivations than mere pleasure and pain. While Jevons used mechanical analogies to explain economic processes, Marshall was more inclined to adopt biological and evolutionary images.

Spencer, Mill, and the Future of Economics

None of the above description is incorrect; yet it is a bit too tidy and simplified. Could Jevons, as some authors have suggested, have ignored the debates about evolution, one of the most important intellectual developments of his day? Charles Darwin's *Origin of Species* appeared in 1859 and Herbert Spencer's *First Principles* in 1862. In fact, Jevons was well aware of these developments and had a high personal and intellectual regard for Spencer. Although Jevons disagreed with some of Spencer's political conclusions, such as his unqualified faith in the virtues of laissez-faire, he was inclined to accept Spencer's philosophical blending of utilitarian and evolutionist ideas.

Jevons certainly preferred Spencer's approach to Mill's revision of utilitarianism; attitudes toward John Stuart Mill were one of the sharpest differences between Jevons and Marshall. While Jevons preferred Bentham's original over Mill's modified utilitarianism, Marshall was influenced by Mill both in his philosophy and in his economic theory. Mill's more complex, multi-faceted view of human character and motivation and his assumption of qualitatively different types of pleasure and pain appealed to Marshall and many of his contemporaries.

Ultimately, the most important difference between Jevons and Marshall lay in their conceptions of the direction in which economics should develop. Jevons favored a division of the field into subdisciplines or even separate sciences, while Marshall envisioned a synthesis of history, theory, and empirical observation. The difference might seem to fit into Amartya Sen's dichotomy between the "engineering-based" and the "ethics-related" origins of economics; but these categories do not capture the entire story.

Jevons unquestionably did see some branches of economic theory in terms of mechanical analogies and proceeded in a manner that could be loosely identified with an engineering orientation. In contrast, Marshall saw economics in organic, biological terms; this perspective is not necessarily related to ethics, although for Marshall it was. However, Marshall's particular view of the relation between ethics and economics may have contributed to the disinterest in ethics on the part of later economists. While Marshall argued for a broad understanding of human nature, behavior, and moral philosophy, he saw the potential for scientific advance as confined to the quantifiable economic realm of motives that could be set against the measuring rod of money.

> It may be contended that it was . . . Jevons whose vision of the reconstructed science of economics in terms of sub-division and specialization contributed most, and most directly, to the narrowing of the subject. In contrast to this, Marshall's vision of an economic biology using a combination of methods and incorporating a social ethic as an integral feature would seem to have pointed towards making economics a much broader discipline. So indeed it did, but Marshall's reluctance to move outside the firm ground of measurable motives, combined with his . . . [use of bland, colorless language to express the ethical implications of economics], made it possible for many later economists to disregard the fact that Marshallian economics was intended to be ethics-related. [15–16]

Summary of

Thorstein Veblen

by E. K. Hunt

[Published in *The History of Economic Thought: A Critical Perspective*
(Belmont, CA: Wadsworth Publishing, 1979), 299–327.]

The rise of neoclassical economics was followed almost immediately by the appearance of one of its most important critics. Best known for his theory of the leisure class and conspicuous consumption, Thorstein Veblen (1857–1929) developed a comprehensive theory of human behavior and the nature of economic and social institutions. This selection summarizes Veblen's economic theories and contrasts them to both neoclassical and Marxian economics. Discussion of the relationship between Veblen and Marx, included in the original, is omitted from this summary.

Veblen's Evolutionary Social Philosophy

Like many late 19th century writers, Veblen was strongly influenced by Darwin's theory of evolution. Veblen, like Marx, saw economics in general terms as the history of our evolving material culture and related social institutions. Although Veblen discussed human "instincts" at length, he emphasized that instincts could not be understood as timeless patterns of behavior; rather, they took on concrete form within a particular historical, institutional framework. Indeed, the role of institutions in mediating and shaping instinctual behavior was what differentiated humans from other animals.

Veblen saw a fundamental, antagonistic dichotomy in the basic traits underlying human behavior. One cluster of traits included what he called the "instinct of workmanship," along with the "parental instinct" and the "instinct of idle curiosity." The other group centered on the propensity to exploit, or the "predatory instinct," and encompassed all forms of conflict and subjugation and gender, racial, and class exploitation. The antithesis between these two sets of traits, manifested in varying institutions, was the core of his social theory.

For Veblen, the conflict between the predatory instincts and the instincts related to workmanship could be seen on many levels. It was reflected in the clash between the economic forces he called "business" and "industry." (The latter term referred to productive activity or the results of industriousness in general, not to manufacturing in particular.) The same conflict appeared in many differences between individuals and classes, particularly in the contrast between the ceremonialism and sportsmanship of the leisure class and the creative and cooperative behavior of the "common man."

Critique of Neoclassical Economics

> Veblen's fundamental criticism of neoclassical economics . . . was that it had an utterly nonhistorical and simplistic view of human nature and social institutions. By attempting to explain everything in terms of rational, egoistical, maximizing behavior, neoclassical economics explained nothing. [303]

In reality, he insisted, production is always a social and cultural phenomenon, based on shared knowledge and skills; the forms of payment, such as wages, rent, and interest, are historically changing phenomena. Capital as an abstraction, distinguished from particular capital goods, is a result of the laws and institutions of capitalism—and therefore, interest and profits are historically specific to the modern era. Wages and wage labor, likewise, could only exist in a society where production was organized by capitalists who hired workers. Neoclassical economics obscured the conflict between owners and workers first by claiming there was a natural harmony of interests in the marketplace, and second by suggesting that the separation of "factors of production" such as capital and labor was a timeless pattern.

Property, Class Society, and the Subjugation of Women

Veblen rejected the traditional justification of private property as based on the productive labor of the owner. Any property results from a social process of production, which can only occur in a community capable of transmitting technical knowledge and production skills. Production, in other words, is a cooperative effort that flows out of the instinct of workmanship; private ownership is an individual right that reflects predatory instincts.

Early in human history, Veblen believed, the instinct of workmanship necessarily prevailed; low productivity meant that cooperative, peaceful efforts were necessary for survival. Only as production became more efficient did predatory exploitation become economically possible. Private property had its origins in coercion and later gained institutional and ideological legitimization. Societies thus became stratified:

> Where this tenure by prowess prevails, the population falls into two economic classes: those engaged in industrial employments, and those engaged in such nonindustrial pursuits as war, government, sports, and religious observances.[1]

A society dominated by the predatory class inevitably thwarts the instinct of workmanship and removes much of the intrinsic enjoyment of work. The values of such a society recognize mastery over others and avoidance of productive work as the leading virtues. Subjugation of women by men and separation of men's and women's spheres of activity were an intrinsic part of this process; marriage in class societies originated in coercion and always involved some concept of ownership.

The Dominance of Business Over Industry

The two basic classes that characterize capitalism embodied Veblen's two basic instincts. Workers, technicians, and any other groups who have to work to earn a living embodied the instinct of workmanship; success for them involved productive creativity. Owners, investors, managers, and their agents (such as efficiency experts) embodied the predatory instinct; success for them involved exploitative advantage over others.

Profit making, or business, was removed from and opposed to the interests of industry or workmanship. Veblen described business as engaged in "sabotage" of industry, defined as a conscious withdrawal of efficiency: since industry could produce more than it was profitable to sell, business was usually holding back production; workers and factories, idled by business decisions, could easily produce additional goods that people needed. Cutbacks in production, though profitable for absentee owners of businesses, frequently led to economic crises and depressions.

Government and Class Struggle

Government, controlled by owners of business, was in Veblen's view dedicated above all to the preservation of property rights. Political parties differed in their detailed aims and in the versions of business interests that they represented. The dominance of business was not primarily based on corruption, but rather rested on widespread socialization into a capitalist worldview and on acceptance of success in business and related pursuits as a leading qualification for holding public office. When property rights were seriously challenged, the state or business interests would respond with armed force.

Imperialist expansion was a dominant feature of capitalism in Veblen's era. He saw it as offering not only increased opportunities for business profits, but also as providing a reason for the promotion of patriotism and militarism. These hierarchical "virtues" were a counterweight to the subversive tendencies toward workmanship, cooperation, and individual autonomy that were inherent in industry:

> Habituation to a warlike, predatory scheme of life is the strongest disciplinary factor that can be brought to counteract the vulgarization of modern life wrought by peaceful industry and the machine process, and to rehabilitate the decaying sense of status and differential dignity.[2]

Social Mores of a Pecuniary Culture

In any class-divided society, the predatory or exploitative activities of the dominant class are held in high esteem, while the necessary industry of the lower classes is deemed unworthy and vulgar. Success, in a pecuniary culture, must be constantly displayed through conspicuous consumption and the conspicuous use of leisure—as Veblen argued in detail in his most famous work, *The Theory of the Leisure Class*. Invidious distinctions of wealth and ostentation come to define status, and emulation of those who have more becomes a powerful and ceaseless motivation of individual behavior. People caught on the treadmill of emulative consumption led lives of chronic dissatisfaction; regardless of their incomes, it was always possible to imagine, and want, more. Like patriotism and militarism, emulative consumption is indirectly a form of cultural discipline and social control, preventing the expression of the cooperative values of workmanship that are continually fostered by industry.

Notes

1. Thorstein Veblen, "The Beginnings of Ownership," in *Essays in Our Changing Order* (New York: August M. Kelley, 1964), 41; cited in Hunt, 309.
2. Veblen, *Theory of Business Enterprise*, 392; cited in Hunt, 319.

PART III

Utility and Welfare II: Modern Economic Alternatives

Overview Essay

Frank Ackerman

The inequality between the rich and the poor is not primarily a matter of utility, or who *feels* what, but one of who *owns* what. There is no obvious reason why abstaining from interpersonal comparisons of utility must have the effect of making it impossible to consider economic inequality in social welfare judgments.

—Amartya Sen[1]

At the beginning of the 20th century, economic theory as expounded by Alfred Marshall offered definite, if at times arbitrary or merely pragmatic, judgments on numerous immediate issues affecting social welfare. At the end of the century, the mainstream of economic theory has become rigorous and elegant in its logic, but indecisive as to the welfare implications of most actual policies. Several interesting alternative interpretations have been proposed, but remain controversial; as Sen suggests, there are many possible bases for welfare judgments, beyond the narrow focus on individual utility that is enshrined in neoclassical economics.

This overview offers a necessarily selective treatment of 20th-century developments in the economics of welfare and well-being. It begins with an exploration of the "ordinalist revolution" of the 1930s, followed by a look at Keynes's philosophy. Subsequent sections address the early development of welfare economics and its contradictions and the theory of social choice that emerged in the wake of Arrow's "impossibility theorem." The final section examines two contemporary alternatives that are somewhat independent of the discussion of social choice. Further applications of welfare economics to problems of externalities, valuation, and cost-benefit analysis are the subject of Part IV of this volume.

Accentuating the Positivists

Two crucial episodes in the history of neoclassical theory are often referred to as "revolutions" within economics. First, the marginalist revolution (see Part II) introduced the assumption that consumers seek to maximize utility, just as firms seek to maximize profits. Values and prices were based on marginal utility, allowing an increasingly mathematical method of analysis. The marginal utility approach was developed in the 1870s and had become widely accepted by the 1890s. The second upheaval, the ordinalist revolution of the 1930s, declared that it was neither necessary nor possible to make interpersonal comparisons of utility, nor even to assign cardinal numbers to utility. All that was needed for economic theory was an ordinal ranking expressing each consumer's preferences.

The first article summarized here, by Robert Cooter and Peter Rappoport, focuses on the change in welfare economics wrought by the second revolution. In the decades of the interregnum—after marginalism but before ordinalism—economics, at least in England, was dominated by what Cooter and Rappoport call the "material welfare" school of Marshall, Arthur Pigou, and others. This school maintained that there were both material and nonmaterial aspects of welfare; economics dealt with the former, though fortunately the two were usually positively correlated. People were assumed to be similar enough in their basic needs that the average utility experienced by large groups, such as the rich and the poor, could be meaningfully compared. This assumption, combined with the declining marginal utility of money, led to an argument for redistribution toward the poor so long as it did not interfere with economic growth.

Although the material welfare school was a British phenomenon, there were other early neoclassical economists who held related views. In France, Leon Walras, who founded the axiomatic mathematical analysis of competitive equilibrium, drew a sharp distinction between the "applied economics" of the market and the "social economics" that should govern questions of equity and public policy. His ideal was a market socialist society in which the state would own and sell natural resources, using the revenues to finance public goods.[2] In Sweden, Knut Wicksell developed a widely discussed critique of the theory that free trade and competition necessarily lead to social harmony. Competition maximizes the value of output, but this does not maximize social welfare unless every individual has the same marginal utility of money, which Wicksell thought unlikely in a world of unequal incomes. Such comparisons of utilities, for Wicksell, provided the "material basis for the idea of *justice*, whether in government or in social distribution."[3]

An opposing, "ordinalist" view of utility could be seen as early as W. Stanley Jevons's writings in the 1870s and was further developed in the work of Irving Fisher and Pareto in the 1890s and early 1900s. Similar perspectives appeared in the Austrian School of economics (including Austrian, German, and central

European authors, largely writing in German) in the early decades of the 20th century.[4] The ordinalists doubted that utility could be measured or compared and emphasized the unpredictable diversity of individual desires rather than the commonality of basic needs. Most important of all, they demonstrated that the technical theory of consumer behavior could be developed without cardinal measurement or interpersonal comparison of utility. When Lionel Robbins reiterated these views in the 1930s, he was soon joined by John Hicks and other leading economists, and ordinalism quickly triumphed.

Cooter and Rappoport emphasize that the ordinalist revolution was not simply scientific progress, but a difference in values on such questions as the importance of equity and the nature of human needs. In some cases, differences in values implied political differences: while Marshall and Pigou were optimistic liberal reformers, Pareto was an affluent aristocrat who believed that substantial inequality was inevitable and cynically dismissed democratic politics as a fraud—and was made an honorary member of the Italian Senate under Mussolini.[5] However, ordinalism was not primarily a political movement, and its adherents certainly did not all share Pareto's extreme opinions.

The abruptness of the shift within the economics profession remains somewhat of a mystery. Why did ordinalism attract only a minority when it was first articulated, but rapidly convert the majority of economists when it was restated in the 1930s? Understanding this paradigm shift is of continuing relevance to contemporary economics, since most economists still work within the ordinalist framework described by Cooter and Rappoport.

Ordinalism succeeded in the 1930s in part because it resonated with other intellectual rhythms of the era. Logical positivism was becoming fashionable in philosophy; this perspective treats all value judgments as subjective expressions of attitude that have no place in science, and calls for a positive, or nonnormative, scientific discourse consisting of empirically falsifiable theories and collections of data. Similarly, psychology was turning toward behaviorism, attempting to eliminate discussion of motivations and mental states in order to create a "hard science" of observable behavior. Behaviorist psychology provided a critique of both the hedonism implicit in simple versions of utilitarianism and the somewhat ad hoc, introspective discussion of human nature employed by the material welfare school. Both positivism and behaviorism have lived on in economics, long after they have fallen from favor in the disciplines that gave rise to them.[6]

This explanation, however, only pushes the question back to a deeper level. Where did the intellectual fashions of the 1930s come from? More broadly and tentatively speaking, the rise of ordinalism, behaviorism, and logical positivism could be associated with the social context of the decade. It was a time of economic crisis and political and cultural conflict. The wounds of the last great war were hardly healed, and the warnings of the next one were increasingly evident.

Traditional liberalism did not flourish in such an era; instead, there was a search for fundamental alternatives. The leading philosophies of the day were logical positivism, which rejected most past philosophical discussion in the name of science; Marxism, which called for sweeping social change; and existentialism, which, at least in some versions, began from the premise of the apparent absurdity of human existence.[7]

In this dark and despairing context, one of the few bright intellectual stars was the recent advance of physics. Using a difficult, technical discourse that defied common sense, intuitive comprehension, both relativity and quantum mechanics had made huge strides in understanding physical reality in the early 20th century. Thus it was not surprising that attempts to imitate the formal, objective methods of science were attractive to scholars in many fields. Logical positivism presumed that natural sciences and mathematics had a privileged, closer relationship to reality than other modes of discourse. Behaviorism sought to bring the same rigorous objectivity to psychology—as did ordinalism in economics.

Turning from the historical context to the content of ordinalism, the new theory's success in driving overt value judgments out of economics can also be traced in part to a weakness of the material welfare school. As Marshall acknowledged, his "higher," nonmaterial values were not amenable to systematic analysis, and thus could not be rigorously addressed within his economic theory. The eclectic versions of utilitarianism and reformist politics developed by Marshall, like the views of Mill before him, or the socialist visions of Walras were all too easily detached from the technical aspects of the same authors' economics. Later writers seeking to introduce ethical concerns into economics have generally attempted to create a tighter connection between moral and technical analyses.

A Macroeconomic Interlude

The most influential book written about economics in the 1930s (and one of the top contenders of all times) had nothing to do with the ordinalist controversy, pro or con. It had a direct relationship, however, to the economic crisis and depression of the day. In *The General Theory of Interest, Employment, and Money*, John Maynard Keynes returned to the broad macroeconomic scope of classical economics, though not to its analytical framework, to produce a novel understanding of aggregate demand, employment, and growth. In the article summarized here, Rod O'Donnell describes the moral and political philosophy within which Keynes developed his economic theories.[8]

Keynes can be viewed as the last in a series of great economists who posed the goal of an ideal future society, in which affluence will allow the development of more ethical behavior and less selfish character traits, replacing the competitive, acquisitive individualism fostered by the market and the regime of scarcity. Mill, Marshall, and Marx, among others, described similarly sharp dichotomies between present and future conditions. Yet none, aside from Marx, were able to integrate the pursuit of the future goals into the analysis of the economy of their times. Keynes's ironic comment (quoted by O'Donnell) on the need to pretend "that fair is foul and foul is fair" to continue capital accumulation only underscores the separation between ultimate ethics and immediate economics.

If Keynes's philosophy were better known, he might also be remembered as one of the first economists to reject all forms of utilitarianism and to begin the exploration of other bases for welfare judgments. As O'Donnell makes clear, Keynes had a detailed conception of the good life and viewed economic and political rights and institutions as means for achieving the good rather than as ends in themselves. That is, his philosophy was consequentialist, since he judged actions and policies solely in terms of their outcomes; but it was also nonutilitarian, since he rejected subjective utility as a measure of the goodness of outcomes. Although Keynes's conception of the good bears traces of the cultural elitism of his class and his times, it also has many aspects of more enduring value. Beneath the differences in style and presentation, there are striking similarities to the contemporary nonutilitarian, consequentialist philosophy of Amartya Sen.

Welfare Economics: Borne in Crisis

Despite his central role in macroeconomics, Keynes's philosophy had no noticeable impact on neoclassical theory and its approach to welfare. Rather, in the 1930s the ordinalist revolution caused a protracted crisis in the newly emerging field of welfare economics. In the heyday of Marshall and Pigou, there had been no great difficulty in making welfare judgments.[9] Intervention in the market could be justified when material and nonmaterial aspects of welfare clashed, when extreme poverty prevented the satisfaction of basic needs, or when externalities or other market failures interfered with the efficiency of competition. There was, as Wicksell put it, a material basis for the idea of justice.

Once the ordinalist objection to welfare comparisons was adopted, however, it was difficult to draw meaningful conclusions about social welfare. The review article by Peter Jackson, summarized here, describes the resulting dilemmas. The sole criterion that ordinalism seemed to allow, advocacy of Pareto-optimal improvements, was ludicrously weak, saying essentially that any policy favored by an unopposed consensus should be adopted or that no valuable resource should be wasted. Two parallel lines of development ensued: the search for more substantial welfare criteria that were compatible with ordinalism and the formalization of the analysis of general equilibrium and its welfare implications.

The search for new welfare criteria led first to several compensation principles and the idea of potential Pareto improvements: was a policy desirable if the winners could *potentially* compensate the losers? This foundered both on technical objections, described by Jackson, and on the ethical objection that, if, for example, the winners are rich and the losers are poor, a potential Pareto improvement may not be desirable unless the potential compensation is actually paid—and if compensation is paid, the change is an actual Pareto improvement, so no new principle is needed. Stepping back from the debate over compensation principles, some economists proposed the creation of a social welfare function that would aggregate individual preferences into society's preferences. Hopes for this approach were destroyed by Arrow's impossibility theorem, which is discussed in the next section.

Meanwhile, the theory of the ideal competitive market became increasingly formal and axiomatic, building on Walras's technical work (while ignoring his social vision). The same behaviorist and positivist impulses that contributed to the rise of ordinalism soon led on to the elimination of all utility functions, ordinal or otherwise. Samuelson's theory of revealed preference asserted that consumers' preferences were revealed by their behavior and that no additional knowledge about utility was needed; economic theory required only that consumers obey a few mild assumptions of rationality. Two problems with revealed preference were noted by Joan Robinson in the essay summarized in Part II. First, despite its apparent behaviorism, a theory based on revealed preference cannot escape the value-laden and controversial assumption that all revealed preferences should be satisfied. Second, removing all reference to utility furthers the tendency to slip from maximizing individual well-being to maximizing money incomes—making it impossible to assess whether these two concepts coincide.

The pinnacle of formalization was reached by Kenneth Arrow and Gerard Debreu in the 1950s, in their proofs of what have become known as the first and second fundamental theorems of welfare economics. First, under a lengthy set of restrictive assumptions, every general equilibrium in a perfectly competitive economy is a Pareto optimum; second, under another set of assumptions, every Pareto optimum is the equilibrium that would be reached by the market, starting from some appropriately chosen initial distribution of resources. These are the mathematical statements of Adam Smith's optimistic vision of the invisible hand, allowing economists to treat the concepts of efficiency, competition, and Pareto optimality as virtually synonymous with each other.

The two theorems provide an interesting illumination of the abstract mathematical structure of neoclassical theory. However, the required assumptions never come close to being satisfied, so neither theorem is necessarily applicable to the real world. (Positivist philosophy, still accepted by many economists, accords little merit to untestable statements such as, "Under the following unattainable conditions, an ideal result would be observed.") Trying to overcome this problem, some economists have suggested that potential competition, or contestable markets, are as good as actual competition for the purposes of theory. This suggestion is rejected by Jackson and by Joseph Stiglitz in another article summarized here.

Stiglitz starts from the "Keynesian" position of acknowledging the existence of persistent unemployment. If significant unemployment exists in reality, then a theory that deduces the existence of full-employment equilibrium must be mistaken in at least one of its assumptions. Stiglitz identifies a broad category of problems of imperfect information and incomplete markets, which are sufficient to undermine the existence and/or optimality of market equilibrium. If market outcomes are not reliably optimal, the Keynesian presumption in favor of government intervention becomes justifiable; practicing what he preaches, Stiglitz himself was appointed to the Clinton administration's Council of Economic Advisors.

Social Choice: Welfare After Arrow's Theorem

The most promising direction for the reconstruction of welfare economics after the ordinalist revolution seemed to be the creation of a social welfare function that expressed society's welfare judgments. Before ordinalism, the "social welfare function" was, in principle, the sum of every individual's utility; although no such function was in fact ever calculated, many versions of utilitarianism imply that it should be possible. After ordinalism, both Abram Bergson and Paul Samuelson separately proposed that some unspecified method of aggregation of individuals' (ordinal, noncomparable) preferences could still lead to a function expressing society's judgments. In 1951, Arrow proved that they were wrong. Using just a few innocuous-sounding assumptions, he demonstrated that any logically consistent social welfare function is dictatorial—that is, there is a single individual whose preferences prevail in every situation, even when all other individuals have opposing preferences. The article by Peter Hammond, summarized here, explores the assumptions used in Arrow's theorem and the subsequent debate over potential modifications of these assumptions. Arrow's conclusion has proved remarkably robust; as Hammond shows, changes in the assumptions that eliminate the paradox often do violence to the concept of the social welfare function as well.

In the wake of Arrow's theorem, a new approach to the problems of welfare economics has emerged. Social choice theory examines the manner in which individual choices, preferences, and well-being should enter into social judgments and decisions about economic matters. It has coincided with the appearance of a new philosophical discussion of ethics, equity, and economics (see Part VII) and has led to syntheses of the approaches of economists and philosophers. Many authors have tried to expand the subject matter of welfare economics to include other criteria besides efficiency and Pareto optimality. To illustrate the importance of going beyond efficiency criteria, Coles and Hammond argue that there is no reason in theory to assume that all economic agents have the ability to survive from one period to the next; a market equilibrium can still be Pareto optimal even if some individuals die of starvation, while others have more than enough resources to save them.[10]

No author has been as important to the development of social choice theory as Amartya Sen.[11] He was a leading participant in the initial discussions of modifications of Arrow's theorem and has produced a new, simplified proof of the theorem that makes its logic more transparent. He has also offered what is perhaps the most insightful interpretation of the Arrow paradox.

Sen attributes the impossibility of a nondictatorial social welfare function to the impoverished informational base allowed by Arrow's assumptions: neither interpersonal comparison nor nonutility information of any sort is allowed. Real decisions are rarely made on such a narrow basis; using only the tools allowed in Arrow's proof, one cannot solve a mundane problem such as the right way to divide a cake among three people. The solutions offered by common sense, either that equal slices are fair or that the hungriest person should get the most, are excluded, one for using nonutility standards of fairness and the other for making interpersonal comparisons of hunger. (Note that majority rule is ethically unattractive here: two people could agree to vote that they should each get half and the third person none.)

Similarly, Sen has argued that utility, or preference satisfaction, alone is an inadequate basis for social choice. His "Paretian liberal" paradox illustrates this point, showing that Pareto optimality is incompatible with even an extremely minimal interpretation of individual rights. Paradoxes seem to be easier to create than to resolve in social choice theory. The article by Pattanaik, summarized here, reviews the Paretian liberal paradox and a related formulation by Gibbard that also finds a conflict between efficiency and individual rights. Pattanaik is skeptical of Sen's own preferred resolution, as well as many others that have been proposed; Sen's paradox, like Arrow's, has proved to be quite robust.

Thus it appears that there is a deep conflict between efficiency (defined as Pareto-optimal satisfaction of individual preferences) and liberty (i.e., respect for a sphere of individual rights), in which economists have traditionally favored the former alternative. Equally problematical, however, is the opposite extreme, as seen in the writings of libertarians such as Nozick. While libertarians claim to evaluate actions purely in terms of processes and rights, Sen points out that Nozick makes an exception for actions with "catastrophic" outcomes and, therefore, is not able to ignore the consequences of actions altogether. Indeed, a (nonlibertarian) decision rule is needed to determine when outcomes are so catastrophic that consequentialist standards must be invoked.[12]

Sen's own philosophy is at least partly consequentialist, judging actions in terms of their outcomes; it is also decidedly nonutilitarian, relying extensively on information other than utility or expressed preferences for the evaluation of outcomes. His concept of human capabilities and functionings (see David A. Crocker's summary in Part VIII) is an ingenious attempt to combine the best of several worlds, including certain types of objective outcomes, subjective experiences, and process standards. Sen's ethical standards for judging economic actions and policies have frequently been elaborated in the course of discussions of poverty and development and will be addressed in Part VIII.

Social choice theory has generated debates that are lively and accessible, but has failed to reach a consensus on most points. An ever-expanding amount is known about social decision rules and procedures that do not make sense, and should not be adopted; little has been settled about what should be done instead. A decision rule that is applicable to all possible sets of individual preferences (Hammond notes Arrow's suggestion that such a rule could be called a constitution rather than a social welfare function) seems all but guaranteed to produce paradoxical results when applied to some particular set of preferences. As a result of these discussions, communication between certain subsets of economists and philosophers has been vastly improved; social choice theory may have had more impact on philosophy than on economics to date. As we will see in Part IV, the application of welfare economics to policy problems in the form of cost-benefit analysis proceeds by ignoring most of the dilemmas that have been raised by theoreticians since the ordinalist revolution. Yet the issues raised by Sen and other social choice theorists should be central to a reconstruction of the economics of social welfare and individual well-being.

Two Alternative Theories

Social choice theory encompasses many, but not all, of the alternative approaches to the problems of welfare economics. Two very different alternatives are examined in the last two summaries included here.

Like a duckling that "imprints" on its mother when it comes out of the shell, neoclassical economics may be inseparable from utilitarianism—the philosophy that was present at the birth of marginal utility theory. John Harsanyi has been working for years to produce a revised, modernized utilitarianism that overcomes the objections to earlier variants. The publication summarized here is one of his most recent and comprehensive; similar themes are expressed in many of his other writings.

Harsanyi derives the existence of cardinal utility functions from the work of von Neumann and Morgenstern, the founders of game theory. Anyone who responds rationally to lotteries has, in effect, a cardinal utility function.[13] Then Harsanyi (like Sen) appeals to the common-sense belief that people's experiences and satisfactions are comparable. The combination of these two principles appears to be enough to overturn ordinalism and allows a restoration of the earlier, unproblematical approach to welfare economics. The social choice paradoxes due to Arrow, Sen, and others would be immediately resolved if it were possible to determine social welfare by adding individual utility levels. Sen's cake would be divided among the three people in the manner that maximizes their joint satisfaction.

Harsanyi is not, however, merely reviving the utilitarianism of the past. He argues for "rule utilitarianism," in which utilitarian calculations determine the choice of society's moral rules, rather than "act utilitarianism" with its impossible burden of evaluation of the social utility of every action. Nor are all preferences created equal in Harsanyi's theory. Only well-informed preferences are counted; more surprisingly, only self-directed preferences are counted in the calculation of the social welfare function. While these modifications are motivated by philosophical debates and objections raised by critics, their effect is to make Harsanyi's utilitarianism less transparent. No simple summation of individual preferences is involved; rather, Harsanyi derives a complex social decision rule, growing out of the utilitarian tradition. A cake should be divided in accordance with moral principles that maximize utility in general, not necessarily on the basis of the actual utility of eating a particular cake today.

Harsanyi is not completely alone in proposing a return to an updated utilitarianism. Bernard van Praag, a Dutch economist working in the same framework, has attempted empirical measurement of the utility of income and finds considerable interpersonal consistency in the responses to his surveys.[14] Game theorists are frequently drawn to the von Neumann–Morgenstern approach to utility functions; some work in game theory could even be seen as suggesting a trial and error model for rule-utilitarian creation of social norms.[15] Support for utilitarianism, however, is restricted to a small minority of contemporary economists.

A different minority of economists has objected to conventional welfare economics on the grounds that preferences are in part endogenous results of economic activity, and thus it is logically circular to use satisfaction of preferences as a standard for welfare judgments. E. J. Mishan's exhaustive survey of welfare economics in 1960 mentioned the complications caused by interdependent utility functions, as proposed by Duesenberry, as one of the unresolved problems in the field.[16] A similar point was raised, from a somewhat different perspective, by neo-Marxist "radical economists" in the 1970s. Herbert Gintis argued that welfare economics was incomplete since it failed to recognize the influence of economic institutions on individual development, and hence on the formation of preferences.[17] (See also the summary of Robert Frank's essay in Part V.)

The final summary is a later analysis that draws on and extends Gintis's approach. Robin Hahnel and Michael Albert offer a detailed critique and proposed reconstruction of welfare economics, including a remarkable mixture of social and philosophical discussion with intricate mathematical derivations. In the portion of their work summarized here, they develop a formal mathemati-

cal model, entirely within the spirit of neoclassical analysis, but assuming endogenous formation of preferences. They use the model to prove three types of
results: first, endogenous preference formation leads to misestimation of the
welfare effects of economic choices; second, under the usual assumptions of
perfect competition plus endogenous preferences, the "fundamental theorems"
of welfare economics still hold; and third, in the presence of market imperfections, endogenous preferences lead to increasing deviations from optimal outcomes over time.

The contrast between the second and third categories of results serves as a
caution for interpretation of optimality theorems in general. Hahnel and Albert
argue that endogenous preference formation alone does not destroy the optimality of competitive equilibria but renders that optimality unstable. Any deviation from ideal competitive conditions—and such deviations are sure to exist—
leads to cumulatively greater departures from optimality.

Other work emerging from a similar perspective (increasingly shedding its
former Marxist assumptions) stresses the significance of institutional inequalities of power, and conflict over market exchange relationships, as well as endogeneity of preferences.[18] There are some points of overlap with the work of
Stiglitz, as described above, and perhaps the potential for the development of a
new paradigm in the future.

The discussion of social choice, and of other recent alternatives, embodies
one clear improvement over the Marshallian welfare economics of a century
ago: contemporary analyses bring ethical concerns, standards, and critiques into
the heart of the theory, rather than leaving the pursuit of higher values to an
unspecified point in the future. Yet there is nothing approaching unanimity
among the alternatives explored here. Nor, unfortunately, has there been much
impact on the practices of mainstream economics. On the one hand, the theory
of welfare economics has played a steadily decreasing role in textbooks and cur-
ricula in recent years. On the other hand, applied welfare economics, in the
form of cost-benefit analyses, often make drastic simplifying assumptions that
ignores the sophisticated debates, largely eliminating the ethical content and insights of the theory—as will be seen in Part IV.

Notes

1. Amartya Sen, "*Social Choice and Justice*: A Review Article," *Journal of Economic Literature* 23 (December 1985), 1764–1776; quote from 1768.

2. Much of Walras's writing on these issues has never been translated into English. See "The Perfect Socialist Society of Leon Walras," Chapter 6 of Ugo Pagano, *Work and Welfare in Economic Theory* (New York: Basil Blackwell, 1985).

3. Lars Pålsson Syll, "Wicksell on Harmony Economics: The Lausanne School vs. Wicksell," *Scandinavian Economic History Review* 41 (1993), 172–188; quote from Wicksell, 180.

4. The rise of ordinalism in the Austrian School is traced in Jack High and Howard

Bloch, "On the History of Ordinal Utility Theory: 1900–1932," *History of Political Economy* 21 (1989), 351–365.

5. Everett J. Burtt, Jr., *Social Perspectives in the History of Economic Theory* (New York: St. Martin's Press, 1972), 267–268.

6. On the influence of positivism, see John B. Davis, "Cooter and Rappoport on the Normative," *Economics and Philosophy* 6 (1990), 139–146. On behaviorism, see Shira B. Lewin, "Economics and Psychology: Lessons For Our Own Day From the Early Twentieth Century," *Journal of Economic Literature* 34 (September 1996), 1293–1323.

7. George Lichtheim, *Europe in the Twentieth Century* (New York: Praeger, 1972), especially Chapters 9 and 11.

8. See also S. A. Drakopoulos, "Keynes's Economic Thought and the Theory of Consumer Behavior," *Scottish Journal of Political Economy* 39 (August 1992), 318–336, summarized in the predecessor to this volume, *The Consumer Society*, eds. Goodwin, Ackerman, and Kiron (Washington, DC: Island Press, 1997).

9. On the greater flexibility of Marshall's welfare analyses, compared to the ordinalists, see P. L. Williams, "Marshallian Applied Welfare Economics: The Decline and Fall," *Economie Appliquée* 43 (1990), 231–245.

10. Jeffrey L. Coles and Peter Hammond, "Walrasian Equilibrium without Survival: Existence, Efficiency, and Remedial Policy," in *Choice, Welfare, and Development: A Festschrift in Honor of Amartya K. Sen*, eds. K. Basu, P. Pattanaik, and K. Suzumura (New York: Oxford University Press, 1995), 32–64.

11. Bibliographic review of Sen's contributions to social choice theory would be a substantial undertaking in itself. Many of his most important papers through about 1980 are collected in Amartya Sen, *Choice, Welfare, and Measurement* (Cambridge, MA: MIT Press, 1982). His 1995 presidential address to the American Economics Association, "Rationality and Social Choice," *American Economic Review* 85 (March 1995), 1–24, is a valuable review article and contains citations of many of his other works.

12. Sen (1995), 12.

13. However, empirical work in psychology has often found that people do not respond rationally to lotteries; low-probability, high-payoff bets are frequently overvalued, for example. See Amos Tversky, Paul Slovic, and Daniel Kahneman, "The Causes of Preference Reversal," *American Economic Review* 80 (March 1990), 204–217.

14. Bernard M. S. van Praag, "Ordinal and Cardinal Utility," *Journal of Econometrics* 50 (1991), 69–89.

15. Ken Binmore and Larry Samuelson, "An Economist's Perspective on the Evolution of Norms," *Journal of Institutional and Theoretical Economics* 150 (1) (1994), 45–63.

16. E. J. Mishan, "A Survey of Welfare Economics, 1939–1959," *Economic Journal* 70 (1960), 197–256. On Duesenberry's model, see the discussion and summary in *The Consumer Society*, eds. Goodwin, Ackerman, and Kiron, Part V.

17. Herbert Gintis, "A Radical Analysis of Welfare Economics," *Quarterly Journal of Economics* 86 (November 1972), 572–599.

18. For example, see Samuel Bowles and Herbert Gintis, "The Revenge of Homo Economicus: Contested Exchange and the Revival of Political Economy," *Journal of Economic Perspectives* 7 (Winter 1993), 83–102

Summary of

Were the Ordinalists Wrong About Welfare Economics?

by Robert Cooter and Peter Rappoport

[Published in *Journal of Economic Literature* XXII (1984), 507–530.]

Two major episodes of intellectual change defined the modern approach to utility theory and welfare economics: the "marginalist revolution" of the 1870s and the "ordinalist revolution" of the 1930s. This article examines the theories of utility and welfare that were accepted by economists between these two episodes and argues that the ordinalist revolution represented a fundamental change in the questions addressed by economics, not scientific progress in pursuing an unchanging agenda.

Utility Before the 1920s

The classical economists of the early and mid-19th century lacked a systematic account of utility and consumer theory. John Stuart Mill, for example, was a utilitarian but did not view utility maximization by consumers as an important part of economic theory.

W. Stanley Jevons, a key figure in the marginalist revolution, was the first to prove (in 1871) that in equilibrium the ratio of each consumer's marginal utilities for any two products must be equal to the ratio of their prices. Further mathematical development of this insight led to Vilfredo Pareto's demonstration that consumption could be treated as a problem of constrained maximization, parallel to production. Analytical tools developed in physics were rapidly assimilated into economics, establishing the mathematical character of the field.

Nineteenth-century economists differed on the question of whether utility was measurable. The affirmative answer can be traced back to Jeremy Bentham, the 18th-century philosopher who founded utilitarianism; he believed that utility was an objective quantity with the same measurable properties as weight. Some of the early marginalists, such as Francis Edgeworth, shared this view, with minor revisions. Others, such as Jevons, Pareto, and Irving Fisher, doubted that it was possible to observe and compare utilities. By 1892, Fisher had established that interpersonal comparisons of utility, and indeed all cardinal measurements of its magnitude, were unnecessary for the technical analysis of market equilibrium, thus laying the mathematical foundations for the ordinalist revolution.

Yet it was not until 40 years later that economists in general accepted the ordinalist approach. The delay was due in large part to the influence of the "material welfare" school of Alfred Marshall, Edwin Cannan, and Arthur Pigou, which had come to dominate the mainstream of English economics by the 1920s. The material welfare economists differed from the modern (i.e., ordinalist) approach in their definition of the subject matter of economics, their methodology, and their understanding of the concept of utility.

The Material Welfare Definition of Economics

For the material welfare school, economics dealt with only a part of the well-being of the community, which Cannan described as "material welfare" and Pigou as "economic welfare." The hierarchy of motives for, and satisfactions obtained from, consumption ranged from purely economic or material at one end to purely noneconomic or nonmaterial at the other; necessities of life were at the former end, while comforts and luxuries were found toward the latter. According to Pigou, the focus on material or economic welfare allowed use of the "measuring rod of money." While nonmaterial satisfactions could not be directly measured and could at times be undercut by policies that promote material prosperity, Pigou thought it likely that material welfare and total welfare were positively related.

In his evaluation of public policies, Pigou argued that redistribution in favor of the poor would lead to more material wants being satisfied, so long as there was no decrease in total national product. Likewise, growth in national product would also lead to increased material welfare, so long as the share of the poor did not decrease. Particularly desirable were policies such as investment in education, health care, and industrial training, which promoted both equity and growth. Relieving poverty was desirable for its own sake, because it often increased growth, and, as Marshall claimed, it allowed people, liberated from the wants of "the brute and the savage," to develop their "higher faculties."

The Material Welfare Conception of Utility

At the turn of the century, two distinct concepts of utility were in use. Pareto made a clear distinction between the two: he maintained the traditional meaning of "utility" in the sense of "usefulness" and coined the term "ophelimity" to describe subjective desire, independent of need or usefulness. He concluded that the science of ophelimity was far more advanced than the problematic analysis of utility.

The material welfare school was clearly concerned with utility rather than ophelimity. Physical needs are measurable and far more comparable between individuals than subjective desires. On the plausible assumption that people spend any increases in income to satisfy their most urgent needs first, it could be shown that additional income is more useful to the poor than to the rich.

For Pigou this created a strong presumption in favor of redistribution, tempered in practice by concern for the negative effects of egalitarian policies on incentives.

Comparisons of utility were not assumed to be possible between two specific, named individuals; rather, the comparisons that mattered for public policy were between broad groups of people, such as "the rich" or "the poor." If a large enough group was examined, Marshall argued, personal peculiarities of individuals would counterbalance one another, and average material welfare would be directly related to income. This use of averages was common, not only to the material welfare school, but also to some of the precursors of the later ordinalist school, such as Fisher.

The material welfare school viewed its policy prescriptions, often including explicit implications for income distribution, as positive scientific conclusions, rather than normative value judgments. They saw themselves as part of the long tradition of British empiricism in believing that knowledge comes from experience rather than from pure reason and favoring, in practice, attention to detail and collection of facts. They differed from modern economists in their approach to problems where empirical data were lacking; the material welfare school accepted common sense and introspection as legitimate evidence in such cases.

The Critique of the Material Welfare School

The tradition of Cannan, Pigou, and Marshall was attacked by Lionel Robbins in 1932. He criticized the material welfare definition of economics for its narrowness; opera tickets were just as fit for study by economists as bread. Robbins introduced the now-famous definition of economics as the relationship between ends and scarce means. No hierarchy of needs was assumed; the expanded definition shifted attention from goods that yield utility to those that produce ophelimity (although Robbins did not make the distinction and used the word "utility" for both concepts). Yet ophelimity cannot be observed or compared, even on average between groups of people. Thus the new definition of economics contained within it the basis for rejecting the interpersonal comparability of utility.

The 1930s was the period when logical positivism began to influence Anglo-American philosophy and social science. Although similar to empiricism, logical positivism had a much narrower interpretation of "observable events," discouraging the use of mental and moral concepts. In the extreme it led to behaviorism, declaring that all subjective concepts were unobservable. Robbins went a long way in this direction, claiming that no *observable* behavior could be explained by cardinal measurement or interpersonal comparison of utility. In consequence, he declared such measurement and comparisons to be outside of science.

For the material welfare school, utility was of course measurable and quantifiable. There is little controversy about the observation of hunger or the measurement of infant mortality. But the shift from utility to ophelimity allowed Robbins to reject this view. Because no one can observe the satisfaction enjoyed by other people, he asserted, no one can demonstrate scientifically that income has a greater marginal utility to the poor, or that redistribution toward the poor is desirable. Statements about redistribution are merely normative for Robbins; if people disagree about the preferred distribution of resources, there is no scientific way to resolve the dispute.

Debate between the two schools of thought, appearing in the economics journals in the 1930s, largely failed to recognize the significance of the differences in definitions that divided them. There is little evidence that the ordinalists persuaded members of the material welfare school to change their views; rather, a new generation of ordinalists gradually replaced the older material welfare economists.

The supposedly value-free economics of the ordinalists, when applied to policy questions, was in fact still based on assumptions about distribution. The so-called "compensation tests" introduced into welfare economics by Nicholas Kaldor and John Hicks favored policies that maximized national income—implicitly assuming that the marginal utility of income was the same regardless of who received it. This is no less normative than Pigou's assumption; it is simply a different assumption.

Evaluating and Explaining the Ordinalist Revolution

The standard history of economic thought views the ordinalist revolution as an attempt to make economics a positive, value-free science and to bring a more rigorous scientific method to the field. This view must be rejected: the material welfare school had a different research agenda and a slightly broader conception of admissible scientific evidence but was no more or less normative than modern economics. Each of the two schools was guided by a different definition of economics, for which a different conception of utility was appropriate. While intensity of subjective preferences (the new conception of utility) cannot be compared or quantified, intensity of needs (the older conception) can be.

One can only talk unequivocally about scientific progress when the same questions continue to be addressed. The gains made by the ordinalists in understanding markets must be balanced against the losses in understanding human welfare, which was better comprehended by the material welfare school.

Summary of
Keynes's Political Philosophy
by Rod O'Donnell

[Published in *Themes in Keynesian Criticism and Supplementary Modern Topics:
Selected Papers from the History of Economics Conference, 1989*,
ed. William J. Barber (Brookfield, VT: Edward Elgar, 1991), 3–28.]

The moral problem of our age is concerned with the love of money, with the
habitual appeal to the money motive in nine-tenths of the activities of life, with
the universal striving after individual economic security as the prime object of
endeavour, with the social approbation of money as the measure of constructive success, and with the social appeal to the hoarding instinct as the foundation of the necessary provision for the family and for the future. [*Collected
Writings of John Maynard Keynes*, IX, 268–269; cited in O'Donnell, 13.]

Discussion of the thought of John Maynard Keynes has usually focused on his
economic theories, with little systematic attention given to his scattered political and philosophical observations. This paper argues that Keynes had a definite
political philosophy that united many of his seemingly disconnected statements.
It describes that philosophy as an unconventional left-of-center liberalism based
in large part on G. E. Moore's ethical theories.

Keynes's Conception of Politics

Keynes's philosophy rested on Moore's *Principia Ethica*, which made a fundamental distinction between means and ends. Social sciences, within this philosophy, were indirect means to the ultimate end of increasing the amount of intrinsic goodness in the world. Politics and economics could not directly create
goodness, but they could establish the preconditions for its creation. Thus politics becomes an application of ethical theory, or a branch of the philosophy of
practical reason. Central to Keynes's philosophy of practice was the doctrine of
consequentialism, according to which the rightness of actions depends on the
goodness of their consequences. As a result, all political principles and rights
were seen only as means, not as ends in themselves. While individual freedom
and security are preconditions of the pursuit of intrinsic goodness, they are not
absolute or inalienable rights, for they are not themselves the ultimate ends of
politics.

For Moore this perspective led to a relatively uncontroversial list of political
objectives (prevention of crime, protection of health, maintenance of freedom,
etc.), and, given his treatment of the uncertain future, to a very conservative

outlook on reform. Because our knowledge of future consequences is so incomplete, he concluded that departures from society's generally established rules could never be justified.

Keynes revised Moore's outlook in two respects. First, he added a number of objectives, such as satisfaction of basic material needs, peace, and economic efficiency. Second, drawing on his early writings on the theory of probability, he adopted a different view of the uncertainty of future events. Even though the future is uncertain, we can still form degrees of rational belief about some future consequences. Such rational beliefs then assist in determining the rightness of actions. Established societal rules are not to be ignored, but individuals can rationally depart from such rules when the available information indicates that departure will lead to higher probability of goodness. This greatly expanded the scope for social change.

A Liberal Reading of Edmund Burke

In a study of this 18th-century conservative, Keynes considered Burke's great discovery to be the view that politics was about means and not end. He welcomed Burke's attacks on the notions of abstract rights and ideal forms of government, as raised by the French Revolution. Burke also emphasized the uncertainty of our knowledge of the future, arguing for extreme timidity in "introducing present evil for the sake of future benefits." [9] Keynes accepted this point, but applied it only to violent means of social change and not, as Burke tended to do, to reforms in general. Keynes also rejected many other aspects of Burke's thought that led to conservatism, including the preference for peace over truth, disbelief in the individual's ability to judge courses of action, and reliance on rigid views of what constituted "natural" social arrangements.

Burke's description of the ultimate end of politics—peace, comfort, and happiness—also differed from Moore's and Keynes's, which focuses on maximizing intrinsic goodness. For Moore, there were two principal categories of intrinsic goods, namely personal affection and aesthetic enjoyment; in short, love and beauty. For Keynes, the economic utopia that would promote the good required a world at peace, where arts of all types were encouraged and humanity's natural and cultural heritage was maintained. Money would still be used, but the love of money, and acquisitiveness for its own sake, would vanish. Far from being static, the ideal society would be constantly experimenting and seeking to improve its conditions of existence.

The Journey to the Ideal

Two fundamental changes were needed in society, according to Keynes. One was economic, to ensure efficient production of the material preconditions of goodness; the other was moral or psychological, to reorient human nature toward the pursuit of intrinsic goodness, particularly love and beauty. The first would be easier to achieve than the second. Yet in order to accumulate enough capital to solve the economic problem, injustice and evil would have to be tolerated for some time to come:

> For at least another hundred years we must pretend . . . that fair is foul and foul is fair; for foul is useful and fair is not. Avarice and usury and precaution must be our gods for a little longer still. For only they can lead us out of the tunnel of economic necessity into daylight. [13]

The link between evil and the love of money is an ancient one in many religious and philosophical traditions. In Keynes, it is related to other important themes in his writings, including the critique of the role of financial capital and rentiers, the attacks on excessive thrift, and a pejorative attitude toward unearned income. He scorned the Benthamite tradition of social theory because it encouraged the overvaluation of an economic criteria of success at the expense of morality and higher ideals.

Keynes's Political Position

Keynes's philosophy led him to be a left-liberal in politics. Achieving Moorean ethical ideals required a massive transformation of both society and individual behavior. But his was a liberal, non-Marxist leftism that called for peaceful, non-revolutionary change and appealed to reason and intelligence, not to class struggle or force.

In his writings on practical politics, he mocked the vestiges of laissez-faire conservatism, a view he saw as appropriate to the 19th but not the 20th century. His moderately conservative views on some questions did not translate into any sympathy for conservatism as a contemporary political doctrine.

Though differing philosophically from many other liberals, Keynes strongly identified with the Liberal Party and assumed that it would have to ally itself with the much larger Labor Party. The solution to the "political problem of mankind," he felt, required economic efficiency, social justice, and individual liberty. Labor would provide a focus on the second, while the Liberals would lean toward the first and third. Others in the Liberal camp emphasized social justice more consistently than Keynes, but this does not mean that he ignored this issue. However, he never saw redistribution as the primary cure for the economic problems of the day.

Keynes described Marxism as "illogical" and was opposed to notions of class struggle, state socialism, and nationalization. Still, he described the ideal economic system he advocated as "liberal socialism," or the "true socialism of the future." His fragmentary descriptions of that ideal involved a restrained form of

private property and enterprise, with an interventionist state engaged in ethically desirable activities ranging from macroeconomic stabilization to support
for the arts and environmental protection. In Keynes's opinion, socialism, like
liberalism, needed to adapt to changing circumstances.

Conclusion

No one would claim that Keynes was a major political philosopher. His great-
ness rests primarily on his contributions to economics that have molded modern societies. Nevertheless, his political philosophy is important because it in-
terlocks with his economics and because it remains relevant to contemporary
discussion. His political legacy may be summed up in two broad propositions:
first, politics should be the servant of an ethical vision combining material and
spiritual objectives; and second, what is needed in politics is a fusion of liberalism and socialism that is appropriate to contemporary circumstances.

Summary of

Welfare Economics

by Peter Jackson

[Published in *What's New in Economics?*, ed. John Maloney
(New York: Manchester University Press, 1992), 101–134.]

Welfare economics, the normative branch of modern microeconomics, addresses the basic question: how should resources be allocated to maximize well-
being? The search for comprehensive theoretical answers has been a difficult
one, as this article makes clear in its review of modern developments in welfare
economics. [Note: this summary omits the original article's discussion of
Arrow's theorem and of distributional questions, since they overlap with other
articles summarized in this volume.]

Traditional Welfare Economics

Welfare economics is usually said to have started, as a distinct branch of economics, with Arthur Pigou's *The Economics of Welfare* (1920). However, Adam
Smith in the *Wealth of Nations* (1776) had already presented the core concept
of welfare economics in his demonstration that the market offered a means to
achieve the common good. In 1932, Lionel Robbins transformed welfare economics with his argument against interpersonal comparisons of utility. Subse-

quently, the "new welfare economics" attempted to separate value judgments from factual propositions and minimized the use of interpersonal comparisons.

The principal results of this endeavor were formalized by Kenneth Arrow in two so-called "fundamental theorems of welfare economics." The first theorem states that a competitive equilibrium, if it exists, is a Pareto optimum. (Proof of the existence of a competitive equilibrium is a separate matter, requiring a set of strong assumptions such as atomized competition, price taking, incorporation of all relevant information into prices, and a process of price adjustments toward equilibrium.) The second welfare theorem is roughly the converse of the first. It states that any Pareto-optimal equilibrium can be achieved via competition, provided the appropriate lump sum taxes and transfers are imposed on individuals and firms.

Do these results make it possible to identify an economic or policy change that leads to welfare improvement, without making interpersonal comparisons of utility? Debate over "compensation tests," beginning in the 1930s, addressed this question. In 1939, Nicholas Kaldor and John Hicks argued that a change implies an improvement if those who gain from it could compensate the losers, potentially making everyone better off. In 1941, Tibor Scitovsky demonstrated the paradoxical result that both a change and its reversal could simultaneously be potential improvements. He suggested that an event was only a welfare gain if it was a potential improvement in the Kaldor/Hicks sense, and its reversal was not. Debate has continued, and no clear set of rules has been established to judge the desirability of economic changes.

One might hope that a comprehensive social evaluation of outcomes could be established, reflecting society's preferences. Along these lines, in 1938 Abram Bergson proposed the use of a social welfare function—a function that converts the individual utilities of all members of society into a single numerical ranking. Although the notion of a social welfare has been used at times in applied studies, it was demonstrated to be a dead end in theory by Arrow's "possibility theorem," often referred to as the third fundamental theorem of welfare economics. In 1951, in his *Social Choice and Individual Values*, Arrow proved that under just a few innocuous-sounding assumptions, there is no logically consistent, nondictatorial social welfare function that ranks all social outcomes. (See the summary of Hammond's article in this section for elaboration.)

First- and Second-Best Welfare Analysis

In the ideal (called, by awkward analogy, "first-best") world of economic theory, all markets are either perfectly competitive or can be made perfectly competitive with suitable government intervention. Under these circumstances, efficiency and distributional issues are logically separate, and policies that address the two areas can be pursued independently of each other.

If some market imperfections cannot be overcome, or the theoretically ideal taxes and transfers are not feasible, then the entire analysis changes. The first-best outcomes developed by economic theory are no longer attainable, and analysis of "second-best" alternatives is necessary. The principal result of such analysis is that under second-best conditions, pursuit of Pareto-optimal outcomes is not necessarily desirable. Other, non-Pareto-optimal economic states could achieve the maximum welfare attainable under the existing constraints. Such conditions as externalities and increasing returns to scale (in technical terms, significant nonconvexities) justify public intervention to restore Pareto efficiency. However, the government still faces the problems of how to aggregate individual preferences and design policies in a second-best world.

Imperfect Information and Incomplete Markets

The mathematical analysis of competitive equilibrium requires perfect information and complete markets. Since these conditions are rarely satisfied, it is difficult to demonstrate that any actual situation is a Pareto optimum. For this reason, a weaker criterion has been proposed, known as "constrained Pareto efficiency." When markets are incomplete, a competitive equilibrium is constrained Pareto-efficient if there is no other competitive equilibrium, based on the same resource endowments, that is Pareto superior.

Can the fundamental welfare theorems be rescued in an imperfect world, on the basis of constrained Pareto optimality? If insurance markets functioned perfectly, or if all economic agents acted as described by rational expectations theory, many of the problems could be overcome; but these assumptions have generated controversies of their own.

Incomplete markets may arise because (1) it is costly to organize a complete set of contingent markets; (2) adverse selection, or hidden information, inhibits market transactions, because buyers cannot confirm quality at the time of purchase (used cars may be "lemons"); and (3) moral hazard, which is the ability of agents to affect outcomes through actions that are unobservable to others (to cheat without being caught), leads to socially inefficient increases in costs.

Potential Competition and Contestability

The basic welfare theorems are not designed to deal with market imperfections; yet most industries are not perfectly competitive. One potential resolution of this problem lies in the concept of "potential competition." Several authors have argued that what matters is not actual competition, but rather potential competition that ensures Pareto efficiency by driving profits to zero. The fear of potential entrants into contestable markets could conceivably force even a monopolist to set prices at the Pareto-efficient level.

However, in the presence of increasing returns, potential competition can be Pareto inefficient. Established producers could respond strategically to potential competitors by overexpanding capacity; the resulting level of welfare could be lower than if there had been no threat of competition, and no excess investment. Potential competition could drive profits to zero but still result in monopoly prices being charged to consumers; the former profits are used up in excessive investment to deter competitors. Theoretical analysis has shown that such perverse outcomes are possible even if the sunk costs, or fixed investments, in the industry are comparatively small.

Conclusion

Beyond the analytical questions addressed so far lie the even more difficult questions of equity and distribution. Once we are forced to leave the first-best ideal world of economic theory, the separation of equity and efficiency concerns can no longer be maintained. There are many rival approaches, including utilitarian, egalitarian, libertarian, and Marxian perspectives, with important differences within as well as between these camps (many of which are discussed elsewhere in this volume). The issue of fairness has been raised, but not dealt with satisfactorily, in recent debates in welfare economics.

> Welfare economics is again an active branch of economics. Establishing the criteria that are to be used to judge the performance of an economy which is characterized by incomplete markets and asymmetric information is at the forefront of current theoretical research. The debate about competing theories of distributive justice is incomplete and enables economists to join with the research agenda of social and political philosophers. . . . Most of the exciting work remains to be done. [127–128]

Summary of

The Invisible Hand and Modern Welfare Economics

by Joseph E. Stiglitz

[Published in *Information, Strategy, and Public Policy* (Cambridge, MA: Basil Blackwell, 1991), 12–50.]

The pervasiveness and persistence of unemployment is, in my mind, the most telling "critical experiment" which should lead to the rejection of the basic competitive equilibrium model which (depending on how you view it) either predicts or assumes full employment. [19]

Although Adam Smith only used the term once in *The Wealth of Nations*, his image of the invisible hand has been perhaps the most influential idea in more than two centuries of discussion of economic theory and policy. Much of economics is an attempt to understand the conditions under which self-interested individuals are led "as if by an invisible hand" to pursue the interests of society. This essay argues that market imperfections, persistent unemployment, and failures of the invisible hand are the norm and proposes that the standard results of welfare economics should be revised or reinterpreted to reflect this reality.

The Framework of Welfare Economics

Arrow and Debreu organized the theory derived from Adam Smith's insights into the two "fundamental theorems of welfare economics." The first theorem says that, under certain conditions, a competitive economy is always Pareto efficient. The second theorem states that every Pareto-efficient allocation can be achieved through the market system. Thus, government need only ensure the desired initial distribution of resources, perhaps through "lump-sum" transfers (i.e., taxes and payments unrelated to income, assets, or other economic variables); the market will take care of the rest. Limited government intervention is justified, in most versions of the theory, to address occasional market failures.

While these theorems have an abstract, logical importance, their empirical relevance and policy implications remain to be demonstrated. Smith was correct to say that the pursuit of individual interests may lead to unintended social consequences, but this does not imply that it leads to Pareto-efficient or socially desirable outcomes. The persistence and pervasiveness of unemployment should at least cast doubt on Smith's optimistic conclusions.

Problems with the First Welfare Theorem

Imperfect Information and Incomplete Markets

If the standard competitive paradigm "proves" that persistent unemployment is impossible, which of its assumptions must be changed to make it consistent with reality? One of the most promising areas for revision is the assumption of perfect, costless information and complete markets in all present and future commodities. Recent research has shown that "in general, when risk markets are incomplete and information is imperfect, markets are not constrained Pareto-optimal[1]: the invisible hand does not work." [22] In such cases, carefully designed market interventions can make everyone better off. Of course, imperfect information and incomplete markets are ubiquitous. Therefore, the analysis of Arrow and Debreu, rather than proving the general applicability of

Smith's conclusions, makes explicit the highly restrictive conditions under which the invisible hand theorem holds.

Technological Change

Another common objection to the invisible hand theorem is that it assumes fixed or exogenously changing technology, an assumption that is clearly not relevant to modern industrial economies. This is closely related to the previous discussion, since technology is a special form of information, and technological expenditures give rise to economies of scale and sunk costs that lead to imperfect competition. Market competition often leads to innovation, but not necessarily to the optimal extent; depending on the assumptions made about the industry and market structure, it can be shown that competition may result in either too much or too little expenditure on research and development.

Human Nature

Even though self-interest is an important aspect of economic behavior, human fallibility and sociability also play important roles. Human fallibility can be viewed as another aspect of imperfect information, not only because of incomplete access to information sources but also because of differing, limited abilities to process and communicate the information that is available. Likewise, human sociability affects economic behavior. For example, individuals' perception of whether they are fairly treated, which is largely a social construct, affects their work effort, with important consequences for productivity and wage determination.

Problems with the Second Welfare Theorem

Absence of Lump-Sum Transfers

Government cannot and does not rely on lump-sum taxes and transfer payments for redistribution, because it does not have enough information to decide who should pay the taxes and who should receive the benefits. Taxes and transfer payments based on income, which are feasible and common in practice, introduce distortions in the ideal competitive equilibrium; once this happens, the separation of efficiency and distribution issues is no longer possible.

Principal-Agent Problems

In the Arrow–Debreu model, incentive problems do not arise: individuals perform according to the terms of a contract or they do not get paid. However, recent economic research has focused on principal-agent problems, in which the provision of appropriate incentives is a fundamental challenge. Incentive issues exist because the consequences of one's actions affect others; for example, a landlord benefits if his sharecroppers work harder. Economies where principal-agent problems arise are seldom Pareto efficient; for example, a more egalitarian land tenure arrangement that allows increased output could easily be Pareto superior to sharecropping. Again, it is impossible to separate issues related to distribution from those affecting efficiency.

Economic Policy

A central assumption underlying standard welfare economics, and the policy recommendations that flow from it, is the existence of competition. Without competition, monopolists will produce too little and charge too much. However, a number of economists have suggested that all that is needed is potential competition, not actual competition, to ensure that the invisible hand enforces efficient prices and production levels.

In other research the author has shown that this view is not well founded; any level of sunk costs, even very small ones, can act as an effective barrier to entry. Profits may be driven down, but without any reduction in prices—an industry's profits can be dissipated by excess entry and investment. The experience of the airline industry after deregulation showed that the potential for new entrants does not hold down prices for long; the incumbent firms matched the entrants' prices for long enough to force them to leave, then quickly restored much higher prices.

> It is only under highly idealized circumstances that the market economy is constrained Pareto-efficient. Some of the inefficiencies of the market economy are small, and some—like the periodic episodes of massive unemployment that have plagued capitalist economies during the past two centuries—are not so small. . . . Now that we see that market failures. . . . are pervasive, that they arise in all aspects of economic life, and that issues of efficiency and equity cannot be neatly separated, these issues of political economy cannot be ignored. But these issues—and not the issue of whether the market economy attains the ideal of Pareto-efficiency—are, or ought to be, the focus of debate and discussion in democratic societies. [37–38]

Note

1. Constrained Pareto optimality is defined in the Jackson article summarized in this section.

Summary of

Social Choice: The Science of the Impossible?

by Peter J. Hammond

[Published in *Arrow and the Foundations of the Theory of Economic Policy*, ed. George R. Feiwel (New York: New York University Press, 1987), 116–131.]

The theory of social choice hardly existed before Kenneth Arrow's pioneering work, particularly his "General Possibility Theorem." This article describes the background and structure of Arrow's theorem and reviews some of the attempts that have been made to escape from Arrow's discouraging conclusion.

The Background to Arrow's Theorem

The fundamental concept of Arrow's social choice theory is his social welfare function (SWF), which is a rule that determines a social-preference ordering for any given profile of individual-preference orderings. Arrow later suggested that it could be called a constitution to distinguish it from Bergson's SWF. The Bergson SWF is a real-valued function, defined on social states for only one profile of individual preferences; in contrast, the Arrow SWF is defined over all possible profiles of preferences, and its values are social-preference orderings.

The simple voting procedure of majority rule appears to give rise to a natural SWF, but Arrow rediscovered the Condorcet paradox, named for its 18th-century author. Voting can give rise to intransitive or cyclical preferences: if individual 1's preferences, in order, are a, b, c, 2's preferences are b, c, a, and 3's preferences are c, a, b, then a majority prefers a to b, b to c, and c to a. On the other hand, a logically consistent but less attractive SWF can be created by selecting a dictator and following his decision on every issue.

Arrow's work can be seen as asking whether there is a middle ground between these extremes. He included the requirement that the SWF must satisfy the Pareto criterion, a weak but familiar condition: in essence, the SWF must not overrule any unopposed vote.

Independence or Irrelevant Alternatives

Is there a nondictatorial SWF satisfying the Pareto criterion and generating a consistent social-preference ordering from any profile of individual preferences? Arrow added one more condition to narrow the search, the most contentious aspect of his theorem: the independence of irrelevant alternatives. That is, the SWF's ranking of a versus b must depend solely on individual preferences between a and b.

The motivation for this condition can be seen by examining a SWF that violates it. The Borda rule, named for another 18th-century writer, begins by assuming that each individual ranks every conceivable social state (assumed to be finite in number), assigning 1 to the least-preferred, 2 to the second-worst, and so on. All the individual rankings are then added to obtain a function that represents the social-preference ordering. This is a consistent, nondictatorial, Pareto-compatible SWF.

The Borda rule, however, is hopelessly unwieldy. Applying it to even a moderately complex state election can require each voter to evaluate more than a trillion possible combinations of outcomes. If the Borda rule is restricted to a smaller set of feasible choices, another rule is needed to decide the (often controversial) question of which alternatives to include. Arrow's requirement that the SWF be independent of irrelevant alternatives cuts through these and other conceptual muddles. Social preferences on any question must depend solely on individual preferences on the same question.

Is Dictatorship Inescapable?

Arrow's theorem proves that the only SWF defined over all logically possible patterns of individual preferences, that satisfies both the Pareto criterion and the independence of irrelevant alternatives, is one in which a single individual's preferences always prevail—in short, a dictatorship.

Numerous escapes from this conclusion have been proposed. One of the least satisfactory solutions is to weaken the requirement that the SWF yields a consistent preference ordering over all social outcomes. This approach violates fundamental assumptions of collective rationality and has not been widely accepted.

Another attempted escape involves abandoning the Pareto criterion. Yet this rejects the whole approach to social choice as based on individual preferences. If someone's preference for a over b is not opposed by any individual, how can the SWF fail to select a over b? Sen's "liberal paradox" (see summary of Pattanaik article in this section) raises questions about the scope of the Pareto principle; but that paradox appears to rest on the inappropriate inclusion of envy, meddlesomeness, or even some forms of altruism and benevolence, i.e., other-directed preferences that are not relevant to an individual's personal welfare.

The only remaining option that maintains both collective rationality and the Pareto principle, while avoiding a dictatorship, is to allow dependence on irrelevant alternatives.

Interpersonal Comparisons

The assumption of independence of irrelevant alternatives combines two important features. One is independence, requiring that only properties of the alternatives under consideration can count in the decision. The other feature is "ordinal noncomparability of utilities"—that is, only the ordinal, noncomparable preferences of individuals can be considered in making the social decision. The latter feature is automatically satisfied by any Arrow SWF, since it relies solely on individual-preference orderings.

Sen has argued that it is the exclusion of interpersonal comparisons, in particular, that leads to dictatorship in the proof of Arrow's theorem. To illustrate this point, Sen has introduced the notion of a "social welfare functional" (SWFL), a broader category than Arrow's SWF. Sen's SWFL derives a social-preference ordering from individual utility *functions*, which may be ordinal or cardinal, interpersonally comparable or not. Any Arrow SWF is a Sen SWFL, but the converse is not true. The utilitarian sum of individual cardinal-utility functions (see summary of Harsanyi article in this section) is a Sen SWFL, but not an Arrow SWF.

Sen has also proposed a modification of the assumption of independence of irrelevant alternatives. The corresponding condition for SWFLs may be called the "independence of irrelevant utilities": the social ordering of any set of outcomes depends only on individuals' *utilities* obtained from those outcomes. Then there are many nondictatorial SWFLs that satisfy the Pareto criterion and the independence of irrelevant utilities; one example is a maximin SWFL, which is related to Rawls's concept of justice.

Which Alternatives Are Relevant?

An additional problem arises in this escape from Arrow's theorem. When the interpersonal comparisons used in the Sen SWFL are placed on a rigorous theoretical foundation, the social decision process appears to include irrelevant alternatives. Application of the Rawls maximin rule to a particular social decision, for example, requires identification of the least well-off member of society; that identification process uses information that is irrelevant to (or independent of) the decision that is being made. In general, if social choice is to depend solely on individual preferences concerning the outcomes under consideration, then personal characteristics must be ignored. A potential solution to this problem is to broaden the definition of relevant alternatives to include personal characteristics as well as social states; the range of relevant alternatives could include those in which individuals exchange places in society and personal characteristics.

> It remains to be seen how social choice theory can be reformulated to preserve as much science as one can while escaping the impossibility of nondictatorship.
> [129]

Summary of

Some Nonwelfaristic Issues in Welfare Economics

by Prasanta K. Pattanaik

[Published in *Welfare Economics*, ed. B. Dutta
(Delhi: Oxford University Press, 1994), 197–244.]

Welfare economics and the theory of social choice normally rest on a philosophical assumption of "welfarism"—that is, the premise that evaluation of a state of affairs can be based solely on individual utilities. This essay explores recent controversies in welfare economics that challenge or transcend welfarism. This summary concentrates on the debate over the reconciliation of individual rights and liberties with utility maximization, the principal topic of the essay. The author's much briefer discussion of the measurement and evaluation of the standard of living has been omitted.

Individual Rights

A number of widely accepted individual rights, such as the rights to choose one's own religion, marriage partner, and many details of one's daily life, cannot easily be expressed in terms of utilities. Amartya Sen, in a series of articles beginning in 1970, was the first writer to formulate and analyze the problem of rights in the context of welfare economics.

Sen argued that liberalism, defined as a political system that respects individual rights, implies that there are some choices that are reserved to individuals, regardless of the preferences and utilities of others. That is, for each individual, there is at least one pair of social alternatives for which society's preference must be to respect the individual's preference. The two alternatives might be the state of the world as it is today versus the state of the world with the sole difference that you were forced to change your religion or the color of your bedroom walls. A weaker condition, "minimal liberalism," assumes only that there are at least two individuals in society who each have final authority over one pair of social choices.

Another formulation of rights, by Alan Gibbard, assumes that social alternatives can be segmented into aspects that lie in the public domain, and other aspects that lie in the personal sphere of each individual (such as the individual's religion or bedroom decor). Under "Gibbard's libertarianism," society accepts each individual's preferences in deciding between alternatives that differ only within that individual's personal sphere.

Paradoxes Involving Individual Rights

Both Sen's and Gibbard's formulations of individual rights lead immediately to logical paradoxes. Sen's "paradox of the Paretian liberal" shows that even minimal liberalism is in general incompatible with a weak form of Pareto optimality (if every individual prefers x to y, then society prefers x to y). It is hard to imagine a version of welfarism that does not imply this weak form of the Pareto criterion; hence the paradox appears to show that welfarism and individual rights are inherently contradictory.

The proof of Sen's paradox is simple: in a two-person society, suppose that individual 1's preference is decisive over the choice between x and y, while 2 is decisive over the choice between z and w. Suppose x, y, z, and w are the only feasible alternatives before the society. If 1's preferences, in order, are w, x, y, z, and 2's preferences are y, z, w, x, then liberalism leads society to reject y (since 1 prefers x to y) and also w (since 2 prefers z to w). However, neither of the two remaining alternatives, x and z, is Pareto optimal—everyone would prefer w to x, and likewise everyone would prefer y to z.

Gibbard's libertarianism similarly can lead to contradictions between the rights of individuals. Surely the choice of which shirt to wear belongs to an individual's personal sphere. Suppose that individual 1 prefers all situations in which 1 and 2 wear different colors of shirts, while 2 prefers all situations in which both wear the same color. Then no combination of shirt colors can be a social optimum—if they match, 1 will prefer a change, while if they differ, 2 will want to change.

Proposed Resolutions

Sen's paradox could be resolved by modifying either the principle of liberalism or the Pareto criterion. In the first category, some authors note that Sen's paradox relies on "meddlesome" preferences about other individuals' personal choices. One solution would be to exclude the preferences of meddlesome individuals from consideration; but this excludes too much, since even meddlesome people have rights that should be respected.

A similar approach can resolve Gibbard's paradox: if an individual's choices in his/her personal sphere must be independent of others' choices in their personal spheres, the paradox vanishes. This restriction, though, does not seem realistic; different people's choices often are interdependent, and there is no reason to rule out such interpersonal effects.

In some of the examples used to establish the paradoxes, it appears that an individual might profit from waiving or contracting away his/her rights over decisions. Several authors have proposed resolutions of the "Paretian liberal" paradox through allowing an individual to waive or trade decision-making rights, and assuming that the individual will do this whenever it is in his/her interest. However, if everyone can engage in such behavior, analysis of expected outcomes requires the solution of complex game theory problems, in which there is no guarantee that the paradox is resolved.

Sen himself has proposed a resolution that modifies the Pareto criterion rather than the principle of liberalism. A distinction can be made between an individual's actual preferences and the preferences that the individual would like to be counted for the purposes of social choice; the Pareto criterion can be redefined in terms of the preferences that individuals would like to have counted for social choice. If there is at least one individual who would like society to follow each person's decisions in their respective personal spheres, then the principle of liberalism is compatible with the modified Pareto criterion. However, no explanation is given for the motivations of this individual, who has to give up expression of his/her own preferences on many issues.

Critics of Sen–Gibbard Formulations of Individual Rights

Another line of criticism has objected to the formulation of individual rights adopted by both Sen and Gibbard. Robert Nozick maintains that individuals do not choose between entire social alternatives; rather, each person has a right to fix the features of the world that lie within his/her personal sphere. Social choices can then be made among the alternatives that remain open, once individual choices have been set. Problems based on meddlesome preferences, such as the Paretian liberal paradox, cannot arise in Nozick's framework—whether or not an individual has meddlesome preferences about other people's actions, he must accept others' exercise of their rights, just as others must accept his.

Nozick's formulation seems more consistent with the intuitive understanding of individual rights. Sen has responded with the claim that the two views of rights are consistent with each other, and that his critics' views logically imply his views as a consequence. Debate over this point is continuing; the author has argued elsewhere that Sen's response has not eliminated the problem in his original formulation of individual rights.

Yet another approach to formal modeling of rights involves the use of game forms (i.e., the matrices or diagrams of game theory, showing the available strategies, but without specification of players' preferences or values of different outcomes). Individual rights may then be represented as limitations on the range of permissible strategies for each player.

The introduction of game theory has provided a more sophisticated analytical apparatus and has cleared up some problems. Gibbard's paradox of inconsistencies between two individuals' rights cannot arise in a game-theoretic model. Each individual's choices are modeled as permissible strategies—each chooses his/her own shirt color—and such choices cannot violate anyone else's rights.

Yet the same approach has not eliminated the Paretian liberal paradox. The familiar prisoners' dilemma game makes it clear that dominant individual strategies need not lead to Pareto-optimal outcomes in the context of game theory. "Sen's seminal insight into the tension between individual rights and even the weakest welfaristic values, such as the Pareto principle, has proved to be very robust." [231–232]

Summary of

Game and Decision-Theoretic Models in Ethics

by J. C. Harsanyi

[Published in *Handbook of Game Theory with Economic Applications*, eds. Robert J. Aumann and Sergiu Hart (Amsterdam: Elsevier Science Publishers, 1992), 671–707.]

Until the 1930s, a utilitarian ethical philosophy was widely accepted among economists. This philosophy often included the assumptions of *cardinal utility* and *interpersonal comparability*, i.e., that it was possible to measure an individual's utility and to make quantitative comparisons of the utility experienced by different people. Since the "ordinalist revolution" of the 1930s, a majority of economists have rejected cardinal utility and interpersonal comparability, leading to considerable problems of reconstructing welfare economics in the absence of these foundational assumptions. A minority has argued for a return to a form of utilitarianism. In this article, John Harsanyi, the best known of the "new utilitarians," argues that rational behavior implies the existence of cardinal utility functions for individuals and a social welfare function for society. He also distinguishes his version of utilitarianism from other utilitarian and nonutilitarian philosophies.

Social Utility

Suppose that people respond rationally to situations like lotteries: that is, situations in which any of two or more outcomes can occur, with known (or subjectively estimated) probabilities. Literally buying a lottery ticket gives rise to an overwhelming probability of simply losing the price of the ticket and a slight probability of winning a jackpot. Driving faster than the speed limit is also a lottery in abstract terms; it leads to some probability of arriving at the destination sooner and increased probabilities of being stopped by the police or having an accident. "Rational" decision making means that an individual is able to compare any two lotteries (either it is clear which one is preferred, or both are equally attractive); if the outcome of lottery *a* is at least as good as the outcome of *b* under every possible situation, then lottery *a* as a whole is at least as attractive as *b*; two lotteries that have the same prizes with the same probabilities are equally attractive; and if *a* is better than *b*, which is better than *c*, then some weighted average of *a* and *c* is exactly as good as *b*.

Any individual who is rational in this sense has an "expected utility" function, such that the expected utility of a lottery is the weighted average of the utility of the prizes, weighted by the probability of obtaining each prize. It is unique up to a linear transformation—that is, once the zero point and unit of measurement have been chosen, the expected utility function is uniquely defined. This result was first proved by John von Neumann and Oskar Morgenstern in their pioneering work on game theory; the expected utility function is often re-ferred to as the *von Neumann–Morgenstern* (vNM) *utility function.*

Building on this result, modern utilitarianism claims that all morality should be based on maximizing social utility, or a social welfare function, which is the sum, or average, of all individual utilities, when measured in the same units. To demonstrate this point, it is necessary to distinguish between an individual's personal and moral preferences. Personal preferences are particularistic, giving more weight to oneself, relatives, and friends than to unknown other members of society; moral preferences are universalistic, giving the same weight to every-body's interests. Moral preferences exist independent of an individual's position in society; they would be equally applicable if an individual did not know who he or she was going to be, but had an equal probability of being in any social role.[1] Under these circumstances, the moral valuation of any situation can only be based on the unweighted average of its utility to every individual. Likewise, public policy, if made rationally, will maximize the policy maker's best estimate of (unweighted) average social utility.

Of course, calculation of average utility is not possible unless interpersonal comparisons of welfare can be made. Comparing the level of satisfaction of two individuals is not a trivial task, but neither is it meaningless. The statement, "he is less satisfied with his career than she is with hers" is difficult to evaluate un-less we know them both well, but, when referring to people we do know well, we frequently make and discuss such statements. It is easier to compare utilities if they are interpreted as measuring amounts of satisfaction, rather than prefer-ence orderings.

A common but mistaken objection to the use of vNM utility functions is that they merely express people's attitudes toward gambling, and thus have no moral significance. If we distinguish between the process utility (positive or negative) obtained from the act of gambling, and the outcome utility derived from the prizes (or losses), it is clear that the outcome utilities are what is im-portant. Despite the definition in terms of lotteries, vNM utility functions de-pend only on outcome utilities: the description of rational decision making, given above, implies that two lotteries differing immensely in process utility, but identical in outcomes, must be evaluated identically.

Rule Utilitarianism and Rawls's Theory of Justice

It is important to distinguish two varieties of utilitarianism. *Act utilitarianism* asserts that the morally right action is the one that maximizes expected social utility in the existing situation, while *rule utilitarianism* requires a two-step process: first, define the moral rule that maximizes social utility in similar situa-tions; second, act according to that rule. Since different moral rules are inter-dependent, rule utilitarianism requires adoption of a utility-maximizing moral code in general.

There are a number of drawbacks to act utilitarianism. It would require an impossible amount of calculation of utilities. It would deprive people of the incentives and assurances obtained from knowing that a given moral code was being followed. It would not allow the existence of any morally protected rights and obligations, nor any binding contracts and commitments, since such considerations could be overridden by a utilitarian calculation at any time. In sum, most of us would much prefer to live in a rule utilitarian world of stable moral codes, which in itself is a utilitarian argument for rule utilitarianism.

Both varieties of utilitarianism are consequentialist ethical theories, defining morally right behavior ultimately in terms of its consequences for social utility. This provides a rational foundation for moral choices that is lacking in nonconsequentialist theories, such as John Rawls's theory of justice. Rawls attributes the principles of justice to a fictitious social contract, adopted under the "veil of ignorance," that is, without individuals knowing what role they will play in society. While this bears some resemblance to the view of moral value judgments presented above, Rawls then argues that a person operating behind the veil of ignorance would not maximize average social utility, but rather would choose to maximize the welfare of the worst-off members of society—the maximin principle. This principle makes the value of any action or situation dependent on its worst possible outcome, not its expected value (which is a probability-weighted average of the value of all possible outcomes). In general, this is a poor guide to both practical and moral decision making.

Reassessing Individual Utilities

Several modifications and clarifications of individual preferences and utilities are required for the full development of a utilitarian ethic. Individual preferences based on mistaken or incomplete information do not correspond to a person's real interests; choosing to drink a glass of orange juice because you do not know that it contains poison does not mean that you prefer to be poisoned. Thus it is fully informed preferences that should be represented in utility functions.

Likewise, malevolent preferences should be excluded; they cannot be rationally supported by a society based on benevolence toward individuals. In fact, all other-oriented preferences, even benevolent ones, should be excluded; failure to do so would mean that the welfare of the most popular individuals, with the largest numbers of well-wishers, would be counted disproportionately heavily in the social welfare function.

> Benevolence toward another person does require us if possible to treat *him* as he wants to be treated. But it does not require us by any means to treat *other people* as he wants them to be treated. (In fact, benevolence toward these peo-

ple requires us to treat them as *they* want to be treated, not as *he* wants them to be treated.) [704–705]

This implies that the social welfare function should be the sum, or unweighted average, of each individual's informed, self-directed preferences.

Note

1. This argument, strongly reminiscent of Rawls's "veil of ignorance," was apparently developed, independently, three times in the 1940s and 1950s—first by William Vickrey, second by Harsanyi, and finally by Rawls. [695, note 7]

Summary of

A New Welfare Theory

by Robin Hahnel and Michael Albert

[Published in *The Quiet Revolution in Welfare Economics*
(Princeton, NJ: Princeton University Press, 1990), 141–202.]

One of the fundamental assumptions of neoclassical welfare economics is that preferences are exogenous, that is, what people want is not affected by their activities as workers or consumers. People have a variety of basic needs such as food, shelter, sex, knowledge, affection, and self-esteem. However, these needs never exist in a pure form; they are always expressed through derived needs for particular commodities, relationships, or experiences. While the underlying needs, based in human nature, are exogenous to economic activity, the formation of particular derived needs is often endogenous. Economic theory is primarily concerned with derived needs, or preferences for particular commodities, and should therefore assume that preferences are endogenous. This paper asserts that preferences are often endogenous and explores the implications of this view for economic theory.

Formalizing Endogenous Preferences

To examine the implications of endogenous preferences, consider a formal model that incorporates such preferences but is otherwise identical to the standard neoclassical model. Specifically, assume that in any time period, an individual's utility, or satisfaction, depends on the individual's current characteristics—personality traits, skills, knowledge, and values—and on the commodities consumed and the types of labor performed during that period. The assumption of endogeneity states that current characteristics may depend on past consumption and/or work experience. Thus, current satisfaction indirectly depends on the ways in which the individual has been shaped by past economic activity. Any economic activity may simultaneously satisfy current preferences and develop future preferences.

Other assumptions of the model are largely the familiar neoclassical ones. Lifetime well-being is a function of satisfaction in each time period. Everyone has perfect knowledge, including knowledge of the endogeneity of preferences. The production side of the model is assumed to be purely neoclassical. The point is not that these assumptions are realistic; important questions have been raised about many of them. However, sticking to the standard neoclassical approach in all areas except for one highlights the effect of that one point of departure.

Implications for Welfare Economics

Eight welfare theorems can be deduced from the endogenous preference model. The first pair shows that conventional theory, based on exogenous preferences, leads to incorrect results.

1. *A theory that ignores the effects of present consumption and work activities on future preferences will systematically misestimate the welfare effects of economic choices.* This theorem is analogous to an important result in human capital theory, e.g., on-the-job training and other human capital effects of current activities will change individuals' future budget constraints. Similarly, the preference-developing effects of current activities will change individuals' capacity to extract satisfaction from future options.

2. *Rational individuals who recognize the endogenous nature of preferences will choose activities that reduce their preferences for expensive items and develop their preferences for cheaper ones.* This undermines the welfare significance of consumer sovereignty, that is, while supply is still governed by current demand (as in the neoclassical model), supply also shapes future demand. The rational adjustment of preferences—learning to prefer what is cheaper—makes the utility of a good depend on its price; this suggests a comparison with conspicuous consumption. However, the two effects point in opposite directions: when the price of a good rises, rational preference adjustment leads to lower demand, while conspicuous consumption may imply increased demand.

The Fundamental Theorems Revisited

The first two theorems confirm the intuitive sense of the importance of endogenous preferences. The next three theorems, therefore, come as a surprise: under standard neoclassical assumptions plus endogenous preferences, the fundamental theorems of welfare economics are still valid. While some of the assumptions of the standard model are unrealistic, endogeneity of preferences does not make these assumptions any less plausible.

3.   *Under traditional assumptions plus endogenous preferences, a general equilibrium exists for any competitive market economy.* The crucial assumptions for the existence proof concern the insatiability, continuity, and convexity of preferences. Recent social and economic analyses lead to questions about insatiability, and even more about convexity. Endogenous preferences, however, only play a minor part in those questions.

4.   *Under the same assumptions, any general equilibrium in a competitive market economy is a Pareto optimum.* The critical premises here are the absence of externalities and "thick" indifference curves. Externalities are important in the real world, but this is true regardless of the endogeneity of preferences.

5.   *Under the same assumptions, any Pareto optimum is a general equilibrium of a competitive market economy with an appropriately chosen initial resource endowment.* The crucial assumptions here are the same as those for theorems 3 and 4.

Theorems 1 and 2 suggest that endogenous preferences have important implications for welfare economics, but theorems 3, 4, and 5 seem to suggest that the effect of endogenous preferences is quite limited. The so-called "fundamental theorems of welfare economics" are still valid in the presence of endogenous preference formation. If that were the end of the story, endogeneity would require minor modifications to standard theory.

Welfare and Imperfect Markets

The strength of the standard results of welfare economics, echoed here in theorems 3, 4, and 5, derives from the high level of abstraction that is employed. All market imperfections and distortions are simply assumed away for purposes of analysis. Economic theory looks very different as soon as we start to move down from this pinnacle of abstraction. The last three theorems reveal the importance of endogenous preferences in an imperfect market economy. For purposes of analysis, we will use the smallest possible market imperfection, a single bias in relative prices (one good is priced above its marginal cost, while other goods are priced at their marginal costs).

6.   *In an economy containing a bias in relative prices, the divergence from optimal resource allocation will be greater than indicated by traditional welfare theory and will increase over time.*

7.   *In an economy containing a bias in relative prices, individual human devel-*

opment patterns will be "warped" relative to those prevailing in an optimal economy; the extent of warped development will increase over time.

8.   *The full welfare effects of any bias in relative prices will not be visible to participants in the economy, nor to observers who believe that preferences are exogenous.*

Although formal proof of these theorems is somewhat difficult, the underlying logic is straightforward. When relative prices are biased, rational individuals will modify their activities aimed at future preference development, as well as current preference fulfillment; neoclassical theory recognizes only the latter effect. The "warping" of human development that occurs in response to market imperfections is individually rational but reinforces the socially suboptimal pattern of resource allocation—the theoretically optimum outcome is not only unavailable on the market, it is no longer even desired. Traditional analysts will fail to perceive the endogenous preference changes that result from market imperfections, and hence (as suggested in theorem 8) will understate the resulting deviation from optimality.

In short, the greatest significance of endogenous preferences is not their effect in the ideal theoretical world of perfect competition with no externalities, but rather the increasingly nonoptimal outcomes that result in a world of market imperfections as people adjust their preferences and thereby aggravate the misallocation that results from any imperfection.

PART IV

Applied Welfare Economics: Externalities, Valuation, and Cost-Benefit Analysis

Overview Essay

by Frank Ackerman

[A] study of welfare which confines itself to the measurement of quantities of goods and their distribution is not only seriously limited, it is—at least in those countries where the mass of people have advanced far beyond subsistence standards—positively misleading. For the things on which happiness ultimately depends, friendship, faith, the perception of beauty, and so on, are outside its range; only the most obstinate pursuit of formalism would attempt to bring them into relation with the measuring rod of money, and then to no practical effect. Thus, the triumphant achievements of modern technology, . . . the single-minded pursuit of advancement, the craving for material success, may be exacting a fearful toll in terms of human happiness. But the formal elegance of welfare economics will never reveal it.

—E. J. Mishan[1]

A definitive review of welfare economics in 1960 ended with an eloquent warning (quoted above) against the attempt to measure and monetize everything that people value. Since that time, however, many have rushed in where Mishan feared to tread. As seen in the previous section, the theory of welfare economics has experienced a protracted crisis and discovered inescapable limitations to its analytical power. Meanwhile, applied welfare economics, in the form of valuation of externalities and incorporation of those values into cost-benefit analyses, has become a rapidly growing field. Useful quantitative tools have been developed—and have been applied far beyond the range of problems for which they are appropriate. As a result, a new round of critiques addresses the theoretical errors and overstatements implicit in the current practice of valuation and cost-benefit analysis.

This section addresses three closely related topics that arise as welfare economics turns from theory to practice: first, the theory of externalities and policies designed to internalize them; second, the debates over valuation of environmental and other externalities, particularly concerning the survey methodology known as "contingent valuation"; and finally, the merits of cost-benefit analysis as a tool for reaching public policy decisions.

Pigou, Coase, and the Invisible Foot

Arthur Pigou's *Economics of Welfare* (1920), a seminal work in welfare economics, introduced the concept of externalities, i.e., cases where private and social costs of economic activity diverge. Since competition does not lead to the socially optimal level of externality-generating activities, Pigou argued, taxes or subsidies that internalize externalities can often lead to welfare gains. The idea of Pigouvian taxes lives on today in proposals for "green taxes" as a policy for environmental protection.

Today, however, Pigou may be more popular among environmentalists than with economic theorists. Ronald Coase's critique of Pigou has won a wide following; indeed, it won Coase a Nobel prize. The so-called "Coase theorem" (codified and named by George Stigler, not by Coase himself) asserts that, if property rights are clearly defined and transaction costs are low, private bargaining can set the optimal price for externality-generating activities, regardless of who holds the property rights in question. Recent textbooks in microeconomics frequently give much more attention to Coase than to Pigou.

Not surprisingly, Pigou's approach appeals to liberals who advocate government activism in response to problems such as pollution, while Coase is correspondingly favored by conservatives who prefer to minimize public intervention and regulation of the market. A lengthy, often unproductive debate has raged between the two camps. Stepping outside of the usual terms of debate, a few recent studies have re-examined Pigou and Coase, concluding that the two authors actually had more in common than one would guess from listening to their followers.[2]

In the first article summarized here, Nahid Aslanbeigui and Steven G. Medema show that both Pigou and Coase thought that markets function reasonably well in most cases, that private bargaining was often a good solution to conflicts between single individuals and that government intervention might be appropriate when large numbers of people are involved and transaction costs are high. The remaining differences, while limited, are still significant. Pigou emphasized problems of equity and the need for protection of the poor, while Coase focused on conflicts between producers and generally ignored distributional questions. Pigou was more likely to consider problems involving large numbers of people, for which both agreed that government intervention might be appropriate; Coase dealt with smaller numbers, for which both agreed that private bargaining might make sense. Pigou was often optimistic about public sector solutions to market imperfections; Coase emphasized the government's own imperfections and suspected that public intervention in the market would often cause more problems than it solved.

To a remarkable extent, Coase's analysis is developed around specific cases, real and hypothetical. One example he discusses repeatedly was a classic 19th-century British lawsuit, involving a doctor's complaint that noise and vibration from a neighboring candy factory made the doctor's office unusable. A careful historical study of that case finds that the doctor, the confectioner, and the judge all agreed that the issue should be resolved in terms of the competing rights to peace and quiet versus the continuation of existing business practices, not the relative costs to the two enterprises. If such cases were to be adjudicated on a Coasian basis of relative costs, the courts would be continually involved in rewriting the laws regarding property rights.[3]

Many of Coase's examples are hypothetical ones; his choice of examples to analyze is just as important as the logic that he applies to them. As noted by Aslanbeigui and Medema, Coase dwells on conflicts between individual producers, while for Pigou, and even more for modern Pigouvian environmentalists, the important conflicts are between producers and large numbers of affected citizens. The fundamental problem with Coase, and even more with his followers, is the implicit assertion that a handful of cases involving narrowly defined conflicts between business enterprises are representative of the broad problem of externalities and that the bargaining strategies appropriate for conflicts between two businesses are generalizable into useful policy recommendations for more complex situations.[4]

This critique of Coase does not simply mean, however, that Pigou was right after all. The Pigouvian tradition does ask the right question: it focuses on externalities that affect large numbers of people, and it recognizes that public policy is often essential in addressing such externalities. Yet when it comes to answering the question of policy toward externalities, difficulties emerge in Pigou's approach as well. In a subtler sense, the treatment of examples, particularly the assumption that externalities occur individually in isolation from one another, shapes Pigou's theory as much as Coase's, as argued in the second article summarized here.

In a 1973 article that deserved far wider attention than it received, E. K. Hunt and Ralph D'Arge suggested that the mechanistic worldview of neoclassical economics has led to a limited understanding of externalities. Competitive equilibrium is assumed as a starting point, and then a single externality is introduced. Either the activist, Pigouvian or the laissez-faire, Coasian response is developed for that externality in isolation. Hunt and D'Arge claimed, in contrast, that externalities are ubiquitous and easily created. Moreover, they maintained that most externalities are at best zero-sum, yielding benefits to the creator that are no greater in value than the damages imposed on others.

In a passage (quoted in the summary) that parallels and parodies Adam

Smith's description of the invisible hand, the authors proposed that an invisible foot leads utility-maximizing individuals to impose externalities on society, increasing general misery more effectively than if they had intentionally set out to do so. The invisible foot would provide an especially painful kick if externalities were often resolved through Coasian bargaining; more people would start engaging in unpleasant behavior if they stood a chance of receiving a financial reward for stopping it. The alternative, only hinted at by Hunt and D'Arge, would involve a restructuring of rights and responsibilities in many areas, recognizing that production is a social process and that current property rights allow private appropriation of many of the benefits without the corresponding costs.

Pricing the Priceless

The Pigouvian agenda appears to require a monetary valuation of externalities. The difference between private and social costs must be known to propose policies that internalize externalities. In recent years, economists have been hard at work estimating such values. The process recalls an old joke. Graduate school in economics is like a black box, within which a mysterious transformation occurs. In one end go sensible people and out the other end come researchers who ask you how much you would pay to avoid having your mother die of cancer. Painful as it may seem to put a price on such priceless qualities as life and health, the logic of economic theory appears to require it to allow quantitative analysis of externalities. The next four articles address the theory and practice of valuation of externalities, a rapidly growing area within environmental economics.

A good place to start, both for a thoughtful critique and for a detailed literature survey and bibliography, is the article by Arild Vatn and Daniel Bromley. They view the process of monetary valuation as a problem of information loss: complex, multi-faceted environmental resources are reduced to unidimensional, numerical magnitudes, and declared comparable to ordinary financial transactions. This process ignores, or tramples on, the interdependence of ecological systems, moral objections to monetization of environmental values, questions of uncertainty and irreversibility, and conventional problems of limited information. Vatn and Bromley propose that discussion about rights and contexts for decision making must precede any particular decision. Moreover, they claim that significant, effective environmental decisions have been made, and will continue to be made, without establishing prices for externalities. The defensive tone of their title, "Choices without Prices without Apologies," reflects the extent to which theirs is a minority opinion within the contemporary world of environmental economics.[5]

The evolving field of ecological economics provides alternative perspectives on this, as on many environmental issues; the August 1995 issue of the journal

Ecological Economics addressed the question of ecosystem valuation. An article by Bromley in that journal points out that the value of natural resources exists independently of any attempts at valuation; economists cannot hope to capture all aspects of the "true" value of the environment but at best can analyze the subset of values that is relevant for particular policy purposes.[6] In this context, he introduces a point that is also discussed in the Vatn and Bromley article: the distinction between "willingness to pay" (WTP) for environmental gains and "willingness to accept" (WTA) compensation for environmental losses. For an ordinary, marketed commodity, economic theory implies that an individual's WTP for gaining a unit and WTA for losing a unit should be identical and equal to the price. However, valuation studies routinely find that WTA is substantially greater—often 3 to 10 times as great as WTP for the same environmental benefit. Bromley observes that many recent environmental laws are designed to provide compensation for damages, implying that the higher WTA measure should be more relevant; instead, use of the lower WTP figure has become standard in U.S. regulatory practice.

The next summary, by the editors of the *Harvard Law Review* (HLR), offers a detailed critique of the dominant technique, "contingent valuation," which consists of surveys of consumers to determine hypothetical market values for nonmarketed goods and services. There is no cost to being wrong in answering such surveys, and there is usually no basis for being right. Valuations of worthy environmental objectives are more like hypothetical donations to charity than like market prices. With billions of dollars at stake in the valuation of nationwide externalities, it is hard for the legal system to accept the common argument that even a rough guess at environmental values is better than no estimate at all. While the article has implications for economic theory, its principal objective is to keep contingent valuation results out of the courtroom.

A response to such critiques is offered in the next summary by W. Michael Hanemann, an advocate of contingent valuation. Survey techniques have improved in recent years, eliminating some of the obvious causes of bias and inaccuracy in earlier studies. The results now appear broadly consistent with other sources of economic information, when it is possible to make comparisons. The goal of contingent valuation is to determine the value that people in general place on particular resources or externalities, not to ask experts for technical analyses. Thus a survey of a random sample of the population is the appropriate methodology, not a second-best or compromise choice.

Hanemann's defense makes a more limited claim for contingent valuation than the ones the critics attack. While Vatn and Bromley examine questions of true social and ecological value, and the HLR editors address the legal valuation of environmental harm, Hanemann merely argues that contingent valuation is the ideal way to find out what individuals think something is worth. Are the two sides in this debate talking about the same thing? To equate the opposing views is to assume that the satisfaction of individual preferences, as revealed by market choices or by contingent valuation, is the sole basis of social, ecological, or legal value. But that assumption begs a basic question of welfare economics and social choice theory (see Part III). If human well-being and economic goals rest on more than individual preference satisfaction, then contingent valuation results need not be decisive in determining ecological value or legal liability.

One of the areas where valuation of externalities has been most extensively studied and has begun to affect public policy is in the electric power industry. Producers must continually choose between several technologies for electricity generation, which cause emissions of varying quantities of a few well-known pollutants, such as sulfur dioxide, nitrogen oxides, and particulates. Large sums of money are at stake, and the regulatory process often requires detailed studies of competing options before investments are made. By the beginning of the 1990s, several state regulatory agencies had begun to approve particular valuations of pollutant emissions for use in planning studies. Most of this work, however, has been published only in specialized consultant studies and regulatory decisions.[7]

In the article summarized here, Andrew Stirling reviews numerous studies that have developed externality estimates for electric power generation. He finds many instances of inconsistent, eclectic methodological choices, destroying the transparency or coherence of elaborately calculated estimates. Embodying widely differing assumptions, published estimates of externality valuations for coal-fired power plants can vary by a factor of 50,000; even if the outliers are ignored, there is no sign of a consensus on the value of emissions per kilowatt hour. The relative ranking of different technologies for electricity generation is subject to dispute; there is not even an "ordinalist" consensus in the field. Stirling's conclusion echoes that of Vatn and Bromley by recognizing the multidimensional nature of environmental effects and calling for extensive public debate and political judgment, rather than mere calculation, as the basis for decision making.

The point is not that studies of electric power externalities have been particularly poorly done. On the contrary, they represent one of the earliest and best developed practical applications of valuation techniques. Yet in practice, as in theory, implementation of the Pigouvian agenda has proved problematical. Better techniques might someday narrow the range of disagreement, but would not eliminate the underlying problem. The Pigouvian response to externalities ultimately embodies the familiar hubris of neoclassical economists: patch up the workings of the marketplace, and competitive equilibrium will make our decisions for us. The environmentally adjusted market will apparently select the optimal amounts of pollution, and of pollution control, as it does with all other commodities.

A better alternative begins with a humbler stance, acknowledging that nothing about being an economist makes one uniquely skilled at discerning society's nonmonetary values. Social goals must be determined through a deliberative process in which the economist is only one person among many. Once those goals have been set, economists have a lot to contribute in analyzing the costs of differing strategies for pursuing the goals. "Green taxes" on polluting activities, for example, might be a cost-effective way to achieve a desired reduction in emissions. (Or some other policy might be more effective; this is an empirical rather than a theoretical question.) But this is crucially different from assuming that technical development of an optimal tax will lead to an optimal outcome. In one case, market incentives may help to reach the goal; in the other, optimally designed market incentives *are* the goal. The former position is far more defensible than the latter.

Costs, Benefits, and Participation

The theoretical concepts of welfare economics and the measurement and valuation of externalities are typically applied in the form of cost-benefit analysis—an increasingly popular tool for evaluation and justification of public policy decisions. The last three summaries in this section examine the meaning and the limits of cost-benefit analysis. As in the discussion of valuation techniques, the critics and the defenders of cost-benefit analysis are not always answering the same questions; despite their differences in emphasis, the authors summarized here might largely agree on what can be accomplished by quantitative cost-benefit techniques, and what cannot.

A profusion of technical issues of measurement and calculation surround the practice of cost-benefit analysis. Yet, as Ezra J. Mishan and Talbot Page observe, technical questions of methodology can raise ethical dilemmas that should not be (but usually are) ignored. The fundamental question of welfare economics that runs throughout the preceding two sections, and throughout this volume as a whole, is the degree to which the pursuit of human well-being can be identified with the maximization of incomes and consumption. Conventional cost-benefit analysis avoids the question by adopting the ostensibly neutral goal of efficiency, which is taken to imply approval of all potential Pareto improvements: if aggregate incomes, adjusted for externalities, would increase as a result of a policy change, then the winners could potentially compensate the losers; this is interpreted as showing that the benefits exceed the costs.

Cost-benefit analysis thus starts by assuming that incomes plus monetizable externality benefits measure well-being, that distributional effects are irrelevant (a consequence of the potential Pareto criterion, as Mishan and Page explain), and that it is safe to ignore the technical objections to the potential Pareto criterion, raised in the debates about compensation principles in welfare economics more than 50 years ago. According to Mishan and Page, however, the list of problems with cost-benefit analysis is even longer than this.

While some conceptual questions affect any cost-benefit analysis, others arise in the analysis of long-term, uncertain, but potentially irreversible environmental impacts, such as the depletion of the ozone layer, which is taken as a paradigmatic problem by Mishan and Page. The use of discounted present values for future events is theoretically legitimate for events within a single generation, or with a bit of a stretch, for two overlapping generations. The authors maintain that there is no way to extend it to multiple, nonoverlapping populations. Likewise, formal responses to uncertainty fail in the face of the long time periods involved, and the irreversibility of some possible outcomes. The "hard," quantitative aspect of cost-benefit analysis is lost in the ozone; Mishan and Page conclude with an appeal for prudence in the face of long-term uncertainties, asserting that it is better to assume that some activities are harmful until proven safe.

In one of the most mathematical articles summarized in this volume, Richard Howarth and Richard Norgaard create an elegant, formal model that further illuminates the problem of intergenerational equity. (The mathematics is omitted in the summary.) They assume the existence of two overlapping generations and one publicly owned, nonreproductive resource, and in most respects develop a standard neoclassical model, calculas and all. Howarth and Norgaard use the model to prove that the optimal allocation of the resource between generations, and the optimal discount rate, depend on the size of the bequest, or resources left by the first generation to the second. The two laissez-faire policies of no bequest—the "maximin" policy of choosing the bequest to maximize the welfare of the worst-off individual (or generation) and the utilitarian policy of maximizing the sum of the welfare of both generations—both lead to a different optimal allocation and a different discount rate. Other variants, a few of which are explored by Howarth and Norgaard, lead to still other optimal outcomes. That is, the market alone is speechless on the questions of intergenerational resource allocation and the choice of a discount rate, until given its cue by the older generation's nonmarket decision about what to leave to its children.

The next summary, of work by Elizabeth Anderson, examines the treatment in cost-benefit analyses of the questions of human safety and environmental quality.[8] While contingent valuation has been applied in many areas, it has not typically been used to establish the value of a human life; even those who emerge from the black box of graduate training in economics do recognize that surveys will not produce meaningful answers to this question. Nonetheless, the logic of cost-benefit analysis requires a price tag on human life—how else could we decide how much it is "worth" spending on safety?

The usual approach infers the value of life from the wage differentials between occupations with different on-the-job death rates. Anderson raises numerous objections to this procedure. To make the inference valid, workers in general would have to be well-informed, autonomous decision makers, unconstrained by seniority benefits, family responsibilities, or other limitations on job mobility. Simply listing these conditions suggests the obvious response. In a world with realistic constraints, choosing a job does not mean choosing everything that goes with it, nor agreeing that fair compensation has been offered for all its accompanying risks.

Anderson distinguishes between respecting people's choices about serious risk on the one hand and believing that those choices are revealed through market behavior on the other hand. The distinction is also relevant to the expanding area of medical economics, where the increasingly cost-conscious health care system is coming to rely on cost-benefit analyses and monetary valuations of diverse health outcomes. In fact, there is no reason to think that there is such a thing as "the" value of something as profound as a human life. It matters how life is lost, or saved: we mourn in very different ways for people who die while skiing down dangerously steep mountains, fighting to defend their country against invasion, or working in a coal mine whose owner refused to install standard safety equipment.

For Anderson, the values at stake in questions of human life, as in environmental protection, are not commensurable with marketed commodities. Thus she advocates a process of institutionalized democratic participation and self-management, rather than technical analysis, for defining and implementing society's decisions in these areas. Others have attempted further elaboration of the participatory processes that would be required, although proposals along these lines still remain somewhat tentative.[9]

The final summary in this section presents a defense of cost-benefit analysis, although from a perspective that accepts many of the criticisms we have just discussed. According to James Campen, cost-benefit analysis, properly performed and understood, is an indispensable part of public decision making. He does not propose monetization of all possible costs and benefits and acknowledges the limitations of quantitative analysis on the types of issues that Anderson discusses. However, he maintains that specific criticisms frequently concern misuse of cost-benefit analysis, not the method itself. The past history of overbuilding of dams by the Army Corps of Engineers and the Reagan administration's sweeping cutbacks in civilian government in the 1980s were both justified by biased cost-benefit analyses; Campen doubts that the use of biased studies advanced the dominant agenda in either episode. More likely, he thinks, debate over the analyses may have slowed down the approval of the desired decisions.

Campen argues persuasively that the systematic, comparative analysis of all readily quantifiable costs and benefits of a proposal is generally worthwhile—even when there are important other aspects of the same proposal that require a different, qualitative style of discussion. In a participatory political framework, cost-benefit analysis has the potential to increase the accountability of decision makers, who can be required to present data and analyses to justify their actions. Campen's alternative has many similarities to Anderson's conclusion but places a greater priority on analysis and debate concerning the quantitative evaluation of policy proposals.

In conclusion, there is a role for the quantitative techniques that have been developed for valuation studies and cost-benefit analyses, regardless of one's philosophical orientation. But there is a distinction between technique and theory. Neither of the two major attempts, by Pigou and by Coase, succeeded in extending the competitive market model to nonmarket values in a satisfactory manner; the actual structure of externalities is more complex and calls for a more elaborately social, deliberative response than either of them imagined. The process of externality valuation extends our knowledge of individual preferences, but that is not the same as knowing what is best for human well-being or ecosystem health. Cost-benefit analysis is too often promoted from useful servant to foolish master of social decision making, reaching far beyond its limited but effective grasp. In the application of these techniques, the dilemmas and contradictions that arise in modern welfare economics and social choice theory are sometimes hidden, but not resolved.

Notes

1. E. J. Mishan, "A Survey of Welfare Economics 1939–1959," *Economic Journal* 70 (1960), 197–256.

2. In addition to the article summarized here, see Allan C. DeSerpa, "Pigou and Coase: A Mathematical Reconciliation," *Journal of Public Economics* 54 (1994), 267–286; DeSerpa, "Pigou and Coase in Retrospect," *Cambridge Journal of Economics* 17 (1993), 27–50; and Federico Aguilera Klink, "Pigou and Coase Reconsidered," *Land Economics* 70 (August 1994), 386–390.

3. A. W. Brian Simpson, "Coase v. Pigou Reexamined," *Journal of Legal Studies* 25 (January 1996), 53–97.

4. The same handful of examples do show up again and again in discussions of Coase's approach. Regardless of who owns a cave, if growing mushrooms is the most profitable use of it, it will be rented to a mushroom farmer. Land use conflicts between ranchers and farmers can be resolved in favor of the higher-value use of the land, no matter who owns it. As one exasperated comment in the literature put it,

> Pure and simple, these are examples in search of a theorem, and they become more and more tedious with each retelling. They *could* become exciting tales. The cave dweller might grow exotic mushrooms, begin to hallucinate, and turn to publishing books in the tradition of Carlos Castaneda. The gentlemanly discussions of voluntary exchanges that leave resources allocated in the same way could deteriorate into range wars—cattle rustling, cowboys dying, and mothers advising their sons not to grow up to be cowboys.

E. Ray Canterbery and A. Marvasti, "The Coase Theorem as a Negative Externality," *Journal of Economic Issues* 26 (December 1992), 1179–1189; quote from 1181.

5. For a review of mainstream approaches, see Maureen L. Cropper and Wallace E.

Oates, "Environmental Economics: A Survey," *Journal of Economic Literature* 30 (June 1992), 675–740.

6. Daniel Bromley, "Property Rights and Natural Resource Damage Assessments," *Ecological Economics* 14 no. 2 (August 1995), 129–135, and other articles in that issue. See also the first volume in this series, *A Survey of Ecological Economics*, eds. Rajaram Krishnan, Jonathan M. Harris, and Neva R. Goodwin (Washington, DC: Island Press, 1995).

7. One extensive study is reported in A. Myrick Freeman III and Robert D. Rowe, "Ranking Electric Generating Technologies with External Costs," *Electricity Journal* (December 1995), 48–53. The studies discussed here are largely concerned with the traditional list of so-called "criteria pollutants," where damages are much more immediate and better known than in the carbon dioxide and global climate change impacts.

8. For a widely cited earlier treatment of the same issues, see Steven Kelman, "Cost-Benefit Analysis: An Ethical Critique," first published in 1981, and reprinted in *The Moral Dimensions of Public Policy Choice: Beyond the Market Paradigm*, eds. John Martin Gillroy and Maurice Wade (Pittsburgh: University of Pittsburgh Press, 1992), 153–164. The same volume contains the Mishan and Page article and many other valuable contributions to the discussion of ethics and public policy.

9. For example, see Sabine U. O'Hara, "Discursive Ethics in Ecosystems Valuation and Environmental Policy," *Ecological Economics* 16 (1996), 95–107.

Summary of

Beyond the Dark Clouds:
Pigou and Coase on Social Cost

by Nahid Aslanbeigui and Steven G. Medema

[Published in *History of Political Economy*, vol. 30, no. 4 (Winter 1998).]

The two classic works that have defined the economic analysis of social costs and externalities are A. C. Pigou's *The Economics of Welfare* (1920) and Ronald Coase's "The Problem of Social Cost" (1960). The traditions based on these works differ sharply, with Pigouvians calling for frequent government action to remedy market failures, while Coasians emphasize the potential benefits of market resolutions to problems of externalities. This paper examines the original writings of Pigou and Coase and finds that the fundamental differences between the two authors are more limited than it might appear from contemporary debates between their partisans.

Coase on Social Cost

Coase wrote his seminal article in 1960 in reaction to the already established Pigouvian tradition of social cost analysis. This orthodoxy proposed the use of government taxes, subsidies, or regulations to force externality generators to internalize the true social costs of their actions. Coase claimed that such Pigouvian policy recommendations were frequently either infeasible or so costly that they might not be preferable to the status quo.

Coase argued that externalities are reciprocal—the polluter's activity harms the victim, while reducing pollution imposes harm (i.e., costs) on the polluter. The real question is, who has the right to harm others or to be protected from harm? Coase demonstrated that, in the absence of transaction costs, regulation is unnecessary for the attainment of efficiency; any clear initial assignment of rights will allow private negotiations that will reach an efficient allocation of resources, maximizing the value of output without government intervention.

Because of the presence of transaction costs, the bargaining solution to externalities may not be feasible. Coase suggested three possibilities for such situations. First, when one producer's actions affect another, they could be combined into a single firm, internalizing the externality and lowering transaction costs. Second, government regulation, in Coase's opinion, could "on occasion" lead to an improvement in economic efficiency, particularly when large numbers of people are involved and transaction costs are therefore high. Finally, given the problems with all other approaches, the best solution in many cases could be to do nothing at all; the social gains from regulation could be less than the cost imposed by its regulation. Comparative institutional analysis is necessary to determine which option to pursue in any given situation. Coase maintained that the market mechanism is more useful than generally perceived, and that its failures might be less harmful than the failures of government regulation.

Pigou on Economic Welfare

Pigou, like his predecessor, Alfred Marshall, saw human welfare as a broad ethical question. Economics addresses a subset of all welfare-related ethical concerns, specifically those that can be compared, directly or indirectly, with the "measuring-rod of money." For the most part, Pigou assumed that what promotes economic welfare also promotes noneconomic welfare (however, the occasional divergences are important to consider). He developed the analysis of public goods and externalities, showing how a reallocation of resources would lead to a welfare improvement.

Pigou's approach to social cost is similar to Coase's, except in terminology. When the number of parties involved is small (and hence transaction costs are low), externalities could be internalized through private contracts. In the case of public goods and externalities, where the numbers of people involved (and the transaction costs) are large, there was a *prima facie* case for government action. Pigou cautioned, however, that government inefficiency, corruption, administrative costs, and distortion of market relations would have to be considered. Even when government action is appropriate, he relied less heavily on taxes than many of his followers. For example, he suggested public subsidies to industries that install pollution control devices.

Comparing Pigou and Coase

Both Pigou and Coase were more pragmatic and more similar in their views than is usually recognized, and Pigou's work was more thoughtful and practical than one would gather from Coase's critique. What, then, were the true differences between them?

First, they differed in their view of policy objectives. For Coase, efficiency and maximization of the value of output is the primary concern. Pigou is interested in promoting increases in output but sees this objective as part of a larger social and moral agenda. He argues that if efficiency is achieved at the expense of lower-income groups, total welfare is likely damaged; that is, his welfare criterion combines efficiency with an ethical preference for protecting the poor. Coase's focus on efficiency alone implicitly assigns equal weights to all individuals and activities, ignoring distributional questions. His focus on disputes between producers makes this perspective a natural one to adopt. Coase offers the familiar argument that economists can only address part of the process of social choice, clarifying the efficiency implications of different proposals; Pigou construes the role of economists in broader ethical terms.

Second, Coase criticizes Pigou for failing to recognize the reciprocal nature of externalities; to protect one party is inevitably to harm the other. Coase is correct in this critique, but remedying this theoretical error would not affect Pigou's approach to policy. Pigou focuses on externalities that affect large numbers of people, such as air pollution or employment practices that force women to work in factories immediately before and after childbirth. Assigning business the right to pollute or to dictate unhealthy labor practices is a clear possibility in Coase's framework, but would seem unethical and anti-social to Pigou.

Finally, despite many points of commonality on the role of government and its limitations, Pigou and Coase part company on the political implications of their analyses. Both acknowledge that government is fallible, corruptible, costly, hampered by inadequate information, and likely to cause market distortions. Coase goes on to conclude that the potential of the market to solve externality problems, either by creating a market in externality rights, or by simply living with market failure, is often (although not always) superior to government intervention. Pigou, in contrast, believes that government intervention often (although not always) succeeds in improving welfare and could be designed in ways that would minimize its limitations.

Conclusion

Both Coase and Pigou assumed that despite working imperfectly, markets function reasonably well. For Coase, this is part of the conventional view of his philosophy, although his pragmatism is often overlooked. For Pigou, the market-affirming passages in his work may come as more of a surprise. However, he argued that there is no such thing as a market independent of the state; all economic activity occurs within a framework of civil government and contract law. In Britain, he believed, the necessary institutional framework had been created in considerable detail, but there were always failures and imperfections that called for further reform.

The genuine differences between Pigou and Coase stem from two primary sources: the ethical underpinnings of Pigou's analysis, as compared to Coase's almost exclusive focus on efficiency, and their differing judgments of the ability of government to improve on market failures. Politically, Pigou supported an activist program of reform, compared to Coase's laissez-faire conservatism. But Pigou's interventions were designed to improve, not replace, the market mechanism. Both shared the broader goal of making the market work more effectively in response to externalities.

Summary of

On Lemmings and Other Acquisitive Animals: Propositions on Consumption

by E. K. Hunt and Ralph C. D'Arge

[Published in *Journal of Economic Issues* 7 (June 1973): 337–353.]

Orthodox neoclassical economics rests on a mechanistic worldview and assumes that atomistic individual behavior is governed by immutable laws of motion. Many alternative approaches to economics are based on a different, contextual worldview and assume that human behavior consists of complex processes and events, connected to other people and things by intricate systems of relationships. This article argues that the difference between the two perspectives is particularly important for understanding the effects of externalities and that only the alternative, contextual perspective can make sense of a world in which externalities are ubiquitous.

The Neoclassical and Contextualist Frameworks Contrasted

The mechanistic worldview, as embodied for example in Newtonian physics, assumes that all movement can be seen as a series of equilibria, governed by a system of natural laws. Such a system is deterministic: all that is needed is a description of its state at any point in time and of the forces operating on it to predict its development throughout all future times.

This perspective dominated early inquiries into social as well as natural sciences. Adam Smith substituted "self-interest" for Newton's law of gravity; in economic life, the invisible hand of the market would harmonize individual actions and lead to an optimal allocation of resources. The later development of neoclassical economics rests to a remarkable degree on this simple assertion, however intricate its modern mathematical expressions have become.

The assumptions underlying neoclassical economics are seldom made fully explicit. The current socioeconomic structure is accepted without question, as setting the boundaries for economic analysis. Social harmony is assumed, and irreconcilable conflicts of interest are assumed to be impossible. Differences between individuals disappear; they become simply homogeneous, utility-maximizing abstractions with given, unspecified preferences. The government has a shadowy existence, vanishing when competitive equilibrium prevails, but appearing when externalities arise to restore the system to a state of bliss.

While mechanism focuses on machine-like functioning of individuals and systems, the contextualist framework takes as its paradigm the "historical event."

Reality, as people experience it, is not atomistic and quantitative; it consists of many linked processes involving diverse human activities, which have connections to past and future events, as well as relationships to other individuals and resources in the present. Synergism between activities, which is exceptional (and mathematically inconvenient) in orthodox economics, appears typical or normal in a contextualist framework.

Externalities in Neoclassical Theory

The traditional neoclassical approach first assumes that competitive equilibrium and Pareto optimality exist everywhere, and then adds the assumption of a single externality. The policy response is either to introduce a tax that restores optimality, or in more recent variants, to establish a "market for the right to pollute" and then let the invisible hand solve the problem.

For this theory, "The critical *coup de grace* . . . comes when one realizes that externalities are totally pervasive. Most of the millions of acts of consumption (and production) in which we daily engage involve externalities." [345] Almost every human activity has some nonmarket effects, positive or negative, on other people's welfare. The benefits of participation in society are a reciprocal positive externality; thus externalities are a normal, inherent part of social life, not isolated or exceptional occurrences.

Consider the implications of the neoclassical model of unrestrained, self-interested competition in a world full of actual and potential externalities. Since there are limits to what can be accomplished within the marketplace, competitive individuals will seek to maximize their gains from nonmarket transactions. Many nonmarket transactions have a zero-sum character, where one person's gain is another's loss; maximizing one's gains from such transactions implies maximizing the negative externalities experienced by others. With many opportunities to create negative externalities for others, each individual will select those with maximum value, i.e., maximizing the negative externalities for the rest of society.

In fact, the problem suggests a paraphrase of Adam Smith's famous presentation of the "invisible hand" metaphor:

> Every individual necessarily labors to render the external costs of the society as great as he can. He generally, indeed, neither intends to promote the public misery nor knows how he is promoting it. He intends only his own gain, and he is in this, as in many other cases, led by an Invisible Foot to promote an end which was no part of his intention. . . . By pursuing his own interest he frequently promotes social misery more effectually than when he really intends to promote it. [348–349]

Neither taxes to eliminate externalities nor the development of legal rights to allow market transactions can possibly correct all the myriad externalities that arise; instead it is necessary to address the underlying incentive structure of the competitive system.

In modern developed societies, consumption is not about actual needs or amenities. Rather, it is a competitive activity, spurred by the unending desire to catch up with, keep ahead of, or protect ourselves from others we encounter. The external diseconomies from such interactions have swamped the earlier external economies of participation in society; the result is a change in incentive structures that manifests itself in our patterns of consumption.

Conclusion

A contextualist analysis starts by recognizing that both consumption and production are inherently social activities. The source of externalities is the fact that, whereas costs and benefits of economic activity are both social, property laws give particular individuals most of the benefits but a much smaller part of the costs. Moreover, quantitative growth leads to qualitative change in the kinds of costs imposed on society by additional consumption; totally new kinds of costs arise, some of which may involve irreversible damages.

Finally, government is not a neutral *deus ex machina* devoted to perfecting the competitive equilibrium. The government enforces private property rights, which are one of the most important sources of externalities. Satisfactory solutions to the problem of externalities may necessitate sweeping changes in property rights, but there may be no alternative if a sustainable society is to survive.

Summary of

Choices without Prices without Apologies

by A. Vatn and D. W. Bromley

[Published in *Journal of Environmental Economics and Management* 26 (1994), 129–148.]

One third of the articles published since 1990 in the two leading journals of resource economics deal with monetary valuation of aspects of the natural environment. This article analyzes the conceptual problems encountered in the process of environmental valuation and argues that environmental choices made without prices are not inferior to those supported by hypothetical valuation studies.

On Valuing Environmental Goods and Services

Collective choices concerning environmental goods and services cannot come from the aggregation of individual preferences obtained from contingent valuation methods. Use of a single metric to value the environment, with its high degree of complexity and interrelations, results in important information losses, "twisting" its individual and collective significance. Thus, pricing environmental goods and services is not a necessary or sufficient condition for coherent and consistent choices.

Economists state that, for society to make efficient choices, there is no substitute for hypothetical valuation. However, prices do not contain all relevant information; likewise, reducing multiple attributes to one measure, and weighting attributes, is not an easy task. How, then, can the use of such prices lead to efficiency?

Information may be lost during the valuation process for three reasons. First is the *cognition problem*, i.e., the difficulty of observing and weighting attributes of the object that is being valued. Second is the *incongruity problem*, due to the mapping of incommensurable characteristics of goods into one dimension. Finally, there is the *composition problem*, where the value of one attribute depends on the level of another.

In addition, context plays an important role in valuation. Preferences are developed as one chooses; valuation studies may therefore construct reality, rather than measuring what already exists. Estimates that do not incorporate the role of context in preference formation will be incoherent.

The Process of Value Calculation

The three problems of information loss during valuation, all affect the process of calculation of environmental values.

The cognition problem includes both the issues of functional transparency and of multiple scales. "Functional transparency means that the precise contribution of a functional element in the ecosystem is not known until it ceases to function." [133] This leads to two difficulties. First, learning-by-doing, a common method of discovery of market values, is very risky when applied to environmental issues. Second, it is hard to describe the good so that all participants in hypothetical valuation studies have the same concept in mind.

The question of multiple scales arises because evidence suggests that people have trouble converting environmental goods and services into monetary terms; they have problems making comparisons across scales. Thus, price bids for goods that are not commonly represented in monetary terms will be randomly dispersed.

The incongruity problem occurs when each of several environmental attributes is in a different dimension; then any single metric, such as price, is unable to include all the relevant information. The moral aspect introduces an important basis for incongruity. The moral dimension of environmental decisions is related to the right to life of all species including humans, aspects of life, personal integrity, and intergenerational equity. Many people refuse to consider monetary valuation of such moral issues.

The composition problem reflects the complexity of ecosystems and environmental values. The authors comment on the economists' suggestion that there are five definite components of value related to the use and existence of a natural resource: (1) recreational use; (2) commercial use; (3) an option demand for maintaining the potential to visit the resource in the future; (4) an existence value derived from simply knowing the resource exists in a preserved state; and (5) a bequest value from knowing future generations will be able to enjoy existence or use of the resource. The first two components may be classified as use values and the last three as nonuse values. None of these components of value is associated with the functional aspects of environmental goods and services within integrated ecosystems.

Hypothetical valuation treats the environment as a commodity. Valuation requires a precise object, with conceptual and definitional boundaries, so that property rights can be attached. Polanyi suggests that in order to assign values and allow markets to work, arbitrary aspects of reality are treated as commodities, an idea he describes as the commodity fiction.[1] However, some environmental goods may be technically impossible or too expensive to "commoditize."

An alternative, holistic approach to valuation would have the following three features: (1) each part of a functionalized system is as valuable as the whole, and its value cannot be separated from the whole; (2) the value of environmental goods and services comes from their function in an ecosystem, not from exchange in a market; furthermore, they do not exist in discrete units; and (3) they do not acquire value from their uniqueness to humans, but from their uniqueness to the system to which they belong. These aspects are routinely ignored by hypothetical valuation studies.

The Multiple Contexts of Valuation

The value of environmental goods and services arises from multiple contexts and is context dependent. Moreover, through the choice of social contexts, individuals shape their preferences and make decisions in the absence of prices. The basic challenge in environmental decision making is to specify the conditions for discourse over what is worth valuing.

The choice of social context determines whose interests are relevant for the decision process. This can be reduced to a discussion of actual and presumed rights. The current structure of rights gives rise to externalities and to differences between willingness to pay and willingness to accept. This is explained by nontrivial income effects: "loss aversion" and/or the structure of actual or perceived rights. Policy measures should focus on compensation through natural resource restoration and not on theoretical monetary measures.

Environmental decisions affect the different choices we make as consumers and as citizens. The results of hypothetical valuation studies may be relevant as long as decisions only deal with consumers choices, but not if citizen choices are also involved. Hence environmental decisions require collective discussion to construct a basis for choice.

The detrimental and irreversible character of environmental choices is often treated as a risk problem, but it is rather one of uncertainty, where probabilities of the occurrence of an event are unknown. Reduction of risks and losses can be attained through the introduction of new options that reduce competition between the economy and the environment. Examples are multiple-use strategies that secure forestry, wildlife and recreation, and zoning policies for industrial development. The choice of a development path is the ultimate question economists should, but rarely do, address.

Implications

Some state that there is a *necessity claim* for valuation. However, there is no proof that prices derived from hypothetical valuation capture all information required to make environmental choices. Prices determined in this way have no more significance than competing claims expressed by interest groups on each side of any discussion.

Many significant choices have been made without prices, such as disease control through water purification, air pollution programs, and reduced chemical contamination of ground water. There is nothing in economics or in hypothetical valuation that addresses the optimal level of environmental protection and use.

> The collective choice problem about environmental goods and services is complex and problematical precisely because it entails aspects of our social existence that defy reduction to the venerable fiction of commodities. Efforts to redefine reality may prove useful in discussing certain aspects of environmental policy in the classroom, but it does not therefore follow that collective choices which reject the commodity fiction are ill-informed, inconsistent, or not in the interest of efficiency. The hypothetical valuation exercise may be its own reward for what it tells us about how individuals value nonordinary aspects of their lives. But the most fundamental environmental choices will continue to be made without prices—and without apologies. [145]

Note

1. K. Polanyi, *The Great Transformation* (Boston: Beacon Press, 1965); cited by Vatn and Bromley, 137.

Summary of

"Ask a Silly Question . . . ": Contingent Valuation of Natural Resource Damages

Harvard Law Review, Editor's Comment

[Published in *Harvard Law Review* 105 (1992), 1981–2000.]

The rise of environmental consciousness over the past several decades has led to legislation that makes despoilers of natural resources liable for both market and nonmarket losses incurred by the public. This creates the need for measurement of those losses. Contingent valuation (CV), a technique that uses surveys to value nonmarket goods, has gained prominence as a tool for assessing damages to publicly owned natural resources. It is the only method currently used in the controversial measurement of nonuse values, such as the preservation of some remote wilderness for potential use, posterity, or for mere knowledge of its existence. This article suggests that CV estimates are biased and unreliable in general and argues that CV measurements of nonuse values are so speculative that the costs of using them in legal proceedings almost always outweigh the benefits.

The Unreliability of CV for Nonuse Values

CV is an approach to valuation of a commodity that relies on individual responses to contingent circumstances posed in a hypothetical market. A typical CV survey introduces a commodity and describes the method by which the respondent is to "purchase" it, be it a one time tax or a price increase. The respondent is then asked to report his willingness to pay (WTP); the sum of such WTP's is averaged and multiplied by the relevant population to produce a total value. In the debriefing, further information is gathered about demographics and the reasons respondents valued goods as they did. As a relatively new method of valuation, CV is still in a rudimentary stage of development.

There are numerous sources of bias and unreliability that are inherent to CV. A fundamental problem is the hypothetical nature of the questions and answers. Unlike the more common marketplace transactions, where consumers must consider income constraints and potential expenditures on other goods, there is no cost to being wrong when answering a CV survey. Therefore, there is no incentive to undertake the mental effort to be accurate. CV surveys are also susceptible to "strategic bias," whereby respondents purposefully misrepresent their WTP in an effort to increase or decrease the amount of money devoted to a resource. For these reasons, a distrust of hypothetical answers and reliance on observed behavior has long been a basic principle of economics.

CV was originally developed for measurement of use values, such as the opportunity to visit national parks or wilderness areas. The extension of the technique to measurement of nonuse values is especially worrisome. The hypothetical nature of the survey is intensified when applied to goods with which the respondent may be entirely unfamiliar. It is not difficult to imagine resource damages to which most people have given little or no thought. Therefore, responses often do not reflect preexisting preferences; rather, they are numbers constructed for the first time while answering the survey. The result is a level of arbitrariness in responses that makes it impossible to obtain legitimate results. In the worst scenario, "if a respondent is unaware of the existence of the resource, a CV survey may *create* the very nonuse value it purports to measure." [1986]

Because CV is the only method available for measuring nonuse values, its reliability cannot be tested through comparison with other techniques. However, it can be tested against economic theory, which assumes that preferences should be continuous and additive. To the contrary, CV estimates for vastly different sizes and types of resources tend to fall within a similar range, while the summation of WTP's for a variety of resources often produces an aggregate WTP that would exhaust the budget of the average individual. An example of the former problem is seen in an experiment that asked three different groups about their WTP to save 2000, 20,000, or 200,000 birds and found that, despite the huge variation in numbers, the average WTP's were virtually identical.

CV estimates purport to measure preferences, but they fail miserably in this task. Determining what they actually do measure requires consideration of the psyche of the respondent. The near constancy of WTP values across widely different quantities of a resource and across vastly disparate resources suggests that people are showing general support for preserving the environment or for whatever good cause a survey covers. "People view the hypothetical bid as an imaginary gift to charity, and that gift creates the 'warm glow' associated with altruism." [1989] This helps to explain the small number of very low nonzero responses, which is similar to the results found in charity drives. People decide whether a cause is worthy and then pick a nice round number to donate to that cause. This problem is inherent to the methodology and renders the results inaccurate, no matter what improvements are made in survey technique.

Economic Effects of Using CV

It has been argued by advocates of the CV method that far from being unreliable, it should rather be considered the *most reliable* method because it is the *only* method available. "It is economic folly, however, to assume that 'some number is better than no number' when assessing damages." [1990] With billion-dollar nonuse values common for virtually any nationwide impact (e.g., a

WTP of $10 per household multiplied by roughly 100 million households), there can be very large social costs to using the wrong number. "In all but perhaps a few limited cases, the costs to society of imposing such uncertain damages are greater than the costs of ignoring the nonuse values measured by CV." [1990]

If awards are consistently inflated, excessive precautions will be taken to avoid environmental harm and excessive funds will be allocated to the restoration of resources beyond economically appropriate levels. These will in turn translate into higher prices, lower dividends to investors, and lost consumer surplus. Even if CV estimates were correct on average, the uncertainty of the results on a case-to-case basis would lead to similar results due to the risk-averse nature of industry.

As the stakes get higher in damage suits due to these inflated values, the marginal benefit of spending a dollar in court also grows. The still questionable admissibility of CV estimates will encourage more defendants to go to court. The widening gap between plaintiffs' and defendants' estimates of expected damages will discourage out-of-court settlements. All of these trends will lead to a significant rise in administrative costs, which are social losses indirectly borne by the public.

The costs of excluding CV studies would lead to an opposite scenario wherein too little precautions are taken against environmental harm, too little is spent on restoration, and prices are too low, encouraging the public to overinvest in polluting industries. Hence, these costs must be weighed against the costs of using CV. In cases where the nonuse values are small, excluding them will be a safer path, with small potential deviations from optimality. This eliminates the possibility of incurring the costs associated with highly inaccurate and often grossly magnified estimates of the CV method.

The Department of the Interior has considered some of these problems in establishing its new rules, the preamble to which states that CV should be used for nonuse values only in cases involving long-term damages to resources that are both unique and well-known. While this is a positive step, it has been shown that CV results vary widely from one study to another, even when measuring the value of a resource as unique and well-known as the Grand Canyon.

Conclusion

A thorough look at the evidence warrants a complete rejection of the CV method. Meanwhile, defendants should have ample grounds for the dismissal of CV estimates from court due to its proven unreliability.

Society's growing concern for the environment and its recognition of natural resources' nonmarket values have elevated the need for accurate methods of measuring those values. CV is a novel and ambitious attempt to do so, but unfortunately, it is a fatally flawed one. Because new data and analyses suggest that CV does not provide even a rough estimate of people's true preferences for nonuse values, CV estimates of nonuse values should be excluded from federal damage assessment regulations and from the courtroom. [2000]

Summary of

Valuing the Environment through Contingent Valuation

by W. Michael Hanemann

[Published in *Journal of Economic Perspectives* 8 (Fall 1994), 19–43.]

The ability to place a monetary value on the consequences of pollution discharges is a cornerstone of the economic approach to the environment. If this cannot be done, it undercuts the use of economic principles. . . . [19]

In many important cases, contingent valuation is the only way to measure how the public values something of importance to public policy. This paper describes current survey research methods, addresses some common objections to survey techniques, and considers the compatibility between contingent valuation and economic theory.

Conducting Reliable Surveys

As in all research, the details are crucial to the success of contingent valuation surveys. Stopping people in a shopping mall and simply asking them what they would pay to preserve a remote wilderness area is unlikely to produce useful results. Vague, open-ended questions such as "What would you pay for environmental safety?" or "What is the most you would pay for . . . ?" are likely to get vague, meaningless answers.

Since the mid-1980s, most major contingent valuation studies have used closed-ended questions like, "If it costs $x, would you be willing to pay for (or, would you vote for) this?" Different people in the sample are confronted with different dollar amounts, allowing calculation of the proportion who are willing to pay each amount. A graph can then be constructed of the cumulative willingness to pay. The closed-end format makes it easier for most people to answer and eliminates the problem of strategic bias (i.e., unrealistically high or low bids designed to influence the survey outcome in a desired direction).

The reliability of a questionnaire can be improved in many ways, including: providing adequate and accurate information; making the survey balanced and impartial; reminding respondents of the availability of substitutes and budget constraints; allowing for "don't know" responses; letting respondents reconsider answers at the end of the interview; and eliminating any perception of interviewer pressure. To check for the respondent's understanding and acceptance of key parts of the contingent valuation scenario, a "debriefing" session is added at the end of the questionnaire. Additionally, the interviewer may be asked about the circumstances of the interview and his/her perception of the respondents.

Other aspects of statistical and survey methods are also significant. For example, while the mean willingness to pay is extremely sensitive to the responses of the higher bidders, the median response is usually very robust. Research on issues of contingent valuation technique has led to many improvements in recent years. "While none of these alone is decisive, taken together they are likely to produce a reliable measure of value." [25]

Objections to Surveys

There are four common objections to surveys. First, surveys are vulnerable to response effects, i.e., small changes in question wording or order may cause significant variations in the answers. Response effects may be classified into several categories: order effects, i.e., bias toward the first item in a list; shift in meaning, where similar words mean different things; or framing effects, where the response varies to situations that the researcher views as equivalent. Other biases may arises from the difficulty of the task facing the respondent; for example, recall of past events or behavior is often inaccurate. Surveys are inevitably sensitive to context and bounded by constraints of human cognition; these limitations affect not only contingent valuation, but also virtually all government data on incomes, expenditures, and employment patterns. However, this is not enough to invalidate their use.

The second objection states that the contingent valuation process creates the value that it is measuring. That is, since there is no real value for the item being studied, respondents just make one up during the interview. However, if an individual responds thoughtfully to a question about voting to raise taxes to pay for a public good, why is this not a valid preference? "The real issue is not whether preferences are a construct but whether they are a *stable* construct." [28] Evidence from test-retest studies shows a high degree of consistency in valuations.

Third, ordinary people are ill-trained for valuing the environment. Yet the goal of a contingent valuation survey is to elicit people's preferences as if they were voting in a referendum. Therefore, prior experience or training are irrelevant since these are not criteria for voting. Who has standing and whose values count cannot be judged by economists.

The final objection is that survey responses cannot be verified. However, there are three ways to validate contingent valuation results: replication, comparison with estimates from other sources, and comparison with actual behavior when possible. Replication can be used even on a small scale to check if results hold and if the survey is communicating as intended. When measuring direct use values, a comparison can be made with estimates obtained through indirect methods, such as hedonic pricing and the travel-cost method. Many studies indicate that contingent valuation estimates are slightly lower than revealed preference estimates and highly correlated with them.

Furthermore, direct testing of contingent valuation predictions against actual behavior is possible. A number of tests have been carried out in which surveys paired real sale offers (e.g., opportunities to buy boxes of strawberries or hunting licenses) with hypothetical questions about what price would be acceptable. Demand curves derived by the two methods have been strikingly similar.

Contingent Valuation and Economic Theory

Critics of contingent valuation sometimes reject it as a method of economic valuation because its results are inconsistent with their views of economic theory. One claim is that only outcomes should matter to people (and should appear as arguments in utility functions), regardless of the processes that generate them. Thus only use values, not existence values, would be legitimate; the "warm glow" of altruism could be seen as obscuring "true economic preferences." From this perspective, contingent valuation is an unacceptable approach because it incorporates existence values. However, this conflicts with the standard economic view that what people value should be left up to them.

A more substantive objection concerns the way that willingness-to-pay estimates depend on other economic variables. Some critics have suggested that the income elasticities measured in contingent valuation surveys are often implausibly low. In fact, measured income elasticities in most surveys are within the range of elasticities typically estimated for state and local government services, or for charitable giving.

The term "embedding effect" has come to be used for several issues. One is the misconception that contingent valuation estimates do not vary with the scale or scope of the resource being valued. Actually, almost all studies do exhibit the expected types of variation; bigger and better resources are given higher values. The two widely cited exceptions suffered from numerous methodological problems. One asked three groups of respondents to value the prevention of deaths of 2,000, or 20,000, or 200,000 out of a population of 85 million birds, describing the numbers at risk as much less than 1 percent, less than 1 percent, and about 2 percent, respectively, of the total population.

Thus respondents had plausible grounds for perceiving these as similar, small numbers.

Other objections included in the discussion of embedding effects include sequencing, i.e., values depend on the sequence in which questions are asked and sub-additivity, meaning that willingness to pay for a group of public goods is less than the sum of the individual valuations. Both of these effects are consistent with the conventional notion that many goods are substitutes for each other; an individual's market demand for goods also depends on what else he/she has bought.

A final theoretical argument against contingent valuation is that it rejects revealed preferences. However, revealed preferences are hard to apply to public goods. Also, they are hardly foolproof, being based on an extrapolation from particular choices to general conclusions about preferences. Nor is there any reason why observing people's behavior and asking them about behavioral intentions and motives should be mutually exclusive. When we want to know how the public values a resource, "a well-designed contingent valuation survey is one way of consulting the relevant experts—the public itself." [38]

Summary of

Regulating the Electricity Supply Industry by Valuing Environmental Effects: How Much Is the Emperor Wearing?

by Andrew Stirling

[Published in *Futures* 24 (December 1992), 1024–1047.]

One of the areas where monetary valuation of environmental externalities has been most extensively applied is in electric power generation. Numerous studies have estimated the value of externalities associated with fossil-fuel burning, nuclear, and renewable technologies. Many proposals have been made, and a few adopted, for use of these estimates in choosing new investments, operating electric power systems, and setting the rates paid by customers. This article examines and critiques both the theoretical arguments for valuation and its practical application in the electricity industry.

Common Problems of All Environmental Assessments

Characterization of distinct categories of environmental effects must precede any analytical evaluation. However, there is nothing approaching a standard classification in the published literature on valuation. One particularly detailed study uses five overlapping, potentially contradictory methods of classifying environmental effects, including the medium (air, water, etc.), agent of harm, originating activity, nature of risk, and manifestation of harm. More systematic approaches have been developed in the field of environmental impact assessment to avoid double-counting. Without a systematic categorization of effects, there is little chance that valuation studies will yield comprehensive or comparable estimates of electric power supply externalities.

Even after environmental effects are appropriately characterized, reducing them to a single quantitative measure presents its own difficulties, as seen in the history of attempts at comparative risk assessments. "The central problem is that environmental effects are inherently and irreducibly multidimensional. A single numerical index fails to convey important contextual information." [1028] For this reason, studies performed for the European Commission in the 1980s recommended moving away from aggregation of environmental effects and quantitative cost-benefit analysis toward qualitative assessment by decision makers rather than specialists.

Methodological Problems with Valuation

There are three common approaches to valuing environmental effects. One method assumes that an equilibrium exists, so the current cost of abating or controlling emissions represents the avoided external environmental cost. However, the appropriateness of current pollution control requirements is debatable. Furthermore, a circularity in reasoning results if current abatement costs are used to estimate the optimal amount of pollution control.

A second approach assumes that current mitigation costs are an appropriate measure of environmental damage. Yet mitigation efforts address only certain aspects of environmental impacts and exclude some important problems altogether—either because they are not readily mitigated or because they would impose prohibitive costs.

The third group of methods attempts to establish, directly or indirectly, the actual social cost of environmental damage. Among the approaches to damage cost estimation are the *travel cost method*, which measures the value of an environmental asset by the amount people are willing to pay to travel to it; *surrogate* or *hedonic pricing*, whereby differentials in property prices or wages are taken to reflect environmental goods, health benefits, or costs associated with a particular property or job; and *contingent valuation*, in which surveys are used to determine a sample population's willingness to accept payment for damages or willingness to pay for benefits. Other calculations of damage costs may be based on market prices for replacement, repair, or restoration of damaged environmental goods. (Discussion of the limitations of contingent valuation, in the original article, is omitted from this summary since it overlaps with the articles by Vatn and Bromley and by *Harvard Law Review* editors, summarized in this section.)

There is no consensus on the appropriate valuation technique to use for the environmental costs of electricity. Several major studies have combined different techniques for different environmental effects in an ad hoc manner; as a result, "[t]he baroque complexity of the exercise does not lend itself to a state of transparency by which any errors are readily detected." [1031] Presentation of results typically features prominent use of phrases such as "full costs" or "true costs," suggesting a degree of comprehensiveness that is simply not available at present. The discount rate has a profound impact on the valuations for technologies with long-term environmental costs; yet the choice of a discount rate is often little more than arbitrary and sometimes varies within a particular study.

Theoretical Difficulties in Valuation

Beyond the numerous methodological problems with valuation lie deeper theoretical difficulties. The value of an object or an attribute is dependent on its context; the market is not always the appropriate context in which to determine environmental values. "[C]an the value of environmental attributes properly be expressed in terms of the price society is willing to pay to avoid destroying them? Or does the environment possess some 'intrinsic' value in itself, reflecting the benefits secured by nonhuman organisms?" [1034] Unlike other methods of environmental assessment that employ physical indicators, valuation reduces these to a single index, monetary value that has no meaning whatsoever beyond the confines of human society.

Some authors protest that failure to ascribe monetary values to environmental attributes amounts to assigning them infinite value; others claim that the same failure implies a zero value. These contradictory interpretations could equally well apply to the refusal of parents to place a monetary value on their children. Rather than being infinite or zero, some values are simply beyond price; a multidimensional whole cannot readily be characterized by a unidimensional index.

Policy Implications in Practice

Are the results of valuation of electricity supply externalities useful to policy makers? The external environmental costs incurred by coal-fired electricity generation have received particular attention; the range of estimates found in published studies extend from a high of $20 per kilowatt-hour (kWh) to a low of 0.04¢ ($0.0004) per kWh, differing by a factor of more than $50,000. Even if a few outliers are arbitrarily excluded, most estimates lie between 0.2¢ and 10¢ per kWh, differing by a factor of "only" $50. "The scale of the disagreement suggests that the accuracy of valuation does not match the precision with which individual authors express their results." [1035–1036]

Moreover, there is a significant overlap between the ranges of external costs attributed to different technologies. The range of variation in published results would support virtually any ranking of coal, nuclear power, photovoltaic, and biomass (wood-burning) electricity generation. Such uncertainty seriously undermines the utility of valuation studies for policy formation.

Conclusion

Valuation as a method of comparison of environmental effects

> . . . is scientific, in the sense that it relies for its authority on the willingness of policy makers and the general public to accept the validity of ostensibly precise numerical results as an adequate expression of complex, context-dependent and multidimensional qualitative issues. It is *technocratic*, in the sense that it delegates important political judgments to specialists to an extent greater than other techniques and is even less transparent to informed public scrutiny. Perhaps most importantly, however, it is *inaccurate*, both in that it is inherently partial in scope, and in that the results generated vary over wide ranges of values. . . .

> The alternative to valuing environmental effects lies in acknowledging their fundamentally multidimensional character. Only a set of discrete weighted decision-making criteria can adequately reflect the complexities of nature. Such criteria are far more effectively identified and prioritized by wide political debate, than by small communities of specialists. . . . [B]y providing an anchor for the iteration of political debate, this procedure at least accepts that calculation is subordinate to judgment. [1038]

Summary of

The Moral Dimension of Cost-Benefit Analysis, with Particular Reference to the Ozone Problem

by Ezra J. Mishan and Talbot Page

[Published in *The Moral Dimension of Public Policy Choice: Beyond the Market Paradigm*, eds. John Martin Gillroy and Maurice Wade (Pittsburgh: University of Pittsburgh Press, 1992), 59–112.]

Seemingly technical aspects of cost-benefit methodology can raise complex questions of ethical judgment, which economists cannot afford to ignore. The methodological dilemmas of cost-benefit analysis, as described in this article, are particularly important in cases of uncertain but potentially serious long-run problems, such as the depletion of the ozone layer.

The Concept of Economic Efficiency

When economists compare alternative proposals, they begin from the assumption that the only necessary data are the orderings or the subjective valuations of the individual members of society, usually measured in terms of money. No other principles of "the general good" are needed; the underlying philosophical position is one of methodological individualism.

Since a large number of individuals are affected by economic changes, there is a need for a criterion that can rank alternative outcomes. Actual Pareto improvements would be uncontroversially welcomed, but in practice they are rare. A more relevant criterion is potential Pareto improvement: if the aggregate value of individual gains exceeds the aggregate value of individual losses, then an economic measure is said to have a net social benefit. This criterion allows the implementation of projects that make the rich richer and the poor worse off, which has led to objection to its adoption. Nevertheless, most economists have adopted it; an increase in economic efficiency usually means a change that meets the (potential) Pareto criterion.

Economic efficiency is a social norm for ranking alternatives, but it is distinct from political processes such as voting. In order for economic efficiency to be useful as a social norm, it must be grounded in an ethical consensus that transcends politics. The defense of potential Pareto improvements rests on the belief that such changes do not generally have regressive distributional effects, or that progressive taxation will provide a safeguard against undesirable redistribution, or that continual pursuit of efficiency will eventually raise the general level of welfare.

Conceptual Problems of Valuation

It is sometimes suggested that distributional weights should be used when aggregating costs and benefits. The proposed weights are necessarily arbitrary, and typically assume diminishing marginal utility of income, weighting impacts on lower-income groups more heavily. While abstractly appealing, this approach would open the techniques of cost-benefit analysis to continual political lobbying and infighting, ultimately tending to discredit the results. There may be perfectly good reasons to approve a project that does not meet standard economic criteria, but it is not helpful to "doctor" the method of evaluation to make this point. Public projects should meet the test of the political process, independently of the results of cost-benefit analysis.

Technical economic analysis, if it is to be accepted by society, must be situ-

ated within the society's ethical consensus. In some cases this may require modifications to the utilitarian framework of cost-benefit analysis; some individual
preferences may be ethically inappropriate to include in calculations of social
welfare. Income gains for one group, for example, may give rise to feelings of
envy and competitiveness on the part of others, but there could be general
agreement that the negative effects of envious preferences should not belong in
a calculation of social welfare.

The Legitimacy of Discounted Present Values

Society's ethical consensus can be difficult to identify; recent controversy appears to have undermined an earlier sense of agreement on many issues. One
such issue is the approach to valuation of future events and outcomes, as embodied in the technique of discounting. There are a number of technical problems (discussed in the original article) regarding the choice of the correct discount rate even within a single generation. Deeper philosophical problems arise
when discounting is used in an intergenerational context, as in the case of cost-
benefit analysis of long-term environmental issues such as ozone depletion.

The difficult question of intergenerational agreement on valuations can perhaps be addressed in a straightforward manner between two overlapping generations, in the years in which both are alive and economically active. However,
over longer time horizons, there is no one year in which everyone affected by a
proposal is alive, and no explicit agreement is possible. Technical analysis no
longer leads to clear answers over long periods of time: for a proposal whose
impacts last for even 100 years, the outcome of a cost-benefit analysis is critically dependent not only on the discount rate but also on detailed assumptions
about the increases or decreases in consumption, savings, and investment that
would result from the proposal.

Intergenerational Equity, Risk, and Uncertainty

Future generations, if asked, would hardly approve of our use of discounting to
analyze intergenerational problems, since any positive discount rate gives a low
weight to future outcomes. Other standards, therefore, should be sought. A
natural criterion is that each generation is entitled to the same per capita income
or to a natural resource and capital endowment that will allow them to produce
that income.

As in the framework of Arrow's theorem, it seems appealing to seek nondictatorial social choice rules that can be applied to intergenerational problems.
Surely no single generation, such as the present one, should prevail in every
case, even if not all future generations are unanimous in opposition. Discounted
present value, "as a rule of intertemporal choice, is a dictatorship of the pre-

sent." [97] An example of a nondictatorial rule would be that infinite majorities of future generations should be decisive over finite minorities; for instance, if a project is beneficial for the next n generations (for any finite n), but damaging for all generations starting with number $n+1$, then it should be rejected. This rule is very future oriented, as can be seen when n is very large.

The role of the discount rate is to help define the acceptable set of intertemporal paths, from which one must choose an equitable resolution of intertemporal conflicts of interest. Once the acceptable set is defined, there is no need for further discounting procedures. This approach is especially important for problems such as ozone depletion, which involve long-term latencies and irreversibility effects.

The analysis of risks of known probability is a straightforward extension of standard theoretical methods. Yet in many cases the probabilities of important outcomes are uncertain. Numerous techniques have been proposed for analysis of uncertainty, including increasing the discount rate, building a probability distribution from experts' informed guesses, applying game theory models, and other mathematical devices. Unfortunately, problems such as ozone depletion may defy all such techniques: they are results of comparatively new, unfamiliar technology; they raise the real possibility of large-scale catastrophic outcomes; and they impose much or all of the damages on future generations.

Conclusions and Recommendations

To address serious long-run problems such as ozone depletion, it is necessary to move beyond the conventional tools of economic analysis. A prudent rule would be that the larger the possible catastrophe and the higher its probability of occurrence, the stricter should be the regulatory regime. In cases involving potential irreversibility, there is a social benefit in not foreclosing irreversible options; this is particularly important and provides grounds for caution, when irreversible events affect multiple generations. One way to proceed in the face of serious, uncertain events is to compare the consequences of unwarranted complacency versus the consequences of unwarranted alarm; there may well be a scientific consensus that the potential losses from complacency are far greater than the losses due to excessive alarm.

What policies should be pursued when there is more than a suspicion that an economic activity may cause serious harm, but not enough information to make a decision with confidence? Broadly speaking, either of two rules could be followed: "Rule A" would allow the activity to continue until it had been proven harmful, while "Rule B" would bar the activity until it had been proven safe. Rule A has generally prevailed in Western economies, at least since the Industrial Revolution. Yet it seems possible that we are moving into an era of more catastrophic risks, resulting from unfamiliar new technologies, making Rule B seem more appropriate. The situation might be different in a poor country where economic growth is satisfying urgent human needs; but a developed country like the United States already has a goods-saturated economy, in which it makes little sense to increase the risk of ecological disaster in exchange for additional economic growth of material goods.

> We are impelled to conclude that a valid cost-benefit calculation of actions to protect the earth's ozone shield cannot be undertaken in the present state of our ignorance concerning the relevant physical relationships and, therefore, in the present state of any ignorance concerning the nature and magnitude of the risks posed by existing economic activities. Nor can the decision techniques devised by economists and others for problems involving future uncertainty shed much light on the issue . . . [Until there is much better knowledge of the causal mechanisms,] any society having a sense of obligation toward its citizens, and a sense of responsibility for generations yet to come, should adopt the prudent course entailed by the B rule. [108–109]

Summary of

Intergenerational Transfers and the Social Discount Rate

by Richard B. Howarth and Richard B. Norgaard

[Published in *Environmental and Resource Economics* 3 (1993), 337–358.]

Cost-benefit analysis incorporates future costs and benefits into current economic calculations via the process of discounting. Thus the problem of evaluation of future outcomes appears to be reduced to the choice of the correct discount rate (as well as the ever-present uncertainty surrounding future events). This article shows that, even under the ideal conditions often assumed in economic theory, the choice of the optimal discount rate depends on nonmarket decisions about intergenerational bequests, or transfer of resources.

Economic Theory and the Discount Rate

The choice of a discount rate is simple in the ideal world of economic theory. If there are no distortions in capital markets, there is no uncertainty about future economic conditions, and the distribution of wealth is socially optimal, then the market rate of interest is equal to both the marginal return on investment and the marginal rate of substitution between present and future consumption. That rate also constitutes the optimal discount rate. The issue is more complex in reality because these ideal conditions arguably do not hold.

Discussion of the choice of a discount rate under second-best conditions has often focused on the problems of taxation and other capital market distortions and on the implications of risk and uncertainty in future outcomes. This paper addresses another concern: the desired distribution of wealth and welfare between generations. Past discussion of distributional questions has often led to calls to reject discounting, or to use a discount rate below the market rate of interest. Here it will be argued that such approaches are based in part on a misinterpretation of the role of cost-benefit procedures.

"[C]ost-benefit analysis is properly concerned with allocative efficiency, not distributional equity." [339] Distribution must be addressed first, through appropriate intergenerational asset transfers; cost-benefit procedures can then be used to improve efficiency, given the desired distribution. Thus sustainability, for example, cannot be evaluated in terms of cost-benefit analysis. "Sustainability is a criterion defining the just distribution of assets between generations; cost-benefit analysis is intended to improve the efficiency of resource allocation subject to the prevailing asset distribution." [340]

Intertemporal Equilibrium: A Simple Model

A simple mathematical model (presented and analyzed in detail in the original article) can facilitate the analysis of these questions. Consider the allocation of a single, socially managed, nonrenewable resource in a three-period economy. There are two overlapping generations that each live for two time periods (generation 1 lives in periods 1 and 2, generation 2 lives in periods 2 and 3). Assume that there are large populations of identical consumers and of identical small firms.

Individuals of the first generation begin with (equal) capital endowments; individuals of the second generation have no initial capital endowment, but may receive public or private bequests from the first generation, in period 2. Each individual chooses between consumption and investment in the first period of her life; in the second period, the first generation chooses between their own consumption and bequests to the next generation. Individuals receive income on their capital at the market rate of interest and wages on their (fixed) supply of labor at the market wage rate.

It is assumed that all agents are self-interested and have perfect foresight regarding future prices and other economic considerations. The utility function, identical for all individuals, is the sum of the logarithms of consumption in the two periods of life. Individuals maximize their lifetime utility, subject to assumptions about bequests to be discussed below. Firms maximize their profits, and the resource management agency sells all of the nonrenewable resource to firms, aiming to maximize the discounted sum of sales revenue over the three periods. Each period's revenues from resource sales are distributed equally to everyone alive in that period.

Given any fixed level of bequests, these assumptions are sufficient to define a competitive equilibrium in each of the three time periods of the model. The equilibria are efficient over time if and only if the social discount rate in each period is set equal to the market rate of interest. Yet different levels of bequests imply different values for the discount rate—and for virtually everything else in the model. Each solution is equally efficient, given its assumption about bequests; the criterion of efficiency cannot select one level of bequest over another.

Three particular policies for intergenerational transfers can be explored: laissez-faire, with zero transfers; maximin, choosing transfers to maximize the utility of the most disadvantaged individual (or generation); and utilitarianism, choosing transfers to maximize the sum of all individuals' (and generations') utilities. The outcomes are quite distinct, with the first generation much better off than the second under laissez-faire, both generations identical in utility under maximin, and the second slightly better off than the first under utilitarianism.

Modifications and Alternatives

Let us now examine a different world, based on different assumptions, especially that individuals are altruistic, so that what they seek to maximize is a weighted sum of their own utility as well as that of their contemporaries, their offspring, and other members of the future generation. Different choices of weights allow different specifications of altruism, and again very different solutions can be calculated.

If parents care only about their own offspring and value their children's consumption almost as highly as their own, then the results, at least in this simple model, are quite similar to the maximin solution. (However, this coincidence is not analyzed further, and may not hold more generally.) If altruism applies more broadly to all members of the present or future generations, then the institutional context for bequests is crucial. No one can make private bequests that correspond to his/her own altruistic interests; everyone will prefer the outcome achieved by public transfers of assets to the results of individual action alone. Broadly diffused altruism is in effect a demand for public goods, which can only be supplied efficiently by the public sector. Something similar arises even under pure parent-offspring altruism, if the time horizon is extended a few generations: the farther into the future you look, the more descendants you will have, and the more your descendants overlap with everyone else's. In short, concern for your own descendants soon merges into a "public good" concern for the future population as a whole.

Consider another modification of the basic model. Assume that there are institutional barriers that prevent the appropriate intergenerational transfers.

What can be accomplished by "second-best" policy making? The social optima defined by the maximin and utilitarian philosophies can be recalculated, subject to the constraints of zero intergenerational transfers. The new solutions are less equitable than the unconstrained maximin and utilitarian solutions; the second generation does worse in the absence of transfers, though it does better than it would under a laissez-faire approach with no attempt at equity. In the constrained, no-transfer solutions, the price of the nonrenewable resource drops over time (while in the unconstrained solutions the price rises over time, as predicted by conventional economic theory). In order to compensate for the absence of transfers, the public agency managing the resource acts as if it were applying a negative discount rate, or "overvaluing" the future. However, this provides only partial compensation and is less efficient than allowing the optimal transfers to be made.

Conclusions

Cost-benefit analysis does not ensure a socially desirable distribution of welfare across generations, and a social optimum will result only if intergenerational transfers are chosen with social objectives regarding the proper distribution of welfare in mind. Furthermore, decentralized private altruism may yield intergenerational transfers that both present and future individuals would agree are too small. This fact suggests a potential role for collective institutions in the provision of intergenerational transfers.

In a world where intergenerational transfers are nonoptimal and policy makers are unable to alter them, second-best policy making may imply a constrained optimum that is inefficient. [354]

Summary of

Cost-Benefit Analysis, Safety, and Environmental Quality

by Elizabeth Anderson

[Published in *Value in Ethics and Economics*
(Cambridge, MA: Harvard University Press, 1993), 190–216.]

In this chapter I examine the application of cost-benefit analysis to public policies concerning the protection of human life and environmental quality. I will argue that these goods are not properly regarded as mere commodities. By regarding them only as commodity values, cost-benefit analysis fails to consider the proper roles they occupy in public life. [190]

Cost-Benefit Analysis as a Form of Communication

Cost-benefit analysis rests on two claims. First, public policies should maximize efficiency. A policy is Pareto efficient if it can improve the well-being of at least one individual without leaving anyone worse off. A *potential Pareto improvement* is reached if enough welfare is generated so that winners could potentially compensate losers and still be made better off. This gives rise to several questions: "Why maximize efficiency and not welfare? . . . Why maximize potential rather than actual Pareto improvements? . . . Why ignore the distribution of gains from public policies?" [190–191] Economists have yet to answer these questions in a satisfactory way.

Secondly, welfare should be measured by an individual's compensating variation, i.e., the maximum that she will pay to bring about a project she favors, or the minimum he/she will accept to put up with a project he/she opposes. Cost-benefit analysis assumes that the best policy will maximize the sum of the compensating variations of all members of society. Thus, applying the rules of the market via cost-benefit analysis results in the selection of potentially Pareto-efficient policies that (hypothetically) have society's consent.

Cost-benefit analysis imitates the market, evaluating health and environmental benefits by studying how much money individuals would trade for commodified versions of these goods: the prices paid for access to private parks are used to measure the value of national parks; the higher wages for hazardous jobs are said to measure the value of increased risks of death. This approach treats health, safety, and environmental quality as commodities in three ways: it measures their value as determined in market transactions for privately appropriated goods; it reduces them to cash equivalents, treating them as substitutable with other commodity bundles that have the same price; and it assumes that market norms and private preferences, rather than ideals, needs, or principles, should shape public policy.

Autonomy, Labor Markets, and the Value of Life

Cost-benefit analysts argue that if we are to behave rationally, we must assign a cash value to risks to life. Distrusting survey responses on such questions, most economists prefer to infer individuals' valuations from the trade-offs between safety and money they actually make in the marketplace, particularly as seen in the wage differentials between more and less hazardous jobs. In a competitive equilibrium, with labor mobility and full information, wage differentials would measure "revealed preferences" for safety.

In practice, the results of such studies have been inconsistent, with estimates of the value of a life ranging from $15,000 to $10,000,000. Yet even if the studies were consistent, the significance of the result would be in doubt. Wage differentials, in reality, do not represent the result of free, informed, autonomous consent to differing risks. Labor mobility is hampered by the need for on-the-job learning, the desire to protect seniority benefits, nontransferability of skills, and other factors. Autonomous decision making is inhibited by lack of information and hierarchical work relations. Particularly for those with families to support, job choices are not made on an egoistic basis, expressing solely personal attitudes toward risk:

> The opportunity to earn a living is not merely another commodity, like a toaster. It is both a need and a responsibility. To the extent that workers' choices reflect this view, wage differentials do not represent the cash values people place on their lives; rather, they reflect the risks people feel obliged to accept so as to discharge their responsibilities. [199]

Nor is there a single meaning to risk, even assuming the other problems could be solved. Risks undertaken voluntarily, for worthy ends, are viewed quite differently from involuntary risks; few workers report that extra pay alone makes them accept additional risks calmly. Risks to life and health often involve ethical considerations, not simply consumer choices about wants and money. It is appropriate to say that people should be able to make their own choices about the value of different risks; it is mistaken to think that all such choices can be expressed through market relations. The choice to accept a particular job at a particular wage does not imply agreement that the accompanying risks are acceptable, fair, or legitimate consequences of employment.

"Cost-benefit analysis therefore does not supply an adequate framework for evaluating public policies that involve risks to human life." [203]

The Value of the Environment

Some environmental goods have explicit market values. For others, values can often be inferred from the prices people pay for similar environmental amenities. Assigning such prices, however, assumes that the values people place on the environment in their roles as producers and consumers are the only relevant considerations. This approach treats the environment as a commodity by assigning it only an instrumental value in promoting human welfare. While environmental goods do have instrumental values, many people also feel that they have other, intrinsic values—the goal of preservation of species, ecosystems, pristine wildernesses, etc. is at least in part independent of any resulting use values for humans.

Some economists have claimed that the existence of markets for art and for nature resorts shows that people can place a price on aesthetic values. These markets, however, express only the value assigned to private appropriation and consumption of aesthetic goods. Beliefs about public policy, or preservation of a valued heritage, are not reflected in private market prices. "Because we value some environmental goods in higher ways than we value pure commodities, they are not indifferently substitutable for the latter." [208] For this reason, the potential economic value of private exploitation of national parks, for example, is not relevant to public policy decisions.

Understanding the differing categories of valuation makes sense out of some otherwise puzzling empirical results. For example, in a survey asking people how much they would demand in compensation for power plant pollution in the Southwest, more than half the respondents rejected the terms of the question or demanded infinite compensation; they interpreted the question as proposing a bribe, not making an inquiry into their values.

People often value environmental goods in different ways than they value commodities, involving public ideals and principles rather than prices. Just as with risks to human life, cost-benefit analysis fails as a framework for public policy decisions about the environment.

Toward Democratic Alternatives to Cost-Benefit Analysis

Supporters of cost-benefit analysis consider it a way to make political institutions more responsive to citizens' values. However, in the case of safety, health, and the environment, citizens' values could be better reflected through democratic institutions, rather than through calculations that mimic the market and its effects. Democratic institutions provide the social conditions of autonomy that people need to express their own values, particularly those related to nonmarket social relations.

One example of a democratic institution is the worker-management model, in which workers have the freedom to determine what risks they will assume, without having to obey orders from people who do not have their interests in mind. Additionally, this approach promotes environmental protection because workers live in or near the communities in which they work and are likely to suffer from workplace pollution. Though it has not been implemented on a large scale in the United States, the worker-management model has been used in many small cooperatives; certain aspects of worker management have been applied more broadly in other countries, such as Germany.

Democratic participation is the best method for exercising collective autonomy and providing a means for expression of concerns about social relations that the market cannot address. Practical implementation problems may arise when large groups are involved, as in the case of global environmental problems in particular. Representative democracy is useful for groups too large for direct participation but also introduces problems of its own.

> Participants in the policy formation process will, of course, need to consult experts to gather facts about potential negative and positive consequences of alternative policy proposals. But these facts are best presented qualitatively, in

terms deemed relevant by the participants. The willingness-to-pay measure of value must be rejected. In fact, no context-independent, global consequentialist formula for identifying and aggregating costs and benefits is generally valid. . . .

There is no reason to think ordinary people are any less capable of correcting their mathematical errors after dialogue with others than are technocrats. If, after dialogue with others, ordinary people's judgments do not conform to consequentialist standards of rationality, this is evidence not that ordinary people are irrational but that consequentialism itself fails to do justice to the diversity of people's values. Our task is not to refine a technocratic standard of rationality alien to people's concerns, but to empower people to speak and act for themselves. [215–216]

Summary of

Selections from *Benefit, Cost, and Beyond*

by James T. Campen

[New York: Ballinger, 1986.]

The progressive potential of BCA [benefit-cost analysis] lies in two of its basic features. The first is its nature as a means of systematically using organized human rationality to identify and evaluate the consequences of proposed collective decisions. The second is its orientation toward valuing all benefits and costs, whether or not they enter into the financial calculations of individuals or firms—that is, its concern with "social" rather than merely "private" benefits and costs. (185)

Critics of conventional economics often suggest that cost-benefit analysis is biased against or incapable of adequate representation of nonmarket values. In contrast, the work summarized here argues that benefit-cost analysis (the term preferred by the author), or BCA, if done properly, is an indispensable part of rational collective decision making and can make an important contribution to a strategy for progressive economic change. This summary draws on portions of Chapters 5, 9, and 10 of a book-length treatment of the politics and economics of BCA.

Evaluating the BCA Debate

Extreme interpretations of BCA have given rise to extreme conclusions: If it means nothing more than systematic thought about the consequences of policy alternatives, who could oppose it? If it is a rigid quantitative rule for mechanically making policy decisions, who could support it? As understood here, BCA produces a single quantitative measure of net benefits expressed in monetary terms, accompanied by descriptive analysis. This result should be used as one of the inputs into a decision-making process; it is a tool rather than a rule.

The quantitative results of BCA contribute to the public interest both by providing helpful information and by allowing increased accountability of decision makers. When dominant political interests have a strong policy preference, no objective analysis will lead to a different outcome; BCA is more likely to make a difference when powerful forces are divided, or are not firmly committed to a single alternative.

Most of the objections from liberal critics concern misuse of BCA, not the appropriateness of the technique itself, as several of the critics acknowledge. In fact, BCA is explicitly designed for cases where private markets are failing. It was first widely used in flood control projects during the New Deal and gained increased prominence as part of the reform agenda of the Kennedy and Johnson administrations in the 1960s. If liberals are right about the prevalence of market failure, they should welcome the opportunity to calculate nonmarket costs and incorporate them in the decision-making process.

BCA does not inevitably have liberal implications; it is essential for the analysis to be done in a way that invites public overview and participation and makes underlying assumptions explicit. Otherwise, it may drive the politics deeper into the technical analysis, hiding real choices from public view. BCA may not be appropriate when intangible effects such as health, safety, and environmental impacts are of central importance; in such cases it may create a false sense that these intangibles can be quantified. In general, if the analysis cannot be done well—if political and bureaucratic constraints prevent the adoption of an open, unbiased approach—it may not be worth doing at all.

Social Change and the Future of BCA

All public policy making takes places within an arena of conflict and struggle. However, BCA, as a tool for policy makers, offers a formal, ostensibly impartial, and objective technique for evaluating proposed alternatives. It tends to favor general over particular interests and to draw attention to the assumptions and procedures used to reach decisions. The dominant political group of any era naturally tries to adapt BCA to its purposes—though often with less than complete success.

For example, in the 1980s the Reagan administration set out to reduce the government's economic role, cutting taxes, civilian spending, and regulations wherever possible. BCAs with carefully manipulated assumptions provided intellectual support for this political objective. Similarly, in an earlier period the Army Corps of Engineers manipulated the assumptions underlying analyses of proposed water projects, in order to show that more dams and canals should be built. In both cases the biases were so obvious and pervasive that many outside observers objected to the studies. Of course, the Corps of Engineers built a lot of dams, and the Reagan administration made many cutbacks. But it seems unlikely that the existence of rigged BCAs advanced the dominant political agenda in either case. More often it was counterproductive, calling critical attention to the details of the policy-making process.

The use of BCA to promote a conservative political strategy is limited by the methodological presumptions that everyone's interests should be considered and that government intervention is an appropriate response to market failure. BCA thus allows attention to be focused in a direction that most conservatives would prefer to ignore.

Toward a Participatory Alternative

Defenders of existing BCAs argue that their critics are unable to offer a superior alternative. But a participatory mode of analysis of public policy would be far better than current practice. It would extend the mainstream paradigm in three directions: toward a more inclusive objective function, a process of dialogue and mutual learning, and an egalitarian set of social relationships. Many of the current analytical techniques would continue to be used, but in a different context, in the pursuit of different ends.

The objective function—the quantity that is to be maximized in a BCA—conventionally includes only a subset of the welfare-relevant consequences of policy proposals. Within the realm of satisfying existing individual preferences, it should be extended to include such "noneconomic" consequences as the changes in people's productive activities and social relations and the ecological, aesthetic, and ethical impacts that would result from proposed policies. In addition, the policy evaluation process ought to be concerned with the effects of public decisions on personal development and on political processes and power relationships.

It is problematical to rest evaluation of social outcomes solely on the satisfaction of expressed individual preferences, as many theorists have noted. A better alternative is to transform, rather than simply reject, individual measures such as the willingness-to-pay criterion. A process of dialogue and learning may lead to a deeper understanding of our true preferences and interests, involving interactions both with people who possess expert knowledge and with the full range of people affected by the proposed decision. The need for dialogue and learning applies to everyone, including economists and others who consider themselves experts, as well as ordinary citizens. This approach to policy analysis is analogous to Paolo Freire's philosophy of education, which calls for a dialogue between teacher and student about their views of the world.

Finally, current BCA practice rests on unequal, nonparticipatory social relationships, in which "rationality" and expertise are used to exclude many of the affected parties from the decision-making process. In a participatory alternative, the people most directly affected by policy proposals would be actively involved in the analysis. "The process of participation is itself a welfare-relevant activity, and it can also contribute to the individual development of those who are involved." [199] Citizen participation requires a reorientation of the role of experts toward clarifying and explaining their work, rather than presenting it in obscure technical formats that confuse and intimidate outsiders. Those most affected by policy proposals may have to learn some of the expert analytical techniques to be effective participants. To secure the social relations of participation, it is necessary to change the structures of power and accountability so that analysts and decision makers are directly responsible to the population whose lives they affect.

These sweeping changes can only be realized as part of a broader movement toward economic democracy and egalitarianism. However, such a movement should not reject BCA techniques because of past abuses. Rather, it should develop new techniques of participatory, collective analysis as a central part of its approach to decision making.

PART V

Economics and the Good, I: Individuals

Overview Essay
by David Kiron

> Economics as a science of human behavior has been grounded in a remarkably parsimonious postulate: that of the self-interested, isolated individual who chooses freely and rationally among alternative courses of action after computing their prospective costs and benefits.
>
> — Albert O. Hirschman[1]

This neoclassical model of *homo economicus* is defended more for its predictive power than for its psychological realism. However, there is mounting concern that the model's simple assumptions, while perhaps adequate for many aspects of economic behavior, fail to explain or promote features of the human condition that are necessary for a good life. This section develops both empirical and theoretical objections to the prevailing "revealed preference" analysis of welfare, challenging especially its assumption that preferences are the correct terms in which to understand human welfare.

As discussed in Part III, the ordinalist revolution in the 1930s seemed to obviate the need for an accurate measure of cardinal utility and a more sophisticated theory of human motivation. Subsequently, economic behavior could be explained with a few assumptions: as long as individuals are rational and their choices reflect their preferences, individuals maximize their utility. Utility was retained as a useful rubric for understanding human welfare, not because problems with earlier formulations had been solved, but because they could be avoided.

Revealed preference theory assumes that the satisfaction of a person's actual preferences must improve her welfare. However, preference satisfaction may in fact fail to improve well-being if preferences are irrational, poorly cultivated, malevolent (based on the misery of others), or based on incomplete or false information. In response to such objections, efforts have been made to improve this theory to account for the many instances in which preference satisfaction detracts from or contributes nothing to human welfare. The main thrust of these modifications is to idealize preferences and model individual preferences as those that a person would have if fully informed about her choices. However, this move brings other significant problems that offer strong reasons to reject any preference-based theory of well-being.

Psychological Realism and Economic Assumptions

The ordinalists were motivated by one especially thorny problem: the measurement of utility. In the early 20th century, the subjective quality of individual experience—pains, pleasures, emotions, and feelings—seemed completely beyond the terrain of empirical study. To logical positivists and psychological behaviorists, entities beyond the empirical pale were mythic substances, objects of rhetoric and unworthy of scientific consideration. However, developments in the discipline of psychology, such as the recent growth of studies of subjective well-being in the past two decades, have opened a window into the nature of individual satisfaction and led to the construction of tools for making interpersonal comparisons. Statistical methods are now used to verify personal reports of satisfaction and measure levels of happiness. As a result, the hedonic quality of experience is more widely accepted as understandable and measurable.

Two leading researchers in this fast growing field, David Myers and Ed Diener, provide an overview of its major findings in our first summary. Their review of empirical work in the psychology of subjective well-being reveals that human welfare is structured by the presence or lack of strong supportive relationships, challenging work, and personality traits that include self-esteem, extraversion, optimism, and feelings of personal control. Consumption plays a more limited role in promoting happiness than is assumed in economic theory: a wealth of studies demonstrate that the correlation between income and happiness is weak above minimum income levels. In wealthy countries, self-esteem is a better predictor of happiness than income.

Myers and Diener also sketch a theory of subjective well-being that incorporates culture, the human propensity to adapt to changing conditions, and the pursuit of chosen goals: elements ignored by the neoclassical theory of consumer behavior. Cultural outlooks on the world tend to shape individual perceptions of satisfaction. Norwegians and Portuguese with similar incomes differ considerably in their self-reports of happiness: the Norwegians are four times more likely to consider themselves happy than the Portuguese subjects. Traumatized accident victims and ecstatic lottery winners both adapt to their respective emotional extremes in relatively short periods of time and then return to baseline happiness levels. Progressive incremental increases in happiness play a larger role in global judgments of well-being than momentous events. They also hypothesize that active involvement in valued activities and making progress toward one's goals contribute more to subjective well-being than does passive experience of desirable circumstances.

The possibility that empirical data from psychology could be used to advance economic theory poses a significant challenge to the neoclassical approach to consumer welfare, given that its founders and later proponents disavowed the need for greater psychological complexity and realism. However, within the discipline of economics a small but expanding group of economists is beginning to place more stock in the uses and value of psychology and its study of motivation.

In the late 1970s and early 1980s, the attention of economists was captured by the work of Tversky and Kahneman, experimental psychologists who examined individual decisions made under conditions of uncertainty. Their findings led some economists to the conclusion that the standard model of the rational economic actor is not always an appropriate explanatory tool; real people make decision errors that result in lower rather than higher utility. Studies in the psychology of decision theory provide dramatic evidence that *decision utility* (i.e., preference satisfaction) may diverge from *hedonic utility*, the subjective experience of good and bad. The upshot is that preference satisfaction implies much less about well-being than assumed by revealed preference theory. A full reliance on the model assumes too much (and as we discuss later, it also assumes too little).

In more recent work, summarized here, Kahneman surveys findings from one area within experimental psychology and argues that hedonic utility is not only measurable, but that measures of it reveal that rational choice does not always promote welfare. He disputes the assumption that individuals are inveterate utility maximizers and provides evidence that individuals neither try to maximize utility functions nor act as if this was their motive. Research demonstrates that, instead of summing utilities that are experienced over time and arriving at a final, cumulative judgment, people often judge their satisfaction according to a "peak and end" rule—combining the most intense experience of an episode with what is experienced at its end. People are also unable to make accurate estimates of the utility they will receive from future consumption. Individuals are vulnerable to *framing effects* (subjects may perceive objectively equivalent options as gains or losses given alternative descriptions) and are susceptible to *endowment effects* (cognitive phenomena in which losses loom larger than gains), a point acknowledged by classical utilitarians such as Bentham, but only recently rediscovered in modern theory.

The adaptation effect noted by Myers and Diener and some of the psychological phenomena noted by Kahneman had been discussed by economists earlier in this century, but none of these early attempts had much of an impact on the mainstream. Today, much of the new empirical research is couched either in the familiar language of rational choice or is based on new sophisticated statistical analysis, both of which are respected by economic theorists. Of course, this does not fully explain why there is a growing acceptance of psychology now, rather than twenty years ago.[2] Among the contributing factors may be a growing sympathy for the claims of social critics who proclaim a modern crisis of values—and a related recognition that simplistic assumptions regarding human motivation diminish economists' ability to predict the contribution of economic activity to human welfare.

In the next summarized article, Robert Frank argues that economic theory should sacrifice some of its parsimony for greater psychological realism. Frank points out that economists ignore the fact that people adapt to changing circumstances, as with the accident victims and lottery winners, and the fact that an individual's consumption is influenced by his or her reference group.

It is evident from Frank's exposition that he believes that the standard neoclassical model need not be sacrificed in order to introduce a number of contextual assumptions. However, it is far from clear that many psychological complexities can be accommodated within this model. For instance, the possibility that some tastes and preferences are endogenous is a frequently raised challenge to the conventional assumption that all tastes are exogenous and relatively stable. The possibility of endogenous preferences, however, undermines standard proofs of efficiency and optimality of competitive outcomes. Will adding this bit of psychological reality complicate economic discourse beyond the capacities of the neoclassical model?

Albert O. Hirschman argues that economic theory omits two features of the human condition that influence various socially desirable activities: the capacity for self-reflection, and the capacity to engage in noncalculating behavior such as voting and collective action. Economic theory has no place either for the idea that individuals may want other preferences than the ones they possess or for the idea that individuals may be moved through rational discourse to change their preferences. The former, sometimes referred to as metapreferences or second order interests, and the latter notion of preference change are central to ethical theory and offer a plausible explanation for behaviors in which individuals seem to act against their own best interests.[3]

Similarly, economists' focus on calculation as a key to rational motivation misses the fact that striving toward and achieving one's goals can be a significant source of personal satisfaction. This point echoes the psychologists claim that having and pursuing one's goals is an important source of satisfaction and central to building one's identity. This cannot be replaced by monetary incentives. As a result, productivity increases that derive from a sense of belonging or loyalty may actually be undermined by incentive-based approaches.

Preference Satisfaction and Human Well-Being

Kahneman's conclusion that measures of subjective utility should be considered as a supplement to the rationality assumption represents a scientist's conservative interpretation of the difficulties faced by the revealed preference model of economic behavior. A less sanguine interpretation of the divergence between preference satisfaction and well-being is that any economic theory based on revealed preferences ought to be abandoned. This perspective is developed by philosopher Mark Sagoff in an article summarized later in this section.

Sagoff vigorously attacks the idea, implicit in welfare economics, that a social optimum can be obtained by maximizing the preference satisfaction of individuals. This approach assumes tight links between choice and preferences (the former reveals the latter) and between preference satisfaction and well-being (the former increases the latter). Sagoff argues that neither assumption is correct. With respect to the first assumption, our visible acts of choice are supposed to reveal subjective mental entities called preferences, but actual chosen behaviors have moral and legal consequences, unlike self-contained preferences that moral maturity often requires us to override.

The problem with the second assumption is that it conflates different meanings of preference satisfaction—what Kahneman refers to as hedonic and decision utility. Preferences are supposed to be the psychological motivation for all behavior, yet the economist must deduce what these preferences are from descriptions of behavior. These inferred preferences are logical constructs, not a causal source of motivation. The belief that maximizing the satisfaction of such preferences increases subjective well-being requires either an empirical or a logical defense. The evidence from psychology is very strong that it is false. If it is nevertheless maintained as a truth of logic, then the economist faces a tautological definition of well-being that destroys the theory's predictive power, since its explanations cannot be falsified.

For Sagoff, preference satisfaction cannot be identified with well-being and thus cannot be the fundamental source of value for economics; therefore it should not be used as a conceptual tool to guide policy. Instead, Sagoff contends that welfare economics can retain its normative significance only if it breaks the tight connection between preference satisfaction and well-being, defining the latter in terms that distinguish humans as responsible citizens from humans as consumers.

Although Sagoff does not explore the possibility, it is possible to abandon revealed preference theory and still argue that some other preference-based theory is the appropriate way to understand well-being. Many such attempts have been made, and they all reject the traditional utilitarian assumption that preference satisfaction or desire fulfillment must be experienced in order for it to contribute to well-being. Preference satisfaction is understood in the logician's sense of having a clause in a contract satisfied. It does not matter whether a person realizes that his or her preference is satisfied, or whether it is experienced—all that matters is whether the desired or preferred state of affairs occurs. To avoid problems associated with defective preferences, such theories also assume that preferences that are relevant to well-being are informed or ideal in some way. Such "corrected" preferences are formed under ideal conditions that permit individuals to be fully informed about the objects of his or her desires. Thus, individuals know and act on what is in their best interests, because they have absorbed all relevant and available information about alternative options.

One significant benefit of this approach is that it avoids the need to distinguish self-regarding and other-regarding preferences. If you desire that a political prisoner be freed from a foreign jail, you are better off if this comes about. But this approach runs into two major problems. The first problem can be illustrated by a classic philosophical example. Consider the situation in which one meets a stranger on a train ride. After a pleasant conversation, you wish him well, say good-bye, and never talk to or think about him again. If his life does go well, satisfying your preference, it is commonly supposed that you are no better off; his success has nothing to do with you, contrary to what is implied by the informed preference theory. The problem becomes one of specifying or restricting informed preferences to those whose satisfaction actually contributes to one's well-being.

Political philosopher Thomas Scanlon, in the next summary, discusses one solution to the first problem. One of the goals assumed by well-being theorists is an answer to the Socratic question: What makes a life good for the person who lives it? This question can be asked and answered from many perspectives, e.g., from an individual perspective, the point of view of friends or parents, from an economic policy perspective, or from a moral perspective. Presumably, one of the virtues of an informed preference account is that it provides an answer for the first person perspective: what is good is whatever is the object of a person's informed preferences. However, there are two possible interpretations of this claim. Either goods are valuable because they are preferred or they are preferred because they are valuable. In each interpretation, preference plays an important role since it is the fact that goods are preferred that is common to or unifies all the values that are relevant to well-being.

One influential but rather eclectic informed desire theory has been proposed by James Griffin.[4] It is eclectic because it tries to accommodate both interpretations—some goods are valued because they are desired, while others are desired because they are valuable. It is influential because it appears to solve many problems associated with restricting the range of desires relevant to well-being. However, as Scanlon argues, in Griffin's account of human good, preferences do not provide a unified account of the good. As a result, Griffin's view resembles less a desire theory of good and more what philosopher Derek Parfit refers to as an *objective list* theory of human good.[5] Objective list theories provide a list of things that are good and bad for people whether or not they want the good things or want to avoid the bad things. Scanlon himself subscribes to one version of this type of theory and believes that citizens should arrange a contract among themselves concerning the kinds of activities, goods, and ways of living that are worth promoting—creating a shared list of substantive goods.

The other significant problem with informed preference theories remains even if such views were to resolve all the problems associated with specifying the correct range of desires. According to Connie Rosati, such views mistakenly assume that it is possible to evaluate different possible lives by adopting a birds-eye view of all such lives.[6] She argues that informed desire theories provide no way to compare different possible lives that contain opposing personality traits and/or conflicting commitments and belief systems. A person cannot simultaneously be fully informed about such different lives. How could someone simultaneously know, even theoretically, what it would be like to? She concludes that it is impossible to value certain intrinsic rewards of a life from any vantage except from within that life.

Well-Being versus Quality of Life

Where does this leave us? Revealed preference theory was introduced as a theory of behavior that had strong ties to human well-being, but the problems discussed by Sagoff and others question the connection between preference satisfaction and well-being. Psychologists make clear that the satisfaction of actual preferences often leads away from well-being. Conceptualizing preferences as informed or rational brings other seemingly insurmountable problems. Is there no coherent structure to be found for what makes a human life good? Are we left with Scanlon's proposal to arrive at some social understanding of what kinds of thing are good and develop some social contract to ensure that society promotes such goods?

One alternative approach is to argue that the subjectivist interpretation of well-being is correct; well-being can be fully explained by referring to mental states, but the significance of well-being may be more limited than commonly acknowledged. This approach avoids having to specify what kinds of desires when fulfilled actually contribute to a person's well-being. Consider the plight of the deceived businessman who dies believing that his life has been a success, that his family loves him, the community respects him, and he has created a successful business. In fact, his family has been nice to him only to safeguard their own interests, the community believes him to be a spy, and his business partner has embezzled all his company's funds. Such examples often motivate attempts to expand the limits of well-being beyond a person's experiences.

In a novel approach, Shelly Kagan draws a different lesson from such examples and argues that those facts that make a person well off (a person's well-being) may differ from those facts that make his or her life go well. Kagan argues that the deceived businessman has a great deal of well-being on his deathbed but a much lower quality of life. Instead of trying to stretch the concept of well-being to account for such examples, Kagan develops the thesis that the concept of well-being should be retained as the correct way to understand changes in a person's mental states. He then introduces the concept of quality of life, as a better way to understand facts about an individual's life that do not impact his or her mental states. His review of familiar examples in the philosophical literature on well-being convincingly argues that a person's quality of life, though related to, may differ from the level of her well-being. Situations that affect one may not influence the other at all. This distinction has serious consequences for economic planning and political policy. To the extent that quality of life differs from well-being, which should be the focus for political and economic analysis and policy?

This section concludes with an essay on the work of Amartya Sen, one of the most influential contemporary writers in interdisciplinary debates on quality of life issues. Sen provides critiques of revealed preference theory and a constructive proposal for an alternative, multidimensional conception of human advantage. He elaborates the relationship between well-being and quality of life and dramatizes the importance of promoting individual freedoms and achievement in economic planning. Sen distinguishes various dimensions of human advantage, a concept that is defined in terms of capabilities to achieve valuable functionings. In his view, quality of life is constituted by what a person is able to achieve in addition to the quality of available choices.

Sen's distinction between well-being achievement (e.g., experienced satisfaction) and agency success (goal achievement, whether or not it results in satisfaction) permits him to argue that a person's goals may extend beyond what directly affects an individual's well-being. One may achieve agency success at the expense of well-being levels (construed narrowly in terms of desire fulfillment or satisfactions) or even of one's standard of living. Although Sen and Kagan do not use precisely the same terms to distinguish well-being from quality of life, they both argue that subjectivist interpretations of well-being are an inadequate guide to social policy.

Conclusion

Both empirical and theoretical objections to the rational egoist model of human behavior call for a more realistic account of individual motivation and a rejection of preference satisfaction as the appropriate concept for understanding either well-being or the broader concept of quality of life. Psychologists as well as philosophers recommend that economists expand their criteria for rational choice beyond the consistency standard, to include measures of subjective well-being and the quality of available choices. Other social scientists also suggest that the revealed preference theory of human behavior offers few tools to explain valuable social outcomes due to the importance of moral preferences and intrinsic motivation. Individual commitments to projects and goals may be relevant to a person's well-being, even if a person does not benefit from his or her success—a possibility that is denied by preference-based accounts of the good. Finally, economic discussions of well-being seem to ignore issues related to self-realization and character development. The conclusion is unavoidable: economists need to develop a comprehensive answer to the question of what makes a person's life go well—the concept of preference satisfaction will not suffice.

Notes

1. Albert O. Hirschman, "Against Parsimony: Three Easy Ways of Complicating Some Categories of Economic Discourse," in *Rival Views of Market Society and Other Recent Essays* (New York: Viking Press, 1987), 142–160; cited from 142.

2. Some might question that there is such a growing acceptance. George Loewenstein describes this recent trend:

> In recent years, despite lingering skepticism, the influence of psychology on economics has steadily expanded. Challenged by the discovery of individual and market level phenomena that contradict fundamental economic assumptions, and impressed by theoretical and methodological advances, economists have begun to import insights from psychology into their work on diverse topics.

Loewenstein, "The Fall and Rise of Psychological Explanations in the Economics of Intertemporal Choice," in *Choice over Time*, eds. George Loewenstein and Jon Elster (New York: Russell Sage Foundation, 1992), 3–34; cited from 3. Robert Frank reinforces this sentiment in his introduction to the recent republication of Tibor Scitovsky's, *The Joyless Economy* (Oxford: Oxford University Press, 1991). Frank says that when Scitovsky's book was first published in 1976,

> most economists were not ready for it. . . . The profession was on a roll, triumphantly extending the neoclassical model into one new area after another. . . . It has become increasingly clear that theories and evidence from psychology have something useful to contribute this reassessment. . . . This time, I think, the profession is primed for Professor Scitovsky's message.

The quotation is from pages iii and iv of Scitovsky's book.

3. For a related discussion, see the comments on the economics of addition in the Overview Essay for Part VI of the previous volume, *The Consumer Society*, eds. Neva R. Goodwin, Frank Ackerman, and David Kiron (Washington, DC: Island Press, 1996), 198–199.

4. James Griffin, *Well-Being* (Oxford: Oxford University Press, 1986).

5. Derek Parfit, Appendix I in his *Reasons and Persons* (Oxford: Oxford University Press, 1984), 493–502.

6. Connie Rosati, "Persons, Perspectives and Full Information Accounts of the Good," *Ethics*, 105 (1995), 296–325.

Summary of

Who Is Happy?

by David G. Myers and Ed Diener

[Published in *Psychological Science* vol. 6, no. 1 (January 1995), 10–19.]

What makes people happy? An abundance of new empirical research offers surprising answers. This article surveys recent findings on the sources of personal happiness, dispels myths about who is likely to be happy, and sketches a theory of happiness that recognizes the importance of adaptation, culture, and personal goals.

In the past two decades scientific interest in the determinants of joy and life satisfaction has surged, leading to thousands of new studies. By the end of the 1980s, nearly 800 articles annually cited "well-being," "happiness," or "life satisfaction" in published abstracts. From these studies, one finding stands out: most people in the industrial world consider themselves reasonably happy, contrary to a tradition of writers who reject the possibility of widespread happiness.

The literature on subjective well-being (SWB) takes seriously self-reports of happiness and dissatisfaction. But can these measures be trusted: do people tell the truth about their happiness? Many considerations confirm their reliability. Over time (from 6 months to 6 years), self-reports of global well-being change little. Individuals who describe themselves as happy appear happy to peers and family members. Positive events are recalled more frequently than negative events. Social desirability effects, such as the desire to please interviewers, do not invalidate SWB measures. In general, "SWB measures exhibit construct validity. They are responsive to recent good and bad events and to therapy. . . . They correlate inversely with feeling ill. . . . And they predict other indicators of psychological well-being. Compared with depressed people, happy people are less self-focused, less hostile and abusive, and less vulnerable to disease. They also are more loving, forgiving, trusting, energetic, decisive, creative, helpful, and sociable. . . ."[11]

Many studies indicate that happiness and unhappiness stem from different sources, or at least are predicted by different variables. Positive and negative emotions are only weakly correlated with one another. These surprising findings suggest that positive and negative affect do not lie on opposite ends of a single spectrum. An individual's global sense of satisfaction may not provide clues about his or her global sense of dissatisfaction.

Happiness Myths

Many beliefs about the relationship between age, gender, race, culture, income, and happiness have been proven false by recent studies. For instance, despite the widespread belief that teenage stress, mid-life crisis, and declining years of old age are unhappy times, interviews with people of all ages reveal that life sat-isfaction is about the same in all time periods. Research also disputes the "empty nest syndrome"—the despondency and lost meaning said to be experi-enced by couples when their children leave home. In fact, most couples find their marriages rejuvenated by an empty nest. Gender and race contribute little to happiness. Men and women share the same distributions of happiness levels, although women seem to experience both happiness and sadness more in-tensely. African-Americans report happiness levels very close to European-Americans and are slightly less vulnerable to depression.

Does happiness vary by culture? In Portugal, only 10 percent of people re-port themselves as very happy, but in the Netherlands, 40 percent make the same assertion. Such marked differences occur even when income variance above certain levels is controlled for and cannot be explained by differences in cultural interpretations of the questions. At low levels of income, SWB covaries with the satisfaction of basic physical needs. But above basic needs levels, SWB is only weakly affected by income; relatively low levels of SWB are observed, for instance, in high-income Japan. "In general, collectivist cultures report lower SWB than do individualistic cultures, where norms more strongly support ex-periencing and expressing positive emotions."[12]

Thus, contrary to the assumptions of policy makers and economists, subjec-tive well-being does not necessarily rise with income. At the national level, the correlation between national wealth and well being is positive (+.67 in a 24-na-tion study reported by Inglehart). This relationship, however, may mask other factors, such as continuous years of democracy, which correlate even better with life satisfaction. At the individual level, studies of happiness levels in the United States, Europe, and Japan indicate that wealth is like health: "Its absence can breed misery, yet having it is no guarantee of happiness."[13] While most Americans express the belief that more money would make them happier, the actual correlation between income and happiness is very weak in both the U.S. and Europe. Americans today average twice the inflation-adjusted income of their counterparts 40 years ago but report themselves as no happier.

Happy People

High levels of subjective well-being are linked with the presence of certain traits, strong supportive relationships, challenging work, and religious faith. Studies consistently show that happy people share the same four traits: self-es-teem, a sense of personal control, optimism, and extraversion. Happy people typically like themselves. When individuals lose control over their own lives, they become less happy compared to those who feel empowered. Optimists tend to be more successful, healthier, and happier than are pessimists. "Com-pared with introverts, extraverts are happier both when alone and with other people, whether they live alone or with others, whether they live in rural or metropolitan areas, and whether they work in solitary or social occupations."[14] Research has yet to determine the extent to which these traits are the cause or result of happiness. Twin studies indicate genetic influences on SWB.

Intimacy, close relationships, and openness to others are all characteristic of happy people. Individuals who can name several friends with whom they share intimate concerns are "healthier, less likely to die prematurely, and happier than people who have few or no such friends."[14] Holocaust survivors who self-disclose enjoy better health than those who cannot discuss their experiences. Married people of both sexes are more likely to say they are very happy than those who are not married. However, it is also true that happy people make better marriage partners and are more likely to marry. Contrary to the myth that men benefit more from marriage than women, European surveys and a meta-analysis of 93 studies indicate that "the happiness gap between the married and never-married was virtually identical for men and women."[15]

Work satisfaction is a major component of life satisfaction. It can provide a sense of identity, community, and purpose. Of course, work can also produce anxiety or boredom if one's skills are challenged too much or too little. The best kind of work engages skills with just enough challenge that motivation is intrinsic to the activity rather than extrinsically driven by rewards. Mihaly Csikszentmihalyi coined the term "flow" to describe the heightened state of consciousness associated with intrinsically motivated, challenging activities.[1]

Religious people report high levels of life satisfaction. Compared with persons of low spiritual commitment, highly spiritual people are twice as likely to say they were "very happy." People with a strong faith have better coping skills, achieving greater happiness after divorce, unemployment, serious illness, or bereavement.

A Theory of Happiness

The human ability to adapt, the cultural context in which one lives, and the advancement of personal goals must all be considered in a viable theory of happiness. Individual happiness is determined more by the frequency of positive affect and less by infrequent events that carry high intensity emotions. For instance, people adapt to euphoric events, such as lottery winnings, as well as paralyzing automobile accidents, returning to baseline happiness levels after periods of adjustment. In addition to adaptation, cultural worldview plays an important role. Cultural worldviews vary; some construe the world as benevolent, while others normalize negative emotions, such as anxiety and guilt. As a result, personal interpretations of life events may be shaped by this cultural template. Finally, progress toward a coherent set of goals is an accurate predictor of SWB. Interestingly, resources such as income, social skills, and intelligence "were predictive of SWB only if they were relevant to a person's goals. This finding helps explain why income predicts SWB in very poor nations, and why self-esteem predicts SWB in wealthy, individualistic nations." [17]

Note

1. Mihaly Csikszentmihalyi, *Flow: The Psychology of Optimal Experience* (New York: Harper and Row, 1990).

Summary of

New Challenges to the Rationality Assumption

by Daniel Kahneman

[Published in *Journal of Institutional and Theoretical Economics*, 150 (1994), 18–36.]

In the domain of social policy, the rationality assumption supports the position that it is not necessary to protect people against the consequences of their choices. The status of this assumption is therefore a matter of considerable interest. [18]

In economic theory it is assumed that rational persons are utility maximizers. However, new empirical evidence challenges the assumption that choices, in fact, maximize utility. Two findings stand out: first, individuals cannot be assumed to be infallible forecasters of future tastes and secondly, they are often unable to accurately evaluate past experience. This paper argues that the traditional hallmark of rationality, i.e., consistency among preferences, is insufficient as a criterion of rationality. Rationality can and should be assessed using substantive criteria, such as experienced utility, that are independent of the system of preferences.

For several decades, debates concerning rationality have focused on the paradoxical implications of the consistency standard. A number of researchers have shown that certain pairs of "reasonable" preferences lead to paradox when combined with the axioms of expected utility theory. Resolution of these paradoxes became the focus of decision theory, reinforcing consistency as the criterion of rationality.

Multiple Notions of Utility

In classical usage, *utility* meant "experienced utility," the hedonic experience of an outcome. Early utilitarian theorists such as Jeremy Bentham focused on the pleasure and pain that accompanied outcomes. Subjective mental states, however, lost their status as a legitimate area of study as behaviorism gained currency in the social sciences during the 20th century. Today, outcomes are evaluated in terms of their desirability rather than the affect derived from them. Two assumptions prevail in the current discourse on utility: people reveal their preferences in the choices they make and people enjoy later what they want now. As a result, *utility* in modern usage means "decision utility," the weight assigned to an outcome of a decision.

Recent work in psychology indicates an empirical basis for revitalizing Bentham's notion of utility. Support is proffered for an additional substantive criterion of rationality—how well do people maximize experienced utility. Substantive criteria of rationality can be assessed in three areas: decision utility, predicted utility, and the relation between real-time and retrospective utility.

Decision Utility

Standard economic assessments of rationality omit key features of the human decision-making process. Research findings indicate three types of deficiency: utility is assigned to gains and losses, not to absolute levels (the main *carriers of utility* are events, not states); losses seem larger than corresponding gains (*loss aversion*); and, the same objective outcomes can be evaluated as gains or losses, depending on the frame of reference (*framing effect*). A set of ingenious experiments reveals two psychological effects that demonstrate the complexity involved in weighting outcomes. First, the framing effect illustrates that wealth is valued in relative rather than absolute terms and that inconsequential differences in the formulation of a problem lead to diverse preferences. Consider these two problems:

> *Problem 1:* Assume yourself richer by $300 than you are today. You have to choose either a sure gain of $100 or a gamble: 50 percent chance to gain $200 and 50 percent chance to gain nothing.
>
> *Problem 2:* Assume yourself richer by $500 than you are today. You have to choose either a sure loss of $100 or a gamble: 50 percent chance to lose nothing and 50 percent chance to lose $200.

Both problems offer the subject a choice between a sure gain of $400 or a gamble with equal chances to increase current wealth by $300 or $500. Mainstream accounts imply that rational people should treat these problems the same, since the amounts of wealth are the same. In fact, people treat these problems differently, favoring the sure thing in problem one and the gamble in problem two.

Second, the endowment effect demonstrates loss aversion and suggests that people are extremely myopic when it comes to weighting future outcomes. In one experiment, some subjects were given a coffee mug and asked the amount of money for which they would be willing to exchange it. Other subjects were offered a choice between owning a mug and receiving an amount of money that they thought the mug was worth. In an important sense, both groups of subjects were offered the same choice: leave the experiment with a new mug or extra pocket money. Owners in the first group evaluated the difference between having a mug and not having one as a loss, while choosers in the second group evaluated the difference as a gain. Consistent with the assumption of loss aversion, mug owners ascribed a much higher average cash value ($7.12 in one experiment) than for choosers ($3.50). Although all subjects chose between the same long-term states ("own this mug" or "not-own this mug") subjects based their decisions on evaluations of short-term transitions ("receive a mug" or "give up your mug"). Such myopia appears to be linked with the emotions involved in making transitions. The endowment effect has implications for both logical and substantive criteria of rationality: given different representations of the same problem people reveal inconsistent preferences and individuals are led to inferior outcomes when they myopically evaluate future consequences.

Predicted Utility: Do People Know What They Will Like?

Experiments show that people are often unable to accurately predict hedonic responses to future stimuli. In one study of the endowment effect, subjects were shown a coffee mug. They were then asked to imagine being given a replica and given the opportunity to either keep it or trade it for money. After subjects decided on an exchange rate for the imaginary mug, they were actually given a mug, and then asked how much money they would be willing to trade it for. The mean selling price after receiving the mug ($4.89) was much higher than that predicted ($3.73), which suggests that people are unable to anticipate that possession of a mug would induce a reluctance to give it up. A different experiment indicates that people are unable to accurately predict their tastes. In this study, most subjects, after tasting a spoonful of plain low-fat yogurt, predicted that their hedonic response to a six ounce helping on the next day would be the same. Not surprisingly, the larger helping was a much worse experience than anticipated.

"The data provided no indication that individuals were able to predict the development of their tastes more accurately than they could predict the hedonic changes of a randomly selected stranger."[27]

Retrospective Utility:
Do People Know What They Have Liked?

In order to know what will be liked in the future, it is invaluable to know what has been liked in the past. However, individuals employ a surprisingly fallible process to represent past experiences. Global evaluations of past experiences require two operations: recollecting the momentary experiences that constitute a given episode and combining the affect associated with these moments. Counter to normative intuitions, experiments strongly suggest that these operations, recollecting experience and combining affect, are performed without adding utilities. In fact, studies support two alternative empirical generalizations: a *peak* and *end rule*, which proposes that global evaluations of past episodes are formed by weighting the experience of most extreme affect and the affect experienced during the final moments of the episode; and, *duration neglect*, which considers global evaluation of total affect unaffected by an episode's duration. For example, in one study colonoscopy patients reported pain every 60 seconds in procedures that took anywhere from 4 to 69 minutes, yet both patients and attending physicians made retrospective evaluations that reflected the intensity of pain at its worst and the intensity of discomfort during the last few minutes of the procedure.

Conclusion

Adding substantive criteria to the current logical standard of consistency makes sense on a number of levels. Substantive analyses permit a more demanding definition of rationality than the consistency standard commonly invoked in economic discourse. Foolish decisions and myopic choices need not be considered rational just because they are part of a system of coherent preferences. A better understanding of hedonics could reveal a great deal about the welfare consequences of institutions and identify which skills derive the most experienced utility from outcomes. "The time has perhaps come to set aside the overly general question of whether or not people are rational. . . . What are the conditions under which the assumption of rationality can be retained as a useful approximation? Where the assumption of rationality must be given up, what are the most important ways in which people fail to maximize their outcomes?" [35]

Summary of

Frames of Reference and Quality of Life

by Robert H. Frank

[Published in *American Economic Review* 79 (May 1989), 80–85.]

Accident victims who suffer severe injury often become accustomed to their new circumstances after a period of depression. Similarly, lottery winners frequently return to a baseline happiness level after a time of euphoria. Although the capacity to adapt to changing circumstances has a powerful effect on well-being levels, this feature of the human condition is overlooked by the standard neoclassical model of choice that asserts that utility depends only on consumption. This article argues that the neoclassical model, which measures well-being by absolute consumption levels, fails to account for contributions to quality of life arising from both the human capacity to adapt and relative consumption.

Despite the fact that psychologists and certain economists have recognized the fundamental relationship between human well-being and sensitivity to change, such insights have yet to make their way into mainstream economic theory. Psychologist Harry Helson underscored the adaptive powers of the human nervous system in his pioneering book, *Adaptation-Level Theory*,[1] which noted that local conditions are relevant to how a given stimulus is perceived. For example, a resident of Havana feels cold on a 60°F day, while a resident of Montreal may find the same temperature warm. A different contextual point is made by economist Tibor Scitovsky who has argued that improving conditions, rather than merely good conditions in some absolute sense, contributes significantly to experienced pleasure.[2] The plausibility of these ideas militates against prevailing economic doctrine, which assumes that only absolute consumption levels are relevant to an individual's utility function. Standard models ignore the significance of relative consumption, even though consuming more than we did in the past, and more than others in similar circumstances, is an important source of satisfaction.

Consider the implications of introducing context into positive and normative economic analysis. In positive analysis, the consumer's frame of reference is significant with respect to both her own consumption over time and her consumption relative to that of others. With regard to the former, the permanent income hypothesis suggests that consumption should be equalized over time to maximize utility. This assertion is based on the implicit assumption that a given level of consumption produces a constant level of utility. By disregarding context, such a view fails to explain or predict that people may demand rising, rather than constant, consumption profiles. A better view considers the influence of previous consumption levels, providing a clear theoretical explanation for the obvious fact that people want to increase their consumption levels over time. Such a consumption pattern could be achieved by saving during the early years and dissaving during the later years, but in practice most people are unable to save sufficient amounts. Instead, people commonly seek out jobs with rising wage profiles. The desire for rising consumption profiles thus can explain the fact that in many occupations wages rise more steeply than productivity over the life-cycle.

Similarly, positive economic analysis would benefit from incorporating the effects of relative consumption on individual well-being. Traditional theories of savings predict no relationship between savings rates and income. Duesenberry argued that a relative income hypothesis, by contrast, implies that savings rates will rise with income.[3] Strong empirical evidence from cross-section studies confirms that savings rates do rise with income. Nevertheless, there is little attention given to the relative income hypothesis in leading intermediate macroeconomics textbooks.

Positional issues may also influence the distribution of wages within firms, as well as the distribution of total compensation between money wages and fringe benefits. Concerns about position may also prevent price increases that would remove excess demand in certain markets.[4] Alan Blinder has suggested that they may even explain the persistence of unemployment in the labor market.[5]

Incorporating contextual considerations would have enormous consequences for normative economic analysis. The most prominent implication would be the rejection of the first theorem of welfare economics, which asserts that competitive equilibrium will be Pareto optimal. Efficiency is no longer guaranteed once relative consumption is accepted as an argument in the utility functions of individuals. If relative consumption is important, each person's consumption imposes negative externalities on others. As a result, excessive resources will be diverted to producing and acquiring positional goods. People will consume too much and save too little. Competitive labor markets may also lead to inefficient outcomes, as people accept undesirable job conditions to compete for positional goods.

An appreciation of context would also benefit public policy, for example, in analyses of tax incidence and economic growth strategies. Traditional supply side arguments for reducing taxation on efficiency grounds miss the potential efficiency gains from taxing positional consumption. Since the acceptability of schools, houses, wardrobes, cars, vacations, and other budget items are determined by how much others are willing to spend, many such positional consumption goods appear more attractive to individuals than to society. Reducing the appeal of these goods through taxation will enhance a zero welfare and generate more federal revenues. Consider a young man in a country in which the custom is to spend two months salary on a diamond engagement ring. If he makes $36,000 a year, then he is bound by custom to pay $6,000 for a ring with a rather large diamond or else be considered a cheapskate. From a social perspective, it would be better if there was a 500 percent tax on what is now a smaller $1,000 diamond. With the tax, everyone would be buying smaller diamonds, while continuing to satisfy the custom of spending two months income. In this scenario, the young man suffers the same amount of economic hardship, his fiancee is no worse off, and the government receives a windfall; the only loser may be the deBeers diamond cartel of South Africa.

Contextual issues also affect the analysis of policies to spur economic growth through increased savings. The United States has the lowest savings rate of any industrialized country. Raising savings rates would lead to higher consumption after a period of adjustment; it is the lower consumption during the adjustment period that creates the practical barrier to achieving higher savings. But given the powerful human capacity to adapt, if everyone simultaneously adopted a savings rate that reduced everyone's consumption levels by, say, 10 percent, the lower consumption level would quickly become the norm. The utility of the lower, but more rapidly rising consumption level would soon overtake that of the relatively static level of consumption we now enjoy.

One theme persistently emerges from many of these examples: a level consumption stream at a given present value delivers less satisfaction than a rising consumption profile of similar total value. Rational utility maximizers can take advantage of this in two ways: by incrementally increasing the quality level of their purchases and by manipulating their consumption-based comparison group. The former strategy will lead to more benefits than following the standard "optimal" procedure, which requires the purchase of a higher quality level whenever its marginal utility compares favorably with other consumption opportunities. For example, if a $5,000 pair of stereo loudspeakers is ultimately your most favored choice, given your tastes and income, your lifetime satisfaction may be higher if you move to that quality level in stages, rather than all at once. Since much of the satisfaction to be derived from the $5,000 speakers stems from the difference in quality between it and your earlier set of speakers, adaptation to the new quality level will quickly eliminate this source of satisfaction. With respect to this latter strategy, individuals may exchange status in one area of life for improvement in another that delivers more value. For instance, an individual who enjoys socializing with friends and family need not acquire a high-ranked position among co-workers, seeking instead a wage premium as a lesser-ranked worker in a highly productive firm.

As all these examples suggest context matters for human satisfaction. Nonetheless, economists have been reluctant to incorporate context into models of consumption, perhaps because it conflicts with their "insistent preference for simple models of behavior." But increased complexity is justified by the greater explanatory power of models incorporating contextual features.

Notes

1. Harry Helson, *Adaptation-Level Theory* (New York: Harper and Row, 1964).
2. Tibor Scitovsky, *The Joyless Economy* (New York: Oxford University Press, 1976).
3. James Duesenberry, *Income, Saving, and the Theory of Consumer Behavior* (Cambridge, MA: Harvard University Press, 1949).
4. See Robert H. Frank, "Are Workers Paid Their Marginal Products?," *American Economic Review* 74 (September 1984), 549–571; "The Demand for Unobservable and Other Nonpositional Goods," *American Economic Review* 75 (March 1985), 101–116; *Choosing the Right Pond* (New York: Oxford University Press, 1985); *Passions Within Reason* (New York: Norton, 1988).
5. Alan Blinder, "The Challenge of High Unemployment," *American Economic Review: Proceedings* 78 (May 1988), 1–15.

Summary of

Against Parsimony: Three Easy Ways of Complicating Some Categories of Economic Discourse

by Albert O. Hirschman

[Published in Albert O. Hirschman, *Rival Views of Market Society and Other Recent Essays* (New York: Viking Press, 1987), 142–160.]

The "economic" or "rational-actor" approach to the study of human behavior draws on the traditional economic view of the individual as self-interested and isolated, freely and rationally choosing among alternatives based on cost-benefit computations. This deliberately parsimonious approach has been applied to an increasingly broad spectrum of human behavior that extends well beyond the economic realm. While this application has yielded useful insights, it is ultimately too simplistic to adequately describe even the basic economic processes of consumption and production for which it was initially designed. In the interest of greater realism, it is time to abandon excessive parsimony and to reincorporate into the economic discourse some of the factors that account for the complexity of human nature. Specifically, two fundamental human tensions should be revisited—the choice between instrumental and noninstrumental modes of behavior and the propensity toward self-interest or public morality—and two basic human endowments should be reincorporated—voice and the capacity for self-evaluation. "Voice"—the capacity for verbal and nonverbal communication and persuasion that can affect economic processes by means other than the traditionally recognized option of "exit"—has been discussed at length in another work.[1] This article addresses the importance of the other three factors.

Two Kinds of Preference Changes

Amartya Sen and others have introduced into economic discourse the useful distinction between first-order and second-order preferences, or, in the terminology that will be used here, between preferences and metapreferences.[2] Economists have traditionally limited themselves to the consideration of (first-order) preferences, that is, the tastes that are revealed by individuals when they buy goods and services. However, this limited scope of analysis ignores the uniquely human capacity for self-evaluation that may lead an individual to question his or her revealed tastes or preferences and form value-based metapreferences that differ with—and potentially bring about changes in—preferences.

There are therefore two types of preference change: unreflective, impulsive changes in tastes, and reflective, tortuous changes brought about by the development of metapreferences that are at odds with previously exhibited preferences. If economists are truly interested in understanding processes of economic change then they must understand both types of preference change. However, traditionally they have focused on the unreflective—and generally minor—changes in taste, ignoring changes of the reflective kind or at best reducing them to the status of mere changes in taste, e.g., the concept of a "taste for discrimination" introduced by Gary Becker.[3]

Two problems arise from this approach. First it impedes efforts to develop an understanding of strongly held values and how they change. Secondly, it leads to the assumption commonly made by economists that human values can best be changed by raising the costs of acting in ways that society deems to be undesirable, rather than by setting standards and imposing prohibitions and sanctions. Economists therefore propose to deal with problems such as pollution by only using effluent charges or other direct costs. Legislators and the public, however, try to change the standards of acceptable behavior through political and regulatory instruments such as laws that limit pollution. In effect, economists assume that individuals are driven purely by tastes in both civic and consumption-oriented behavior and that these tastes are either unchanging or change, such as in response to price and income differences. The possibility that preferences are influenced by values and that people are capable of autonomously and reflectively changing their values is ignored. Yet, such changes in value do occasionally occur and their effects on consumption behavior are worth exploring.

Two Kinds of Activities

In evaluating the productive activities of firms, a clear distinction can be made between inputs and outputs, or costs and revenues. However, with respect to the productive efforts of individuals, the distinction between inputs and outputs, or between work/effort and pay/reward, may be less clear. For firms, inputs (costs) are clearly entered as negatives in company accounts. For the individual, the effort of production may be seen either as a positive or negative, i.e., the means to the end of a productive effort are *not necessarily* a negative entry in the calculation of satisfaction. The positive and normative implications of this for income differentials have long attracted the attention of economists, and it is necessary to understand the sources of this ambiguity if the complexity and full range of human activities are to be properly interpreted.

One way of understanding the extent to which the means (work or effort) is seen as a negative cost or as a positive benefit may be found by considering the predictability of the outcomes of this effort. If an activity has a perfectly predictable outcome in the short or long run, then the clear separation of the productive process into means/costs and ends/benefits seems to make sense; the work appears to be essentially instrumental. However, for activities with uncertain outcomes such as the pursuit of truth, beauty or justice, *striving* becomes an important component of the inputs, and the clear means-ends distinction breaks down. Noninstrumental activity is thus characterized by a certain fusion of, and confusion between, striving and attaining.

In a similar way, traditional economic thinking has typically assumed that utility accrues through the actual consumption or use of a good. However, in reality there is often much utility gained in *savoring* expected future consumption, use, or achievement. This can be true whether or not the expectation is certain to be fulfilled. This savoring—the fusion of striving and attaining—thus explains much of the existence and importance of noninstrumental activity. A complementary view developed in part by Pizzorno[4] suggests that much of noninstrumental behavior, e.g., working in a political campaign, is valuable because it enhances either the feeling of belonging to a group or simply of being human. In other words, noninstrumental behavior can be understood as an investment in individual and group identity.

The importance of this for economists is its usefulness in explaining both collective action and productivity changes. Analyzing political action without an understanding of noninstrumental behavior leaves economists unable to explain why people vote or engage in collective action. However, in the context of noninstrumental behavior it becomes apparent that

> since the output and objective of collective action are . . . a public good available to all, the only way an individual can raise the benefit accruing to him from the collective action is by stepping up *his own input*, his effort on behalf of the public policy he espouses. Far from shirking and attempting to get a free ride, a truly maximizing individual will attempt to be as activist as he can manage.[5]

Accordingly, collective action becomes a less surprising phenomenon. For example, shifts in labor productivity can be explained by the fact that the assumed connection between instrumental and routine activities and noninstrumental and nonroutine ones does not always hold; some routine activities may take on noninstrumental components, and vice versa. Fluctuations in this component may then affect labor productivity, such as through the extent to which people see their work as just a job or as part of a "collective celebration."

Love: Neither Scarce Resource nor Augmentable Skill

The need of any economic system, including capitalism, for the "input" known as morality, civic spirit, trust, or observance of elementary ethical norms is widely recognized. Differences arise, however, over the question of what happens to this input as it is used in the production process. Two standard models of factor use apply. The first is for inputs such as scarce material resources that are depleted during the production process. The second is for inputs such as skills that are improved by use and hence increase in availability during the production process. However, neither of these models adequately accounts for the important input of public morality, or "love."

Love, or public morality, has occasionally been treated as a scarce resource, the use of which must be economized. The near absurdity of this approach is clear; certainly the supply of this input is not fixed or limited. Hirsch has approached this problem from the opposite perspective.[6] He suggests that if a system such as capitalism convinces people that self-interest is all that is required for adequate performance, and that morality and public spirit are unnecessary, then the system will undermine its own viability since these civic-minded inputs are more important to the system than the official ideology acknowledges. Yet, this alternative view based on the "atrophy dynamic" (which equates love or public morality with a skill that improves with use and atrophies when ignored) also has weaknesses since it seems unlikely that increasing the use of public spirit can indefinitely increase its supply. At some point this practice would conflict with self-interest or even the requirements of self-preservation. In fact, it seems that love and public spirit exhibit a complex, composite behavior, atrophying when inadequately called upon by the socioeconomic system, but susceptible to overuse if they are relied on to excess. The problem lies in locating these outer boundaries, a challenge that may correspond to the weaknesses of today's capitalist and centrally planned economies. Nevertheless, it is necessary for economists to recognize both the importance of and the limitations on this resource in the economic production process.

Conclusion

Economists have tended to ignore the human capacities for voice, communication, and for self-evaluation. They have thus overlooked the existence of values and metapreferences that shape and change tastes and preferences. In addition, they have focused excessively on the instrumental aspects of behavior while neglecting noninstrumental modes. This has championed the role of self-interest, while it neglected the importance of benevolence and public morality to all economic systems. In the interests of better reflecting and understanding reality, it is time to reincorporate these missing elements into the economic discourse.

Notes

1. Albert O. Hirschman, *Exit, Voice, and Loyalty: Responses to Decline in Firms, Organizations, and States* (Cambridge, MA: Harvard University Press, 1970).

2. Amartya K. Sen, "Rational Fools: A Critique of the Behavioral Foundations of Economic Theory," *Philosophy and Public Affairs* 6 (1977), 317–344.

3. Gary S. Becker, *The Economics of Discrimination* (Chicago: Chicago University Press, 1957).

4. Alessandro Pizzorno, "Sulla Razionalità della Scelta Democratica," *Stato e Mercato* (1983) 3–46; English version in *Telos*, (Spring 1985).

5. Albert O. Hirschman, *Shifting Involvements: Private Interest and Public Action* (Princeton: Princeton University Press, 1982); cited by Hirschman, 152.

6. Fred Hirsch, *Social Limits to Growth* (Cambridge, MA: Harvard University Press, 1976).

Summary of

Should Preferences Count?

by Mark Sagoff

[Published in *Land Economics* 2 (May 1994), 127–145.]

A leading assumption of welfare economics, which presents itself as a normative discipline, is that satisfying preferences (our natural inclinations, desires, drives, etc.) should be an important consideration in resource allocation. Welfare economists justify this assumption with reference either to the concept of choice or to that of well-being. This article argues that the concept of preferences is neither clear nor useful. Preferences do not necessarily correspond to the choices people actually make, and satisfying people's preferences bears little relationship to increasing their well-being.

Definitions of Preferences

Psychologists view preferences as the underlying motivations for our actions. Psychologists also recognize that these motivations usually cannot be empirically determined in humans. While a rat's simple behavior can be described as revealing underlying preferences, the preferences of humans are far more complex. Human preferences are private mental states that are not observable and that cannot be scientifically tested. Thus, a father standing with his son in line for a ride at Disney World may be described as preferring to stand in line as opposed to walking around, or he may be described as preferring to fulfill a promise to his son rather than live with the guilt of refusing to take him. The way the action is described will determine which preferences can be said to cause the behavior.

In contrast to a psychological definition of preferences, social choice theory does not speculate on the causes of behavior. It defines preferences not as a state of mind but as theoretical attributes of a person or thing that are inferred logically from stipulated descriptions of behavior. Descriptions of particular behaviors are selected as starting points, and preference orderings or maps are constructed for each individual. Since the preference rankings are logically derived from the descriptions of behavior, they imply nothing about underlying motivation. Social choice theory concerns itself with logical reconstruction, not psychological motivation.

Problems arise if preferences as constructed in social choice theory are confused with preferences in the psychological sense in which they cause human action. Welfare economists use the social choice methodology to construct preference rankings from stipulated descriptions of behavior. However, they then assert that these logical constructs are the psychological causes of what people do. This practice confuses the ranking of descriptions of behaviors with the mental entities supposed to cause those behaviors. An indefinite number of ways to describe and explain a given behavior are consistent with the motions one can observe. Preferences are little more than rhetorical constructs based on ad hoc descriptions. But this sort of epistemological construction is not a psychological explanation. Preference maps exist in the eye of the observer, not in the mind of the observed individual.

Should Allocations Be Based on Preferences or on Choice?

A principal goal of resource economics is to maximize the satisfaction of preferences. Yet the choices we actually make are often quite different from our preferences. Many preferences are simply selfish drives and desires that moral maturity often requires us to control rather than to satisfy. Choice involves the exercise of liberty in an open society, while maximizing the satisfaction of preferences could be a goal of a benign despot.

Critics of resource economics argue that the choices people make have value beyond simply revealing underlying preferences. Choices have moral qualities—consent, responsibility, and liberty—that are not involved in the satisfaction of preferences. To identify choices with preferences is to confuse acts that have moral and legal consequences with private mental states. A society in which individual choice guides resource allocation would include responsibility, consent, free will, cooperation, commitment, accountability, social interaction, and self-reliance, as well as other virtues. A society that leaves it to experts to elicit preference and thus "correct" market may possess none of these virtues.

Further, preferences constantly change in response to the creation of new desires by the market. Like markets, the processes of public discussion and debate in a democracy often modify preferences. Even if free markets and democratic institutions fail to satisfy preferences, they still encourage and facilitate individual and collective choices and their attendant virtues.

Preference Satisfaction versus Well-Being

Microeconomic theory assumes that when a person's preferences are satisfied in the sense of being met, that person's well-being is increased. Individuals are thought to be the best judges of how to increase their well-being, as expressed by their preferences. Resource economists tend to assume that people are concerned only with their own well-being—as if larger political and moral questions were beyond them.

There is ample evidence to show that merely fulfilling preferences does not increase happiness. For example, there is no correlation between happiness and increased income (which should allow the individual to meet more of his wants). The evidence proves what wisdom already suggests: "[T]he things that make one happy—friends, family, achievement, health—depend largely on virtue and luck; they are not available on a willingness-to-pay basis." [137]

Yet, well-being in the economic sense is not a function of happiness, but of willingness to pay. When formulated in this way, the entire exercise meant to maximize well-being simply allocates resources to the highest bidders. Asserting that increased willingness to pay reflects increased welfare thus turns environmental economics into a trivial tautology.

The relationship between welfare and preference satisfaction is further strained when environmental and other community issues are considered. Consumer theory assumes that individuals prefer what they believe will increase their own well-being. Yet people often make choices based on what they believe will benefit the good of the whole, rather than their own personal welfare. Choices made for the benefit of others reflect commitment values. As Sen says, commitment values drive "a wedge between personal choice and personal welfare, and much of traditional economic theory relies on the identity of the two."[1]

Resource economists have sought to find ways to include such commitment values in the welfare function. They have developed such concepts as existence values, vicarious benefit, bequest, and stewardship to describe people's willingness to pay for causes other than their own personal welfare. Resource economists regard these values as providing some sort of psychic satisfaction for which people are willing to pay. Yet to construe such ideal-regarding or commitment preferences as somehow always serving to increase personal welfare denies the ethical and political nature of human beings. It confuses the concept of humans as citizens with that of humans as consumers.

In the end, preferences are only theoretical constructs. Attempting to describe and understand them, much less base policies on them, is a futile exercise. The choices we actually make demonstrate that responsibility and ethical concerns often override self-interested preferences. Basing allocations on choices rather than preferences enables moral maturity to be exercised by individuals and society. Further, the mere satisfaction of preferences cannot bring happiness. Attempting to explain all personal motivations on the basis of self-centered preferences denies that people are ethical beings who will make personal sacrifices for the common good and who entertain goals more important than their own personal welfare.

Since welfare economics defines well-being in terms of preference-satisfaction, it loses any normative significance, since it can no longer cite well-being as the justification for satisfying preferences. We must thus return to the question with which moral philosophers since Plato have grappled: What is happiness and how can it be achieved? Concepts such as virtue, knowledge, faith, love, and luck, rather than preference-satisfaction, have been suggested in answer. We must also consider the further question of what constitutes a good society. Neither of these questions can be answered by contemporary welfare economics.

Note

1. A. K. Sen, "Rational Fools: A Critique of the Behavioral Foundations of Economic Theory," *Philosophy and Public Affairs* 6 (1977), 327–344; cited by Sagoff, 139.

Summary of

Value, Desire, and Quality of Life

by Thomas Scanlon

[Published in *Quality of Life*, eds. Amartya Sen and Martha Nussbaum (Oxford: Oxford University Press, 1991), 185–200.]

"What makes a life good for the person who lives it?" Answers will vary depending on whether the question is asked from the point of view of the individual, the policy maker, or from the standpoint of morality. This paper contends that desire theories of the good, while amenable to economic and policy analysis, should be rejected as the appropriate account of well-being for individuals and also for moral argument. For the latter, an alternative, substantive theory of good is proposed that makes claims about what things, conditions, and opportunities make life better.

In his 1984 book, *Reasons and Persons*, Derek Parfit identifies what have become the three standard alternative theories of the good. Hedonistic theories hold that changes in quality of a life must affect personal experiences. "Desire theories reject the experience requirement and allow that a person's life can be made better and worse not only by changes in that person's states of consciousness but also by occurrences elsewhere in the world which fulfill [sic] that person's preferences." [186] Objective list theories recognize that a person may be mistaken about what makes his or her life proceed in the best way and that assessments of well-being must involve substantive judgments about the goodness of things. Desire and objective list theories differ with respect to who makes judgments of goodness. Desire theories require that assessments originate with the individual, while objective list theories are not so constrained.

This "standard" approach to classifying well-being theories glosses over important similarities among the different categories. For instance, there is a strong sense in which hedonistic theories typify Parfit's "objective list" category, which might be more aptly labeled "substantive good theories" since they make claims about what things are good. The conceptual line between hedonism and substantive good theories collapses once it is recognized that hedonism makes a substantive judgment about the kind of good, i.e., pleasure, that constitutes well-being.

A similar collapse occurs at the conceptual line between James Griffin's informed desire account and substantive good theories. Central to desire accounts is the claim that things are good because they are objects of desire. However, informed desire theory makes a different claim. It holds that goodness can arise from certain features of an object, features that will be desired and appreciated by the appropriately informed person. Griffin thinks his account represents a desire theory because it is flexible, allowing different objects to be viewed as good by different people. However, substantive good theories can also accommodate flexibility, as well as the position that it is sometimes a good thing to get what you want.

What then is the objective of a philosophical theory of well-being? One objective is to describe a class of things that makes lives better. A second, more ambitious, objective is to give a general account of what it is that makes a life a good life. Most substantive good theories aim only to achieve the first objective. The justification for this more limited objective is the perception that it is unlikely that there are any good-making properties that are common to all good things. Thus rather than seeking a general theory of goodness, it may be sufficient to describe characteristics of things that are conducive to well-being.

A Critique of Desire Theories

Desire theories should be rejected as theories of well-being appropriate to the individual's point of view. Individuals and benevolent third parties assess well-being in terms of substantive goods, not desire fulfillment. Desire theories imply the false claim that desire fulfillment confers a basic reason for wanting a certain outcome. Consider an outcome that satisfies the desire to improve life quality. The fact that this outcome fulfills a desire does not motivate an individual to want it. Rather, a preference for this outcome is due either to the pleasure it is expected to bring or to the substantive judgments that this state of affairs is desirable for some reason other than the mere fact that it is preferred, such as the judgment that it is morally good.

Support for this argument comes from the observation that both past and future preferences often matter very little to well-being. Past desires that carry no weight in the present provide little reason for action and their fulfillment does not contribute to well-being. For example, a child [person] who desires to ride a roller coaster to celebrate his fiftieth birthday finds that as the date approaches he prefers other kinds of activities. Fulfilling the childhood desire will not contribute to the adult's well-being, just because he once desired it. Future preferences may seem to have more weight in present discussions than past preferences do. For example, if a youth believes that in 30 years he will prefer to have a set of family photographs that he cares little about now may seem to provide him with reason to keep them. But insofar as the reason in such cases is matter of future well-being what is in fact providing this reason is in most such cases future happiness, not the satisfaction of future preferences as such. Suppose, for example, that while the youth knows that in future he will prefer having the photographs, he also knows that they will make him miserable. If he still has reason for saving the photographs in this case, the reason seems to be a regard for the autonomy of his future self, not a concern with his future well-being.

Desire theories are also inappropriate as accounts of individual well-being from the point of view of third-party benefactors. Benevolent third parties, such as friends or parents, often promote well-being by aiming at the happiness of the intended beneficiaries rather than the fulfillment of their desires. The aim is not always to please, since there are cases in which it is best to aim at a person's overall good, though this may require going against a person's preferences. This commonly occurs when parents make choices for their children that are not well liked.

Desire theories are most plausible when we consider people whose role is solely that of agents for other adults. It is reasonable to suggest that officials who must choose social policies should do so with respect for the preferences of the people whom they represent. These preferences can count as ultimate sources of reasons from the point of view of the decision maker, whatever the considerations that have led members of society to express these preferences. "Here, then, is a natural home for desire theories." [195]

A Contractualist Moral Theory

The role of well-being in moral argument differs from its use in social policy. Decision makers know the stated preferences of the individuals they represent and combine these preferences to formulating policy. In contrast, according to certain nonutilitarian moral theories, such as contractualism, the rightness or wrongness of an action depends on what an indefinite range of individuals whose detailed preferences are not fully known would have reason to agree to. On this view people are moved to do what is right "the desire to be able to justify one's actions to others on grounds that they have reason to accept if they are also concerned with mutual justification." [196]

Well-being enters into moral calculations if individuals have reason to reject a principle on the ground that following it will result in harms or burdens from the point of view of their substantive judgment of what makes a life good. Such rejection is reasonable if there are alternative principles that would not entail comparable burdens for other members of society.

Given a pluralistic society, individual members are bound to disagree on what counts as moral goods and bads, although there may be common ground with respect to judgments that certain losses of basic functionings are bad. The contractualist's objective is to build consensus on the assignments of moral weights to conditions, goods, and kinds of activity, by formulating abstract categories of good and bad, using a vocabulary that is understandable to all. "The aim then is to develop a set of goods and bads that we all, in so far as we are trying to find a common vocabulary of justification, have reason to accept as covering the most important ways in which life can be made better or worse." [198] Such a system of moral goods and bads is not an expression of any individual's preference, and the process of constructing the system may yield different outcomes in different societies.

Summary of

Me and My Life

by Shelly Kagan

[Published in *Proceedings of the Aristotelian Society*, 94 (1994), 309–324.]

The concept of well-being is central to issues in moral philosophy. Despite its importance (or because of it), there has been little consensus on the nature of well-being. This paper argues that efforts to define well-being have confused what it means for a person to be "well-off" with what it means for a person's life "to go well." In contrast to the mainstream view, this article argues that the concepts of quality of life and well-being are different and provocatively suggests that the standard of evaluation for each may differ as well.

Theories of well-being range from the narrow, which value only isolated properties of the mind, to the broad, which value states of the world, including nonmental properties. Hedonism, the most familiar and narrow account, defines well-being in terms of a single mental property, pleasantness. Many reject this view, since it disregards the value of all other mental properties. Still, many do find compelling the idea that mental states, broadly defined, constitute well-being. This more general mental state view implies that only changes in one's mental state can affect levels of well-being. The appeal of this view lies in the intuition behind the platitude: "What you don't know can't hurt you." It is not clear, however, that the mental state view is sufficiently broad. Consider the plight of a man who dies contented, in the belief that he is loved by his wife and family, is respected in the community, and is successful in business. But in reality his wife cheated on him, the community only pretended to respect him because of his charitable donations, his children were only nice to him so that they could borrow the car, and his business partner embezzled funds from his nearly bankrupt company. If one's mental state is all that matters, the man's life has gone well; but this conclusion is clearly unacceptable.

The standard response to this type of example is to broaden the concept of well-being to include events and states of affairs that occur in the world, factors that do not involve mental properties. Since it matters whether or not the businessman really achieved what he wanted, it is important to consider whether his preferences or desires were actually satisfied. Desire or preference theories take seriously the idea that well-being consists in states of the world, not just states of mind. However, preference or desire accounts fail to distinguish between those satisfied desires that do and those that do not contribute to well-being. Suppose I meet a stranger on the train, discuss her work, and desire her success, but I never think about the person again. Whether or not the stranger succeeds has nothing to do with me or my well-being. Apparently, the satisfaction of certain desires is relevant to well-being.

This example suggests that changes in well-being must involve changes in the individual. After all, well-being constitutes a final, rather than an instrumental, benefit to a person. For instance, changes in wealth or political power may be of instrumental benefit, potentially leading to changes in well-being, but they are not in and of themselves the pay-off. In contrast, well-being is the pay-off itself, the ultimate benefit. Final or ultimate benefits require intrinsic, nonrelational changes in a person. If we then accept the plausible view that a person is no more than a body and a mind, it follows that changes in well-being must involve changes in a person's body or mind. This narrow view of well-being implies that external changes that do not alter the internal properties of the individual cannot effect her well-being.

This conclusion calls for a revision in the standard way of interpreting examples, such as the case of the deceived businessman, which have been typically used to illustrate changes in well-being. A better approach is to acknowledge that there is a difference between a person's well-being and her quality of life and that it is possible for a person's quality of life to be low, while her well-being is high. This does seem possible, given that a person's life is more encompassing than the person himself. Thus, even though a person's well-being can only be affected by intrinsic changes in the person himself, in principle, it seems, the quality of that person's life can be affected by facts that alter the intrinsic content of the life without involving intrinsic changes in the person's body or mind. For example, the lack of success of the deceived businessman and his very failure to perceive this lack of success were significant factors in his life, but they had no impact on his body or mind. So although it may be appropriate to conclude that the businessman's life went poorly, nonetheless the businessman himself was well-off.

Obviously, none of this shows that goods or states of affairs that extend beyond the individual are unimportant. If the deceived businessman's family, community, and business partner had really loved, respected, and treated him fairly, these facts would have contributed much value to his life. Accordingly, some external, relational goods may be more significant than well-being itself.

Intuition itself reveals the distinction between the concepts of well-being and quality of life. Intuitively, the deceived businessman is well-off, but his life goes poorly. Similarly, consider a severely retarded individual who does not realize how constrained his/her life is but is content. His/her personal well-being does not suffer, yet his/her life does not go well. It also seems possible that one's life can be improved by a change, even if this change is not considered an improvement from one's perspective. Though the force of this evidence may be weak by itself, when combined with the earlier argument, it strongly suggests that the concept of well-being is more limited in scope and importance than formerly recognized.

Three lingering issues remain: First, it is not clear which among many external factors may be relevant to a one's life, though not to one's well-being. Second, while it has been suggested that standards for evaluating lives and persons may differ, it has not been shown that they do in fact differ. Third, it is not clear how well-being and quality of life relate to one another, and whether we should aim to promote individual well-being, or the quality of lives. One practical application of this question concerns the case of legislation that paternalistically implements restrictions to promote well-being. Suppose that promoting well-being through regulation does not promote the quality of life of the coerced individuals. Would this undercut the justification for the legislation? Alternatively, would it be plausible to justify such legislation on grounds that it would improve quality of life, but not increase well-being?

These questions suggest "that the topic of welfare is even more complex than has been previously recognized. For if there are two subjects where previously it has been thought that there is only one, then things are much more than twice as complicated. We will need an account of what is good for me, an account of what is good for my life, and an account of the relationship between me and my life." [324]

Summary of

Amartya Sen's Contributions
to Understanding Personal Welfare

by David Kiron

Amartya Sen's primary contributions to the literature on well-being, both critical and constructive, were produced during the 1970s and 1980s in a series of
lectures, books, and published articles. These are represented in many places in
this volume, with focused attention in the following four places:

- A review by Robert Sugden, summarized in Part VII, looks at Sen's contributions to the literature on justice and equality, with comparisons to
  Rawls and Nozick. Sugden also discusses Sen's critique of the effort to
  construct a social welfare function based on models that assume that relevant economic goals can be discerned through the preferences revealed in
  purchasing behavior.

- Two long essays by David Crocker, summarized in Part VIII, discuss the
  work that Sen developed with philosopher Martha Nussbaum. The focus
  here is on an ethic to be used in plans and assessments of economic development. Sen and Nussbaum base this ethic on the Aristotle-inspired concept of *capabilities* (a subtle term that is discussed in each of the essays).

- The essay by Prabha Pattanaik, summarized in Part III, and related portions of the Part III Overview Essay, address Sen's contributions to the development of social choice theory, including his famous "Paretian Liberal"
  paradox.

- This essay was written to give more coverage to two topics. One is Sen's
  major critiques of the revealed preference theory of behavior (the theory
  that undergirds the type of welfarism that Sen criticizes, as discussed by
  Sugden). The other is his alternative theory of well-being—the concept
  that Sen calls "human advantage," within which he distinguishes between
  standard of living, well-being achievement, and agency success. This set of
  distinctions provides an important way of assessing the contributions of
  economic activity to human well-being.

Critiques of Revealed Preference Theory

The revealed preference approach to behavior is widely accepted as the basis for
the microeconomic theory of behavior. It asserts that a consumer reveals
his/her preferences by what he/she chooses to buy. Sen's critique of this approach focuses on its impoverished informational foundations, specifically its as-

sumptions concerning rationality and self-interest. He has described the theory and its implications as follows:

> If you are observed to choose *x* rejecting *y*, you are declared to have "revealed" a preference for *x* over *y*. Your personal utility is then defined as simply a numerical representation of this "preference," assigning a higher utility to a "preferred" alternative. With this set of definitions you can hardly escape maximizing your own utility, except through inconsistency.[1]

Revealed preference theory appears to offer a circular definition of behavior, in the sense that a given behavior can be explained in terms of preferences that are then explained in terms of behavior. However, it is not a meaningless theory since it is theoretically possible that an irrational person would reveal inconsistent preferences.

In his 1973 article, "Behavior and the Concept of Preference,"[2] Sen argues against the fundamental assumption of the revealed preference approach—that personal choice, as a matter of fact, reveals personal preferences. He uses the classic "prisoners' dilemma" story to illustrate that selfish choice may both fail to reveal a person's real preferences and also fail to maximize utility. In the story, police separately interrogate two prisoners, who are known to have been co-perpetrators of a crime. If neither confesses, they will each get light jail sentences; if both confess, they will get medium-length sentences. If only one confesses, he will be freed while the nonconfessor will get a very long jail term. If both prisoners act selfishly, then each will confess to the crime. However, each would be better off if neither confessed. But other behavioral rules would yield better results for both. In fact, both prisoners would be better off if each acted to maximize the welfare of his partner, rather than his own.

Sen develops this objection further and adds new criticisms in a 1977 article[3] in which he argues that economic agents sometimes want different preferences than the ones they have. Carnivores who wish that they liked vegetarian foods more or smokers who wish that they did not enjoy smoking so much have preferences that cannot be represented within the revealed preference approach. As a result, the theory misses important information that is relevant to understanding and assessing personal welfare.

Implicit in revealed preference theory is the idea that personal choice is identical to personal welfare. Sen argues against this by distinguishing the concept of sympathy from that of commitment. "If the knowledge of torture of others makes you sick, it is a case of sympathy; if it does not make you feel personally worse off, but you think it is wrong and you are ready to do something about it, it is a case of commitment."[4] Sympathy is more closely tied to egoistic concerns but is linked to the welfare of others, while commitment is linked to the welfare of others but is not necessarily connected with an individual's own subjective well-being. The existence of commitment has a crucial effect on many economic issues, including problems of work motivation, optimal allocation of public goods, and collective bargaining. Economics treats individuals as "social morons" when it ignores the role of commitments in human behavior.

Sen objects that revealed preference theory inappropriately uses a single preference ordering to represent a person's welfare, one's idea of what should be done, and one's actual choices and behavior. All of a person's interests are thereby reduced to selfish concerns. Efforts to broaden this approach to include other-regarding preferences, such as Harsanyi's distinction between what a person thinks is good from an impartial point of view and what the person thinks is good from a personal point of view (a person's ethical and subjective preferences, respectively) represents an admirable if unsuccessful attempt to bring the breadth of human experience into economic theory.[5] The concept of commitment demonstrates that the range of human concerns includes more than the polarities of concern for oneself, on the one hand, and for all of society, on the other. Individuals may also act according to a sense of commitment to their neighborhood or social class.

Sen then expanded his critique of revealed preference theory to include a range of objections to the rationality assumption and the theory from which it sprang—the utilitarian conception of well-being. These criticisms appeared in his 1985 article, "Well-Being, Agency, and Freedom."[6] Due to space limitations, only two of these critiques are represented here.

Sen asks whether the concept of well-being is best understood in terms of utility. His answer is that we must be careful to avoid confusing "well-being" with "being well off," a confusion that could occur if a person's state of mind is identified with the extent of his or her possessions. A related confusion might occur if well-being is identified with what goes on in an individual's mind. Classic utilitarians believed that mental states such as feeling pleasure constitute or reflect the whole of well-being. A person who is ill-fed, undernourished, and unsheltered may learn to have limited desires, finding as much pleasure in occasional opportunities for "small mercies" as a more affluent person experiences in a better provisioned daily life. The pleasure-taking abilities of the chronically deprived hide the real extent of their substantive deprivation, when the measuring rod is pleasure or fulfillment of desire. Yet preference-based accounts of well-being do not distinguish between these cases; they discount the compromises that are often made with unpleasant circumstance. Sen therefore argues that utilitarian conceptions of human welfare typically imply well-being judgments that suffer from "physical condition neglect."[7]

Another critique from "Well-Being, Agency, and Freedom" is that the mainstream economic theory of consumer behavior judges the contribution of a set of feasible choices according to the value of the best element in the set. Thus, if all other elements besides the best one are eliminated, there is no loss in value. In reality, however, an individual's freedom (and even well-being) can be enhanced by the opportunity to make choices. A more adequate account of well-being would place a higher value on this freedom.

Sen's Alternative Theory: Capabilities and Functionings

Sen is interested in developing a theory of the good life that can be used to assess a person's ability to achieve valuable functionings. This is not an abstract theory unmoored from daily concerns. It is specifically designed for application to such social problems as inequality and poverty.[8] Sen believes that one significant advantage of his theory over rival conceptions of human welfare is its directness. It provides a framework for assessing what people actually succeed in doing or being, rather than using consumption levels and income as proxies for well-being. Others have found his approach useful; for instance, the United Nations Development Programme (UNDP) uses the capability approach in its assessment of national welfare and also in various development strategies (see Part X).

The origins of Sen's capability approach can be traced to the Aristotelian conception of human good, which holds that human lives involve unique functioning in the world, and defines happiness in terms of worthwhile activities—being able to be or do the things one has reason to value. However, the ability to achieve valued functionings in Aristotle's account of the good is different from Sen's notion of capabilities. Aristotle's restrictive claim that there is a single, correct list of valued functionings (i.e., activities) that comprises good living.

One issue that Sen takes as basic to the set of problems he is addressing concerns the problem of ensuring that individuals have a wide range of desirable, feasible choices. A theory of human advantage must be able to distinguish between the experience of a person who is involuntarily starving and one who is voluntarily fasting. As a result, Sen's analysis of human advantage consists of many dimensions, including but not limited to the dimensions of pleasure, preference satisfaction, and well-being. In Sen's view, human advantage is a function both of a person's capability set (representing the freedom to achieve one's goals and the freedom to achieve happiness) and of a chosen combination of functionings (success in achieving one's goals and achieved levels of happiness). Certain functionings are intrinsically valuable; these include health related beings and doings, such as being well-nourished or taking care of oneself.

In 1985, when Sen delivered the prestigious Tanner lectures on the topic of the standard of living,[9] he distinguished three components of human advantage. The narrowest component is a *standard of living*, which concerns an individual's self-interest but does not admit the effects of sympathy or the emotions that arise in connection with others. The pleasure you receive from eating your favorite ice cream contributes to your standard of living; that is, the pleasure, not the ice cream, is a constituent of your standard of living. However, this term does not cause sympathy-based happiness (e.g., when your favorite political prisoner is freed). A somewhat broader notion is the concept of *personal well-being*, which also incorporates sympathy-based affect. Well-being includes both the enjoyment of ice cream and the happiness you receive from your favorite political prisoner being freed.

Broadest of all is the notion of *agency*, which focuses on one's success in the pursuit of any objective that one has reason to promote, whether or not one receives any psychic benefit or loss in the process of achieving it. For instance, if you sacrifice yourself for some cause that you believe in, there may be no contribution to well-being, but you would have agency success.

The relation between these components is complex. In general, well-being includes standard of living; however, agency is a somewhat different type of category and may or may not overlap with the others. Certain agency goals may be strictly personal, and pursuing them might bring increases in both well-being and standard of living. However, it is not necessary that assessments of well-being and judgments of achievement lead in the same direction. People may have objectives other than the pursuit of their own well-being. Similarly, judging achievement of either well-being or agency success is a different process from and may have different results from the evaluation of the freedom to achieve, since a person can be advantaged by having more freedom but still end up achieving less.[10]

Sen's work is of critical importance to recent efforts to reconceptualize human welfare and, thus, to many parts of this book. It should be clear that in his analysis different aspects of human advantage require distinct modes of evaluation. Sen is thus one of the few economists who has laid out a conceptual framework for discussions of multidimensional measures of national welfare (see Part X essay).

Sen's work is also significant for recognizing the economic value of commitment and of social norms. His arguments concerning commitment provocatively suggest that the question of whether the pursuit of self-interest maximizes the social good fails to account for intermediary interests that influence both individual and national welfare. For instance, commitments to community, social norms, and moral codes of behavior all influence economic activity. These topics and more will be discussed in Part VI.

Notes

1. Amartya Sen, "Rational Fools: A Critique of the Behavioral Foundations of Economic Theory," *Philosophy and Public Affairs* 6 (1977), 317–344; quotation is from 322.

2. Amartya Sen, "Behavior and the Concept of Preference," *Economica* 40 (1973), 241–259.

3. Sen, "Rational Fools," op. cit.

4. Sen, "Rational Fools," op. cit., 326.

5. John Harsanyi, "Cardinal Welfare, Individualistic Ethics, and Interpersonal Comparisons of Utility," *Journal of Political Economy* 63 (1955), 309–321.

6. Amartya Sen, "Well-Being, Agency, and Freedom: The Dewey Lectures 1984," *The Journal of Philosophy* 82 (1985), 169–221.

7. This term also appears in Amartya Sen, *Commodities and Capabilities* (Delhi: Oxford University Press, 1987), Chapter III, 12–16.

8. Exposition of this application can be found in Crocker's article, summarized in Part VIII.

9. These lectures were published with commentary in Amartya Sen, *The Standard of Living*, ed. Geoffrey Hawthorn (Cambridge and New York: Cambridge University Press, 1987).

10. These ideas are developed in Amartya Sen, "Capability and Well-Being" in *The Quality of Life*, eds. Martha Nussbaum and Amartya Sen (Oxford: Clarendon Press, 1993), 30–53.

PART VI

Economics and the Good, II: Community

Overview Essay
by David Kiron

Economic textbooks typically describe individuals as rational, self-interested agents who spend their lives satisfying their own preferences. Yet, as many critics have pointed out, this conception of the economic actor neglects the influence of social relations and institutions, assuming individuals to be undersocialized agents who shape but are not shaped by social arrangements and cultural values. Of course, economists have long recognized that a trusting citizenry, the existence of strong social norms, and a sympathy for human values can mediate efficient outcomes, but the relationship between economic activity and social structure remains, by and large, a mystery that is little understood within modern economic theory.

Since the early 1970s, economists have made numerous attempts to locate the production and maintenance of trust, norms, and moral values within the paradigm of neoclassical economic theory. The articles in this section provide an overview of the issues that economists confront when trying to understand the impact of social organization and social relations on the economy and the impact of economic activity on social arrangements. Three questions emerge from this collection of articles. First, what evidence indicates that social structure is relevant to economic success? Second, what are the advantages or disadvantages associated with applying economic models of human behavior to social problems, such as crime, or to efforts to promote a community's willingness to accept certain necessary, but locally undesirable, projects, such as prisons or hazardous waste facilities? Finally, is the economist's "undersocialized" conception of human motivation sufficiently flexible to accommodate social influences, or must it be abandoned and replaced?

In the economics literature, one optimistic approach to all of these questions is to argue that social organizations, out of which values and norms emerge, follow the same principles of rationality that regulate human economic behavior. Proponents of this new institutional economics school attempt to explain the development of social institutions and arrangements as efficient solutions to certain types of social problems. They advocate policies to solve social problems using standard economic assumptions about human behavior.[1] On the one hand, this approach recognizes the economic importance of social relationships, but on the other hand, it simply transfers an undersocialized conception of economic agents to a social setting, abstracting away from the culture and history of concrete interactions and characterizing individuals in a stylized way.[2]

Strong Communities, Economic Vitality

The idea that social relations, especially political activity, is a critical factor in a community's economic success has been strongly urged by Robert Putnam, who argues that a community's social capital can be a critical force behind economic growth.[3] Social capital exists in various forms: as obligations and trust, as social norms and conventions, and as networks through which information is exchanged. It allows groups of people to accomplish things they could not do individually. Unlike other forms of capital, no one individual possesses social capital; it is a functional feature of relations among social structures, such as friends, community organizations, and governments. Similar to a public good, its benefits may accrue to those who do not contribute to it. As a moral resource, the more it is used the more plentiful it becomes. It can enhance the efficient allocation of community resources by fostering reciprocity norms, by facilitating trust information, and by providing the means to solve problems of collective action.

Putnam argues that when similar government institutions were established in different Italian regions in 1970, the relative success of each could be explained by the regional quality of civic engagement. Communities that had a history of strong associational networks and trustworthy leadership were successful, and those with weak civic activity and untrustworthy leaders did poorly. Putnam's central point is that communities become rich because they are civic, rather than the reverse. Similar findings emerge from studies of rural development, of rapid growth countries in East Asia, and of urban renewal projects: development strategies that build social networks or enhance preexisting ones are successful, while those programs that tend to destroy social capital do less well. Putnam concludes that informal structures such as social networks and grassroots associations, as well as political involvements, can be critical for economic success.

Some economic writings resonate with Putnam's findings that economic success depends on community vitality. For example, Sen defends the view that successful operation of an exchange economy depends on mutual trust and implicit norms. When these behavioral modes are plentifully there, it is easy to overlook their role. But when they have to be cultivated, that lacuna can be a major barrier to economic success. This can be illustrated by (1) the development problems of the third world, (2) problems of economic reform in the second world, and (3) variations in productivity and corruptibility in the first world.[4]

Social capital may also contribute to economic success through its impact on individuals. Many economists argue that higher productivity levels can be brought about not only through improvements of physical capital, such as tools and machines, but also through improvements of human capital, such as changes in the skills and abilities of persons. However, human capital itself is dependent on the social context in which it is formed and sustained. The late James Coleman, a leading proponent of the view that social capital is essential to the functioning of social systems, argued that the development of human capital requires adequate levels of social capital. His findings reinforce the idea that economic strategies that do not build up social capital have little chance of succeeding in the long run.

When Economics Worsens Community Life

Economic activity may not only fail to develop social capital but may also destroy it. As discussed by Robert Frank and Philip Cook, the explosive growth and proliferation of winner-take-all markets, in which top performers are rewarded much more than close competitors, have increased competition among economic actors. As a result, more and more people waste efforts, talents, and skills pursuing the grand prizes awarded to a chosen few in such diverse industries as entertainment, athletics, fiction writing, and education. Another consequence is a wide spread deterioration of cooperation norms that formerly restricted competition. Their policy solution to the inefficiencies and inequalities that result from these markets is to institute social interventions, such as laws, taxes, or social norms, since individuals who have the power are not likely to have the incentive to limit opportunities for a big payoff.

The traditional economic solution to problems of inefficient outcomes is to find the correct incentive structures. Many economists believe that price signals can be used to reduce socially undesirable outcomes, such as criminal activity, or to promote socially desirable outcomes, such as community acceptance of prisons or other not-in-my-back-yard (NIMBY) projects. Attach costs to crime, and demand for it will drop. Or, offer sufficient compensation to communities, and they will accept socially necessary if locally undesirable projects. The next two summaries criticize such incentive-based approaches to social planning that fail to consider elements of social capital.

Criminal behavior is in many instances a local phenomenon. Without a consideration of the institutional context in which crime occurs, economic approaches can make recommendations that may worsen rather than alleviate crime. Social planners have paid a good deal of attention to Gary Becker's economic model, which assumes that criminal activity among gangs will diminish as the likelihood of getting caught increases. The policy conclusion is obvious: increase police activity to reduce crime. In work summarized here, George Akerlof and Janet Yellen take issue with this approach, arguing that if community values and social norms are not taken into consideration, then policy recommendations based on Becker's model may generate more rather than less criminal activity.

Akerlof and Yellen contend that a crucial deterrent to crime is knowledgeable and cooperative citizens. In their model, gangs are willing to commit crimes only up to the point where they alienate the community in which they reside. Crime reduction strategies that either ignore this dynamic or alienate community members may lead to more crime, especially if the community is surrounded by other high crime areas. In such communities, residents may not want to weaken their neighborhood gang if that makes them vulnerable to gangs operating in nearby areas. Akerlof and Yellen recommend strategies that both foster community integrity and build norms of cooperation between civic institutions.

In the next summary, Bruno Frey demonstrates that incentive-based economic approaches fail to explain levels of tax evasion and community willingness to accept nuclear waste facilities in Switzerland. In cantons where trust in the political system is high, levels of tax fraud are low; where trust is low, levels of fraud are high. These differences cannot be accounted for by incentive differences. Also, contrary to economic expectations community willingness to accept a socially undesirable project was diminished by the mere prospect of significant financial incentives. Economic strategies that use incentives as the guiding principle of social planning appear to omit the importance of noncalculating motives (such as intrinsic motivation and civic virtue) that are endogenous and related to an ethical commitment to one's community. Attitudes toward paying taxes or accepting undesirable projects indicate a deeper concern with what citizens ought to do, rather than with the potential costs of tax evasion or the benefits of financial remuneration.

Together, these articles offer strong evidence that a thriving community reinforces and is reinforced by a successful economy. Effective social networks, a trusting citizenry, and a commitment to community contribute to the support of socially productive projects and even increases tax returns. Winner-take-all-markets and incentive-based planning undermine norms of cooperation and a sense of community membership. Yet a successful economy does not require community vitality of the sort typically associated with strong communities in Western countries. Certain authoritarian countries in Asia, such as South Korea and Malaysia, have enjoyed economic growth, while placing strict limits on individual liberties.

A strong rule of law prescribes citizen activity by imposing obligations and restricting freedoms, but in liberal societies citizens play an active role in organizing social structure and taking advantage of voluntary organizations. Thus, citizenship occupies a significant place within liberal societies and may be a central feature of the relationship between social arrangements and economic activity. In their summarized article on citizenship theory, Will Kymlicka and Wayne Norman advance the idea that good citizenship depends on both the preservation of rights and the political exercise of one's obligations and responsibilities to community. Taking stock of the fact that government would be impossible if it were not for responsible citizens, they review how postwar citizenship theory has moved away from an emphasis on rights and toward an emphasis on the value of cultivating a more responsible and politically involved citizenry.

Economic Theory and Social Capital

The final group of articles considers how economists might accommodate within the existing framework of economic theory such concepts as trust, social norms, and moral values. In the next summarized article, Partha Dasgupta analyzes the production, exchange, and use of trust as a commodity. His main point is that a rational, self-interested individual will pay to acquire trust by investing in his or her reputation. The market provides incentives even to dishonest people to build a reputation as trustworthy, especially if they expect to live a long time in a close-knit community. Similarly, Frank has argued that being known as honest is helpful in situations where partners are being sought.[5] However, community investment in trust tends to achieve less than ideal levels, since no one person invests to make others more trustworthy.

A more expansive view of trust production is suggested by sociologist Mark Granovetter, who argues that the formation of trust has less to do with self-interest than with the fact that mutual obligations and psychological bonds develop from repeated exchanges.[6] In his view, economic actors not only care whether someone is reliable or trustworthy (as argued by Dasgupta and Frank) but also want trusted sources from which to obtain this information. That is, individuals are often interested in obtaining information from trusted members of their community, such as friends and family. Although consumer decisions based on this advice sometimes lead to unwise purchases,[7] looking to such sources for information often saves time and permits individuals to focus on other more important decisions.

In fact, people seldom investigate all possible alternatives and calculate which would optimize results: if they did little would be accomplished. As Koford and Miller note, "life would be too complex if agents had to carefully consider each daily action from an optimizing point of view. If, at any given time, people con-

sciously make decisions about only a small fraction of their actions, then it is unlikely that their actions taken together will be optimal."[8] Economist Herbert
Simon has for many years pointed out that for reasons such as this individuals
adopt decision-making strategies that satisfice rather than optimize results.[9] In
the behavioral domain most habits, customs, and social norms serve a similar
function, reducing complexities in life that would otherwise paralyze action.
Koford and Miller argue that an explicit recognition of habits, customs, and
norms would lead to an economic model of human behavior that represents individuals as satisficers rather than maximizers.

Currently, economists tend to emphasize the rational nature of social norms,
explaining their existence in terms of either selfish interests, collective interest,
or genetic fitness. In other social sciences, researchers are more diverse in their
opinions about the origins and purposes of norms. A rationalistic approach is
discussed by Coleman who analyzes norms as a type of social capital that results
from externality-producing actions.[10] In his view, norms tell individuals or
groups what should or should not be done—they prescribe or proscribe actions.
Norms can be internalized, i.e., learned so well that they become a routine part
of life; or followed for such external reasons as seeking social approval or avoiding disapproval; or violated and either internally sanctioned (e.g., guilt) or externally sanctioned (e.g., ostracization). A less rationalistic approach to norms is
developed by political scientist Jon Elster who contends that many norms exist
for reasons that have little to do with instrumental rationality: some norms
remain in use long after they served their original purpose, while others arise
randomly.[11]

Economists usually represent norms and values within the standard microeconomic theory of behavior as either preferences, constraints, or decision
rules. In the final summarized article, economist Robert Goldfarb and philosopher William Griffith assess these three approaches and argue that none are
entirely successful. Instead of trying to fit such nebulous concepts as values
and norms into utility functions, or to interpret norms as decision rules, economists ought to begin with a more robust theory of human behavior. Goldfarb
and Griffith are less sanguine than other economists represented in this section about the prospects of expanding the neoclassical paradigm to accommodate norms and values. They align themselves with Amitai Etzioni, Sen,
and Hirschman in "refusing to accept the defensive posture of shielding
basic assumptions in economics from direct evaluation, criticism, and potential
revision. . . ."[12]

Trust, social norms, and moral values—the main ingredients of social capital—constitute part of the social glue that holds society together, but economists have only recently begun to grapple with the relationships between these
elements and economic activity. The neoclassical model constructs a social welfare function by aggregating up from individual welfare, yet it may well be that

social welfare is a much more dynamic entity than this. As the articles in this section suggest, social structure also has a downward impact on individual welfare. Thus, the interactive forces that shape social capital and human interests may not prove amenable to economic theories of well-being based on individualistic preferences. Consequently, as economists become more interested in and gain a fresh perspective on the elements of social capital, it is questionable whether the economist's tool kit can be expanded to include them.

Notes

1. An approach sometimes referred to as "economic imperialism." For instructive discussions of this movement, see G. Radnitzky and P. Bernhoz, *Economic Imperialism: The Economic Method Applied Outside the Field of Economics* (New York: Paragon House, 1987); also Jack Hershleifer, "The Expanding Domain of Economics," *American Economic Review Directory* (December 1985), 53–68.

2. This argument is developed in Mark Granovetter, "Economic Action and Social Structure: The Problem of Embeddedness," *American Journal of Sociology* 91 (1985), 481–510.

3. As discussed earlier, the idea of social capital and its central role in the structure and function of social systems is developed in great detail by the late sociologist James Coleman.

4. Amartya Sen, "Moral Codes and Economic Success," Discussion Paper no. 49, Development Economic Research Programme, Suntory-Toyota International Centre for Economics and Related Disciplines (London, 1993).

5. Frank, Robert, "If *Homo Economicus* Could Choose His Own Utility Function, Would He Want One with a Conscience?" *American Economic Review* 77 (1987), 593–604.

6. Granovetter, op. cit.

7. Akerlof has argued that trusting information from friends may not produce optimal results. See George Akerlof, "Procrastination and Obedience," *American Economic Review* 81 (1991), 1–19.

8. Kenneth J. Koford and Jeffrey B. Miller "Habit, Custom, and Norms in Economics," in *Social Norms and Economic Institutions,* eds. Kenneth J. Koford and Jeffrey B. Miller (Ann Arbor: University of Michigan Press, 1991), 21–38. The quotation is from p. 24.

9. Herbert Simon, *Reason in Human Affairs* (Palo Alto: Stanford University Press, 1983).

10. James Coleman, "Norms as Social Capital," in *Economic Imperialism: The Economic Method Applied Outside the Field of Economics,* eds. G. Radnitzky and P. Bernhoz (New York: Paragon House, 1987), 133–153.

11. Jon Elster, "Social Norms and Economic Theory," *Journal of Economic Perspectives* 4 (1989), 99–117.

12. Robert S. Goldfarb and William B. Griffith, "The 'Theory as Map' Analogy and Changes in Assumption Sets in Economics," in *Socio-Economics: Toward a New Synthe-

sis, eds. Amitai Etzioni and Paul R. Lawrence (New York: M. E. Sharpe, 1985), 105–130. The quotation is from p. 107.

The works of cited authors are, respectively:

- Amitai Etzioni, "The Case for a Multiple Utility Conception," *Economics and Philosophy* 2 (1986), 159–183;
- Amartya Sen, "Rational Fools" (1977) (see review essay of Sen's work in Part V); and
- Albert O. Hirschman, "Against Parsimony" (1985) (see Part V for summary and full citation).

Summary of

The Prosperous Community:
Social Capital and Public Life

by Robert Putnam

[Published in *The American Prospect*, (Spring 1993), 35–42.]

The importance of social cohesiveness to both economic prosperity and personal flourishing has long been ignored by mainstream economic theorists. Other social scientists have begun to analyze the problems of collective action using the analytic rubric of social capital, which are those features of social organizations that facilitate coordination and cooperation for mutual benefit, such as social networks, norms, and trust. Social capital has proven to be a scarce and fragile resource that is difficult to cultivate in some communities. This summary examines the relationship between social capital and economic growth in a variety of contexts and calls attention to the idea that civic engagement is central to economic progress.

Lessons from Italy

In 1970, similarly structured government institutions were established in regions all over Italy. The author and a number of other researchers examined quality differences among these regional institutions as they developed in diverse social, economic, political, and culture contexts. As expected, some proved to be dismal failures—inefficient, lethargic, and corrupt; while others were remarkably successful—efficient, creative, and productive. For example, the latter institutions helped produce innovative day care programs and job training centers, while promoting investment and economic development. Surprisingly, differences in institutional quality cannot be accounted for by political ideology, political harmony, levels of affluence, or social stability. Rather, the hallmark of a successful regional government is civic engagement.

Successful institutions are led by relatively trustworthy individuals committed to equality. Citizens in these communities (e.g., Tuscany and Emilia Romagna) actively participate in public issues and trust one another to act fairly and lawfully. Social and political networks are arranged horizontally, rather than hierarchically. History suggests that these regions have a long tradition of civic involvement that can be traced back to the 11th century when civic solidarity was important to the self-defense of medieval communes. In the 20th century, this tradition can be seen in neighborhood associations and choral societies.

The upshot of the Italian study is that prosperous communities did not become civic because they were rich, rather they became rich because they were civic. Social capital is instrumental to economic prosperity on many levels. First, civic engagement fosters strong norms of generalized reciprocity, which lead to greater efficiency. A classic example involves farmers who help each other bale hay. Each can get more work done with less physical capital. Second, civic engagement can facilitate the coordination and communication of trust information about individuals. For instance, in dense networks of social interaction, reputation and trust information are crucial to economic exchanges such as diamond trades, where the possibilities for fraud are extreme. Finally, a tradition of civic engagement provides a cultural template for solutions to novel problems of collective action. Stocks of social capital tend to be self-reinforcing and cumulative. As noted by Albert Hirschman, they are a "moral resource" whose supply increases rather than decreases with use.

Social Capital and Economic Development

"Scores of studies of rural development have shown that a vigorous network of indigenous grassroots associations can be as essential to growth as physical investment, appropriate technology, or (that nostrum of neoclassical economists) 'getting prices right.' " [38] Studies of rapid economic growth among countries in East Asia indicate the important role of dense social networks based on extended families or close-knit ethnic communities. In advanced Western economies, network collaborations among workers and entrepreneurs have led to highly efficient industrial districts within such diverse environments as high-tech Silicon Valley and high fashion Benetton.

Current development strategies for the formerly Communist economies of Eurasia tend to focus exclusively on strengthening market economies and democratic institutions through loans and technical assistance. These strategies will probably fail in the long run because they do nothing to improve social capital. Similarly, economic reconversion programs, such as factory closings, that ignore the possible effects of destroying social capital can lead to the shredding of communities. "Worse yet, some government programs themselves, such as urban renewal and public housing projects, have needlessly ravaged existing social networks. . . . Shred enough of the social fabric and we all pay." [39]

Social Capital in the United States

Inequality with respect to social capital can be as portentous as income inequality. In poor ghettos across the United States, an exodus by the middle and working classes leaves those who remain even further behind with fewer opportunities to access social networks that lead to jobs. Socially inherited differences in community networks and norms can render individually-targeted "equal opportunity" programs ineffective.

Education is another arena in which social capital can be decisive in determining opportunity. For instance, improving parental involvement and civic engagement in the schooling of children greatly increases a child's academic success and future potential. Many proposals for increased school "choice" are deeply flawed by their individualist conception of education. School vouchers can only aid education if they are spent in ways that strengthen community organization, not merely enhance individual choice.

Efforts to revitalize American democracy need to recognize that political dissatisfaction reflects an erosion of social capital. This can be observed in national surveys that show a multi-decade decline in trust and the tendency of socially mobile two-career families to use market services, such as child care services, that were formerly available from family and neighborhood networks.

> Our political parties, once intimately coupled to the capillaries of community life, have become evanescent confections of pollsters and media consultants and independent political entrepreneurs—the very antithesis of social capital. We have too easily accepted a conception of democracy in which public policy is not the outcome of a collective deliberation about the public interest, but rather a residue of campaign strategy. The social capital approach, focusing on the indirect effects of civic norms and networks, is a much-needed corrective to an exclusive emphasis on the formal institutions of government as an explanation for our collective discontents. [41]

Summary of

Social Capital in the Creation of Human Capital

by James S. Coleman

[Published in *American Journal of Sociology* 94 (1988), S95–S120.]

Most sociologists tend to view human behavior as the product of a social environment governed by social norms, rules, and obligations. Economists tend to view humans as independently motivated by rationally determined, wholly self-interested goals. The social capital concept combines elements from both streams of thought. It assumes that rationality is a primary motivating force for human behavior both at the level of individual action and social organization.

This article introduces the concept of social capital and provides examples of its use. It then explores how social capital embedded in the family and community helps explain the level of human capital—represented by educational achievement—in the next generation.

What Is Social Capital?

Social capital refers to characteristics of social structures that facilitate the actions of people and institutions within those social structures. Although social capital can reside in relationships between and among people and institutions, this paper concentrates on the relationships between and among people. As with human capital and physical capital, social capital enables societies to achieve some actions that would not be possible without it. For example, social capital allows for the relatively intangible properties of relationships, such as trust, which enhance the productive activities of those involved.

Social capital exists in at least three forms. One form is concerned with obligations, expectations, and trust. People who perform many favors for others may be considered to have a large number of credits on which they can draw. These interconnections of obligations and expectations give members of the social structure additional capital to assist them in meeting their goals. This form of social capital depends on the level of trust within the social environment and on the extent to which individual actors are able to accrue credits as payment for favors.

Information channels constitute a second form of social capital. Because acquiring information is costly, it is often acquired through social relations that are maintained for other purposes. A busy woman who wants to be fashionable may rely on her friends to keep her up to date on fashion trends.

Finally, norms and sanctions constitute a third form of social capital. Norms may enable powerful forms of social capital to develop, including those norms that enable people to walk in public without fear of crime. The norm that leads people to forego their own personal interests and to act for the common good is particularly important. These norms may be internalized or they may be maintained through an external system of reward for following the norm and/or punishment for acting selfishly.

Social Structures and the Formation of Social Capital

Certain aspects of social structures are particularly conducive to building social capital. One of the favorable properties of a social structure is closure. Closure of a social structure means that the affected people have an ongoing relationship with each other. When people know each other, effective sanctions and rewards can be applied to monitor and guide behavior. Norms are far less likely to be effective when the social structure lacks closure. In that case, the people negatively affected by some action do not know each other and are far less able to join forces to sanction the action. Closure of the social structure also raises the trustworthiness of social structures, enabling the interconnections of obligations and expectations to increase.

Another structure that facilitates the formation of social capital occurs when an organization formed for one purpose is subsequently used for another. This is known as an *appropriable* social organization. For example, tenants in a public housing project built during World War II who had joined together to fight for better housing conditions kept the organization together even after its initial goals had been met. The members realized that the social capital inherent in the organization improved the quality of their lives.

Social Capital and the Creation of Human Capital

Social capital within the family and the community plays a particularly important role in creating human capital in the next generation. Three different types of capital within the family affect the educational achievement of children: financial capital, human capital, and social capital. Financial capital may be measured by the parents' wealth or income. Human capital may be considered the potential of the parents to create an environment that aids learning. It may be measured more or less by the level of parental education.

Social capital is another element in family background that contributes to the level of human capital in the next generation. Some parents have the ability to increase the educational achievement of their children even when the human capital of the parents is not particularly high. Parents can do this by taking the time and effort to instill learning and discipline in their children. This extra time and effort exerted by the parents represents an additional resource of social capital within the family.

The effects of social capital in families and in communities were measured in a study of high school dropout rates. Significantly lower dropout rates were found in families with two parents in the home rather than just one, with one sibling rather than four, and with a mother who expects her child to attend college. Each of these variables is assumed to help foster social capital in the family and thus increase human capital as measured by the educational level of the children.

Lower dropout rates were also found at high schools where there appeared to be greater inter-generational closure, meaning that the parents of the children know each other. Students whose parents know each other are thought to have access to greater social capital to aid them in developing their human capital. Thus, these two examples demonstrate that social capital within the family and within the community can increase the human capital of children.

Public Goods Aspects of Social Capital

While the benefits of private capital and human capital primarily accrue to the owner, the benefits of most forms of social capital accrue not just to those who contribute to it but also to society at large. It may make financial sense to a family for a mother to return to work outside the home and withdraw from active involvement in the parents' association at school, but that withdrawal means decreased social capital is available for the community. Because social capital is created by people who often are not the primary beneficiaries, it is often formed as a by-product of other activities and societies tend to underinvest in its formation. With the weakening of formerly strong families and strong communities, the undersupply of social capital worsens. It may then become necessary to substitute some kind of formal organization for the voluntary and spontaneous organization that in the past was the major source of social capital.

In summary, the concept of social capital preserves the paradigm of rational action but avoids the assumption of atomistic elements lacking social relationships. An important aspect of social capital is its public goods nature.

Summary of

Winner-Take-All Markets
and
The Growth of Winner-Take-All Markets

by Robert H. Frank and Philip J. Cook

[Chapters 1 and 3 in *The Winner-Take-All Society*
(New York: The Free Press, 1995), 1–22; 45–60.]

Winner-take-all markets, in which the rewards for being the top performer(s) are vastly greater than for even close competitors, have long been common in sports and entertainment. In these markets, the rewards are based on relative, rather than absolute performance. This article shows how technological innovations, expanding global trade, and changes in social norms are making these markets increasingly common in fields as diverse as law, journalism, consulting, medicine, investment banking, corporate management, publishing, design, fashion, and higher education, among others. It argues that winner-take-all markets increase income inequality, waste talents and resources, and affect the culture in disturbing ways, all of which profoundly affect individual well-being. However, solutions are suggested to diminish both the allure of the top rewards and the pernicious effects of cutthroat competition.

Causes of the Increase in Winner-Take-All Markets

In today's economy, decreasing transport and tariff costs, combined with advances in information processing and telecommunications, mean that what were formerly local or regional markets for many products and services are now

global, with far greater amounts of money at stake. At the same time, technological and marketing capabilities enable the mass customization of products,
spawning greater specialization of markets, each one of which may have a winner-take-all structure. These changes have dramatically increased the rewards
for top performers, while competition for top performers has become more
open and intense.

Further, changes in production methods mean that the benefits of increased
productivity flow not to laborers, but to those who design, direct, and finance
the production process. These are the group whom Robert Reich has referred
to as "symbolic analysts," who engage in "problem-solving, identifying, and
brokering."[1] The salaries of these professionals rise more quickly than do those
of other workers. As their salaries rise, they demand more *positional goods*—
goods that have additional value based on their reputation as the best or most
prestigious in their category. Because only a small number of products can make
this claim, this increased demand promotes winner-take-all markets.

In winner-take-all markets for products, only barely detectable differences in
quality may mean the difference between success and failure. While the public
may care little about which product wins, the stakes are enormous for the man-
ufacturers and producers. This produces a new class of experts capable of making the difference between corporate success and failure. Given their pivotal positions, competing firms attempt to outbid each other for their services. The
result is a winner-take-all reward structure for those in this field.

In addition, social norms that once restricted competition have eroded. Old
norms of loyalty that caused people to stay with the same company, team, or
university have been replaced by bidding wars for the top talent. Norms that
prevented CEOs from making much more than others in their company are far
less powerful. Norms against sensationalizing the news and exploiting people's
private lives are also deteriorating as journalists and entertainers compete for
winning ratings.

Negative Consequences of Winner-Take-All Markets

Consumers benefit when technology enables the most talented writers, musi-
cians, entertainers, and scientists to disseminate their works widely, but there
are also many socially harmful results when the rewards for success are so high,
the competition for these rewards is so intense, and the rewards depend on relative performance. They include the following:

• *Growing income inequality.* Wage theory holds that pay rate is related to
productive contribution. However, this relationship is broken in winner-take-all
markets. An Olympic runner may win first prize by mere fractions of a second,
earning thousands of times more than the runner-up, yet the difference in talent is barely perceptible. Wealth and power are increasingly concentrated in the
winners; those who are merely very good earn far less. Increasing income in-

equality caused by the prevalence of winner-take-all markets is undermining social cohesion.

- *Misallocation of talent.* The allure of spectacular rewards in winner-take-all markets has attracted some of the most talented people to enter these markets but has also caused too many contestants to compete for a limited number of top positions. The rising stakes in litigation, for example, have led people to pay more and hire the best lawyers, thereby attracting many of society's most talented people to careers in litigation. Yet this influx of talent has created no new social value or wealth. By siphoning talented people from productive careers in traditional markets, it has actually reduced our national income.

- *Unproductive consumption and investment.* In military arms races, countries fear losing position if they do not buy more arms, yet everyone is worse off if each country buys more arms. Similarly, *positional arms races* in winner-take-all markets increase the losses caused by overcrowding the field. Competitors invest in products and practices that may help them win but that have little or no social value. In the end, everyone pays more just to maintain the same relative ranking.

- *Stifling of social mobility and elitism in higher education.* Without elite undergraduate or graduate degrees, it is increasingly difficult to gain entrance to competitive graduate schools or firms. With a winner-take-all mentality, elite colleges and universities have assumed the role of gatekeeper for the top job prospects. To attract top students, universities engage in bidding wars for professors who are academic superstars, thus participating in positional arms races that do little or nothing to increase social value.

- *Mediocrity in popular culture.* Success in popular culture is often based not on quality but on hype, with success measured as rapid market triumph. People want to read the book or see the movie they have heard about. The more people do this, the more popular the book or movie will be, vastly increasing the payoffs. The search for rapid market triumph makes the success-breeds-success feature so pernicious. Products must achieve success early or they are considered failures. Thus, the emphasis is on hype and on relying on tried-and-true formulas and sequels, stifling creativity.

- *Increased competition and changing norms in private life.* Ordinary citizens also compete for rewards based on relative, rather than absolute performance. People spend more and more for a limited number of houses in the best locations, pay more to dress better than others, and undergo plastic surgery to look better, yet their relative ranking in housing, dress, and appearance may remain the same. They simply spend more to remain in the same position. Plastic surgery may serve to enhance individual appearance, but it also changes the norm of appearance. What used to be acceptable appearance no longer is, causing people to want to make more money simply to keep up with community standards.

Positional Arms Control Agreements
to Limit Wasteful Competition

Just as pollution causes externalities, most of the inefficiencies of winner-take-all markets are due to the costs participants impose on others. To mitigate the harms of winner-take-all markets, the best remedies will be those that redirect individual and social incentives, while preserving freedom of choice as much as possible.

A number of strategies used to control wasteful competition have been used and are referred to as *positional arms control agreements*. These strategies seek to reduce the benefits winners receive and control the competition. They include:

- *Legal mechanisms.* Higher income taxes and luxury goods will decrease the rewards of upper incomes and thereby reduce the attraction of entering these competitions. This would encourage the marginal contestants to enter other fields where they could add greater social value. Conservative economists argue against a more progressive tax system by saying that it would inhibit growth. But if, as appears, most of the highest earners work in winner-take-all markets, the effect of more progressive taxes may actually be to stimulate economic growth. The time-honored trade-off between equity and efficiency is far less agonizing than it appears. Consumption taxes on houses, clothes, cars, and plastic surgery increase the cost to individuals for participating in positional arms races, thus reinforcing whatever residual social norms against conspicuous consumption may remain. In addition to tax reforms, other legal mechanisms for controlling these markets may include campaign finance rules and health and safety regulations.

- *Private agreements,* such as dress codes or uniform requirements, may also be used. Sports leagues may enact pay caps and revenue sharing agreements, or industry groups may work out strategies for sharing basic research costs.

- *Social norms* may play an important role. In some communities, for example, social norms discourage dueling, conspicuous consumption, and cosmetic surgery.

In general, detailed, prescriptive government regulation is not the preferred approach to moderating the effects of winner-take-all markets. Policies that internalize the social costs of individual actions, altering the reward structures to discourage socially damaging activity, are better policy tools.

Note

1. Robert B. Reich, *The Work of Nations: Preparing Ourselves for 21st-Century Capitalism* (New York: Knopf, 1991).

Summary of

Gang Behavior, Law Enforcement, and Community Values

by George Akerlof and Janet L. Yellen

[Published in *Values and Public Policy,* eds. Henry J. Aaron, Thomas E. Mann, and Timothy Taylor (Washington, DC: Brookings Institute, 1994), 173–209.]

This article examines the role of community norms and values in controlling crime. It argues that community cooperation with the police is essential for controlling crime. A model of inner-city gang behavior is developed that emphasizes the gangs' pursuit of economic gain, as well as the rational behavior of both gangs and community members. The model assumes that the primary limitation on crime is the gangs' unwillingness to alienate their own communities. It explicitly includes factors that influence the likelihood of citizen cooperation with the police and concludes that managing community norms to enhance cooperation with the police is as important for controlling crime as harsh punishments or additional police activity. In addition, crime-control approaches that undermine community values may prove counterproductive in the long run.

A standard economic view of appropriate levels of punishment and police presence was developed by Gary Becker.[1] He created what came to be known as the *principal-agent model of behavior.* This model is applicable to many different two-role interactions, such as managers and workers or voters and politicians. According to this model, the principal (the police) sets out incentives to which the agent (the criminal) responds. The outcome of the interactions depends on who knows what about whom. Becker assumes that the ability of the police to detect criminals depends directly on the level of law enforcement effort, referred to as monitoring expenditure. Becker also assumes that criminals view the risk of their detection as outside their control.

However, the most important deterrent to crime is not the presence of police, but the presence of knowledgeable civilians who are willing to cooperate with police. A third element—the community—must also be included in the model. This amended version of the model assumes that criminals view their chances of being detected as dependent on both law enforcement monitoring and community behavior. It further assumes that gang members think that they can influence the community's willingness to cooperate with the police.

The roles of the three protagonists in the model—gangs, community, and government (represented by the police)—are described in the following sections.

Modeling Gang Behavior

The model assumes that gangs, as agents, calculate the costs and benefits of criminal activity to determine the optimum number of crimes to commit. The attractiveness of noncriminal activities is a key determinant of these costs and benefits. Residents of poor neighborhoods earn little money for legitimate work, so the differential reward for committing crimes is higher there than in wealthy neighborhoods. In addition, the departure of the middle class from the inner city has led to a decline in acceptance of the work ethic and in norms against imprisonment.

Gangs calculate the costs of each crime committed based on three elements: the potential penalty (jail sentence) associated with the crime, the amount of police monitoring, and the level of community cooperation. Local residents are aware of certain illegal activities conducted by gangs since some require a degree of openness, such as the selling of drugs. Gangs realize that they must secure community support, otherwise citizens will cooperate with police. Rent-seeking behavior of gangs is also constrained by other factors, such as relationships through blood, marriage, or friendships with community residents.

Under the simplified assumptions of the model, as the level of crime increases, a critical point is reached where the representative community member changes from being uncooperative to cooperative with the police. This point defines the cooperation/noncooperation boundary. The gang has an incentive to commit crime up to this critical point; beyond that level, the community cooperates with government and crime does not pay.

Modeling Community Behavior

Community residents, the second protagonist in the model, are aware of gang activities. Among the significant number of residents with middle-class aspirations, two opposing motives determine the degree of cooperation with the police. First is the fear of retaliation for informing the police, which is measured against the hatred of gangs and their activities. This tendency is weighed against secondary motives. For instance, there may be sympathy for gangs because they sometimes make positive community contributions: preventing undesirable outsiders from entering the neighborhood, using their power and money to support positive local activities, and even restraining drug selling to children. Community attitudes toward the police also influence the tendency to cooperate. Residents often view the police as an alien, hostile force that uses unfair procedures and imposes inappropriate punishments.

Community residents who are potential informants are modeled as "representative agents" with identical preferences. This assumption requires two simplifications of the model. First, community diversity is undervalued. The differences between residents with middle-class aspirations and a work ethic and those residents who espouse street values and hustling are disregarded. Another simplification is that the model accepts norms as given; this ignores factors that form and shape values, such as community leaders who demonstrate the value of a strong work ethic. Unfortunately, the black middle class, which might have helped form these values, has fled the inner city; those who remain have less belief in these norms and little hope of increasing their status.

Accordingly, the principal-agent model of behavior assumes that there are four factors that influence the willingness of community members to reveal information to the police:

(1) Fear of reprisals from gangs.

(2) Consequences of a weakened local gang. Community members may not wish to weaken the local gang if they believe that the level of crime in nearby similar neighborhoods is higher than in their own. Residents may prefer to deal with a gang they know than to take their chances with an outside gang. If local crime is perceived as higher than in other nearby neighborhoods, citizens will tend to cooperate with police.

(3) Perception of fairness of the criminal justice system. Community members are assumed to be less willing to cooperate if penalties against offenders are felt to be either too high or too low.

(4) Attitudes toward police and community norms concerning the criminal justice system. This is relevant when the police are perceived as playing an ambiguous role in poor neighborhoods—the police may preserve order to some extent, but they also imprison citizens, sometimes unfairly.

Modeling Government Behavior and Community Cooperation

The government, as the principal, plays the third role in the model. The government, represented by the police, establishes the procedures for catching, sentencing, punishing, and paroling offenders. It also determines law enforcement budgets and penalties for offenses. The model views the government as balancing two separate aims: controlling the level of crimes and controlling spending. Although not included in this model, a more general framework might also include the possibility of kickbacks between gangs and government agents.

The level of law enforcement monitoring has an ambiguous effect on cooperation. Higher monitoring levels may increase reporting because there may be a greater likelihood that the information reported will lead to convictions. However, if penalties are considered unfair, higher monitoring may decrease reporting because the information may lead to unfair sentences.

Community Norms and Crime Fighting Strategies

This principal-agent model of behavior can be used to determine the optimal strategy for fighting crime, assuming that community norms cannot be changed in the short run. The optimal strategy depends on three factors that have been used in previous economic models of crime and punishment: the social cost of crime, monitoring costs, and neighborhood income. In addition, the model also includes two new factors: a norm of fair punishment and the community's tendency to report crime. The tendency to report crime is assumed to depend on the norms of cooperation with police, the severity and probability of retaliation against informants, and crime levels outside the neighborhood.

The model presents the possibility of an upward spiral of crime in the absence of strong reporting norms in communities surrounded by high crime neighborhoods. In such communities, residents are less likely to cooperate with police. Residents fear that they will be worse off if they punish their local gangs, thus allowing nearby gangs to enter their neighborhood. Without community cooperation, law enforcement efforts are less effective and gangs have less reason to moderate their criminal activity.

The model suggests that traditional methods of crime prevention and control—increased police presence and more severe criminal punishments—may be counterproductive because they have the potential to undermine community norms for cooperation with the police. On the other hand, nontraditional strategies—such as enhancing the roles of churches, parent support groups, citizen patrols, neighborhood cleanups, and community policing—may offer high payoffs by strengthening community norms for cooperating with the police.

Note

1. Gary S. Becker, "Crime and Punishment: An Economic Approach," *Journal of Political Economy* 76 (March–April 1968), 169–217.

Summary of

Institutions and Morale: The Crowding-Out Effect

by Bruno S. Frey

[Paper presented at Conference on the Relationship between Economic Institutions and Ethical Values and Behavior, 1996, Yale University.]

Economists use the concept of relative price to explain institutional effects on a wide variety of behavior, including criminal activity and community acceptance of noxious facilities. Although the relative price effect is a fundamental proposition in economics, it fails to explain many important behaviors that are driven by noncalculative motives such as intrinsic motivation. This paper demonstrates through empirical work on tax evasion and community acceptance of NIMBY (not-in-my-backyard) projects that the economic analysis of institutional effects must include factors that go beyond relative price. It is shown that under certain conditions, external interventions such as reward or punishment may result in a crowding-out effect that undermines the intrinsic motivation to perform socially desirable activity. Two questions are discussed: do compensations increase community acceptance of NIMBY projects, and does increased deterrence raise (gross) tax revenue?

Relative Price and Institutions

The *relative price effect* asserts that price increases reduce demand for a good or activity and raise its supply, other things being equal. This implies that increasing the penalties of crime or the expectation of detection will lower crime rates and that offering compensation to communities will increase their tendency to accept projects, such as prisons and nuclear waste repositories, that are recognized to be socially desirable but are undesirable in one's own neighborhood. Coase clearly makes the point: "An economist will not debate whether increased punishment will reduce crime; he will try to answer the question, by how much."[1]

Institutions determine the magnitude of relative prices, such as the size of a punishment. Institutions can be understood in a variety of ways, but they are essentially social regularities. These are manifested in the form of decision-making systems, such as democracies or markets; formal rules, such as those embodied in constitutions, laws, and regulations; informal rules, such as social norms or traditions; and organizations, such as firms, government, or bureaucracies.

Economic Relevance of Noncalculative Motives

Noncalculating behavior is motivated by considerations other than short-run benefits and costs. The existence of such behavior is clearly evidenced by Emily Dickinson's desire to write poetry without the intention to publish it, and the mathematician Galois, who forsook a good night's sleep before a duel to write down major discoveries in algebra. The hallmark of noncalculative behavior is intrinsic motivation, which implies an interest in performing an activity for its own sake. Intrinsic motivation is different from but compatible with the calculating motivation underlying optimization behavior. Although conceptually distinct, calculating and noncalculating motivations are difficult if not impossible to distinguish in actual behavior. The most salient examples of noncalculative motives consist of morale, in the sense of work or tax morale; civic virtue or public spirit; social capital, which includes norms and networks of civic engagement; and trust.

The relevance of intrinsic motivation to economic analysis is suggested by the failure of the deterrence model to provide a satisfactory explanation of tax-paying behavior.[2] Despite the fact that the probability of apprehension and the size of punishment for tax evasion is low, there is a high compliance rate with tax payments in most countries. Some economists have attributed this seemingly nonoptimizing behavior either to tax morale (a commitment to citizenship and respect for law) or to a lack of opportunity to evade taxes. An erosion in tax morale has been suggested as an important factor in the noted decline of tax compliance in the United States. Further support can be found in the vast literature on why people obey the law. Social psychologists have forcefully argued that criminal activity cannot be explained by deterrence variables and that individuals will engage in lawful behavior if procedures are considered fair, even if outcomes are unfavorable to them.

One might object that intrinsic motivation poses few problems for economic analysis so long as intrinsic motivation is considered to be exogenously given. As is argued later, this is not the case. Intrinsic motivation is determined endogenously and influenced systematically by pricing instruments and regulations.

The Crowding-Out Effect

The main idea behind the *crowding-out effect* is the notion that rewards can have hidden costs that reduce intrinsic incentives to perform an action. In one study, asylum patients who were paid to make their bed or clean their room were less inclined to do these activities on their own without payment. External rewards can undermine intrinsic motivation in two ways: if individuals perceive a reward as controlling in the sense that they perceive their actions to be determined by others; or if a reward fails to acknowledge a person's intrinsic motivation and leads to impaired self-esteem. Paying a friend to come over for dinner, for example, would destroy the intrinsic motivation of friendship.

In addition, there may be *indirect* damaging effects from external intervention. A *motivational spill-over effect* may lead people to lose intrinsic motivation when they observe rewards or penalties being applied elsewhere. For example, effluent charges or tradable permits may be effective where they are applied but may reduce intrinsic motivations to control pollution in areas where no external incentives exist.

Empirical Evidence

In 1992, the Swiss government considered four different communities as possible sites for an underground repository to store low- to mid-level radioactive wastes. The author and three other researchers conducted a survey in one community to discover its civic interest in accommodating the facility. The survey took place one week prior to a referendum on a regional constitutional amendment to permit the construction of underground facilities. This survey, which consisted of in-person interviews, in effect asked respondents to say how they would vote on permitting a nuclear waste dump in their community. Slightly more than half the respondents (51 percent) agreed to the repository, while 45 percent opposed the siting (4 percent did not care where the facility was built).

Subsequently, these respondents were asked the same question but were given the additional information that the Swiss parliament would compensate all residents of the host community. The compensation was substantial: while the median income of respondents was CHF 5,250 per month, the amounts offered ranged from CHF 2,500 (N=117), to CHF 5,000 (N=102), to CHF 7,500 (N=86) per individual per year. With compensation, only 25 percent of the respondents agreed to the facility in their community—a significant reduction from the 51 percent majority who agreed to the facility without compensation. Increasing the compensation amounts by half led only a single respondent to accept the higher offer. Similar results were found in a survey among communities that were being considered for a second repository for highly radioactive wastes.

Other research supports the hypothesis that financial incentives do not necessarily increase acceptance of hazardous and nuclear waste repositories. In the United States, hefty compensation has failed to persuade communities to accept such facilities, and states that rely on compensation-based siting have been no more successful than those that do not.[3]

Econometric analysis of tax compliance suggests that the intrinsic motivation to pay taxes depends on citizen trust in the political system. In Switzerland, research that utilized various methods to assess tax fraud indicates that tax morale is high in those cantons where political participation (popular initiatives and referenda) is extensive and low where opportunities for political participation are few. Further, rates of tax evasion were not significantly affected by detection probability (as measured by audits per 1,000 tax payers) or by the penalty tax rate. Corresponding evidence exists for tax compliance in the United States.

The empirical results presented here are consistent with the crowding-out effect. While the relative price effect remains important, it is not the only relevant link between institutions and behavior. These results suggest that an effect working in exactly the opposite direction should also be taken into account. Crowding-out theory allows empirical testing of a connection between institutions, ethical values, and human behavior.

Notes

1. Ronald H. Coase, "Economics and Contingent Disciplines," *Journal of Law, Economics, and Organization* 4 (Spring 1978), 33–47.

2. The deterrence model was first proposed in Michael Allingham and Agnar Sandmo, "Income Tax Evasion: A Theoretical Analysis," *Journal of Public Economics* 1 (November 1972), 323–338. Surveys of empirical evidence showing the limitations of the deterrence model appear in *Taxpayer Compliance,* eds. Jeffrey Roth, John T. Scholz, and Ann Dryden Witte (Philadelphia: University of Pennsylvania Press, 1989); D. J. Pyle, "The Economics of Taxpayer Compliance," *Journal of Economic Surveys* 5 (1990), 163–198; and *Why People Pay Taxes: Tax Compliance and Enforcement,* ed. Joel Slemrod (Ann Arbor: University of Michigan Press, 1992).

3. See for example Michael B. Gerrard, *Whose Backyard, Whose Risk: Fear and Fairness in Toxic and Nuclear Waste Siting* (Cambridge, MA: MIT Press, 1994); Howard Kunreuther and Douglas Easterling, "Gaining Acceptance for Noxious Facilities with Economic Incentives," in *The Social Response to Environmental Risk: Policy Formulation in an Age of Uncertainty,* eds. Daniel W. Bromley and Kathleen Segerson (Boston: Kluwer, 1991); and Kent E. Portney, *Siting Waste Treatment Facilities: the NIMBY Syndrome* (New York: Auburn House, 1991).

Summary of

Return of the Citizen: A Survey of Recent Work on Citizenship Theory

by Will Kymlicka and Wayne Norman

[Published in *Ethics* 104 (January 1994): 352–381.]

Citizenship defines the status of an individual in society and is thus of fundamental importance for enhancing individual well-being. Postwar citizenship theorists defined citizenship primarily in terms of rights. In more recent years, two major critiques of this dominant view of citizenship have arisen and are summarized in this article. One set of critiques concerns the need for more active assertions of citizen responsibilities and virtues, such as economic self-reliance, political participation, and civility. The other set of critiques involves the need for the citizenship concept to adjust to the social and cultural pluralism of modern societies.

Rights, Responsibilities, and Virtues of Citizenship

T. H. Marshall was the most influential thinker of the postwar citizenship theorists. He advocated state guarantees of social rights, including rights to public education, health care, unemployment insurance, and pensions, to enable the disadvantaged to enter the mainstream of society and to exercise their political and civil rights. This conception of citizenship is often thought of as passive or private citizenship. It emphasizes passive entitlements without obligations.

The New Right argues that these rights have produced passivity and dependency among the poor, without improving their life chances; such passive citizenship overlooks ways in which people need to fulfill obligations, such as supporting themselves, to be accepted as full members of society. To ensure the full social and cultural integration of the poor, society must look "beyond entitlements" and focus on the responsibility to earn a living.

In response, critics of the New Right argue that the welfare-dependency model ignores other forces, such as global restructuring, that lead to unemployment. In addition, New Right reforms of the 1980s—tax cuts, deregulation, and freer trade—appear to have done little to promote responsible citizenship. Rather, unprecedented greed and economic recklessness have resulted, leaving many citizens disenfranchised and unable to participate in the new economy.

Many left and feminist critics of the New Right agree that citizenship entails not only rights but also responsibilities. However, they contend that rights must first be ensured before people can be expected to fulfill all their responsibilities. Many leftists hesitate to impose obligations such as work requirements, believing that lack of jobs, not lack of motivation, prevents people from working. Many feminists believe that the rhetoric of economic self-sufficiency often masks underlying assumptions that men should be breadwinners and that women should care for children and the home, thus increasing women's dependence on men and reinforcing barriers to women's full participation in society.

In addition to acknowledging the importance of both citizen rights and citizen responsibilities, critics of postwar citizenship concepts also recognize that numerous personal lifestyle decisions affect basic public policy concerns: families need to take care of their members, or the state will be overwhelmed; citizens must adopt responsible habits of resource use or public environmental goals cannot be met; and there can be no progress toward a more just society if citizens are prejudiced and intolerant. At the same time, civility and public spirit appear to be in decline. Thus, citizenship theorists recently have considered how to instill those virtues that enable citizens to carry out their responsibilities in both the private and public spheres. Recommendations have been developed from a variety of perspectives, including the following:

• *The New Right* appears to depend on the market to teach responsibility and related virtues necessary for citizenship. Critics say that market forces alone are inadequate for this task.

- *The left* emphasizes freedom and the devolution of power through participatory democracy, but it has been criticized for assuming that responsibility will be learned through political participation alone. Participating citizens may still be irresponsible—pushing for tax breaks and other benefits for themselves while scapegoating the poor or certain ethnic groups.

- *Civic republicans* view political life as of great intrinsic value for those who participate in it; they also view public life as superior to private life. However, most people in the modern world find their greatest pleasure in their private lives, not their public activities—a view shared by citizenship theorists of virtually all other perspectives. Civic republicans believe that this has resulted from the decline of public life, but it may have resulted more from the enrichment of private life.

- *Civil society theorists* emphasize the importance of civility and self-control but believe that these virtues are best learned through the voluntary organizations of a civil society. Such groups, by relying on personal approval and disapproval rather than legal punishments, enable a sense of personal responsibility to be internalized. Yet there is little empirical evidence to show that exposure to and participation in a civil society creates civic virtue. Neighborhood groups, families, and churches may foster prejudice, intolerance, domination, submission, and other attitudes presumably incompatible with civic virtues.

- *Liberal virtue theorists* say that the necessary civic virtues should be taught in schools. Students need to be taught not only to obey authority but also how to participate in public debate, as well as how to question authority and traditions, as necessary. But teaching children to question authority and their own background is controversial—groups that depend on unquestioning acceptance of their traditions do not want the open debate of a liberal education.

In postwar political theory, justice and democracy were the basic normative political concepts, with citizenship derivative of these two concepts. Many have now come to believe that citizenship is itself an independent normative concept, with urgent measures required to foster it. Yet the few suggested solutions in the current citizenship debate are usually not new and appear timid. It is not even clear that a genuine crisis exists. Crime may be increasing and voting rates down, but society also appears to be more committed to tolerance, democracy, and constitutionalism than in previous generations. Thus, it is not clear how urgent the need is to promote citizenship, nor how it could or should be done.

Citizenship, Identity, and Difference

The well-being of minority groups is related to unique needs and circumstances that are not readily accommodated in majority-rule democracies. Even though they possess common citizenship rights, many members of these groups still feel excluded. Defining citizenship only in terms of individual rights and responsibilities does not resolve this problem. *Cultural pluralists* argue that citizenship theory must consider those differences that make people feel excluded and that some citizen rights should depend on group membership. Such group-differentiated citizenship directly challenges the prevailing notion of citizens as individuals with equal rights. In fact, it is a return to historical notions that conferred rights based on religious, ethnic, or class identity.

One of the leading exponents of such differentiated citizenship, Iris Marion Young, gives two reasons why group differences need to be affirmed rather than denied to promote genuine equality. First, traditionally oppressed groups start out with a disadvantage in the political process and require institutional measures to ensure full recognition and representation. Second, groups that have been excluded by culture have distinctive needs, such as language or land rights.

Critics of cultural pluralism fear that granting special group rights threatens the ability of the citizenship concept to integrate society. Citizenship would no longer supply a common sense of purpose; a group rights system would encourage a "politics of grievance," rather than mutual striving to overcome differences.

Three different types of groups and group rights need to be identified to evaluate the appropriateness of any recommended measures. *Special representation rights* would apply to disadvantaged groups. The special rights would enable groups to overcome past oppression and would last only as long as the oppression exists. *Multicultural rights* would enable people to express their unique cultures and identities without restricting their opportunities in the dominant society. *Self-government rights* would apply to cultures, peoples, or nations with a valid claim to self-determination.

Both special representation rights and multicultural rights are demands to promote inclusion in the larger society. Self-government rights, on the other hand, appear unlikely to promote integration. Insofar as citizenship provides identity, then self-government rights may promote feelings of dual citizenship and conflicting loyalties.

Few multi-nation democracies (meaning countries containing minority groups with valid claims to self-government) today truly follow a "common citizenship" strategy; most make some allowances for minorities of one kind or another. What is the source of unity for such countries? Rawls claims that modern societies are united by a shared sense of justice.[1] But two countries may have similar conceptions of justice and still wish to remain separate countries. An important challenge for citizenship theory is thus to understand what gives citizens common identity in countries where some citizens belong as individuals while others gain their identity through special group membership.

Note

1. John Rawls, "Kantian Constructivism in Moral Theory," *Journal of Philosophy* 77 (1980), 515–572.

Summary of

Trust as a Commodity

by Partha Dasgupta

[Published in *Trust: Making and Breaking Cooperative Relations,*
ed. Diego Gambetta (New York and Oxford: Basil Blackwell, 1988), 49–72.]

Trust is usually taken for granted by economists, yet it is central to all transactions. It is essential for the smooth functioning of society and for ensuring individual well-being. This article discusses how people pay to acquire trust by enhancing their reputation. An approach is presented that treats reputation as a capital asset in which people are willing to invest. The article shows how both dishonest and honest people invest in their reputations and both may exhibit honest behavior, even though their underlying motivations are different.

Trust and Reputation

While there is more than one type of trust, this article focuses on the category of trust in which a person does not know the disposition of a potential partner. People must then rely on a person's reputation, which in turn is based on knowledge about the person, such as background, motivations, and available options.

A model based on selling cars is used to make several points about the nature of trust. It is assumed that salesmen are either honest or dishonest; each type is assumed to have different payoff structures for selling good cars or faulty cars. The payoff to the dishonest salesman for selling a good car is lower than for selling a faulty car. However, customers will not even enter the showroom if they believe the salesman to be dishonest.

This model shows that both honest and dishonest salesmen would be willing to invest money to increase their reputations so that customers would be willing to enter into a transaction with them. Salesmen would be willing to invest up to the level of payoff they would receive for selling a car to the customer (with differential returns for honest and dishonest salesmen selling good or bad cars).

Since people are willing to invest in their reputations and perceive a benefit for doing so, reputations are a type of capital asset. When people invest in enhancing their reputations they are only willing to spend up to the point that an enhanced reputation benefits themselves. Yet trust is a public good that creates externalities. Increased trust in the seller also benefits the buyer (who benefits from buying the car), but the buyer would not invest to increase trust in other people. This results in market failure, with chronic underinvestment in building trust.

While there may never be enough investment in trust, Albert Hirschman says that trust is like other moral resources "whose supply may well increase rather than decrease through use."[1] How does trust increase with use? First, sometimes people have a sense of personal obligation to not betray someone's trust. Second, people who repeatedly transact business with each other develop psychological bonds that will inhibit the tendency to cheat. Third, people form their opinions about someone's trustworthiness based on experiences with others in that group. Thus, if a consumer's first several encounters with people of a particular group show them to be honest, then the consumer infers that the chances are that others in that group are also honest and will continue dealing with them. If the first several encounters are with dishonest people, then the consumer infers that others in the group are also dishonest and may terminate any future transactions with them. The increase in trust through use is reflected in this case as the increase (or decrease) in the perceived proportion of honest people in the particular population.

The Acquisition of a Reputation for Honesty

When it is common knowledge that a seller has the payoff structure of a dishonest person and is in business for a limited time, no one would enter into a transaction with him. However, consider a situation in which a dishonest salesman is known to intend to stay in business forever and also discounts future benefits at a low rate. Because future customers would refuse to enter the showroom if the dealer ever sells a bad product, it is in the dealer's interest to sell only good cars. An equilibrium outcome is then possible in which the salesmen sells a good product and receives a lower short-term payoff. To sell one bad car would mean a greater return for that time period but would risk losing an infinite flow of future benefits. Customers may know that the salesman is dishonest, but they also know that he acts honestly because the punishment for being dishonest (loss of customers) is high.

This example deals with only one aspect of trust—customers trust a salesperson to sell them good merchandise, even when they know that his payoff structure is that of a dishonest person. However, it does not deal with another aspect of trust in which the merchant wishes to convince people that he really is an honest person, as opposed to simply acting honest as the only way to remain in business.

Assume another case, in which all customers could be made aware of a salesman's practices and that he is in business for a finite period of time. All salesmen would then sell reliable cars in the initial periods, independently of whether or not they are truly honest. Selling reliable cars at this stage does not indicate the underlying disposition, so the salesman's reputation does not change. During later periods, honest salesmen would continue selling good cars. On the other hand, dishonest salesmen would choose randomly between honest and dishonest strategies after the initial periods. At some point, a bad salesman would choose the strategy of selling a bad car, thus ending future transactions. Finally, a dishonest salesman would have no incentive to be honest in the last period of time if he is still in business. His reputation is only valuable to him if it helps ensure future customers.

This model illustrates how people invest in building a reputation for honesty. Within each time period, the dishonest salesman has a higher payoff if he chooses a dishonest strategy. However, he invests in his reputation by foregoing these short-term gains.

A serious weakness of this model is that there is no way to distinguish honest from dishonest salesmen (before the later periods). The role of commitments in distinguishing honest from dishonest salesmen could be explored. Another weakness of the model is that it does not include all credible strategies, thus excluding potential outcomes. In the real world, there are many sellers, customers, and transactions, making the model far more complex. Salesmen who behave dishonestly may be able to stay in business, because not everyone is aware of their reputation.

This problem of complexity can be simplified by assuming only a limited number of strategies. Sociobiologists argue that each person has only one strategy; no one has any real choice about which strategy they follow. Yet people in the real world are not nearly so restricted in the strategies they choose. Neither are strategies chosen completely randomly. Rather, outcomes can be predicted based on factors such as moral codes, which rule out certain behaviors. The role of moral codes in building analytical models of trust may thus be a valuable avenue for future research.

Note

1. Albert O. Hirschman, "Against Parsimony: Three Easy Ways of Complicating Some Categories of Economic Discourse," *American Economic Review Proceedings* 74(1984), 88–96.

Summary of

Amending the Economist's "Rational Egoist" Model to Include Moral Values and Norms

by Robert S. Goldfarb and William B. Griffith

[Published in *Social Norms and Economic Institutions,* eds. Kenneth J. Koford and Jeffrey B. Miller (Michigan: University of Michigan Press, 1991), 59–84.]

Incorporating moral values and social norms into economic analysis presents various challenges to the traditional model of microeconomic behavior. In this model, human actors are considered to be rational egoists; economists therefore analyze moral values in terms of preferences and view norms either as decision rules or as constraints on individual choice sets. This paper evaluates the various attempts to integrate moral values and economic preferences and discusses the efforts of economists to explain the development of moral values and social norms.

Norms as Decision Rules

Norms are generally considered to be shared rules of conduct that constrain the aggressive pursuit of self-interest. Economic models that fail to incorporate the influence of norms will lack predictive accuracy and will be unable to provide a satisfactory analysis of market function.

Researchers in a variety of disciplines, including economics, philosophy, political science and sociology, have treated norms as decision rules akin to those governing strategic interactions in repeated, two-person "prisoner's dilemma" situations. This treatment of norms has two important problems. First, in more realistic situations involving many participants, norms are more likely to break down since cheating is less likely to be detected and is thus more likely to occur. Second, this analysis makes the false assumption that all norms are chosen in order to achieve materially advantageous results. As suggested by James Coleman, there is a difference between those norms that are chosen and internally sanctioned and those that are externally sanctioned by others at the time of an action.[1]

Norms as Constraints

Internalized norms are similar to budget constraints in the sense that they restrict the range of available choices. The difference is that budget constraints are usually perceived to be externally imposed, while internalized norms are absorbed through behavioral conditioning. The interpretation of rules as constraints is consistent with the economist's notion of a rational agent as one who optimizes, given constraints.

This approach to norms gives rise to three major concerns. First, economic analysis traditionally holds that choice is subjectively determined by preferences and externally determined by constraints. However, norms have both subjective and external characteristics, so it is not clear that they fit into the constraint category. Second, if norm violations result in psychological discomfort, as is commonly presumed, then it seems to follow that it feels better to obey norms. If so, then it is hard to distinguish norms as constraints from norms as preferences. Third, the interpretation of norms as constraints is not useful in making predictions unless there is some explanation about the conditions under which norm constraints appear. Research in this area is ill-suited to economic analysis.

Moral Values as Preferences

The effort to incorporate values as preferences requires a more complex economic model of humans as rational egoists. Some economists have found it useful to analyze moral values as preferences, while challenging the assumption that individuals act to maximize the satisfaction of all preferences, which are understood as given, exogenously determined, and not subject to dispute. Albert Hirschman, for instance, forcefully points out that economists typically focus on unchanging, unreflective tastes, such as a taste for oranges, and ignore the endogeneity of value as preferences, that is, the fact that experience and rational persuasion can influence or change values.

Values as preferences may also necessitate a change in the standard form of utility functions. For instance, Amartya Sen has argued that values can be analyzed in terms of metapreferences, which are those preferences an individual rationally desires to be the case, for himself or for others.

The values as preferences approach also implies a modification of the egoistic aspect of the rational egoist economic model. Moral values such as honesty suggest that actors do not always act selfishly, since honesty implies restrictions on the pursuit of personal advantage. Also, the inclusion of the moral value altruism, which by definition is the opposite of egoism, suggests a substantial revision in the model.

Generation and Maintenance of Moral Values and Norms

The emergence of moral values and norms is important for both positive and normative economics. On positive grounds, a theory on the generation of values and norms will increase the accuracy of economic predictions. Many researchers have argued on normative grounds that such a theory will help explain and/or lead to "better" functioning markets.

In general, economists tend to borrow theories from biological evolution and cultural development to explain the emergence of values and norms. Two central issues arise in this tentative and developing literature: the optimality of the norm-generating process and the nature of cross-generational transmission mechanisms for values and norms.

Researchers disagree on whether a social optimum is promoted by evolution through norm generation. Some, notably Dennis Mueller, argue that norms represent a collective effort to maximize the probability of group survival. Thus, evolutionary pressures play a significant role in the adoption of mores and values. Others, notably James Coleman, argue that the process of norm generation need not be optimizing, especially where parents lack incentives to internalize norms in their children. This occurs when parents do not reap sufficient benefits from appropriately socializing children.

Any comprehensive theory of norm generation must take into account the wide variety of possible transmission mechanisms. Some norms are transmitted through behavioral conditioning, while others are chosen and sustained within a cultural context. Still others may be created via an invisible hand mechanism; although it is far from clear that these norms tend toward a social optimum, as is commonly argued in economic contexts. Alternatives to invisible hand accounts focus on group selection and the fact that individuals may adopt rules that favor a group only if they are advantageous to the individual.

Conclusion

It is far from clear that treating moral values and norms as either decision rules, constraints, or preferences fully and accurately represents their complexity and their relation to self-interest. None of these approaches alone can provide an appropriate analytical framework for understanding moral values and norms. Economists have yet to face head on the relationship between a self-interested life and a moral life and to what extent they are consistent with one another. Finally, moral rights are either part of the background social structure within which individuals pursue their selfish concerns or are themselves amenable to change by selfish individuals engaged in rent-seeking behavior. The attempt to fit rights into the rational egoist model obliges us to confront the issue of what conditions justify a particular structure of moral rights.

The attempt to incorporate moral values and norms into economics aims at a more realistic and comprehensive picture that incorporates both the limitations of human knowledge and concern for others, as well as the ways in which humans seek to compensate for these limitations. This effort will undoubtedly complicate the model of economic decision making and possibly make it less appropriate for prediction. But it may yield a more accurate picture, for example, by making clear that the benefits commonly attributed to well-functioning markets are at least in part due to well-functioning moral codes. Interdisciplinary cooperation, with a significant potential payoff both in economics and in moral philosophy, will be required to achieve this improved understanding of social coordination.

Note

1. James S. Coleman, "Norms as Social Capital," in *Economic Imperialism,* eds. Gerald Radnitsky and Peter Bernholz (New York: Paragon House, 1987).

PART VII

Economics and the Good, III: Society

Overview Essay
by David Kiron

Finding out what should be done is no less important than estimating what will happen. Hence, normative economics is no less important than positive economics. But the normative side of academic economics is nowadays heavily handicapped by its still being dominated by an outlook that is logically untenable . . . the utilitarian one.

—Serge-Christophe Kolm[1]

For over a century, mainstream economic theorists have adhered to the philosophy of utilitarianism. Today, however, utilitarianism finds little support among political philosophers. During the past three decades critics of utilitarianism have increasingly objected to its core idea that the goal of a moral society should be to maximize utility. A central focus for these critics' objections is that utilitarianism is ill equipped to address matters of justice. Although these problems have been well-known, they were not considered by many to be decisive until 1971, when political philosopher John Rawls proposed a modern alternative to utilitarian moral theory.

Rawls's work opened the way for other alternative conceptions of justice, which together challenged utilitarian hegemony within political philosophy. Collectively, these alternative theories of justice helped kindle an interdisciplinary debate on how to reconcile social goals such as equality, freedom, and rights with the economic goals of efficiency and wealth maximization.

This essay discusses the intersection of economic and social goals. It begins with a look at philosophical challenges to utilitarianism and moves to responses by selected economists. Next, the discussion focuses on the alleged trade-offs between efficiency and equity. It ends with a review of a significant recent debate within political philosophy—whether the design of social institutions should start from a clear definition of what makes for good living or from a conception of individuals that secures the rights of all.

239

The Rawlsian Challenge to Utilitarianism

The tendency of economists to neglect issues of distributive justice was challenged by the 1971 publication of Rawls's *A Theory of Justice*. For Rawls, a just society does not aim at a specific ideal of human good. Rather, its goal is to provide an institutional framework that embodies a set of basic freedoms and rights that allow individuals to pursue their diverse plans and objectives. To achieve this, he proposed that the design of social institutions should be based on two principles of justice. The first principle, commonly referred to as "equal liberty," states that each person is to have an equal right to the most extensive basic liberty compatible with a similar liberty for others. This principle is intended to guarantee that the rights of the few will never be sacrificed for the good of the many; as Rawls notes, this is a guarantee that is not secure within utilitarian doctrine.

Rawls's second principle of justice, called "fair equality of opportunity," states that social and economic inequalities are to be arranged so that they are both (a) reasonably expected to be to everyone's advantage and (b) attached to positions and offices open to all. This principle requires that distributions maximize the benefit of the least advantaged members of society—the so-called maximin rule. This view, however, assumes what was denied by the ordinalists: the possibility of interpersonal comparisons.

Rawls defended his two principles of justice with a thought experiment that has garnered almost as much attention as the principles themselves. He claims that these are the principles that would be chosen in a hypothetical situation by rational, self-interested, free, and equal representative agents who, though ignorant of their own particular circumstances in society, are fully informed about the framework in which the society operates. Because their decisions will have ramifications over their entire lives, these representatives will be very risk averse and will choose principles of justice that will ensure for them the highest possible quality of life even if they find themselves in the worst circumstances their society has to offer. This argument builds on a tradition of social contract thought, represented by John Locke and Immanuel Kant, and is therefore referred to as a contractualist theory.

Rawls presents his theory of "justice as fairness" as an alternative to utilitarianism, which he contends permits morally unacceptable trade-offs between liberty and welfare. His first principle of justice denies any moral justification for such trade-offs. He also argues that utilitarianism does not take seriously "the separateness of persons" when it treats the contribution of each person's well-being as only a means to achieving the social optimum.

Another of Rawls's objections to utilitarianism is that it implies that if an individual can give up all his/her preferences to have a different set that would create more utility, he/she ought to do so. Individuals are thus seen as "bare persons" without allegiance to their values and goals, except insofar as these promote their own utility. Consequently, utilitarianism slights an individual's moral personality.

In Rawls's theory, a moral personality consists of two moral powers—a capacity for a sense of justice and a rational power to organize and revise one's plan of life in a social context. In order to develop and exercise these moral powers, every individual requires a number of primary social goods, which include basic liberties, rights, income and wealth, access to office, and the social bases of self-respect. Interpersonal comparisons of well-being are based on an index of these goods. Thus, Rawls neatly ties the basis of interpersonal comparisons to a person's moral powers that embody the capacity for cooperation—an element that is central to his vision of a fair society.

Other Ideas of Justice

Nozick followed Rawls in defending the inviolability of a private sphere of rights but extended this sphere far beyond what is implied by Rawls's two principles of justice. Nozick defends the libertarian position that the state's role in achieving social aims should be minimal: it should act only as a nightwatchman, guarding the security of its citizenry and preserving individual rights. A free market becomes an important arena in which individuals can exercise their rights and exchange their possessions without unjust state interference.

Nozick's fundamental objection to utilitarianism also applies to Rawls's conception of justice. Both of these views, Nozick contends, require that judgments regarding the justice of a given distribution depend on comparisons with some ideal, such as equal utility. Nozick rejects such *end-state principles* as fictions, unsuitable for determining the justice of a given distribution. His alternative is a theory that consists entirely of procedural principles, which determine the justice of distributions according to whether property holdings have arisen through just acquisition and transfer.

In another approach, Sen argues that the informational base of welfare economics is too narrow, focusing only on information related to preferences. In his view, the appropriate informational base for normative economics should be not welfare or good, but rather capabilities—the ability of individuals to achieve valuable functionings, which for Sen are the essential constituents of human well-being. According to his Aristotelian-inspired vision of a just society, benevolent governments must take a stand on a particular conception of what makes for a good life and take steps to ensure that everyone has a reasonable chance to achieve it. One implication is that the capability sets of all persons should be made as equivalent as possible.

Taken together, these alternative conceptions of justice—Rawls's, Nozick's, and Sen's—present different ways of defining the goals of institutions in a just or good society. Their respective views of justice imply different goals, but they all share the belief that justice requires equality in one sense or another.

Although economists have been reluctant to accept the possibility of interpersonal comparisons of subjective utility, many economists have worked at incorporating Rawls's maximin rule within a utilitarian framework that makes the heroic assumption that everyone has the same utility function. Such an effort exemplifies a common economists' response to recent major philosophical writings on distributive justice: they have worked at producing theories of justice that preserve the utilitarian roots of welfare economics.[2]

We have summarized several articles by economists grappling with challenges from philosophy. In the following section we will see Hal Varian's response to, and use of, Nozick's ideas of procedural justice. Later we will see John Roemer responding to Ronald Dworkin's work on equalizing resources; and Marc Fleurbaey taking up the ideas of Richard Arneson and Gerald Cohen on equalizing opportunities for human advantage. The summarized article by John Broome presents an attempt to reconstruct utilitarian theory to accommodate matters of justice without reference to preference satisfaction.

Economists Reply to the Challenge:
The "Envy-Free" Approach

Since Rawls's major work, a tradition within economics has developed that defines just distributions in terms of a single criterion—the absence of envy. In a survey of this movement, one recent commentator states that

> [t]he criterion of envy-freeness, according to which no agent should prefer any of his neighbors' allocation to his own, has become a central part of the economic theory of distributive justice. It essentially corresponds to the need to express an ideal of equality in societies where preferences and endowments are heterogeneous.[3]

The economic literature on envy-free justice witnessed its major developments in the mid-1970s, as academics debated whether the push for social and economic equality was driven by envy or by some loftier purpose. After a short hiatus in interest, this subject has flourished again in the 1990s.

Varian's early work, summarized here, was seminal in analyzing fair allocations in models of complex economic environments. Previously, it had been mathematically demonstrated that envy-free allocations were possible in models of exchange economies that excluded production factors; however, once production was brought into the model, there was no guarantee that a fair allocation would exist.[4] This problem arises because people with less talent might wish they had the larger resource bundles of goods that can be achieved by those with more talent. Varian's solution to the production problem was to argue that everyone would be satisfied with his or her own resource bundle (i.e., the distribution would be envy-free) if the definition of resource bundles included not only the goods and services contained in a given bundle but also the work effort required to attain those goods and services. An individual with lesser endowments would then prefer the resource bundle of the more talented only if he or she would be willing to make the efforts and sacrifices necessary to achieve it. Thus, it is impossible to model a competitive equilibrium in which no person prefers the resource bundle of another.

Varian's article was also significant in demonstrating that a libertarian theory of justice, such as Nozick's, fails to adequately consider the justice of initial distributions. He attempts to remedy this lacuna in his own theory by assuming an initial distribution of consumption goods to all individuals that is equal in the sense that it will not give rise to envy (as defined herein).

A Deeper Look at Equality

The envy-free approach to distributive justice has led many to question whether it accurately captures the nature of egalitarianism. Clearly, envy plays a role in certain egalitarian claims. A child who does not receive his/her fair share of cake may be envious of the larger shares of his/her siblings. However, there are many types of egalitarian claims, not all of which are concerned with envy.

Michael Walzer's famous book, *Spheres of Justice*, partially summarized here, makes the case that most egalitarian claims arise not from envy but from the harms that follow from inequalities. It is not that the poor desire equality because they desire the wealth of the rich (although they may); rather it is because the rich can grind the faces of the poor. Also, he disputes the very assumption with which the envy-free theorists begin their project—that goods simply appear in the hands of hypothetical agents in mathematically formalized models. Instead, justice requires an appreciation of the cultural meanings of goods and the historical conditions in which they develop. Consequently, the ideal of equality is better understood as a struggle for being free from the domination of those who have misappropriated the meanings of goods. In Walzer's articulate vision of an egalitarian society, more importance is placed on diminishing the effects of inequalities and less on eliminating the inequalities themselves.

The question—equality of what?—may be variously answered: e.g., equal welfare, freedoms, social primary goods, resources, or capabilities.[5] As we have seen, Rawls wants to minimize inequalities among individuals' holdings of primary goods, the resources that every rational agent needs to pursue his or her life aims. In situations where inequalities must obtain, he defends a difference principle, which requires that inequalities benefit the least advantaged. Sen argues for equalizing individuals' capability sets. Nozick seeks equal respect for property rights. Each of these thinkers uses "equality" in different ways, and for different purposes—a point adeptly made by Robert Sugden in the summarized review of Amartya Sen's book *Inequality Reexamined.*

Along lines comparable to Rawls, philosopher Ronald Dworkin developed arguments opposing the idea, implicit in welfare economics and the envy-free literature, that preferences, utility, and welfare are the appropriate terms in which to define egalitarian distributions. Although welfare economics often sidesteps issues of equality, its assumptions can be used to construct a distributive criterion aimed as equalizing differences among the utilities achieved by different individuals. However, Dworkin argues that the appropriate target of egalitarian concerns is resources, not welfare.

Prominent among Dworkin's criticisms of the equal welfare school (including, of course, the utilitarian) is the objection that this approach fails to hold people responsible for either offensive or expensive tastes. That is, if one of the objectives of a just society is to ensure that its citizens obtain equal welfare, then both misanthropes (who derive happiness from others' misery) and people who require the finest foods to be happy must receive more goods and services than others who have more average tastes. Dworkin argues that these examples demonstrate that the concept of equal welfare fails to acknowledge the importance of personal responsibility in developing one's tastes and pursuing one's goals. Moreover, he takes these objections to imply that justice need not be responsive to individual tastes and preferences.

Dworkin's own view is that just social institutions should be willing to compensate individuals only for the effects of circumstances over which they have no control, such as being born with poor health or few talents, or suffering the effects of a natural disaster. This implies that people should be compensated for inequalities among natural endowments over which they have no responsibility, but that people should be held responsible for their ambitions. Roemer (see summary) agrees with Dworkin that a theory of distributive justice should focus on responsibility but argues that Dworkin's equal resource view cannot escape the need to address welfare, since a person's innate characteristics include the ability to convert resources into utility. In fact, Roemer questions any approach that distinguishes handicaps from tastes, since preferences arise from many factors over which individuals have little control, such as genetic endowments and education.

The idea that welfare and responsibility are both relevant to issues of distributive justice is defended by proponents of the equal opportunity school, which seeks to equalize *individuals' opportunities for welfare.*[6] Proponents agree with Dworkin that an adequate conception of justice needs to distinguish talents from ambitions, but they also maintain that a concern with responsibility is compatible with a concern with preferences and welfare.

Fleurbaey, in a summarized article, objects to the equal opportunity principle on the grounds that it is simply impracticable to equalize the opportunity sets of all individuals over the course of their lives, given that individuals change their preferences, suffer bad luck, make poor judgments, and may or may not have free will. His alternative egalitarian theory avoids the need to distinguish talents from ambitions—a problem that has plagued both the equal opportunity school and Dworkin's equal resource theory. Instead, Fleurbaey argues that social institutions should equalize those outcomes for which they are responsible, a view that turns on the more feasible distinction between private and social realms. This is one of the few theories of justice sponsored by an economist that avoids the language of preferences and utilitarian ideals.

A final approach is to reformulate utilitarianism in terms that avoid the language of preferences. In the summary of selections from *Weighing Goods*, Broome argues for a teleological theory of the good that emphasizes the structure rather than the content of good. He defines the structure of good in terms of a "betterness relation" (see summary) that allows him to avoid analyzing the concept of utility in terms of preferences or anything else. A normative economics built on Broome's utilitarianism need not define Pareto optimality on the basis of preferences and avoids problems relating to Sen's *Impossibility of a Paretian Liberal* argument (discussed in Part III).

In the past, utilitarians gave lukewarm support for redistributive transfers. They could justify transfers from the wealthy to the poor on the grounds that the poor will benefit more than the wealthy from the same incremental benefit; however, as the 19th-century economist Frances Edgeworth pointed out, this is true only if the wealthy and the poor have similar benefit functions. In his view, as a utilitarian and an aristocrat, they did not: the wealthy could do more with more. Broome has offered a more convincing approach to utilitarian equality; in his view, equality is desirable in itself, as part of the general or social good. It follows that inequality can be a harm to a person at any income level whether or not the rich can do more with more.

What Is the Relationship between Equity and Efficiency?

As long ago as the 18th century, economists considered the social goal of equality (broadly understood) to be directly opposed to the economic goal of efficient resource allocation. The question of how to balance efficiency goals with the distributive goal of equality is often interpreted as a question of sacrifice: should well-being levels be traded for justice? And whose well-being? Would an individual living in a just society be better off (if other things could remain the same) than the same person living in an unjust society? If so, it is not clear whether this is because justice is a component of, or in a more fundamental way a condition of, one's well-being or quality of life.

A common belief implied or stated in the teaching and practice of economics is that where equity and efficiency are concerned, we face a zero-sum game in which it is necessary to settle for less of one to get more of the other. A justification for this view is the assumption that redistributive transfers (aimed at equalizing material resources) eliminate the differential rewards necessary to motivate people to be productive. However, many recent thinkers have come to question not only this motivation argument but also the idea that these goals are opposed to one another.

A basic philosophical issue arises when we consider the possibility of making a trade-off between equality and efficiency.[7] Such a trade-off makes sense if we believe these to be values or goals of similar standing: i.e., if both are regarded as final goals, or else if both are seen as intermediate. However, recent writing in philosophy and among philosophically-inclined economists has emphasized that, while equality may be regarded as a means to other ends, it is often also held as an end in itself. By contrast, while economic theory is often taught and promulgated as though efficiency were a final goal, few commentators overtly defend such a position. If equity is a final goal and efficiency is only a means to other, final ends, it should be possible to find ways to avoid a trade-off between them.

Kenneth Arrow has been a strong advocate of the view that modern equilibrium theory implicitly supports the compatibility of equity and efficiency. In a summary included here, Arrow contends that the motivation argument relies on the mistaken assumption that a person is always entitled to the value of his marginal product. In fact, an individual's marginal product depends on substitute or complementary factors beyond his or her control. Justice does not require assigning the full value of their product to individuals who are not responsible for the value of these factors.

Another practical observation is that, in many sectors of the economy and in many types of firms, changes in productivity levels and in wages are not closely related to each other. Therefore, appropriate redistribution strategies need not reduce productivity levels. Arrow also defends the idea that transfers from the wealthy toward investment in social and human capital formation among the poor will raise society's productivity levels in the long run, if not in the short run. Far from being a trade-off, efficiency and equality are interdependent and mutually reinforcing.

Martha Nussbaum also argues (in an article summarized here) that issues of justice and well-being go hand in hand. She defends a capabilities-based conception of human good in which the political planner must satisfy Aristotle's primary condition for a just polity—that no one lacks for sustenance. This requirement of political justice, also found among institutional theories of the welfare state (see Part VIII), implies a wide safety net for the disadvantaged and places extra emphasis on the importance of education, for it is here that the powers of mind are cultivated. Beyond these basics, it is crucial to Nussbaum's view (though not to Sen's) that the political system ought to promote everyone's capability to live an experientially rich human life.

The Good Life and Economic Theory

It was assumed, by many of the great economists from Adam Smith and his precursors up through the early part of the 20th century, that an understanding of economic systems, and a measure of their success, must be rooted in moral and political philosophy. As markets play an ever larger part in everyday life, this assumption seems more, not less, relevant today; but utilitarianism and positivism—the two major philosophical influences on economics—are withering or have already withered on their original philosophical vines. This essay and the summaries it introduces represent the leading modern alternatives. Among these we have stressed Rawls's theory of "justice as fairness" and Sen and Nussbaum's "capability ethic" as of particular relevance for the field of economics.

Economists might have come closer by now to understanding the relationship between the goals of efficiency and justice if philosophers could offer a widely accepted answer to the Socratic question: What makes for a good life? Modern answers may be divided along the lines of a debate that is sometimes represented by the technical-sounding question: Does the right have priority over the good?

On one side of this debate are those such as Nussbaum and Sen who, with Aristotle, believe that, from the point of view of political institutions, it is necessary to define what it means to have a good life before one attempts to figure out which political arrangements best serve this goal. On the other side are those, such as Rawls and Scanlon, who believe that it is necessary for a political planner to accept that citizens may have life goals that conflict with one another; this puts the priority on establishing social institutions that preserve the rights and liberties of individuals even while they pursue their different aims.

Much of the recent debate about the respective virtues of the capability ethic and social contract theory concern just this issue: Can the good life be defined independently of the concepts of rights and liberties? For normative economic theory, this debate is important. The contractualist approach has advantages when applied to the design of political, social, and economic institutions within constitutional democracies, but it has limits in other parts of the global arena. On the other hand, the capability approach has advantages when applied to issues of international economic justice.

The challenge for philosophy and economics is to work together to promote, simultaneously, the goals of freedom, justice, security, and prosperity. The question is still open whether there is a unified social philosophy that will usefully replace utilitarianism in guiding economic theory and policy for all parts of the world; or whether for a variety of circumstances economics requires a variety of philosophical underpinnings.

Notes

1. Serge-Christophe Kolm, *European Economic Review* 38 (1994), 721–730; quote is from 721.

2. The major exception to this trend is the reaction of economists to Michael Walzer's theory of justice, discussed below and represented in a summary. Communitarian economists have been especially responsive to Walzer's work.

3. Christian Arnsperber, "Envy-Freeness and Distributive Justice," *Journal of Economic Surveys* 8 (1994), 155–186; quotation is from 155. This article is also a good resource for anyone interested in an overview of the major issues in this field.

4. This literature defines a "fair allocation" as one that is both equitable (envy-free) and Pareto efficient.

5. The philosophical literature on equality, and on the appropriate target of egalitarian concerns, is vast and wide-ranging. For an illuminating discussion of problems that crop up in comparing and contrasting these theories see, Norman Daniels, "Equality of What: Welfare, Resources, or Capabilities?" *Philosophy and Phenomenological Research* 1 (1990); Fall Supplement.

6. Richard Arneson, "Equality and Equal Opportunity for Welfare," *Philosophical Studies* 56 (1989), 77–93. Gerald Cohen, "On the Currency of Egalitarian Justice," *Ethics* 99 (1989), 906–944. There are subtle differences between their respective views. Cohen believes that the equal opportunity principle applies to a slightly broader concept than welfare, namely, human advantage. Strictly speaking, neither view seeks to equalize opportunity sets; rather the aim is to make them equivalent.

7. Arthur Okun popularized this notion in his book *Equality and Efficiency: The Big Trade-off* (Washington, DC: Brookings Institute, 1975). For two similar opposing views, see Julian Le Grand, *Equity and Choice: An Essay in Economics and Applied Philosophy* (New York: HarperCollins, 1991). Also, Zamagni, "Efficiency, Justice, Freedom: A Perspective from Modern Economic Theory," *Giornale Degli Economisti e Annali di Economica*, 52 (1993), 455–477.

Summary of

Welfare, Resources, and Capabilities: A Review of *Inequality Reexamined* by Amartya Sen

by Robert Sugden

[Published in *Journal of Economic Literature* 31 (December 1993), 1947–1962.]

For the past three decades, Amartya Sen has been a leading critic of welfarism, the orthodox theory of normative economics. In a recent book, *Inequality Reexamined*, Sen continues his probing attack on the foundations of welfarism, arguing that its "informational base," which consists entirely of information about preferences, is too weak to support an acceptable or even coherent account of the social good. Instead, he argues that normative economics should be grounded on an enriched informational base that describes the capability of individuals to achieve valuable functionings. This review selectively analyses Sen's alternative normative theory and some of its implications for justice and equality.

Critics of welfarism fall into two main categories. Some believe that the economist's role in shaping government policy has changed over the past few decades as doubts about the ability of government to plan for the social good have grown. Government is seen as an organization with limited powers, whose behavior economists ought to explain, rather than treat as an autonomous power for good. This approach is reinforced by the legacy of political philosophy in the 1970s, contractualist and libertarian thought, which turns away from assessing social good or individual good, and turns toward evaluating the rules that govern social choice and maintaining a framework of rules within which individuals are left free to pursue their own ends. Others, most prominently Sen, have resisted this approach. Sen believes that the government should promote the overall good of society and that economists should produce an operational definition of that good and identify policies that will best promote it.

Sen develops the second strategy in an alternative normative theory that focuses on capabilities. "One is to start from a conception of what makes a good life for a human being, and to build up from this to a theory of the social good: this is the enterprise to which Sen's work belongs." [1961] He defines well-being as the achievement of valuable functionings, consisting of various "beings" and "doings." Some functionings are intrinsically valuable. These include the utilitarian values of "being happy," the liberal values of "acting freely," the Rawlsian value of "having self-respect," as well as more concrete functionings such as being well-nourished. Cultures may vary with respect to what is necessary to achieve certain functionings. For instance, Sen discusses Adam Smith's 18th-century observation that in Scotland, but not in England, women of the lowest classes could appear in public without shoes or shame. For Sen, appearing in public without shame is an intrinsically valuable function.

A person's state of being is represented by a vector of functionings. Individuals choose from a set of feasible functioning vectors. This *capability set* represents a person's opportunity to achieve well-being and contains information about a person's positive freedom to do or be certain things. A person's well-being consists of the achieved functionings given the capability set. Sen's aim is to show that information related to capability sets is the appropriate "informational base" for normative economics. Although Sen's subtle analysis adroitly covers complex material, there remain problems of clarification.

For instance, it is not clear whether capabilities or functionings have priority in his scheme. At one level of analysis, well-being is defined exclusively in the dimension of functionings, yet freedom matters to well-being, but not because it is a property of functionings. A different problem relates to the issue of weight assignments to different vectors of functionings. Everyone may agree that "being able to appear in public without shame," "being happy," and "being well-nourished" matter to well-being. The question remains: how are these different functionings to be ranked or valued? Sen attempts to disarm this type of criticism by arguing that a fully developed theory of the good life need only provide a partial ordering of functionings. It may even be impossible to rank some functionings. Rankings must be established through agreements based on reasoned deliberation.

Finally, Sen's discussion concerning how to value capability sets is incomplete. Sen wants to rely on information other than individual preferences and choices. However, he offers few alternatives and fails to endorse any method for evaluating capability sets. Without some guidance on this point, it is difficult to see how his view can be to provide an alternative to real income measures that include an operational metric for weighting commodities (i.e., the metric of exchange value).

Justice and Capability: Sen and Rawls

Sen proposes a theory of justice that provides an alternative to both utilitarianism and Rawls's [1971] theory of justice as fairness. Sen believes that the appropriate evaluative domain in which to consider issues of justice should address capabilities rather than utility or resources. He argues that the best utilitarian accounts, those based on desire-fulfillment rather than experienced pleasure, fail because they neglect the effects of physical conditions on shaping desire. For instance, individuals who suffer extreme deprivation may adapt to their situations and want only what they have a reasonable opportunity to achieve. Sen claims that from the point of view of justice, such deprived individuals are worse off because they have an impoverished capability set. Utilitarianism misses this important point because it relies entirely on information regarding the fulfillment of desire; as indicated earlier, fulfilled desires do not indicate well-being.

Sen considers Rawls's view to be the most credible alternative to his own but rejects it in part because the capabilities approach is more direct in assessing what matters to human well-being. Rawls's theory of justice relies on the concept of primary goods, which are those resources (such as income, education, and self-respect) that every rational agent normally needs to achieve his or her ends. According to Rawls, issues of justice concern fair distributions of primary goods. Unequal distributions of these resources are permissible only if they work in favor of the least advantaged, and only if in the absence of these inequalities the least advantaged would be even worse off.

Sen objects that at a fundamental level matters of justice concern valuable functionings and not, as Rawls claims, a command over resources. Resources are only a means to valued functionings. To show this, Sen relies on examples in which people vary in their ability to convert resources into functionings. For instance, someone confined to a wheelchair needs more resources than an able-bodied person to participate in community life. This type of example is supposed to show that Rawls's resource approach concentrates too much on the means to freedom and not enough on what is intrinsically valuable: the extent of achieved freedom.

In his criticism of Rawls, Sen underestimates the differences between their respective approaches to justice and equality. According to Sen, justice requires a theory of individual good that answers the Aristotelian question: What is a good life? In his vision of a just society there must be fair distributions of capabilities. Thus, the concept of well-being is central to Sen's account. In contrast, the idea of cooperation is central to Rawls's political conception of justice. Rawls argues that in a democratic society composed of free and equal persons pursuing diverse ends, justice is "a system of fair rules within which individuals with different ends can cooperate to their mutual advantage." [1957] In this scheme, just or fair distributions center on the benefits and burdens of social cooperation. Further argument is necessary to show that matters of justice must rest, as assumed by Sen, on issues of well-being.

Thus, it is not surprising that Rawls's theory fails to measure up to the standards set by Sen's capability approach, especially since Sen interprets Rawls within the context of his own program to define the social good—a goal that is not shared by Rawls.

Summary of

Distributive Justice, Welfare Economics, and the Theory of Fairness

by Hal R. Varian

[Published in *Philosophy and Public Affairs* 4 (1974–1975), 223–247.]

Theories of justice emphasize either end-state or procedural principles. End-state principles, as found in John Rawls's theory of "justice as fairness" and also in welfare economics, evaluate current distributions in light of future ideals. Procedural theories assess current distributions according to the justice of past distributions and past transfers. In the year prior to the publication of his famous treatise on libertarian political philosophy, *Anarchy, State and Utopia*, Robert Nozick wrote an insightful piece defending a distributive theory of justice based on procedural principles.[1] End-state theories, Nozick argued, ignore historical and procedural aspects of justice. This article defends welfare economics from Nozick's criticisms and offers a theory of fairness that pays more attention to the matter of equity in initial allocations.

Nozick's Entitlement Theory

According to Nozick, a valid theory of justice must include principles of acquisition, transfer, and rectification. Distributions can only be just if they arise from other just distributions obtained through legitimate transfer. Past injustices must be redressed. The primary restriction on these principles is that they cannot violate agents' rights. This is a procedural theory in the sense that whether a given distribution is just will depend entirely on the justice of the process that leads to it. By contrast, proponents of end-state principles, such as Rawls, contend that we must first decide what a perfectly just state is and then try to move toward it.

Nozick's theory of acquisition implies that nearly any appropriation is legitimate so long as it does not make others worse off by preventing them from freely using their own goods. The concept of private property plays an important role here. Once property is appropriately acquired, it becomes permanent and inheritable subject to the constraints of legitimate transfer within a free market economy. Nozick defends the idea of private property by invoking the market mechanism.

Nozick explains that some of the critical problems with a theory of distributive justice that focuses on a fixed social product (a current time-slice) arise from considerations of whether people have done things in the past to deserve the shares they have today. He goes on to argue that welfare economics ignores the interaction between distribution and production.

In fact, welfare economics does deal explicitly with this issue. To see that this is so, let us consider the intersection of two sets: the set of all possible allocations of goods (including all possible redistributions of initial endowments) and the set of all Pareto-optimal allocations. This intersection will be extremely large. It does not take us very far toward answering the basic problem of welfare economics: At which feasible allocation should the economy operate?

Here we can introduce the basic idea of welfare economics, which is "to assume that there is a welfare function which evaluates the 'goodness' of the social states as a function of the utility evaluations of those states by the agents in the society." [139] Because of the way welfare functions are defined, the choice of the best Pareto-efficient point is assured by the selection of a feasible allocation of maximum welfare.

The use of the market mechanism is an alternative approach to that which starts from the definition of a social welfare function. The weakness of the market approach is that it is also purely procedural and does not deal with the fact that any given allocation to which it gives rise must reflect the endowments with which the present agents began. "We are interested in justice precisely because we live in an unjust world; injustices have occurred in the past and are occurring now. The question is what should we do about them." [137] Nozick's analysis seems to depend on the market mechanism—whose outcomes are strongly determined by the initial allocation—to "solve" the distribution problem. This is unreasonable.

An alternative is a concept of "people's capitalism," which uses the market mechanism as a means of allocating resources, but does not rely on permanent, private ownership of property. "It is perfectly possible to use prices for allocation, while basing distribution on factors other than the blind-chance assignment of initial endowments."[147]

> The interesting result of welfare economics is that we can relate an end-state principle of justice—maximum 'social welfare'—to an allocative procedure—the market mechanism. Nozick's own theory is most deficient in failing to provide such a relationship: the first part—how agents come to acquire legitimate holdings—seems to require some sort of end-state principle and is crucial in determining the entire outcome.
>
> Unfortunately, welfare economics is itself too arbitrary in that it leaves unanalyzed the basic normative question of the choice of the social welfare function. [147–148]

The Theory of Fairness

A fair allocation, as defined here, would be both equitable and efficient. To be equitable, the allocation must be one in which every agent is content with his own bundle of goods, i.e., would not prefer the bundle held by any other agent. Such an outcome could, in theory, be achieved using the price system and allowing agents to trade to a market equilibrium, as long as all agents start out with identical endowments. However, even this does not address another justice-related question: How to match each individual's final allocation with his/her contribution to the social product.

We can extend this concept of equity to include rewards to production if we describe each individual's position in terms of labor contribution as well as of consumption. A fair distribution would exist if, after all desired trades had been made, we found that no agent preferred the consumption-labor bundle held by any other agent. Unfortunately, it would often prove impossible to arrive at such an equilibrium, because agents' abilities may not coincide with their tastes, and because abilities cannot be transferred.

This difficulty can be overcome if we ask agent x, when evaluating each of the other agents' bundles, to consider y's outcome in light of how much time and effort x would have had to put in to produce y's output. In effect, "each agent compares his consumption-output bundle to the consumption-output bundle of each other agent." [151]

"If an allocation is such that each agent prefers his consumption-output bundle to that of every other agent, I will say that allocation is wealth-equitable; if the allocation also happens to be efficient, I will say that the allocation is wealth-fair."[151] The feasibility of a wealth-fair allocation can be proven in a similar manner to the earlier fair equilibrium allocation, with similar provisos: that the initial distribution must be an equal allocation of all consumption goods, and the agents buy and sell consumption goods—and also, in this case, their labor—at market rates. (Other solutions, such as insurance, will have to be found for problems that arise with agents so handicapped that they are unable to produce another's output by any substitution of their own labor, no matter how much effort they offer.)

"People's capitalism" thus depends on a combination of government interventions for ensuring an equal distribution of material resources, along with market procedures for allocating material resources, including the products of each person's labor. The major requirement for a nonmarket intervention is that some entity (presumably the state) has the power to prevent agents from making nonmarket transfers of property—e.g., gifts and bequests—because those would upset the pattern of wealth-fair allocation. It specifies the principles of acquisition, transfer, and rectification as follows:

(1) At some stated point (birth, maturity?) each agent is endowed by the state with a share of society's material resources identical to the shares received

by all other agents at the same points in their lives. All property reverts to the state when its owner dies.

(2) Agents can transfer ownership of goods and services only through the market mechanism; there are no "private" or nonmarket transfers.

(3) If some agent finds that he prefers another agent's consumption-output bundle to his own, this is counter to the expected outcome. A complaint along these lines would be taken seriously by the state, which would consider rectification measures.

One other alternative has been suggested by Pazner and Schmeidler, who propose that each agent should start not only with an equal share of all goods but also with an equal claim on the labor of each and every agent in the economy. This "income-fair" scheme totally corrects for differences due to ability—in contrast to the wealth-fair allocation that equally allocates all goods but allows each person complete control over his/her own time and the benefits accruing from the use thereof.

The wealth-fair allocation seems preferable to the income-fair scheme, mainly because it is easy to organize. This approach to distributive justice is compatible with the form of Nozick's entitlement theory but goes farther in determining the initial distribution faced by each agent. It does, however, leave open a number of questions:

> What are we going to do about acts of God, children, mistakes, small gifts, lies, malicious envy, and so on? If these questions can be answered in a satisfactory way, the idea of fairness may provide a very attractive theory of justice that combines the considerations of both procedural justice and distributive justice. [153]

Note

1. Robert Nozick, "Distributive Justice," *Philosophy & Public Affairs* 3(Fall 1973), 45–126.

Summary of

Complex Equality

by Michael Walzer

[Published in *Spheres of Justice* (New York: Basic Books, 1983), 3–30.]

Theories of justice can be distinguished on the basis of whether they imply that distributive principles are universal or pluralistic in nature. The traditional approach to justice is to look for a single set of universal principles that is applicable across circumstances, i.e., to a wide range of goods. An alternative approach is to look for principles as they are practiced in a given culture or society and draw a connection between the social meanings and appropriate distributions of goods. This essay adopts the alternative perspective and argues that every society creates many kinds of social goods, each of which has its own sphere of distributive principles, procedures, and agents.

Contemporary industrial societies create a range of social goods that includes political membership, security and welfare, money and commodities, hard work, free time, education, kinship and love, divine grace, recognition, and political power. Egalitarian concerns focus on maintaining autonomy among the spheres and preventing individuals who get ahead in one sphere from dominating others. Domination is the root problem for egalitarians. "It is not the fact that there are rich and poor that generates egalitarian politics but the fact that the rich 'grind the faces of the poor.'" [xiii] Inequalities can be tolerated within spheres so long as the spheres are relatively autonomous, and a person who gets ahead in one sphere is unable to convert this advantage in another. Complex equality is achieved when no one is able to convert advantages from one sphere into another. In such a society, one is free from domination.

One consequence of this approach to justice is that theorists must remain closer to the beliefs and understandings of ordinary people than is usually the case with abstract theories of justice. Social criticism is possible, but critiques must highlight the divergence between the ethical code espoused by society and what actually transpires.

A Theory of Goods

Traditional approaches to justice assume that goods simply appear in the hands of distributive agents, devoid of meaning and history, and are then distributed according to universal principles. However, every political community attaches its own social meanings to goods before distributing them. In a sense, the social meanings of goods determine their system of distribution. Once the social meaning of a particular good is known, the specific distributive principles associated with this good are also known. Thus, the role of a distributive theory is to interpret the social meanings of goods. This requires a theory of goods that recognizes six principles:

- Distributive justice is only concerned with social goods, the meanings of which are shaped by society.
- Personal identity is bound up in goods.
- Across cultures and times, there is no single set of primary or basic goods.
- Distribution is determined by the social meanings of goods.
- Social meanings are historical in character.

- Every set of social goods constitutes a distributive sphere within which only certain criteria and arrangements are appropriate.

Dominance and Monopoly

Most societies organize their distributive arrangements according to a social version of the gold standard: one set of goods is dominant and determines the value of other goods. In capitalist systems, capital is the dominant good; it can be readily converted into other goods such as prestige or power. A good is dominant if the individuals who have it, because they have it, can command other goods, with other social meanings, in other spheres. Monopolistic control of dominant goods permits exploitation of their dominance. Ruling classes monopolize dominant goods.

Simple Equality

Men and women who claim that a given monopoly is unjust challenge the monopoly, but not the dominance of that social good. If the good is wealth, the claimants seek a simple kind of equality: let wealth be shared. Societies that focus on the problems that follow from monopoly, rather than dominance, will forever substitute one monopoly for another. For instance, if everyone is given the same amount of wealth in a free market society, inequalities will follow almost immediately. Market winners and the talented will have to be constrained by state forces, but then state power will become the object of monopolistic concerns. State power might be shared widely, but then diffused state power will be unable to cope with the emergent monopolistic claims of social groups such as technocrats and meritocrats.

Tyranny and Complex Equality

An alternative is to focus on the claim that dominance is unjust, which implies that limits should be placed on the convertibility of social goods. A complex egalitarian society prevents the conversion of goods such as beauty into respect, strength into love, power into belief. Implicit are two assumptions. First, goods with different social meanings should have relatively autonomous spheres of distribution. Second, disregard of these principles is tyranny. A ruler should not be able to command opinion because of the power he wields. Complex equality is the opposite of tyranny.

> In formal terms, complex equality means that no citizens standing in one sphere or with regard to one social good can be undercut by his standing in some other sphere, with regard to some other good. Thus, citizen x may be chosen over citizen y for political office, and then the two of them will be unequal in the sphere of politics. But they will not be unequal generally so long

as x's office gives him no advantages over y in any other sphere—superior medical care, access to better schools for his children, entrepreneurial opportunities, and so on. [19]

For goods, this amounts to the open-ended distributive principle: "No social good x should be distributed to men and women who possess some other good y merely because they possess y and without regard to the meaning of x." [20] Outcomes will not be determined by this principle, but it focuses attention on the pluralistic nature of social goods.

Three Distributive Principles

Three criteria or principles that are commonly invoked to guide distributions— free exchange, desert, and need—exemplify the open-ended principle for some, but not all goods. Each has been defended, incorrectly, as a distributive principle that ranges over all goods. For instance, free-exchange is appropriate for market goods, less so for goods such as welfare or honor and respect. Desert is appropriate for education, less so for goods such as kinship and love. Need is appropriate for medical care, less so for political power.

Setting of the Argument

Issues of justice arise chiefly in bounded political communities. This is true for two reasons: (1) unless there is a determinate membership, there are no shared meanings to shape distributions; and (2) unless the society is politically organized, a theory of justice cannot be applied since there is no state institution to maintain the boundaries between the spheres of distribution. It is possible to imagine societies, such as the old caste systems in India, in which the meanings of goods are so intertwined that their intertwined differentiation is impossible. In these societies complex equality cannot arise.

Summary of

Equality of Talent

by John E. Roemer

[Published in *Economics and Philosophy* 1 (1985), 151–187.]

The debate over what an egalitarian philosophy should seek to equalize—welfare or resources—was sharpened by a famous pair of articles published in 1981 by Ronald Dworkin. Dworkin's analysis provoked interest among economists, in part because he used a hypothetical insurance market to determine levels of compensation. This paper examines Dworkin's position, which captures the resourcist intuition that it is right to compensate individuals who, through no fault of their own, enter society with poor resource endowments. This position becomes more complicated when inalienable traits, such as talent, are included in the jurisdiction of an equality-of-resource theory. Roemer's examination of these complications leads to the conclusion that:

> There is no acceptable conception of resource egalitarianism that does not reduce to recommending equality of welfares. Thus the dichotomy between welfare egalitarianism and resource egalitarianism is misconceived at a level of abstraction appropriate for establishing a first-best standard of egalitarianism. [156]

Dworkin: Equality of Resources

> Following Dworkin's discussion . . . , the point of equality-of-resources theories is to give everyone an equal share of what is scarce in society, but then to insist that people pay the true social costs required to satisfy their preferences. Thus people are considered responsible for their preferences, as it were, but not responsible for their resource endowment. Society should indemnify people to the extent of guaranteeing each an equal endowment of resources but after that, the true social cost of one's demand for a good, which is measured by its value at market-clearing prices, should be borne by the person. [157]

Resources are either transferable (e.g., money and food) or nontransferable (e.g., talent or a biochemical constitution (such as endorphin levels) that may affect one's ability to derive utility from other resources). The scope of egalitarian concerns is assumed, to start with, to cover both kinds of resources. Because it is impossible to reallocate the talent or (probably) the biochemistry components of a social pie, it is necessary to specify a mechanism that allocates transferable resources so as to compensate people with inferior bundles of nontransferable resources.

Dworkin considered two mechanisms for equalizing resources. One is the "equal division of property" mechanism, which equally divides the property rights to the total package of transferable and nontransferable goods in a society. In this case, each person owns a partial share of the labor power of every person, a share that is valued at the wage rate that each person earns at equilibrium. Allocations are thus both envy-free, in the sense that no agent will prefer the resource bundle of another agent to his own, and Pareto optimal. Dworkin objects to this mechanism on the grounds that it leads to "slavery of the talented." For instance, a person who is born with a socially valuable talent has a certain labor capacity, 99 percent of which is owned by others than him- or herself. Because of this shared possession of resources, the individual is forced to pay off his or her debt by performing this highly valued skill, whether or not he/she prefers some other less valued activity, such as writing indifferent poetry.

Dworkin's alternative approach proposes an insurance mechanism for allocating resources. He supports this approach for three reasons: it avoids the slavery of the talented problem, it removes concern over the appropriateness of allocating rights to one's labor, and it is presumed to make the less talented better off. In a hypothetical insurance market individuals start from a position behind a veil of ignorance and insure themselves against the possibility of drawing an impoverished bundle of talents. Insurance purchases are based on knowledge of individual preferences and insurance costs. Premiums represent equilibrium prices that are determined by the demand for insurance and society's productive capacity or total supply of income. Although no society could actually implement such an insurance market, insurance premiums represent a guide to the shape of just income distributions. Progressive taxes could be used to achieve the post-insurance incomes that would have occurred had people been able to insure themselves against bad luck draws of talent. Dworkin stops short of recommending such a tax because he believes that decisions made behind a veil of ignorance cannot provide ethical justification for the implementation of policy.

Problems with Dworkin's Proposals

Under the equal division model people who are more productive than average will suffer, as they are made to trade much of their productive labor for part of the slackers' labor, while those who are less productive will gain, for the inverse reason. Although everyone's initial endowment is of equal value, the less productive workers also benefit from being able to "buy" leisure at a much lower rate, equal to their own productivity; while the more productive workers lose more if they want to cut back their hours of work. This outcome is clear if we consider that:

> A highly talented person is exactly like a person with an involuntary expensive taste: the only kind of leisure he likes to consume is expensive leisure, his own. His leisure is expensive because it has an alternative use which is highly valued by society. The utilitarian objective function of the insurance problem will require, for reasons of productive efficiency, that the talented work longer hours than the untalented, which thereby relegates the talented to lower welfare. . . . [165]

Under Dworkin's alternative insurance mechanism it turns out to be possible for individuals who are less talented to wind up actually being worse off in a case where the set of nonalienable resources includes factors that directly affect utility. For example, consider a two-good world with two persons, Andrea and Bob. Behind a veil of ignorance these individuals may agree to own equal shares of all resources, including a resource we will call "the capacity to enjoy corn." Suppose that, due to a higher level of endorphins, Andrea is better able to enjoy corn than Bob. When each assumes his or her identity in society, each will buy back the other half of their own capacity for enjoyment in exchange for some amount of corn. Bob, the happiness-impaired member of the duo, has much less capacity for enjoyment; his capacity is a scarcer good than Andrea's and should command a higher price per unit. Bob is thus buying fewer units of enjoyment capacity from Andrea, but at a higher price per unit than vice versa. Depending on how much higher the per unit price is, Bob could end up paying more corn for his meager capabilities than Andrea pays for her grander but cheaper (per unit) abilities. In this case Bob would end up with less than half of the corn. The resource egalitarian is thus faced with an inconsistency: compensation for differences in nontransferable resources can lead to inegalitarian distributions of transferable resources.

> One might object: What kind of insurance is this that can penalize the person who ends up with the low "talent"? The answer is: expected-utility-maximizing insurance. Dworkin . . . does not propose this kind of insurance (which economists consider to be rational insurance), but rather a minimal floor insurance policy where a person insures himself not to maximize expected utility, but to guarantee some minimal income. [175]

Equality of Resources Implies Equality of Welfare

Dworkin did not spell out the details of his minimal income guarantee, leaving open the question: "Is there a way of defining an insurance mechanism which would implement equality of resources, not behave perversely and inconsistently as described above, and still preserve Dworkin's division between resources eqalitarianism and welfare egalitarianism?" [175–176] That question is answered in the negative: the only way to fulfill the requirements of resource egalitarianism is to allocate resources specifically so as to equalize welfare. [The proof for this conclusion is found in Roemer, 1986, "Equality of Resources Implies Equality of Welfare."[1]]

A deeper problem is that the difference between preferences and resources becomes very hazy once resources are taken to include innate capacities. If it turns out that the preferences over which we are thought to be responsible are actually resources that we cannot control, then, again, there is no coherent distinction between resource and welfare egalitarianism. This problem can be illustrated with Dworkin's suggestion that, under equality of resources persons are entitled to the returns from their ambitions, but not from their endowments. But what is ambition? If ambition levels are determined by some bio-logical propensity, then this propensity must, logically, be treated as a resource, rather than as a preference.

The theoretician is saved from the requirement of having to apply such diffi-cult conclusions by the reality that it is impossible to obtain much of the infor-mation on which they would be based, e.g., accurate, quantifiable data, compa-rable across individuals, regarding talents, tastes, and levels of pleasure or utility. Nevertheless, it is still worthwhile to refine further our understanding of where to draw the line between those resources for which an individual is and is not responsible.

Note

1. John Roemer, "Equality of Resource Implies Equality of Talent," *Quarterly Journal of Economics* 101 (4) (November 1986), 751–784.

Summary of

Equal Opportunity or Equal Social Outcome?

by Marc Fleurbaey

[Published in *Economics and Philosophy* 11 (1995), 25–55.]

The traditional approach of normative economics to issues of distribution is to seek to equalize outcomes, defined in terms of subjective well-being, or welfare. However, recent debates over the appropriate object of egalitarian concerns have shifted away from welfare toward problems related to the selection of other relevant variables.

The notion that egalitarianism must be selective applies on two levels. First, the individual outcome to be equalized must be identified. For instance, nor-mative economics selects welfare, while Amartya Sen's capability view asserts that the thing to be equalized is appropriately defined choice sets. Second, once the outcome is selected, the factors that influence it must be specified. Most re-searchers now divide these factors into three main categories: resources, factors controlled by social institutions that can be allocated to and redistributed by agents; talents, factors controlled neither by government nor individuals, such as inheritable traits or irreducible social circumstances; and will, factors over which individuals have control and responsibility, such as ambitions. The frame-work of "factor selective egalitarianism" identifies these three factors and seeks to compensate for differences in talents—but not in will—by appropriate allo-cation of resources. Disagreements among authors pursuing factor-selective egalitarianism are mainly to be found in the area where the line is drawn between talents and will, and in the means recommended for compensating talent differentials.

Although there are many important differences between the positions of the following theorists, their views can generally be divided into two camps that compete over where to draw the line between talent and will. The "equal resources" school is exemplified by Rawls and Dworkin, who place goals and ambitions espoused by individuals in the will category. The resources needed to pursue these two factors are located in the talent category. On the other side, the "equal opportunity" school, which includes Arneson, Cohen, Roemer, and Sen, places all factors for which individuals are morally responsible in the will category and all factors (aside from resources) that are outside of the individuals' control in the talent category.

The debates over what to equalize are similarly divided. The equal resources school advocates the equalization of extended bundles of resources and talents across individuals, while the equal opportunity school contends that choice sets rather than resource bundles are the appropriate objects of compensation.

Equal Opportunity View

"The equal opportunity approach is generally empty, inefficient, unfeasible, and it relies on a shaky sociological and philosophical basis." [27] The main feature of this approach is its focus on options. Equal opportunity is achieved only if each person faces an array of options that is equivalent to every one else's. Because people may differ in their awareness of available options, in their ability to choose among these options, and in their character strength to follow through on chosen options, the equal opportunity view must seek to accommodate these differences. This challenge can be met in one of three ways: (1) equalize the ability to negotiate equivalent options; (2) allow the choice sets to be non-equivalent so as to counterbalance differences in ability to negotiate options; or (3) equalize the choice sets and hold that any inequalities in people's negotiating abilities are due to causes for which individuals are personally responsible.

Separability Condition

The equal opportunity view implicitly assumes that resources can compensate for talent differentials independently of differences among individual motivations or wills. This assumption is known as a separability condition. For instance, compensating for blindness with extra income should be independent of the effort made by a blind person. As an example, if 10 percent more income makes blind person i as well-off as sighted person j, both of whom make little effort in their lives, then the same 10 percent more income will benefit i in the same way as *j* if both are ambitious. In fact, the separability condition is realistic only in a small number of cases where resources and talent have the same nature and are additive. For example, there may be sound reasons to apply the separability condition to compensate for inherited wealth inequalities through money transfers. However, this reasoning does not support its application to situations involving more generalized social inequalities. It turns out, also, that the separability condition becomes both more necessary and logically harder to achieve as we consider larger groups.

Problems with the separability condition go to the heart of the choice set approach to equality. Factor-selective egalitarianism assumes two goals: more resources for less talent, and better outcomes for better wills. Without the separability condition, these two goals are incompatible. Other problems arise when this approach is studied in a market setting, or if one attempts to achieve factor selective egalitarianism at the same time as Pareto optimality.

Problems for Equal Opportunity

There are a number of other problems with the equal opportunity approach. One is that it implies results that are too callous. Consider Bert who recklessly drives a motorcycle without a helmet, is uninsured, and gets into an accident. Bert has no money to pay for the necessary life-saving operation. According to equal opportunity, Bert is fully responsible for his injury and so deserves no health care or transfer of funds. This result conflicts with our moral intuition that "however criminal or stupid his behavior may have been, there is a limit to the kind and amount of suffering he should endure." [41] One could argue that Bert should still receive some compensation for reasons of charity, but not under the norms of justice. However, this response ignores the fact that Bert has a basic need that demands ethical consideration.

Another problem is that individuals are constantly changing, and it is hard to bound them to consequences of earlier choices made with a different frame of mind. To make them suffer only the consequences of the virtual choices that they would have made in the past with their current frame of mind is overwhelmingly complex. This illustrates the fact that, in addition to nonseparability difficulties or counterintuitive implications, the apparently unbounded complexity of the equal opportunity approach makes it impossible to implement in the real world.

Outcome-Selective Egalitarianism

Given the inappropriateness of factor-selective egalitarianism for global issues of distributive justice, let us return to a focus on egalitarian outcomes. To do this, it is useful to employ a particular concept of responsibility—that which relates to the decisions allocated by society to its various members. "[T]he way I dress is my own daily responsibility. Probably my choice is influenced by many factors, including the remarks of my fellows, but whatever happens at the moment I pick my clothes from the closet, I remain, from the viewpoint of society, the decision maker in this domain." [44]

A society based on outcome-selective egalitarianism would design a set of institutions aimed at equality, across individuals, in the outcomes for which society assumes some responsibility, while not seeking, in this respect, to influence the outcomes that are the individual's responsibility. The relevant outcomes to be divided up between societal and individual responsibility would include, for example, "health, living standards, education level, career, family life, sense development, preference satisfaction, cheerfulness, etc." [45]

Such an approach differs from factor-selective egalitarianism in a number of significant ways. For example, according to this approach, if cheerfulness is deemed a private matter, the person who is naturally sad, but otherwise leads a perfectly normal life, will not be compensated with any social resources. Similarly, the naturally cheerful person would not be penalized for this trait of personality. But if their social outcomes (job, income, family life, for instance) are affected, then social institutions may intervene. In contrast, since none of them has chosen to be sad or joyful, equal opportunity would immediately subsidize the former and tax the latter. [52]

An outcome-selective egalitarian principle does not require information on the causes of individual behavior (such as the distinction between talents and will). This avoids the practical difficulties of allocating subsidies according to whether a person was born with a special need (such as the born Muslim whose required trip to Mecca might be subsidized) or choose it for him/herself (e.g., an individual who converted to Islam, knowing the cost of travel to Mecca, and is therefore responsible for paying the full fare). This makes outcome-selective egalitarianism much easier to apply, since outcomes are more easily observed than causal factors.

A source of difference between the two approaches is the type of responsibility emphasized in each. Factor-selective egalitarianism in effect assumes free will and gives rewards and punishments for choices freely made. Outcome-selective egalitarnianism does not have to grapple with free will, basing its allocations of social responsibility on the decision-making expectations and powers described above as a practical (rather than a moral) responsibility. It gives people a substantial amount of choice without attaching thereto any moral desert. At the same time, social institutions retain the responsibility to fight against undesirable influences and provide individuals with good conditions within which to make their private choices.

The effectiveness of outcome-selective egalitarianism depends largely on how a society decides to divide responsibility between individuals and social institutions. An appropriate division would value autonomous choice, self-esteem, and privacy and would leave individuals with responsibility over their own goals and degrees of satisfaction. Most subjective outcomes would remain private, but their spillover effects on society would be in the public domain. Thus subjective and intellectual outcomes would be private, but considerations of mental health and education level would be public. The life-style and consumption of individuals would be private, but institutions would be needed to circumscribe the externalities caused thereby.

Summary of

Coherence Against the Pareto Principle and Equality

by John Broome

[Published in *Weighing Goods: Equality, Uncertainty, and Time* (Cambridge, MA: Basil Blackwell, 1991), 151–164 and 174–201.]

The economics profession initially relied on an early version of utilitarianism as the basis for theories of choice and welfare. As problems emerged with the resulting philosophical and behavioral assumptions, neoclassical economics attempted to retreat to a positivist formalism, supposedly grounding its theories on nothing more than stylized observation of individual choices. Yet, as many critics have observed, the economists' retreat into positivism did not entirely succeed in eliminating controversial and contradictory traces of the earlier philosophical perspective.

This selection is part of a rigorous reconstruction of a modern form of utilitarianism and an examination of its implications for such economic questions as equity, distribution, and social choice. In earlier chapters the author identifies utilitarianism as a leading example of the broader category of teleological, or consequentialist, ethical theories. Teleological theories are those in which the goodness of an act and its consequences determine what should be done (i.e., other ethical principles such as rights, fairness, and obligation can be subsumed into the notion of goodness). Utilitarianism assumes that the goodness of an act depends solely on the total good it provides to people, independent of distribution.

In any teleological ethical system there is an ordering of alternatives, consisting of statements like "A is as good as or better than B"; this ordering can be said to define the "structure of good." If the ethical system is consistent, then the ordering satisfies the assumptions of expected utility theory (see the Harsanyi article summarized in Part III), and it is possible to define a cardinal (quantitative) mathematical representation of the degree of goodness; the author refers to such a representation as a "utility function." Note that this definition of utility involves individual or collective good, not preferences; the distinction is a crucial one. If people were perfectly rational, well-informed, and self-interested, then their preferences would coincide with what is good for them; the fact that these assumptions are not satisfied, however, affects both preferences and concepts of the good.

The chapters summarized here explain how these ideas lead to a critique of the principle of Pareto optimality and to a utilitarian basis for egalitarianism.

A Problem with Pareto's Principle

The Pareto principle is familiar to students of economics everywhere: two alternatives are equally good if everyone is indifferent between them; if someone prefers the first of two choices, and no one prefers the second, then the first is better than the second. It has been pointed out that if individuals disagree about the probability of events, and each person has coherent (logically consistent) preferences, then it is easy to construct examples in which the general "betterness" relationship cannot both be coherent and conform to the Pareto principle. This is a serious contradiction, since both the Pareto principle and logical coherence are widely accepted as desirable features of social choice.

The contradiction arises from the sloppy formulation of the Pareto principle, which mixes statements about preferences and about good. It is easily confused with two related but less problematical principles, one dealing with good and the other with preferences. The *principle of personal good* states that two alternatives are equally good if they are equally good for everyone, and that if one alternative is at least as good as another for everyone and better for someone, then it is better. The *democratic principle* states that if no one prefers the second of two choices and someone prefers the first, then the first should come about.

There is no contradiction in maintaining both of these principles while recognizing their possibly divergent outcomes, since people do not always prefer what is best for themselves, and democracy involves doing what people want, not what is good for them. The structure of general, or societal, goodness is coherent, but as Arrow demonstrated, the choices made by a democratic social system need not be.

Welfare Economics

The Pareto principle is untrue when expressed, as above, as a statement about the general good. It is more often stated as a condition on social preferences— if someone prefers the first alternative, and no one prefers the second, then the first is socially preferred. John Harsanyi, for example, argues that if individual preferences are coherent, and social preferences are coherent and Paretian, then social preferences can be represented by a utility function that is the sum of individual utility functions. But the concept of social preference used by Harsanyi and others is an ambiguous one: either it means betterness (in which case it suffers from the problems suggested earlier), or it is a statement about what should come about. The latter interpretation reduces it to the "democratic principle."

Attempts to base welfare economics on social preferences require abandonment of either coherence of social choice or the Pareto property; both alternatives have been tried, but neither is entirely satisfactory. The problems can be
avoided by reformulating welfare economics on the basis of good rather than
preferences. The analogue of Harsanyi's theorem, expressed in terms of goodness—assuming coherence and the principle of personal good, the general good
can be represented as the sum of individual goods—is more defensible than his
original form.

A Utilitarian Case for Equality

The principle of personal good, a Pareto-like principle expressed entirely in
terms of individual and general goodness, appears to say nothing about distribution. Utilitarianism in general seems concerned with the total amount of
good, not with the equity of its distribution. How, then, does a utilitarian ethical theory argue for equality?

A traditional answer rests on additional assumptions about the structure of
the good. Assume that each person has the same individual benefit function, in
which his/her individual good is an increasing but strictly concave function of
her own income. That is, the additional benefit of an increase in income is always positive, but diminishes as income rises. Then, as utilitarian economists
such as Alfred Marshall and Arthur Pigou pointed out, redistribution from rich
to poor would increase the total amount of good. However, this is true only if
each person has the same benefit function. If benefit functions differ, the total
good might be maximized by a very unequal distribution of income that equalized the marginal utility of income for all. Francis Edgeworth, an early neoclassical economist, made crudely aristocratic and sexist assumptions about differences in benefit functions, so that his argument for equalization of marginal
benefits implied preservation of historic inequalities.

Two more sophisticated utilitarian arguments for equality have been offered.
One approach, communal egalitarianism, suggests that equality is a communal
good: at any fixed level of total individual good, the more equally it is distributed, the greater the general good. This can be true even if the general good
depends solely on individual goods. For instance, if the general good is a sum
of increasing, concave functions of the individual goods, then more equality in
the distribution of good means more general good.

A second approach, individualistic egalitarianism, challenges the assumption
that a person's good depends on his/her own income alone. In this view, inequality itself is bad for those at the bottom, if no one else, independent of the
absolute level of income. Since income inequality is bad for those below the average, an increase in equality increases the general good. The same arguments
apply, with only a little more complexity, to inequality of individual good rather
than of income. Most generally, "a person's good consists partly in how fairly

she is treated; unfairness is bad for a person, whatever she may feel about it."
[182] Individualistic egalitarianism avoids certain problems involving the treatment of risk and uncertainty that arise under some versions of communal egalitarianism; thus the individualistic theory appears to be the stronger of the two.

Equality and Fairness

Why is equality good in the first place? Utilitarianism seems to imply that any
scarce commodity should be allocated in a manner that maximizes the resulting
benefits; but this alone would overlook the question of fairness. The reasons
why a person would benefit from obtaining the commodity can be divided into
claims, or duties owed to the individual him/herself, and all other reasons.
There is ample room for debate about the nature and extent of claims: do they
arise solely from historical agreements and contracts, from an analysis of basic
needs or prevailing standards of living, from capabilities, as discussed by
Amartya Sen, or from other considerations? It seems unlikely that all sources of
individual good are equally worthy claims on society.

The definition of claims answers the question, "Equality of what?" Whatever
answer is chosen, fairness requires that claims be satisfied in proportion to their
strength. When resources are scarce and many people have vital claims (e.g.,
there is usually a scarcity of replacement organs for sick people who need trans-
plants), a lottery among all qualified applicants may be the fairest means of distribution.

If people have equal claims to the satisfaction of needs, then unfairness is
plainly an individual harm, corresponding to the discussion of inequality in the
individualistic egalitarian theory above. While fairness affects an individual's
good, it cannot be determined by examining the individual's own resources
alone. Consequently, theories that base utility solely on an individual's own resources or consumption, as is common in economics, cannot incorporate the
notion of fairness, which is one crucial aspect of egalitarianism.

Summary of

Distributive Justice and Desirable Ends
of Economic Activity

by Kenneth Arrow

[Published in *Issues in Contemporary Macroeconomics and Distribution*,
ed. George R. Feiwel (Albany: State University of New York, 1985), 134–156.]

The purpose of the economy is the welfare of the consumers, public and private. In no sense is mere production as such a proper measure, rather it has to

be production for the ends that people want. Output, income, and consumption are important aims and preconditions for achieving other goals of individuals; that is, they are only a part of what people live for. [134]

Economic policy must address the aspects of consumer welfare that depend on factors that lie outside of the economy, as well as the three goals that are endogenous to a market system: economic stability, the efficient allocation of resources, and egalitarian income distributions. The last of these has been relatively neglected in modern economic analysis. It is the principal focus of this paper, which concludes that the need for government intervention and collective responsibility is suggested by market failures that prevent just distribution.

Justice, Equality, and Freedom: The Trade-Off between Efficiency and Equity

Modern neoclassical general-equilibrium theory can be used to argue that efficiency and equity are distinct goals. It assumes that, if some significant conditions are met, independent private decisions coordinated through the market will achieve a Pareto-efficient allocation, employing all available resources, especially labor. However, this definition of efficiency implies nothing about the justness of a given allocation.

Desirable income distributions cannot be achieved through the automatic workings of the market system. The price system fails to provide a defensible income distribution mechanism and ignores the fact that low income restricts freedoms in important ways. In addition to constraining the freedom to consume, poverty also restricts job opportunities and limits influence in a political setting that favors ideas acceptable to the rich. Unequal distributions of power and money result in the curtailment of many aspects and types of liberty. Justice therefore requires equality—in both wealth and power—as well as liberty.

The Case for Redistribution

The theory of social choice aims at providing a normative rationale for making social decisions when a society's individual members have different preferences. The central problem for the theory is how to define a social optimum by aggregating individual preference orderings, including, for example, preferences regarding one's own consumption, social attitudes, and perspectives on the provision of public benefits to others. In spite of the lack of generalizable conclusions, and in spite of uncertainty as to how to define equality, the desirability of redistribution policies to redress inequality can be defended on the strength of the following five points.

First, it is clear that ethical judgments lean toward equality in income distribution. Economists William Vickerey and John Harsanyi, along with philosopher John Rawls, show that members of society would choose social arrangements that lead to equal outcomes if they were placed in an "original position" where individuals know all the possible social conditions (including circumstances of wealth and of talent) they might be born into but do not know which particular role they will, in fact, be given. When all members are presented with similar sets of possible scenarios, it is predicted that the group will arrive at a mutually beneficial contract of sharing, in which those who turn out to be more fortunate will give to the less fortunate. The ethical judgments that emerge from this approach suggest a moral obligation to redistribute income and other goods more equally.

The choices made from Rawls's original position can be expected to converge on a system that would, in effect, insure against disaster. This implies an allocation of awards that is independent of individual productivity levels. To a certain extent this approach rejects the productivity principle, which asserts that an individual is entitled to what he or she creates. Our second point regards the limitations of the productivity principle, recognizing, for example, that it ignores the dependence of an individual's marginal product on complementary or substitute factors beyond his or her control, as well as on inborn talents or family advantages. Being, thus, less than fully responsible for their marginal products, individuals do not have a just claim on the full value of their product.

A concern for incentives seems to support the productivity principle, on the grounds that people will create less if they do not expect rewards for what they create. However, this confuses rents with incentives. In fact, there is no reason to believe that the able scholar or artist requires a higher incentive payment than the mediocre one. Most very high incomes found in capitalist systems do not necessarily represent incentive payments; they are more likely to represent a form of rent than to be a reflection of productivity. (The failure of competition to eliminate such high incomes may be due to monopolistic elements or uncertainty.) Our third point, therefore, is that appropriate redistributions need not diminish performance incentives.

The fourth issue to be addressed is the trade-off between efficiency and equity considered across generations. Here the fundamental concern is the problem of how much one generation should save to increase the welfare of the next generation. Market economies score reasonably well on this overall, generating levels of aggregate investment (public and private) that approximate a just and efficient intertemporal allocation. However, when we look at the composition of investment we see that uncertainty reduces the willingness of lenders to give credit, especially for the critical functions of human capital formation and technical development. This observation leads to the conclusion that transgenerational equity can be improved by appropriate tax-based redistribution, even if growth and aggregate savings are hurt by the attendant market distortions.

For instance, taxes levied on high incomes will reduce wealth concentrations and lower total savings, but the poor who benefit from these taxes will have a greater incentive to invest in their own human capital formation and will increase their future income. However, private investment by the poor will only go so far. Redistribution should also focus on improving social capital to raise their productivity—e.g., technical education, healthcare, and housing. A larger role for the government in the development of basic civilian technology will also increase both equality and efficiency. Because of market imperfections, large pools of capital are usually required to bear the risk of technical progress. When government supplies the capital for such investments, the resulting technical progress can be made available on a more equitable basis.

Our fifth point addresses the question: "To what extent does the nature of capitalism, its institutions, its functioning, or its ideology facilitate or inhibit the achievement of justice?" [144]

> The ideology, and to a considerable extent the practice, of the capitalist system do encourage equality of opportunity. But since the opportunities have a strong element of uncertainty about them, this very equality of opportunity is apt to lead to inequality of outcomes. As stressed earlier, inequalities of present possessions in turn impede equality of opportunity; wealth achieved from earlier success increases opportunities for oneself and one's children both directly and through family influences and connections. [151]

Unemployment, private property, lack of social responsibility by corporations, and investment speculation all contribute to unequal incomes. Most income inequality is due to inequality in the returns to labor, but the ability to acquire profits through property income also increases inequality. The capitalist drive to maximize profits tends to suppress the expression of altruistic motives, even though competition itself depends on an intricate network of reciprocal obligations.

Market Failures and Collective Responsibility

According to textbook theories, any economic actor in a well-functioning economy is able to conduct any transaction at a given set of prices. In reality, this is not the case. For instance, workers are often unable to sell all the labor they want and are restricted to selling that labor for which there is effective demand. This kind of serious macroeconomic failure points to an irreducible need for collective decision making or government intervention. Government stimulation of insufficient demand is preferable to letting valuable resources, such as unsold labor, remain idle. The private sector cannot solve the problem of market failure, the inefficiencies of unemployment, or the equitable redistribution of incomes. Progress toward these goals can only be achieved by a mixed economy that makes sufficient room for government and for social institutions.

Summary of

Aristotelian Social Democracy

by Martha Nussbaum

[Published in *Liberalism and the Good,* eds. R. Bruce Douglass, Gerald M. Mara, and
Henry S. Richardson (New York and London: Routledge, 1990), 203–252.]

This article argues that political institutions should focus on developing the capabilities of its citizens and assuring that every citizen has access to the necessary circumstances for good human functioning. This Aristotelian perspective contrasts with other liberal approaches that define social goals in terms of increasing wealth and welfare or equalizing the distribution of resources.

Basic Elements of Aristotelian Political Theory

An Aristotelian conception of political institutions is based on a theory of human good, i.e., on what it means to function as a human being. Such a theory describes at a suitably general level the functionings and goals that individuals in all societies pursue. The task of the political planner is to make sure that every citizen has the capability to choose a life of good functioning. This objective is accomplished by making available the relevant material, institutional, and educational circumstances, while treating all citizens as free and equal. These circumstances will vary across cultures and societies.

Priority of the Good

In contrast to the major liberal theories, the Aristotelian view first defines what makes for good human functioning and then designs political arrangements to advance this good. The basic intuition behind this approach of giving priority to the good is that it is necessary to understand what makes for a good life before developing the institutions to promote it. Since this view is concerned with all members of a given society, the purpose of political arrangements is both broad and deep: *broad* in that its goal is to bring every citizen across a threshold into conditions in which a good human life may be chosen and lived; *deep* in that it is concerned with the totality of functionings that constitute the good life, not merely with money, land, opportunities, and office.

The Aristotelian conception differs in several important ways from opposing views that define the good either in terms of wealth, wealth and distribution, or utility. First, although no major contemporary liberal theorist defines the good in terms of wealth, GNP is widely used by liberal democratic governments as a measure of economic development. This approach mistakes wealth (a means) with goodness (an end) and fails to consider how and to what extent wealth contributes to people's lives. Second, the liberal political theories of Dworkin and Rawls describe the goodness of political arrangements in terms of resources and their distribution among citizens. The Aristotelian conception objects that possessions are not good in themselves and that answers to interesting questions about distribution require an examination of how resources affect human functioning. "Even to answer the question 'Which things that we have to hand are the useful and usable resources?' requires *some* implicit conception of the good and of good human functioning." [212] Lastly, utilitarian theory supports the Aristotelian view that resources have only instrumental value but takes a different turn when it argues that an individual's good can be achieved by satisfying his or her actual desires and preferences. The central problem with the utilitarian approach is that desire is an unreliable guide to human good. Desire adapts to both good and bad circumstances, and it tends to constrain the imagination. As a result, political arrangements that focus exclusively on actual preferences lead inexorably to a reinforcement of the status quo.

The Thick Vague Conception of the Good

Any political view that questions the reliability of desire as a guide to human good must face the liberal charge of paternalism, i.e., that some life projects are favored over others. The Aristotelian view meets this criticism head on by sketching a "thick vague" outline of a good life that embraces the important life functions shared by everyone and captures the important ends in all areas of human activity. This escapes the charge of being excessively metaphysical because it is based on commonalities found in the myths and stories of different societies that answer the question: "What are the features of our common humanity, features that lead us to recognize certain others, however distant their location and their forms of life, as humans . . . ?"

The shape and structure of our shared humanity can be approximated with an open-ended list, which includes various capabilities, such as being able to live to the end of a complete life, have good health, avoid pain and enjoy pleasure, use the five senses, to assess and critically revise a conception of one's own good, care for others and nature, play and laugh, live one's own life and no one else's, and live one's own life in one's own circumstances. "[O]ur working list is meant not as systematic philosophical theory, but as a summary of what we think so far, and as an intuitive approximation, whose intent is not to legislate, but to direct attention to certain areas of special importance." [219] It is evaluative because it is selective, and it implies that a life without any of these capabilities would be lacking in humanness. It is irreducably plural, but it contains two elements—practical reason and affiliation—that serve to organize and arrange all the others.

The charge of paternalism also suggests that Aristotelianism, because it advocates a single conception of the good life, does not permit individuals to choose a plurality of conceptions of the good life. It allegedly tells people what to do with their lives. The Aristotelian response is first, that the account of the good is a list of capabilities or opportunities for functioning, precisely in order to leave room for choice of when and whether to exercise the function. Second, that there is a plurality of concrete specifications of the thick vague account of the good in different cultures and societies. Individuals endorse the thick vague conception in the way they conduct their lives, even though the variance among individual lives may be very great. The Aristotelian conception of the good life is grounded in the humanness that all members of our species share at a fundamental level. Contrary to the charge of paternalism, Aristotelianism does not prescribe a certain way of life, and it celebrates choice in at least four ways. Citizens are assumed able to choose (a) whether to function well; (b) whether to participate in the political design of institutions; (c) what kind of life they would like to lead; and (d) where to draw the limits of personal spheres of privacy and nonintervention.

The Task of Politics

The aim of Aristotelian politics is consistent with institutional, rather than residual, welfarism. It designs institutions to provide comprehensive support to individuals over the course of their entire lives. Unlike residual welfarism, it does not wait to see who fails under a given institutional arrangement to then bail them out. Instead there is a focus on getting more individuals to have the capability to choose a good life, rather than improving the lives and choices of those who have already fallen below a minimum threshold of choice.

The Aristotelian view has important implications for the areas of labor, property, political participation, and education. According to Aristotle, some forms of labor are so incompatible with good human functioning that compensation in the form of money and commodities cannot undo the damage wrought by such work. As a result, the Aristotelian conception excludes labor opportunities that are inimical to good functioning. With respect to property, Aristotle advocated both private and common property—that each person should be able to live in an environment that is his/hers alone, but that a person in need ought also to be able to help herself to someone else's crops with impunity. Citizenship in the Aristotelian view extends to the political sphere. All citizens share the ability to participate in making and administering laws, since it is in the political arena that the conception of good that shapes a citizen's life is formulated. Finally, the most important focus of political planning concerns education because it is here that the capacity to choose is developed and the powers of mind are cultivated.

Summary of

Social Unity and Primary Goods

by John Rawls

[Published in *Utilitarianism and Beyond*, eds. Amartya Sen and Bernard Williams, (Cambridge: Cambridge University Press, 1982) 159–185.]

[This article resolves certain points of ambiguity identified in the author's *A Theory of Justice* (1971). The author published a number of articles during the 1980s that represented an extended discussion of this work—an evolution of ideas that eventually turned into *Political Liberalism* (1993). This article represents a midpoint in the transition: it was published exactly eleven years after the earlier book and eleven years before the later one. The summary of this article, in which Rawls distinguishes his approach to justice from that of utilitarianism, is informed by explanations that were elaborated on in articles during the second half of this period.]

Normative economics, following a common utilitarian approach to justice, assumes that all rational members of society pursue a single common good: the maximization of social utility. Issues of justice that arise in these theories are considered in terms of this goal. An alternative approach is to view society as a cooperative venture for mutual advantage, and to consider issues of justice in terms of maintaining fair terms of cooperation. The author proposes the Kantian concept of "justice as fairness" as one version of this alternative, making the case that his approach to the nature of just claims and interpersonal comparisons is substantially different from that of utilitarianism and normative economics.

Justice as Fairness: The Basic Idea

A central thesis of justice as fairness is that issues of justice apply to basic institutions, rather than to individuals, individual acts, or private exchanges. This is a political conception of justice, to be distinguished from metaphysical conceptions that are tied to a particular moral theory, such as utilitarianism. This conception starts with three assumptions. First, it can be developed and applied only to the basic institutions of a constitutional democracy. Second, people accept this political conception on the basis of fundamental ideas that already exist in a culture; an important example is the idea that society is a fair system of social cooperation in which citizens are free and equal and capable of cooperating over a whole life. Finally, different individuals may have opposing conceptions of their life objectives.

In dropping the assumption that there is a single common good to which all aspire, justice as fairness assumes that citizens with different ends will seek fair terms of cooperation to advance their mutual goals. However, cooperation is only possible if citizens are able to exercise the two powers of moral responsibility: the capacity and desire to honor fair terms of cooperation; and the capacity to decide upon, revise, and rationally pursue a personal conception of the good. Morally responsible individuals who exercise these two powers will regulate the pursuit of their ends as well as their demands on others in light of the two public principles of justice.

These principles are chosen from behind a veil of ignorance by parties representing the highest order interests of citizens, namely, to develop and exercise the two moral powers just cited. The first principle of justice recognizes that all citizens in a well-ordered society have the same, equal basic liberties. This is prior to the second principle (sometimes called the difference principle), which holds that any social and economic inequality must (a) benefit the least advantaged members and (b) attach to offices and positions that are open to all under conditions of fair equality of opportunity. The benefits and advantages mentioned in (a) are to be understood in terms of primary goods that may include basic liberties, such as freedom of association, freedom of movement and choice of occupation, positions of political and economic responsibility, income and wealth, and the social bases of self-respect. Primary goods are features of social institutions; they represent the background conditions for the development and exercise of the two moral powers.

Fair terms of cooperation can only be established when there is a fair distributions of primary goods—those resources that are necessary for the pursuit of one's rational life plan. The choice and ranking of primary goods require a general account of rational plans of life—an account that shows how our lives depend on primary goods for their formation, revision, and execution.

An index of primary goods permits interpersonal comparisons. This is a necessary basis for ensuring fair distributions of opportunities and freedoms. With justice as fairness, everyone's social situation can be assessed using the same index of primary goods. The appropriateness of claims to primary goods is settled by the two principles of justice. Thus, claims of justice turn on distributions of primary goods, not on welfare considerations (as in utilitarian formulations).

According to justice as fairness, rights to certain basic freedoms are prior to conceptions of the good in the sense that they limit permissible conceptions of the good to those that do not violate the fundamental (public) principles of justice. Normative economics has no such limitations—it implies that, so long as the design of institutions realizes the greatest good, individuals may pursue whatever goals they choose. However, since it is easy to describe realistic social institutions that allow the greatest satisfaction to arise without the preservation of basic liberties, basic liberties are more secure in a theory of justice as fairness.

A Welfarist Objection

Some people have expensive tastes and can only be satisfied with a diet of exotic dishes and fine wine. Others have plain tastes and can be satisfied with a diet of milk, bread, and beans. One objection to justice as fairness is that it is said to imply that everyone can be equally satisfied with the same resources. This objection is not fatal, first because justice as fairness is committed neither to the view that income and wealth are good indicators of satisfaction, nor to the claim that primary goods are a measure of psychological well-being. Justice as fairness rejects the idea that comparing and maximizing satisfaction is central to issues of justice. Second, the theory is committed to the idea that people are responsible for the ends they pursue. If citizens are unable to find satisfaction with their income because of their expensive tastes, this gives them no claims to additional resources. The appropriate use of primary goods relies on a capacity to assume responsibility for one's goals and preferences. This capacity is implied by the moral power to form, revise, and rationally pursue a conception of the good.

A theory of justice that holds individuals responsible for their goals is plausible only if (1) it is assumed that persons can regulate their goals and preferences in light of their expectations of primary goods over the course of a life; (2) interpersonal comparisons are based on an index of primary goods that are tied to the highest-order interests of citizens as moral persons; and (3) everyone accepts, as an ideal underlying the public principles of justice, the conception of persons as moral citizens.

This view implies a social division of responsibility. Society is responsible for maintaining the public principles of justice, and individuals are responsible for revising and adjusting their conception of the good to their expected fair share of primary goods. Claims of justice attach to primary goods, rather than to desires or wants, no matter how strongly felt. Strong feelings about goals, or their intensive pursuit, do not constitute justification for a claim on resources.

Interpersonal Comparisons: Kolm versus Justice as Fairness

The dramatic and substantial differences between two approaches to issues of justice—the utilitarian and justice as fairness—can be illustrated by considering their respective views on interpersonal comparisons. For instance, Serge Kolm argues for the utilitarian position that normative economics should use "fundamental preferences" as the basis of interpersonal comparisons.[1] The basic idea behind fundamental preferences is that everyone has, at bottom, the same preferences. In a given society each citizen has a preference ordering over all possible situations that affect any person's well-being. According to this view, it is possible for a representative individual to construct a social welfare function by sympathetically identifying with everyone's preference ordering. All citizens promote a single conception of the good that is common to all rational citizens.

Justice as fairness assumes a completely different conception of persons from that of Kolm's utilitarianism. Where Kolm assumes that every individual has the same basic preferences and goals, justice as fairness recognizes that individual's goals may be incommensurable. Where Kolm assumes that a representative individual can assess the good of others, justice as fairness assumes that persons can assess only their own overall situation. Finally, interpersonal comparisons based on an index of primary goods have nothing to do with preferences.

Conclusion

The major difference between justice as fairness and utilitarian conceptions of justice is that justice as fairness begins with a shared conception of justice and is linked to a conception of the moral individual: someone who is responsible for his or her own goals, some of which may oppose the goals of others. It offers a more realistic and complex view of rational individuals as citizens who are more than a collection of utility maximizers out to satisfy their aims and desires. In pluralistic democratic societies, justice must be based on principles that support cooperation rather than on principles that define what is right in terms of a social good that obliterates differences among persons, their goals, and overall worldviews.

Note

1. Serge Kolm-Christophe, *Justice et Equité* (Paris: Editions du Centre National de la Recherche Scientifique, 1972).

PART VIII

National Development: From Basic Needs to the Welfare State

Overview Essay

by Frank Ackerman

Why does national economic development matter? Offering a precise answer is more difficult than it appears at first glance. If, as argued throughout this volume, human well-being cannot be achieved through private consumption alone, then economic development cannot be justified solely in terms of growth in per capita incomes. What else is needed, in addition to (or perhaps, in affluent societies, in place of) economic growth? What development objectives should a government pursue, in addition to (or in place of) promoting increases in national income?

Two separate discourses address these fundamental questions about development. They emerge from opposite ends of the income spectrum but raise a number of similar issues and concerns. On the one hand, discussions of development economics have frequently observed that a nation's average per capita income is not an adequate measure of the well-being of the poor. This has led to an interest in problems of equity and distribution of resources and to measures of development that encompass more than money income. Several of the articles in this section examine the questions of human needs, equity, and the goals of development from the perspective of low-income, developing nations.

On the other hand, even the most affluent nations continue to experience political conflict over issues of equity and distributional justice and have resolved these conflicts in very different ways. The resulting role of government varies from the welfare states and social democracies of northern Europe, to the welfare cutbacks and increasingly laissez-faire, "anti-social" democracy of the United States. Critiques of U.S. policies in the area of equity and social welfare address only one end of the spectrum; to explore the limits of what can be accomplished in developed countries, it is necessary to look elsewhere. Several articles in this section deal with the economic theory and political philosophy of the welfare state, involving concepts of equity and needs that are remarkably similar to those found in the development literature. (The important relationship between human welfare and environmental sustainability is largely omitted here; it was central to the first volume in this series, *A Survey of Ecological Economics,* and will again be the focus in a later volume on sustainable development.)

Needs, Rights, and the Good Life

In a discussion of the philosophy underlying development economics, Ajit Dasgupta outlines four bases for the use of varying indicators of the standard of living.[1] An emphasis on the satisfaction of preferences, the conventional approach in economic theory, leads to the use of national income (GNP or GDP) per capita or similar measures. The alternative approaches assign top priority to the satisfaction of basic needs; the protection of human rights; and the creation of "excellence" or the good life, often embodied in a set of particularly meritorious goods and services. Each of these alternatives appears in the articles summarized here.

Development economics, when it arose as a separate field of study in the 1950s, initially focused on promoting growth of per capita incomes. Growth, it was assumed, would eventually solve the problem of poverty. In the words of the classic metaphor, a rising tide lifts all boats. Critics of the tidal theory of poverty alleviation appeared almost at once, arguing that an emphasis on growth alone ignored issues of human development and did not lead directly to the satisfaction of basic needs.

Paul Streeten has been a leading proponent of the "basic needs" perspective, spelling out its implications in numerous publications over the years. For Streeten, there is a set of universal, basic human needs, such as food, shelter, clothing, health care, and basic education; satisfaction of these needs is far more urgent than satisfaction of consumer desires in general. Thus equality of resources in general is less important than the guarantee of the necessary minimum to all. Provision of that minimum should be the top priority for development policy:

> The hypothesis of the basic needs approach is that a set of selective policies makes it possible to satisfy the basic human needs of the whole population at levels of income per head substantially below those required by a less discriminating strategy of all-round income growth—and it is therefore possible to satisfy these needs sooner.[2]

The first article summarized here is a recent review of the evolution of development economics by Streeten, examining contemporary debates and restating his perspective. Since human development is not solely a matter of financial resources, alternative indicators are needed. Streeten and others have created the widely used Human Development Index (HDI), about which more will be said in Part X, which combines per capita income (up to the world average level), literacy, and life expectancy. Development looks different when measured by the HDI rather than by income alone.

Streeten raises the important distinction between absolute and relative measures of poverty.[3] While there is a tendency for socially accepted poverty thresholds to rise along with average incomes—defining poverty, perhaps, as a fixed percentage of the national average—the basic needs approach seems to imply that an absolute measure should be used. Poverty thresholds may rise with general affluence, both because socially expected standards of appearance and lifestyle tend to increase, and because the costs of satisfying the same basic needs may become greater. For example, compared to most people in developing countries, Americans require more expensive clothing to feel respectably dressed and are more likely to need a car in order to buy food. The latter effect, at least, is an increase in the cost of providing basic needs.

More generally, Streeten suggests that to understand the welfare significance of income, one must consider real purchasing power, adjusted for the particular local spending patterns of the poor. Even this does not capture all of well-being, however, since it omits the provision of public goods, the role of nonmarketed activities and resources, levels of health and education, and distribution within and between households.

The question of rights and freedoms is mentioned briefly by Streeten; his observation that basic needs could in theory be met in a well-run prison highlights the significance of the issue. The second article summarized in this section, by Partha Dasgupta, addresses the relationship between freedom and the market, in a manner that is relevant to developed as well as developing countries. (See also the related Dasgupta article in Part VI.) Dasgupta starts from Isaiah Berlin's famous distinction between negative freedom (the freedom from coercion or interference) and positive freedom (access to resources and capabilities). The former is more obviously compatible with the market, since the policies needed to maintain negative freedoms are largely public goods—unlike the overtly redistributive policies needed to provide positive freedoms.

Yet as Dasgupta points out, the questions of rights are more complex than this in several respects. The libertarian approach, emphasizing negative freedom and celebrating the efficiency of the competitive market, overlooks the fact that an efficient outcome can be reached from any initial distribution of resources. Thus, even for advocates of laissez-faire efficiency, a separate theory of the ethically appropriate initial distribution is needed to determine whether redistributive public policy is necessary. On the other hand, an emphasis on positive freedom does not reduce all questions of political rights to patterns of resource distribution. Human well-being is not created solely by economic goods and services; it is for this reason that most people would not welcome Streeten's image of basic needs being met in a prison. Dasgupta also offers a provocative discussion of the implications of uncertainty about individual needs, concluding that when there is great inequality of incomes, it is better for positive-rights goods to be distributed in kind rather than via income transfers. Similar issues of uncertainty appear in Barr's analysis of the economic theory of the welfare state, discussed below.

The distinction between theories of basic needs, human rights, and merit goods or "excellence" is in part simply a matter of degree. A sufficiently elaborated list of basic needs, or of positive rights to which everyone should be entitled, would amount to prescribing a menu of merit goods that should be provided to all. For example, the detailed theory of welfare and human needs developed by Ian Gough, discussed in Part I, includes 11 categories of "intermediate needs" and leads to the identification of 18 quantitative indicators of need satisfaction. Gough and Theo Thomas have collected data on these indicators for more than 100 countries and correlated these indicators with a number of economic, political, and demographic variables. They find that the extent of need satisfaction is strongly correlated with income per capita, the degree of democracy, gender equality, and other explanatory factors.[4]

A subtle and distinctive conception of the good life, defined in terms of "functionings" and "capabilities," has been introduced into development theory by Amartya Sen. The lengthy two-part article by David Crocker, summarized here, explains the views of Amartya Sen and philosopher Martha Nussbaum in this area. (Some of the work described by Crocker was coauthored by Sen and Nussbaum, while other parts were written separately, expressing minor differences between the two authors.) While sympathetic to the basic needs approach of Streeten and others, Sen and Nussbaum argue that basic needs theories incorporate the same fallacy as conventional economics, confusing commodities with human experience.

What is important for well-being, according to Sen and Nussbaum, is not the possession of a certain level of commodities, but rather the achievement of a certain level or ensemble of essentially human functionings. The quantity of food consumed does not matter as much as the adequacy of nutrition that it provides; the relationship between the two varies widely from one individual to another. Even more important is the set of capabilities, or functionings, that an individual could have chosen to achieve: choosing to fast when one has the capability of obtaining adequate nutrition is different from starving for lack of food—even if the physical experience on a particular day is the same. The identification of a desirable set of capabilities, constituting a fully human existence, has much in common with theories of positive freedoms, particularly in Sen's version of the theory.

The development ethic based on functionings and capabilities provides an elegant solution to a number of philosophical problems and offers a satisfying account of human nature, needs, and the role of economic goods in promoting well-being. Yet as Crocker concludes, its specific implications remain to be worked out; it is not yet clear whether it will lead to unique results of its own or merely provide a more rigorous basis for theories of basic needs and positive freedoms.

Developing Visions of Equity

All the theoretical perspectives reviewed here point to the central importance of equity in addition to economic growth. The next two articles offer different, but complementary, visions of equity and its implications for development. For Naila Kabeer, the failure to recognize gender inequality is the blind spot of both standard approaches to development and many of the alternatives proposed in developing countries. She sees development as a process of social transformation as well as redeployment of resources. Power over resources, ideas, and participation in the development process are mutually reinforcing and serve the interests of existing hierarchies rather than the poorest and most needy members of society.

Like several of the authors discussed here, Kabeer decries the confusion of means and ends implied by the use of marketed output and income as measures of success in development. The use of market indicators ignores nonmarketed resources, such as the natural environment, as well as many women's activities, such as domestic labor and informal sector production. Changes in the lives and economic activities of women are thus ignored in the standard paradigm. A focus on the ends rather than the means of development would recognize the satisfaction of needs through a variety of institutions, including but not limited to the market; it would give poor women a voice in the process of social transformation, helping not only women but all oppressed groups.

In the 1970s, Irma Adelman presented a widely discussed comparative analysis of equity and development. Based on a review of experience throughout the developing world, she concluded that the early stages of economic development were likely to cause worsening inequality; the relationship between equity and growth was at best a U-shaped curve. Many obvious public policy initiatives seemed to have little if any effect on the degree of inequality. Examining the rapidly growing countries with the most equitable income distributions, Adelman identified a pattern to their success. All started with radical redistribution of assets, usually land, combined with limits on the accumulation and use of financial capital, before the era of rapid growth; they then invested heavily in human capital (education and training) and pursued labor-intensive industrial growth strategies, aided by large amounts of foreign capital.[5]

The next summary, by Nancy Birdsall, David Ross, and Richard Sabot, is a recent analysis continuing along the lines of Adelman's work. Birdsall et al. examine the success of eight rapidly growing East Asian countries, finding positive interactions between the rate of growth, investment in education, and comparatively equal distributions of income. Not surprisingly, the relationship between education and economic growth is strongest when there is an increasing demand for skilled labor; that demand resulted from the promotion of manufactured exports in the countries being studied. Spending on education was no greater as a percentage of GDP than in other developing countries, but the combination of declining population growth rates and rising per capita incomes allowed a sharp increase in educational spending per student.

Contrary to the common notion of a trade-off between equity and growth, Birdsall et al. identify several mechanisms by which an increase in the incomes and power of the poor may promote growth. Greater income opportunities for the poor may mean more savings, greater productivity, and better incentives for hard work, while broadened political participation can lead to more sensible and stable government policies. The trick is not to rely on income transfers, but rather to eliminate subsidies to the elite, and to expand real opportunities and incentives for both the rural and the urban poor, as several East Asian countries have managed to do.

The View from the Top

Turning from the bottom to the top of the world income distribution inverts the perspective on many economic problems. In the affluent countries of North America, Western Europe, and the Pacific Rim there are ample resources to satisfy basic needs for all. Poverty, while not eliminated, is almost always a matter of relative rather than absolute deprivation. Agriculture has become one of the smaller industries, and reservoirs of rural poverty no longer loom over the urban economy.

Yet in other respects, many of the underlying issues about development and well-being persist even in the most affluent societies. If the growth of average incomes alone is not an adequate justification or goal for development when countries are poor, how urgent can growth be when societies are richer and the marginal utility of income is presumably lower? Questions arise at every income level about the definition of and provision for basic needs, the balance between positive and negative freedoms, and the ability to prescribe a bundle of merit goods or to describe a good way of life. These issues often surface in the debates over the welfare state, which can be viewed as a form of development economics for the already developed.

The article by Nicholas Barr summarized here is an exhaustive review of the economic theory of the welfare state, combined with an empirical comparison of selected social welfare programs in ten developed countries (most of the latter topic is omitted in the summary). Barr rests the justification for state intervention on a category of market failures involving imperfect information and unpredictable, uninsurable risks. This analysis elaborates in greater detail on themes raised by Stiglitz in Part III.

In essence, Barr argues that people want things—his examples are stability of real income in business cycle downturns and in retirement, and universal health coverage regardless of pre-existing or congenital conditions—that the market cannot efficiently or profitably provide. Faced with such market failures, government intervention is not only redistributive but can contribute to efficiency in satisfying consumer desires. However, it is particularly difficult to define the appropriate incentive structure for the efficient provision of health care, since the service that people need is so unlike a conventional, marketed commodity. Emphasizing the limitations of the commodity approach, Barr observes that the developed country that relies most heavily on the market for health care, the U.S.A., has the most expensive and inequitable system and provides the least complete coverage. Unfortunately, comparative analysis does not lead to identification of a single, unambiguously superior alternative.

American readers who are astonished to find that their team is not a contender for the gold medal in social welfare would do well to consult Robert Kuttner's very readable introduction and survey of the subject, in the chapter summarized here. Kuttner defends the Northern European model of universal entitlements to social welfare, maintaining that it is often superior to the American style of rigorously means-tested benefits. There is little empirical evidence, he asserts, that universal entitlements lead to wasteful public expenditure or undermine work incentives. On the other hand, means-tested programs lead to isolation and stigmatization of recipients and create a dual society of rich and poor—undermining political support for the provision of essential services. Government assistance to middle and upper income groups is not absent in the U.S. but takes the form of tax provisions and other benefits that are of little value to the poor, making it possible to cut social welfare spending without harming the more comfortable majority. European-style universal programs, like Social Security in the U.S., are more likely to receive universal support and, in Kuttner's view, combine efficiency in spending and dignity for recipients even in times of austerity.

Like Barr and Kuttner, most theorists analyze and advocate a universal welfare state, as opposed to the minimalist or "residual" model of narrowly means-tested safety net programs. An exception is Robert Goodin, who has developed a detailed political philosophy of the residual welfare state, based in part on a critique of more universal approaches.[6] For Goodin, there are flaws in the claim that the state should provide for basic needs; the distinction between high-priority needs and lower-priority desires becomes ambiguous and ill-defined on close examination. Other justifications for universal programs likewise fail to persuade him; arguments for equality typically do not provide or motivate a clear answer to the question, "Equality of what?" The sole grounds for social welfare programs, according to Goodin, derive from consideration of negative freedoms. Society should protect everyone from harm, including the vulnerability to exploitation that arises when an individual is impoverished and economically dependent on others. That is, the safety net of benefits for the very poor is essential to their autonomy.

Inside the Scandinavian Model

If provision of adequate social welfare were an international athletic competition, it would best be held as part of the Winter Olympics. Europe's northernmost countries, in Scandinavia, routinely top the lists in comparisons of the extent and success of welfare state activities. To cite one example, Barr finds that the fraction of poverty eliminated by the government's efforts ranges from roughly one-fifth in the U.S. to four-fifths in Sweden.[7] It is worth exploring, therefore, the Scandinavian model of the welfare state both in theory and in practice.

Sweden, in particular, is often taken as the leading example of the welfare state. Its Social Democrats have governed the country for most of the 20th century and have had an unparalleled opportunity to put their ideas into practice. In the chapter summarized here, Tim Tilton describes the distinctive features of Swedish Social Democratic ideology; though the vocabulary is often unique, there are many similarities to philosophical positions that appear elsewhere in this volume. Tilton outlines five central themes of the Swedish ideology. First is a belief in "integrative democracy," implying full participation of the working classes in political, economic, and social life. Second is the concept of society and state as the "people's home," characterized by solidarity, cooperation, and equality. Third is the complementarity of economic equality and efficiency, reflected, among other places, in innovative labor market policies. The last two themes are the preference for a socially controlled market economy, with active but incremental development of regulation and planning, and the perception that expansion of the public sector can be designed to extend freedom of choice.

The extent of the resulting welfare state comes as a surprise to those from the U.S. or other countries with more minimal public sectors. The "Scandinavian model" includes free or heavily subsidized medical care, child care, higher education, family allowances (cash benefits paid to all parents with minor children, regardless of income), public pensions, publicly built or subsidized housing, guaranteed sick pay and vacations for all workers, extensive worker rights on the job, active government retraining and employment referral services, and more.[8] Not only is poverty drastically alleviated by such measures; the demographics of the income distribution are changed. The elderly, and families with children, are almost never in the lowest income brackets. Rather, the poorest members of society are often childless young adults—suggesting that being on the bottom is a transitory stage of a normal life cycle, rather than a lifetime condition.[9]

It may seem difficult to believe that such a sweeping commitment to equality is compatible with economic efficiency, as suggested in Tilton's account of Social Democratic ideology. Yet there are at least two specific ways in which the welfare state may lead to increases in efficiency, in addition to the general benefits of investment in education, health, worker retraining and job referrals, etc. One economic advantage of the welfare state involves attitudes toward risks. Extensive income guarantees may encourage a risk-averse population to take more chances, since they know that they will be provided for even if they fail; this, in the view of many economists, is important in stimulating innovation and economic growth.[10]

The second factor involves the so-called "solidarity wage policy" or "egalitarian wage compression," which was a feature of the Scandinavian economic model until the 1980s. Nationwide wage bargaining by labor and employer federations allowed the labor movement to push successfully toward equalization of wages between industries. While fulfilling a political commitment to equality, this also acted as an indirect subsidy to expanding, high-productivity industries and a corresponding tax on stagnant or low-productivity industries.[11] For example, paying similar wages to metalworkers and restaurant waiters is a bargain for metalworking industries and a disaster for restaurants (assuming the wage is based on average productivity). And in fact, Sweden has long excelled in various metal-based industries but has relatively few, and quite expensive, restaurants. Nationwide wage bargaining broke down in the 1980s, when more profitable industries began to pay more to attract more labor.

Scandinavia, like the rest of Europe, has been in a prolonged state of economic crisis in the 1990s, forcing retrenchment and cutbacks in numerous areas. The description of the "Scandinavian model" offered here, and in much of the literature, is not as completely applicable after about 1990 as before. Critics have suggested that some of the problems are self-inflicted and that stagnation represents in part the emergence of inherent contradictions in the welfare state. The Swedish economist Assar Lindbeck maintains that the welfare state, with its provision of such a lengthy menu of positive freedoms and merit goods, decreases consumer welfare by limiting the freedom of choice and dampens work incentives by providing excessively generous income guarantees.[12] However, the crisis of the 1990s has led to economic stagnation throughout Europe, with no obvious difference in the impact on countries with more and less extensive welfare states. Even if global economic pressures force a permanent retreat from the classic Scandinavian welfare state of the 1970s and 1980s, the model has, unlike many philosophical proposals, been tested in practice and shown to be successful when economic conditions permit.

The last word on the subject, for this section, belongs to Gøsta Esping-Andersen, who has written widely on the economics of the welfare state. In the final summary, Esping-Andersen examines several interpretations of the rise of the welfare state. The logic of industrialism cannot be said to make the welfare state necessary as a replacement for traditional communities; for welfare programs arose long after the destruction of older communities. Nor is the provision of social welfare a simple result of progressive, redistributive majority politics in modern democracies; some of the earliest welfare states emerged in quite undemocratic contexts, such as Germany under Bismarck. Esping-Andersen argues that the welfare state must be seen as the result of a particular configuration of class alliances in the history of political development, which worked out differently in Scandinavia than elsewhere.

There are, for Esping-Andersen, three clusters of different types of welfare states. The minimalist, "liberal" (in the 19th-century sense) approach taken in the U.S. provides primarily means-tested, stigmatized benefits, perpetuating economic and social dualism. Many continental European welfare states provide more extensive social rights but remain tied to the institutions of the market and the traditional family, failing to challenge existing values in these areas. Finally, the Scandinavian social democratic model, best developed in Norway and Sweden, is committed to the principles of universalism and decommodification. The goal of this model is to provide an increasing number of benefits as human rights or entitlements independent of market transactions, thereby "decommodifying" a growing area of human life and potential. This generates social solidarity and support for public policy, far more than in the other modes of welfare provision.

Many of the same issues arise in development economics and in the discussion of the welfare state. Questions of rights are important at every income level, both as ends in themselves and as means to democratic decision making. Most governments intervene to address a range of market failures, embodying a vision of welfare and the good life that extends far beyond the satisfaction of consumer preferences in the marketplace. Equity, in many senses of the term, is on most lists of social goals; analyses discussed here suggest that, both in developing countries and in affluent welfare states, judicious pursuit of equity may promote rather than impede efficiency. Finally, there is a similarity between Streeten's provision for basic needs and Esping-Andersen's decommodification: both seek to reduce the dominion of the market, to provide as much as possible of the material basis of human life on the basis of needs rather than wealth.

Notes

1. Ajit K. Dasgupta, *Growth, Development, and Welfare* (New York: Basil Blackwell, 1988), Chapter 3. The discussion of the fourth category here deviates substantially from Dasgupta's summary treatment of that issue.

2. Paul Streeten, *First Things First: Meeting Basic Human Needs in the Developing Countries* (New York: Oxford University Press, 1981), 37–38.

3. See also Amartya Sen, "Poor, Relatively Speaking," *Oxford Economic Papers,* 35 no. 2 (July 1993), 159–169.

4. Ian Gough and Theo Thomas, "Why Do Levels of Human Welfare Vary Among Nations?," *International Journal of Health Services* 24 (1994), 715–748.

5. Irma Adelman, "Development Economics—A Reassessment of Goals," *American Economic Review* 65 no. 2 (May 1975), 302–309; "Economic Development and Political Change in Developing Countries," *Social Research* 47 no. 2 (Summer 1980), 213–234.

6. Robert E. Goodin, *Reasons for Welfare: The Political Theory of the Welfare State* (Princeton: Princeton University Press, 1988). For a related argument, see Brian Barry, "The Welfare State versus the Relief of Poverty," *Ethics* 100 (April 1990), 503–529.

7. Using 50 percent of median income as the poverty line, Barr considers the population that would have been below the line in the absence of government taxes and transfer payments and calculates the fraction of that population that was moved above the poverty line by taxes and transfers.

8. See Robert Erikson, Erik Jørgen Hansen, Stein Ringen, and Hannu Uusitalo, eds. *The Scandinavian Model: Welfare States and Welfare Research* (Armonk, NY: M. E. Sharpe, 1987).

9. Björn Gustafsson, "Poverty in Sweden, 1975–85," *International Journal of Sociology* 23 (Summer–Fall 1993), 53–71; Gustafsson and Hannu Uusitalo, "The Welfare State and Poverty in Finland and Sweden from the Mid-1960s to the Mid-1980s," *Review of Income and Wealth* 36 (September 1990), 249–266.

10. Hans-Werner Sinn, "A Theory of the Welfare State," *Scandinavian Journal of Economics* 97 (1995), 495–526.

11. Jonas Agell and Kjell Erik Lommerud, "Egalitarianism and Growth," *Scandinavian Journal of Economics* 95 (1993), 559–579.

12. See, among many other articles, Assar Lindbeck, "Individual Freedom and Welfare State Policy," *European Economic Review* 32 (1988), 295–318. On the rise of individualism and anti-social attitudes, see Pekka Kosonen, "From Collectivity to Individualism in the Welfare State?" *Acta Sociologica* 30 (1987), 281–293.

Summary of

The Evolution of Development Thought

by Paul Streeten

[Published in *Thinking About Development* (Cambridge, New York, Melbourne: Press Syndicate of the University of Cambridge, 1995), 5–56.]

Development thinking has evolved over the years from its original focus on economic growth, to emphases on employment, jobs and justice, redistribution with growth, basic needs, and, most recently, human development. This review traces the evolution of some of the most important ideas in the field. In particular, it discusses the concept of human development as a model for thinking about development, identifies some of the weaknesses of current poverty measures, and proposes some alternative indicators.[1]

Human Development

Economic growth has never been regarded as the objective of development but rather as its principal performance test. Poverty reduction has always been the core concern; economic growth was believed to help achieve this goal through trickle down effects or through government intervention to redistribute the gains. However, as it became increasingly clear not only that these mechanisms for linking growth and poverty reduction were inadequate, but also that direct investments in the human capital among the poor could be productive, GNP was "dethroned," and more direct approaches to poverty reduction were pursued.

One approach focuses on human development, defined as "the enlargement of choices, the presentation of options." [22] Income is one means of achieving this enlargement, but health, education, self-respect, participation in the common life, and cultural identity are also important components. It is "development of the people, for the people and by the people," where "of the people means jobs and incomes; for the people means social services; and by the people means participation." [22] Human development and poverty eradication are beneficial not only as ends in themselves but also because they can contribute to higher productivity, lower reproductivity (lower population growth), and environmental sustainability, as well as to the growth of civil society and of social and political stability.

The Human Development Index (HDI), introduced by the United Nations Development Programme in 1990, is a composite indicator that measures income per head, life expectancy, literacy rates, and years of schooling. While there are some criticisms of this index, and no single index can fully capture the depth and richness of the concept of human development, the greatest value of the HDI (apart from the political value of highlighting a single figure) is in demonstrating the inadequacies of measures based on GNP alone. For example, analysis of the HDI indicates that there is much greater scope for reducing international gaps in human indicators than in income. It shows that in human terms, development in the last three decades has actually succeeded, as life expectancy, literacy, nutrition, and mortality levels have all increased substantially during this period despite the persistence of wide income gaps; average income in the South is only 6 percent of that in the North, but life expectancy is 80 percent, literacy 66 percent, and nutrition 85 percent.

It is important to remember that the HDI, like GNP, is also an average indicator, and we must look beyond it at the implications of the underlying income distribution for the poorest, especially rural inhabitants, women, and children. Even so, the HDI has additional advantages because the distributions of literacy and life expectancy are generally much less skewed than that of income, so, for example, a high HDI does tell us something about distribution, and an increase in the HDI is a better indicator of actual improvements than an increase in average income. But the most important advantage of the HDI is its political and policy implications; it can shift attention to social sectors and policies that are left out in income alone.

There has been some debate about whether and how freedom should be treated in measures of human development; it is clear, for example, that basic material needs could be satisfied in a well-run prison. However, it is difficult not only to measure freedom but also to compare its importance with that of other social indicators; freedom can also be highly volatile. Nor does guaranteeing freedom require commitment of scarce resources in the way that protecting positive rights does. Freedom might therefore best be treated as an issue separate from, but related to, development. It is not a necessary condition for development, but neither is its absence. Moreover, increasing levels of human development almost invariably lead to greater demands for freedom by the people, as recent experiences in Latin America, East Asia, Eastern Europe, South Africa, and the former Soviet Union clearly demonstrate.

Poverty: Concepts and Measurement

Before we can consider policies to reduce poverty, we must analyze the concept of poverty and its measurement. First, do we identify the poor and measure the extent of poverty? This has most often been done by using fractiles of income recipients, an approach that has some uses but also serious weaknesses: how do we measure income distribution (e.g., by household, individual, or adult equivalent)? Moreover, income statistics alone cannot capture the essence and causes of poverty, even when they are well used. For example, poverty may be related to an individual's or household's location, control of physical assests, stock of human capital, ethnic group, position in the age cycle, or characteristics of the household head. In addition, poverty may be dynamic rather than static, as incomes fluctuate year by year or as a household progresses through various life-cycle stages of greater and less poverty, or faces a year of particular misfortune. This suggests that consumption expenditure will serve as a more consistent measure of poverty than income and that understanding poverty requires knowing how long any given segment of the poor population has been in that position, how long it is likely to stay there, and what adaptations are available, such as borrowing to alleviate hardship during the most difficult periods.

The distinction between relative or absolute poverty is also important. The assumption that higher poverty lines in countries with higher income levels reflect only relative poverty is mistaken. Absolute poverty levels can also rise with rising incomes as "the capability of appearing in public without shame, of participating in the life of the community or of maintaining self-respect will vary with the conventions, regulations, and material comforts of society." [36] For example, if access to educational television programs becomes the norm in schools, it becomes necessary for gaining the full benefits of a primary education and to have access to a television set. This is not a case of rising income creating new needs (for television), but of satisfaction of the same need (to be educated) requiring more income. While viewing shame as an indicator of absolute poverty can be taken too far, it is clear that absolute poverty is at least partly a function of average living standards. Relative poverty is an evil but is a different and lesser evil than absolute poverty.

Another important distinction was made by the turn-of-the-century economist Seebohm Rowntree between primary and secondary poverty. Primary poverty is the inability to command enough income to obtain the minimum necessities (i.e., insufficient resources) while secondary poverty exists when there is an inefficient use of adequate resources (for example, owing to lack of education or to addictions such as drinking and gambling). Amartya Sen builds on the concept of secondary poverty when he identifies the importance of "capabilities" and "functionings" when he discusses the capacity to convert resources into well-being. The ability to convert income into a high quality of life will also depend on the availability and quality of education, health, and other social services.

There are considerable difficulties in measuring primary poverty; should income or consumption be the focus, should households, individuals, or adult equivalents be the basic units, determining how poor (i.e., how far below the poverty line) the poor are, and dealing with how poverty is distributed among the poor. To overcome these complexities, it may be useful to measure poverty through the removal of six veils; "the removal of each veil gets us nearer the facts that we want to measure, but the outer veils are not therefore unnecessary." [42] We must therefore evaluate poverty as it is associated with each "veil," and then proceed beyond it. The first such veil is money income, which has some relevance, but which also obscures a great deal about differences among the poor and about how conditions for the poor change as incomes rise. The second veil is real income or money income adjusted for changes in the general price level, and the third is real income adjusted for the region- and commodity-specific purchases of the poor and for the nonavailability of some items.

However, even real income misses some important components of well-being and poverty; it ignores the welfare benefits of leisure, often does not include nonmarketed subsistence income, free social services, and benefits derived from pure-public goods and does not account for distribution. The fourth level or veil is therefore the direct measure of the physical inputs required to meet basic needs (e.g., calories consumed) that "penetrate behind the veil of money," [43] while the fifth incorporates impact measures of health, mortality, literacy, and morbidity to "look behind income and what it is spent on, at the inputs in relation to requirements, and the skills and abilities of converting goods and services into human functionings." [44] While average income per head often is not very closely correlated with these human indicators, the indicators are highly correlated with one another, which has important implications for policy selection, especially when it comes to granting priority to income generation or to provision of social services. Finally, the sixth level evaluates distribution of benefits and costs within the household.

Human impact indicators have some advantages over income or consumption indicators, but the former should serve to complement rather than replace the latter. There is no easy way to aggregate these indicators into a single composite measure similar to GNP, but this should not discourage their use. Several approaches to aggregation have been attempted, including the HDI discussed above, and the Physical Quality of Life Index (PQLI), which aggregates life expectancy, infant mortality, and literacy, giving equal weight to each. Another approach develops profiles of lifetime expectations of years of schooling, marriage, employment, retirement, etc. that can then be compared across different groups or countries.

An alternative approach that highlights the shortcomings of those listed above is to evaluate poverty from the point of view of the poor by, for example, asking households not only what they consume but also what they think is an adequate level of well-being. Indices of satisfaction determined in this way often are not highly correlated with other measures of poverty, in part because a number of nonmaterial benefits other than income and consumption influence an individual's perception of his or her well-being, including independence from patrons, mobility, security, self-respect, good working conditions, and freedom to choose jobs and livelihoods. This should warn against efforts to measure poverty by single indicators and against an excessive concern with income levels, which may or may not influence an individual's ability to meet these other needs. It also demonstrates that "any attempt to understand poverty must include the way in which poor people themselves perceive their situation." [50]

Finally, it should be clear even in the best conditions that no policy maker can guarantee the achievement of all of these goals, but policy can create opportunities for their fulfillment. Policy makers must recognize that "in assessing and measuring successes or failures in the pursuit of these objectives, it is important not to fall victim to the twin fallacies that only what can be counted counts, and that any figure, however unreliable, is better than none. . . . The ability, or capability, not only to keep alive, but also to be well nourished, healthy, educated, productive, fulfilled, these are the objectives of good policy, and incomes or the goods they buy are only one type of instrument to achieve them." [51]

In the light of the earlier discussion, three measures are proposed for use by donors in monitoring poverty and the effectiveness of policies aimed at poverty alleviation. The first is income or consumption per capita (or, preferably, per-adult equivalent) in conjunction with the definition of a poverty line. The second is calorie consumption relative to requirements, again preferably on a per-adult equivalent basis. The third measure is the proportion of income or expenditure on food; high levels (e.g., above 75 percent) indicate poverty, and levels that remain unchanged even as income increases indicate extreme poverty.

These three indicators often will not identify the same groups of people as poor, in which case more analysis is called for, including measures such as weight for age of children, land area per capita, literacy rates, and life expectancy (which are in any case useful supplements to the indicators suggested above). Monitoring poverty is constrained by the fact that there are trade-offs between accuracy and the costs of gathering information, but the cheapest indicators will probably also be the least accurate ones. Monitoring, especially by outside donors, may also be politically sensitive in the eyes of host governments. Creating monitoring institutions that can gain the trust and meet the needs of both sides may therefore be necessary. At the same time, a degree of competition in the monitoring process that encourages the testing of a variety of methods would also be productive. Enhancing indigenous capacity to monitor and conduct research on poverty issues should be a priority, since research and action on poverty tend to go together.

Note

1. This article covers a broad range of issues encompassed by the debates about development. This summary focuses primarily on the last two sections of the paper that deal most directly with understanding and measuring human well-being.

Summary of

Positive Freedom, Markets, and the Welfare State

by Partha Dasgupta

[Published in *The Economic Borders of the State,* ed. Dieter Helm
(Oxford: Oxford University Press, 1989, 110–126).]

The debate about the proper mix of market and nonmarket resource allocation mechanisms, especially for the commodities whose public provision has come to represent the welfare state, is central to the continuing discussion about the kind of society we aspire to live in. This article reviews a number of theoretical arguments that have shaped thinking and justified various positions in this debate. For example, the right to one type of liberty, negative liberty, has frequently been used, along with some instrumental arguments, to justify exclusive reliance on market allocations. Positive freedom and welfarist approaches, on the other hand, may both support more government intervention. The practical implications of these two approaches may, however, still differ; in general, welfarism suggests that states should allocate positive-rights goods via transferable coupons, while positive-freedom arguments advocate their allocation in kind.

Justifications for Market Allocation

In addition to Nozick's justification for market allocations and a minimal state[1] based on the necessity of protecting negative freedom (i.e., the right to be free of coercion or interference by others) there are several instrumental arguments for this position as well. Hayek argues, for example, that the real end is progress, and that the market mechanism and negative freedom are merely the best means to this end.[2] A more prosaic view simply argues that competitive market mechanisms produce, under certain conditions, the most efficient allocation of resources with a minimum of state interference. Bauer, meanwhile, promotes the market based on both preservation of negative freedom and on the grounds that it is the best means for achieving material well-being for those who seek it, without corroding self-reliance or an individual's sense of responsibility and self-respect.[3] He does not, however, suggest that negative political freedom (or political democracy) either leads to or derives from efficient economic markets.

Of these justifications, the second argument, which focuses on markets as the means to efficient allocations, is the most ambiguous with respect to the justifiable role of the government. The criterion of Pareto efficiency alone may produce a number of feasible economic states with no basis for ranking among them. Moreover, the Second Fundamental Theorem of Welfare Economics argues that under certain conditions any efficient resource allocation can actually be sustained as a market equilibrium if the government appropriately redistributes wealth in advance. Thus, a commitment to efficiency alone can be consistent with massive government intervention. The other positions, however, advocate strictly limiting government activity to public goods, such as security, legal systems, and some support of information channels.

Positive Freedom

Isaiah Berlin distinguished between negative freedom—freedom *from* coercion and interference—and positive freedom, which guarantees access *to* certain resources and to the abilities that they permit one, especially the ability to function and to "be somebody."[4] Goods that are necessary for a person to be capable of functioning, i.e., to ensure positive freedom, are "basic needs" and comprise a category of "natural-rights goods" known as "positive-rights goods." A positive-rights doctrine emphasizes the right to positive freedom, requiring that each individual have sufficient access to and command over certain resources, in particular those typically provided by the welfare state. There are also natural-rights goods needed to secure negative freedom, including security and an effective legal system, that are known as "negative-rights goods," but the need for state provision of these goods is already widely accepted. Negative and positive rights may clash with each other or with other goals of society. Also, since both require some command over resources, resource allocation problems and trade-offs are inevitable when both types of freedom are sought.

A key distinction, however, is that negative-rights goods do tend to more nearly approximate pure-public goods, which are well-known sources of market failure. This explains why no conflict necessarily arises between negative freedoms and economic efficiency. The same is not true, however, for the commodities that are necessary to secure positive freedoms, which include some that are only partially public, such as certain health care services, and others that are totally private, including food and shelter. Economic efficiency and protection of positive freedoms are therefore not necessarily compatible goals. Moreover, while the competitive-market mechanism may produce an efficient resource allocation (although it will not necessarily do so), it can never guarantee distribution that ensures positive freedom for all members of society.

Welfarism

Welfarism has been the source of the dominant moral framework in the economics literature. It focuses on the production and distribution of individual welfare via access to and use of goods and services and judges or ranks social and economic states based on their welfare characteristics. Utilitarianism, a spe-

cial case of welfarism, evaluates states based simply on the sum of individual utilities (or welfares). One common critique of Utilitarianism is that it is indifferent to variations in the distribution of welfare among individuals; i.e., if two
economic states have the same total amount of welfare, but great differences in
the distribution, one being very egalitarian and the other highly unequal, Utilitarianism suggests no preference between the two.

The focus here, however, will be on another type of indifference problem
that is common to welfarism in general. It occurs when different commodity allocations produce not only the same level of total welfare, but the same distribution of welfare among individuals as well, yet result in differences in the distribution of rights-based goods among individuals. Welfare and freedom are not
the same, and similar distributions of welfare can be associated with very different distributions of freedom. The chain linking commodity availability to use,
the ability to function, and welfare or utility is very complex, and the entire
chain must be carefully scrutinized when evaluating social states; both welfarist
and rights-based theories, when taken alone, are too limited to make this moral
evaluation effectively.

Like negative-rights approaches, welfarism in general justifies resource allocation by the market. The First Fundamental Theorem of Welfare Economics
states that competitive equilibrium is Pareto efficient; given initial endowments
and technological possibilities, individual utilities or welfares will determine
equilibrium allocations. However, some welfarists may still find competitive-
market allocations unappealing, because they do not get the distribution of welfares right (while Utilitarians are unconcerned with this issue, this is not true of
all welfarists). Thus, unlike those concerned exclusively with negative freedoms,
these welfarists might, on the basis of the Second Fundamental Theorem of
Welfare Economics, advocate that the state correct this problem via massive redistribution of initial allocations prior to allowing competitive markets to function freely. In practice this will, of course, be quite difficult, not least because of
the vast amount of information that the state must know to redistribute effectively, including individual utility functions, technological possibilities, and initial endowments. In fact, if the state has all of this information, then questions
arise as to why it should bother to resort to markets at all. If, however, we relax
the expectation that the state should get things exactly right, and instead aim
only for getting things approximately (or statistically) right, then at least in
some cases a combination of state taxes and subsidies with reliance on markets
is indicated.

Uncertainty about future possibilities and the unequal distribution of information about uncertain events also have important implications for the welfarist
attitude toward reliance on competitive markets. People "*know* different things
and are uncertain *about* different things" and, as a result, information becomes
a tradable commodity. [122] However, markets for information, like those for

risk, are prone to inefficiencies and failure, and in some cases may not even exist. This therefore supplies welfarists with another justification for the non-market allocation of certain commodities that are most affected by these problems and that are also critical for personal welfare, including insurance, health care, and basic food and shelter. Advocates concerned only with negative freedom may remain uninterested in these arguments, but proponents of positive freedom would appear to be in general agreement with the welfarists on this point, and both types of moral theory have therefore been used to justify a streamlined welfare state.

Provision of Positive-Rights Goods

In addition to these apparent similarities in the practical implications of the positive-rights and welfarist approaches, however, there are some important differences as well, particularly with respect to whether positive-rights goods should be provided in kind, as positive-freedom advocates argue, or via tradable coupons, as welfarists suggest. Positive freedom relates to the ability of individuals to function, and access to commodities is merely a means to this end. Rights to commodities are therefore derived rights that vary among individuals depending on their *needs;* individual *preferences* for goods or commodities are relatively unimportant to positive-rightists in determining a just distribution of resources.

If the state had complete information about people's needs, then it could simply implement a just distribution according to needs, but this, of course, is not the case. The best alternative given lack of information is, therefore, equal allocation. But there is more than one way to do this, including distribution of tradable coupons (i.e., the price mechanism) and distribution of nontradable goods or services in kind (i.e., the rationing mechanism). Each results in different final distributions. Thus, the question for positive-rights approaches is which of these mechanisms will come closest to producing a just distribution (i.e., one based on needs) of the positive-rights commodity.

It turns out that if the dispersion of income is small relative to that of needs, then tradable options produce the best results. But in the more realistic case in which income inequalities are large relative to differences in needs, nontradable allocations in kind produce the best results; tradability would result in people with high needs but low incomes consuming less of the positive-rights good than those with low needs and high income. Coupons are the preferred approach of welfarists, and even of proponents of negative freedom once they have accepted state control over a particular positive-rights good. However, when income variability is large, positive-rightists insist on the nonexchange-ability of rights to this good. Thus, while a coupons approach has long been accepted as the more justifiable method of distribution, positive-freedom and positive-rights approaches, which have been ignored for too long in these de-bates, challenge this assumption, and require a reevaluation of these issues.

Notes

1. Robert Nozick, *Anarchy, State, and Utopia* (New York: Basic Books, 1974).
2. Frederick Hayek, *The Constitution of Liberty* (London: Routledge, 1948, 1960, 1976).
3. P. Bauer, *Dissent on Development* (London: Weinfeld, 1971, 1984).
4. Isaiah Berlin, "Two Concepts of Liberty," in *Four Essays on Liberty* (Oxford: Oxford University Press, 1969).

Summary of

Functioning and Capability: The Foundations of Sen's and Nussbaum's Development Ethic, Parts 1 and 2

by David A. Crocker

[Part 1 published in *Political Theory* 20 (November 1992), 584–612; Part 2 published in *Women, Culture, and Development: A Study in Human Capabilities,* eds. Martha Nussbaum and Jonathan Glover (Oxford: Oxford University Press, 1995), 153–198.]

This paper draws on the broad body of work produced by economist Amartya Sen and philosopher Martha Nussbaum to present and evaluate a new and im-portant ethic for international development. Sen and Nussbaum argue that global poverty, deprivation, and hunger represent not just scientific, technical, or political failures but conceptual and ethical ones as well. Their "capability ethic" is intended to provide a new normative perspective on the theory and practice of international development based on the Aristotelian and Marxist tra-ditions and the associated concept of human flourishing. The review begins with an evaluation of the moral assumptions of a number of different develop-ment approaches and situates Sen and Nussbaum's ethic within this context, before turning to a more detailed development of the capabilities and function-ings perpective.

Part I: Alternative Ethical Approaches

According to Sen and Nussbaum, development is an inherently value-laden concept, because it provides criteria for defining good social change and for achieving a better life for people. It is, therefore, especially important to distin-guish means, such as increasing per capita GNP, from ends, such as greater

well-being and the freedom to achieve these ends. Ethics are essential to defining and giving meaning to such objectives. Development is then best defined in
terms of "functionings," and "capabilities" ("what human beings can and
should be able to do"), and the goal of development policy is "the enhancement of certain human functionings and the expansion of human capabilities to
so function." [586] Before developing this approach in more detail, we will first
review the alternatives.

Commodity Approaches

To evaluate different ethical approaches to the concept of development it is necessary to begin with some fundamental questions about how humans should be
able to live their lives, what sorts of things are intrinsically rather than just in-
strumentally valuable, and what the ultimate goals of development should be. It
is necessary to identify fundamental ethical categories (e.g., meeting particular
needs or respecting certain rights) that will serve as the basis for defining and
evaluating other ethical concepts. Sen and Nussbaum argue that this fundamental category is "the ethical space of human functionings and capabilities."
[590]

The "crude" commodity approach defines fundamental ethical categories in
terms of goods or commodities that are seen as intrinsically good or basic. This
approach correctly recognizes that material prosperity is essential for development, but it gives too much attention to commodities, turning them from
means into ends. Sen and Nussbaum argue that goods are of no value in and of
themselves, but only in terms of what they can do for people or what people can
do with them. In addition, consistency problems arise because of individual and
cultural variability in the need for and utilization of goods—different packages
of goods may be able to promote the same human functionings for a given individual, while the same package will promote different capabilities for different
individuals. Certain commodities may harm some and help others, and in many
cases goods can be bad when we get too much of them.

John Rawls offers a more sophisticated model of the commodity perspective.
He identifies "social primary goods" such as rights and liberties, income and
wealth, and opportunities as the things that rational individuals want and need.
He conceives of these goods not as ends, but as means that are essential for realizing each person's conception of the good life, whatever it happens to be.
This can be referred to as a "thin theory of the good," in contrast to a "thick
theory," which would define specific concepts of human excellence toward
which individuals and government should aspire. Rawls thus does much to recognize the ethical importance of individual freedom. However, Sen points out
that individuals vary not only with respect to the ends they choose but also in
how they convert goods into freedom to pursue these ends; we have "unequal
powers to build freedom in our lives even when we have the same bundle of

goods."[1] Rawls limits himself to a concern with negative freedom or absence from restraint by others, but positive freedoms, or freedom from constraints imposed by conditions such as poverty and ignorance, are also necessary if individuals are to have genuine options to choose different ways of life.

The Welfare (Utilitarian) Approach

The commodities approaches overemphasize goods while neglecting people. The welfare approaches, including utilitarianism, recognize well-being and goods development as features of individuals themselves, but they overemphasize individual utility—a mere mental state of individuals—while neglecting other aspects of human well-being. Sen identifies two major problems with welfarism's focus on levels of individual utility. First, welfarism deals only with well-being, ignoring human agency, but Sen believes that both are fundamental dimensions of being human. "Humans are not only experiencers or preference satisfiers; they are also judges, evaluators, and doers." [600] Secondly, utility, happiness or desire fulfillment are not, in any case, adequate measures of well-being; a person who has very little may still experience happiness, and vice versa, but this is an imcomplete basis for judging that individual's well-being or, more importantly, the state of social justice. Utility therefore "at best captures part of the good life but at worst justifies severe deprivation and inequality." [607]

The Basic Needs Approach

The basic needs approach (BNA) does recognize the importance of the kind of lives that individuals are able to lead and the choices that are available to them. It argues that enhancing human well-being is a matter of meeting certain basic or human needs that promote a good life for all *and afford individuals the freedom to choose it.* Sen is quite sympathetic with this approach but argues that it lacks a solid foundation because it fails to specify the nature of needs or to justify treating them as a more fundamental ethical category than commodities, utility, rights, or human functionings. However, reinterpreting needs as capabilities, and reconstruing meeting needs as promoting the freedom to pursue valuable functionings, could overcome this weakness.

Another weakness of the BNA is the tendency to reduce it in practice to a commodities approach, with the same inherent problems. It also puts too much emphasis on bringing individuals up to a certain *minimal* level of needs satisfaction, while ignoring lack of opportunities for higher functioning and levels of inequality that are incompatible with human flourishing and self-respect. Sen also argues that the concept of needs is too passive in contrast with the active concept of capabilities. "[A] capability ethic enables us to say that good public action does not always dole things out to passive recipients but increases people's choices and enhances people's capabilities, including their capability of choice." [607]

Part II: The Capability Ethic: Foundations

Turning to the capabilities and functionings ethic, we find that Sen and Nussbaum offer slightly different interpretations of *functionings*. Sen includes both purposive human activity and a person's states of existence (or mental state); in the case of food, for example, he identifies functionings related to choosing to eat, eating itself, enjoyment of eating, digestion, and the social activities related to eating. Nussbaum takes a narrower view, treating neither choosing nor the experience of pleasure as separate functionings, leading her to somewhat different conclusions about the nature of human well-being and the role of agency. Nevertheless, both would agree with Sen's claim that "the primary feature of a person's well-being is the functioning vector that he or she achieves."[2]

Capabilities are closely related to but still distinct from functionings:

> A person's combination of actual functionings, her "functioning vector," is the particular life she actually leads. . . . The person's "capability set" is the total set of functionings that are "feasible," that are within her reach, that the person could choose. [159]

Two people can thus possess the same capability set, but choose to realize different sets of functionings, or they may achieve the same sets of functionings with different capability sets. A classic example of this that highlights the importance of capabilities is the difference between starvation and fasting; for an individual with a limited capability set it may be the only choice, but for someone with an expansive capability set, fasting may be one choice among many options. Capabilities are also important because, consistent with an Aristotelian ethic, functionings are *chosen* from among options, not determined or enforced. Moreover, capabilities also have *intrinsic* value because they add positive freedom (i.e., worthwhile options) to life.

Capabilities can be defined in relation to general character traits and opportunities, and Sen and Nussbaum interpret this concept differently. Both agree, however, that choice is an essential component of capabilities. Sen restricts his notion of capabilities to the possibilities or opportunities facing an agent. "Hence, for Sen, capabilities are not powers of the person that might or might not be realized in different situations. They are, rather, options . . . for actions." [163] Nussbaum, however, conceives of capabilities as a combination of the internal *powers* possessed by an individual and the material and social conditions that make options possible, or *external capabilities*. The concept of external capabilities might have been better expressed as a requirement that functioning both realizes *internal* capabilities and requires *external* opportunities, the latter depending on access to resources, enabling rights, and absence of interference, but Nussbaum's approach—with its greater emphasis on valuable personal powers—is still the stronger of the two.

Several distinct types of functioning and capabilities have been identified by

Sen and Nussbaum. Sen distinguishes between levels of opportunity that are more or less feasible, and between positive and negative functionings, and he also describes actual and possible functionings at different levels of generality, from the most inclusive level (being able to function well), to the more specific (e.g., being able to move about or to ride a bicycle). Both Sen and Nussbaum stress the belief that various functionings and capabilities are incommensurable (i.e., they cannot be measured and compared by some common, "deeper" measure such as utility) and that each is distinct and important in its own right, so that the absence of one cannot be made up for by increasing the amount of another.

Sen also distinguishes between the well-being and agency functionings and capabilities of humans. Well-being freedoms and functionings concern an individual's choices driven by self-interest, while agency freedom and functionings may concern both an individual's own well-being and also goals (e.g., the well-being of others) that may be at odds with self-interest. Sen's Smithian and Kantian view thus breaks with those—especially economists—who conceive of humans as mere maximizers of self-interest narrowly defined and instead makes room for altruism and sacrifice.

Sen and Nussbaum also rank capabilities and functionings by importance and argue that the aim of development is to expand and promote *valuable* capabilities and functionings, although in practice sometimes valuation proves difficult. Thus far, Sen has refused to offer a definite list of valuable capabilities and functionings, since that decision is partly political and calls for a democratic procedure to deal with unobvious cases.[3] Nussbaum, on the other hand, lists ten valuable capabilities (see Nussbaum summary in Part VII), aiming to articulate "an Aristotelian view of 'good human functioning' that precedes and is the basis for considering the responsibilities and structures of a just political arrangement." [170]

> For Nussbaum . . . the aim of government goes beyond fairly distributing Rawls's primary goods and Sen's positive freedoms, as important as both these tasks are. The more determinate and guiding aim of just legislators should be that of promoting [170] 'the capability to live a rich and fully human life.'[4]

She seeks to build international consensus about a universal definition of good human functioning that is nonmetaphysical and that can recognize and reconcile different religious and metaphysical traditions. Such a cross-cultural definition could provide "the basis for a global ethic and a fully international account of distributive justice."[5]

The resulting "thick vague conception" of the human being developed by Nussbaum is presented at two levels. The first deals with the "shape of the human form of life" or the "constitutive circumstances of the human being" [171] and includes factors such as recognition of and aversion to mortality,

basic bodily needs, affiliations with others, and the capacities to experience pleasure, pain, and humor, and to reason and play. The second level identifies "basic
human functional capabilities" [174], or in other words, the particular
"virtues" associated with the constitutive elements of the first level (Sen frequently mentions many of the items on this list). Nussbaum is concerned with
identifying two distinct thresholds, a lower one below which a being is so impoverished in (potential) capacities as to not be human at all, and a second,
somewhat higher level, beneath which a life may be judged human, but not
good. It is this second threshold that is of particular interest when making public policy, for the task of good government is to ensure that everyone (who is
able) can live, if they choose, above the second threshold.

One potential challenge to Sen's and Nussbaum's pluralistic and diverse vision of well-being is the "conflict of principles" problem, which arises if two or
more valuable capabilities cannot be simultaneously chosen as actual functionings. Sen argues, however, that it is possible, based on an appeal to shared values, to formulate at least partial orderings of valuable functionings, moreover,

> Sen . . . makes the point that it is better to be "vaguely right" than "precisely
> wrong." It is better to be correct in identifying the diversity of good function-
> ings and be beset with the problem of ordering them than in using one ho-
> mogenous quality like utility that, at best, does justice to only one intrinsic
> good and, at worst, is wildly inaccurate with respect to human well-being and
> other goods. [178]

Nussbaum adds that it is often possible to change the social order and eliminate
or at least alter some of these "tragic choices." She also notes, however, that
some value conflicts may be irresolvable, reflecting our individuality and our
human limitations.

Implications for Needs, Freedom, Rights, and Justice

Sen hopes to use the capabilities ethic to provide a sounder foundation for the
basic needs approach, but Nussbaum argues that needs themselves do still have
a role in contributing to human well-being. First, she argues that "humans *need*
to develop their nascent valuable capacities into mature ones." [181] Underdeveloped capabilities represent "needs for functioning," because "actual capabilities are more valuable than merely latent ones." [181] Needs are also essential
because they reflect human limitations, and without them there is no basis by
which to measure human achievement.

Sen places a high value on freedoms, especially positive freedom, which is
closely linked to his notion of capabilities. He argues that negative freedom
(though important in the sense of freedom from external interference) is not
enough if a person still does not have valuable options (positive freedoms). In
fact, "some policies of noninterference actually extinguish human freedom to

choose what is valuable."[6] Sen also distinguishes between well-being freedom—"the real opportunity to choose and achieve well-being" [184]—and agency freedom, or the opportunity to choose *for or against* one's own well-being. These freedoms have both intrinsic value as ends in themselves and instrumental value as they contribute to achieving other goals. A good society should provide the conditions for both types of freedom and ensure the development of the human ability to have and make choices.

There are different conceptions of how the notion of rights fits together with that of capabilities and functionings. Nussbaum takes a purely instrumental view, arguing that rights are only justified when they promote valuable functionings and capabilities. Others, especially rights-based (deontological) theorists such as Nozick, give primacy to rights while arguing that they are neither means nor ends, but constraints on both of these. Sen, however, conceives of rights (like freedoms) as both means and ends and defines a basic or capability right as the right to minimum levels of basic capabilities or freedoms. He then constructs a consequentialist "goal rights system" in which fulfillment of rights is included among the goals and criterion for evaluation of states of affairs or government actions.

Sen and Nussbaum are beginning to develop theories of distributive justice consonant with the capability ethic. Sen argues that individual claims must be evaluated not in terms of utility, social primary goods, or negative rights but in terms of the freedom to choose among different options or ways of living. Justice is thus concerned with the distribution of freedoms and functionings and with equality of basic capabilities. Governments should therefore protect the claims of *all* citizens to basic levels of freedom and well-being and promote their ability to rise above Nussbaum's second threshold, rather than protecting the rights of a few to advance to higher levels while the rest are left behind. There is, however, still a need for further elaboration of these theories, especially with regard to issues of international distributive justice. The pluralistic capability ethic that Sen and Nussbaum are forging offers new and important challenges to practitioners and ethicists of international development.

Notes

1. Amartya Sen, "Justice: Means versus Freedoms," *Philosophy and Public Affairs* 19 (1990), 111–121, p. 121.

2. Amartya Sen, "Well-Being, Agency and Freedom: The Dewey Lectures 1984," *Journal of Philosophy* 82 (1985), 169–221, p. 198.

3. Sen sees this kind of decision partly as a subject for "social choice." See Amartya Sen, "Rationality and Social Choice," *American Economic Review* 85(1), 1–25.

4. Martha Nussbaum, "Aristotelian Social Democracy," in *Liberalism and the Good,* eds. R. B. Douglass, G. R. Mara, and H. S. Richardson (New York and London: Routledge, 1990), 217.

5. Martha Nussbaum, "Human Functionings and Social Justice: In Defense of Aristotelian Essentialism," *Political Theory* 20(2), 202–246.

6. Martha Nussbaum, "Nature, Function, and Capability: Aristotle on Political Distribution," *Oxford Studies in Ancient Philosophy* (1988, suppl. vol., 145–184).

Summary of

Connecting, Extending, Reversing: Development from a Gender Perspective

by Naila Kabeer

[Published in Naila Kabeer, *Reversed Realities: Gender Hierarchies in Development Thought* (New York and London: Verso, 1994), 69–94.]

There are many flaws in the core assumptions of standard development paradigms, as well as in alternative paradigms called for by the South. One of the most important of these flaws is the continuing confusion between the means and the ends of the development process, a problem that is fostered by the use of GNP as the key indicator. Another is the recognition of only certain kinds of inequalities in the development process while others, such as gender inequality, are largely ignored. Development must be reconceptualized starting from the vantage point of poor women before equity and a real transformation of society can be achieved.

Power, Resources, and Knowledge in the Development Process

Development is a problematic concept. "In its narrow meaning, it refers to the *planned* process by which resources, techniques and expertise are brought together to bring about improved rates of economic growth." [69] In its broader sense, development can be conceived of as a far reaching process of social transformation with varied and often conflicting goals that can have both negative and positive connotations and outcomes. For some it may mean the expansion of individual choice, while for others it has simply "defined new conditions of constraint, enriching a few, impoverishing the many, and in the process eroding both cultural and biological diversity." [70]

Power in the development field, as in others, is derived from control over both resources and ideas, each of which reinforces the other. Gandhi observed that the world has enough resources to meet everyone's basic needs, but not enough to satisfy the greed of a few. Yet the power wielded in the development process by particular members of international financial institutions precludes the global redistribution that is seen by the South as a prerequisite for poverty alleviation and meeting basic needs. Assistance therefore flows to countries that best represent donor interests, rather than to the poorest and most needy. Furthermore, significant shares of aid expenditures must often be made in the donor countries themselves, rather than in recipient countries where they can produce more good. However, though the South and the North often pursue substantially different development goals, they have still both managed to ignore gender inequalities.

Power has influenced the development process through the control of perspectives and ideas. The dominant worldview espouses a hierarchy of knowledge that privileges scientific, positivist knowledge over local, experimental understandings and rewards detached, neutral observers over involved, committed participants. This reductionist approach treats both natural and scientific phenomena as mechanical and divisible parcels, rather than dynamic elements in an organic system. Social reality is thus partitioned into component parts—politics, culture, and economy—and policy analysis is separated into means and ends. This approach ignores the blurred boundaries between these areas and the complex interactions that relate the parts and the whole.

Methodological reductionism has served dominant interests. It has allowed the linkage between the exploitation of elements—material resources or human beings—and the whole to be concealed or overlooked. This is demonstrated by the global effects of capitalist exploitation of resources and the domination of the poor by those who control material resources. The supposedly gender-neutral models and development paradigms that arise from this reductionist approach explain why gender has been neglected as a category of analysis and why this failing has been so successfully obscured from view.

Confusing Means and Ends

With the exception of a brief respite in the 1970s when the focus shifted to basic needs and redistribution, economic growth has generally stood at the core of influential development models. Although proponents of this approach acknowledge that economic growth is a means toward development rather than an end in itself, the conceptual separation of means and ends still causes more attention to be directed toward the *rate* of economic growth than toward its *pattern*. As a result, there has never been any serious implementation of redistribution measures at the national or international levels. Moreover, "[t]he confusion between means and ends, between growth and development, has served a very real political agenda." [75] Energy and resources are diverted to maintaining economic growth, which is pursued with little concern for equity, while redistribution is continuously postponed. This is justified on various pretexts to support the preference of elites for continued growth and their satisfaction with the status quo. Thus distributional issues are neglected on conceptual, political, and economic grounds with serious implications for equity, especially gender equity.

This means-ends confusion can be traced to the long-standing use of GNP as a convenient and simple indicator of a country's level of development. However, per capita GNP growth has not solved the social and political problems of development, leading Seers to challenge the positivists' value-free view of development. He argues that "[d]evelopment is inevitably a normative concept, almost a synonym for improvement. To pretend otherwise is just to hide one's value judgments."[1]

GNP is not a value-free measure "because the market itself is a highly partial mechanism for assigning value." [76] GNP only measures activities and resources that are exchanged; it equates the value of goods with the market prices they command (or could command), while consigning a wide variety of goods and activities, especially many of the activities performed by women in the household, to a "black hole" in economic theory. This pricing mechanism is a deeply value-laden measure of worth. It implies that the value of a good lies not in its ability to meet human need, but in the price it commands in the marketplace.

This approach is not only unwilling but also *unable* to recognize the value of goods and services not supplied by or demanded in the market. This fosters an ideology that only those values that can be measured in monetary terms matter. As a result, "within a market-led framework of development planning, certain categories of 'demand' and 'supply' are given secondary status in defining the means and ends of economic growth because the market is not capable of assigning a value to them." [77] Since the housework of women does not earn income and their labor in the marketplace is often confined to casual and low-paying sectors, the productive activity and demands of women are not adequately measured in GNP; women are consequently ignored by planners. The same holds true for other nonmarket-oriented assets such as domestic labor and the natural environment that are afforded no recognized value.

This conflation of prices and values not only distorts macro-level analyses but also micro-level project planning that focuses on GNP components. For example, many subsistence and networking activities that occur outside of the formal market system, upon which the market (and many of the poor) rely, are neglected or incorporated only to the extent that "shadow" prices can represent them. These uncounted prior activities include the production, care, and well-being of the human labor force, activities that are neither marketed nor likely to be responsive to market prices. Economists obscure these prior activities by treating labor as a "given" factor of production.

This orientation toward development thinking and planning, and the resource allocations it legitimates, begins to make sense when we consider the interests served by this approach, i.e., interests that link power and ideas in the development field. Development efforts and resources focus on "tip of the iceberg" activities where women, especially poor women, are underrepresented. Women's work is thus taken for granted, and the voices of women are ignored. They only enter the policy debate as unproductive recipients of welfare assistance that do not have legitimate claims to the national development budget.

Reversals in Thinking

Transforming development possibilities requires reversing the hierarchies of values embedded within the conventional methods of analysis, beginning with the generation of knowledge. Knowledge is constructed, not discovered, and reflects the interests of the dominant classes by justifying their position with particular interpretations of reality and the sources of poverty. Alternative development theories and practices should be nurtured by giving poor women a voice and viewing issues from their vantage point—not to the exclusion of all other viewpoints, but to realign the basis of development thinking more closely with "the real order of things." [81] It is not that only the dispossessed women of the Third World matter, but rather that without the transformation of their lives, there can be neither development nor equity. Such reversals will not only help poor women, but all oppressed groups.

Critics of dominant development paradigms do not always agree on how to produce alternatives. Some take the position that all methods of gathering knowledge are inherently oppressive, that objectivity is unattainable, and that research and the creation of theoretically informed policy and practice is therefore impossible. This reasoning concludes that unified thought cannot emerge because knowledge is dependent on values. An alternative approach is to acknowledge the influence of underlying values and to make them explicit, rather than denying their presence and shrouding them in neutralizing, positivist language.

Focusing on the ends of the development process reveals the need to reverse allocational priorities and the advantages of making human life and well-being the focus of planning, i.e., valuing means in terms of their contribution to the goal. Human activities should be valued on the basis of how well they satisfy present or future human needs; markets should be recognized as simply one of a variety of institutional mechanisms for meeting these needs, rather than as the sole arbiter of value. While economic growth is a necessary foundation for investment in human welfare, growth likewise requires human health and well-being. If the growth rate declines because of increasing investment in human welfare, this should be regarded as a "trade-off between different kinds of development." [84] Evaluating the terms of trade-off will require a view of development based on complementary indicators of GNP that monitor sustainable human welfare as the end, rather than a means to increase the volume of marketed goods and services.

The required reversals go beyond criticizing the neoliberal agenda of free-market promotion or the hostility toward interventionist policies that seek to equalize access to the market or welfare services. These reversals provide a new paradigm that calls for the "social management of the market."[2]

Notes

1. D. Seers, "The Meaning of Development," *Development Theory: Four Critical Studies,* D. Lehman, ed. (London: Frank Cass, 1979), 9–24.

2. D. Elson, "Market Socialism or Socialization of the Market?" *New Left Review* 172 (1985), 3–44.

Summary of

Inequality and Growth Reconsidered: Lessons from East Asia

by Nancy Birdsall, David Ross, and Richard Sabot

[Published in *The World Bank Economic Review* 9 (1995), 477–508.]

Conventional wisdom has long held that there is a necessary trade-off between increasing economic growth and reducing income inequality in developing economies. However, using cross-economy statistical studies of eight "high-performing East Asian economies" (Hong Kong, Indonesia, Japan, the Republic of Korea, Malaysia, Singapore, Taiwan (China), and Thailand), as well as theoretical analyses and microeconomic studies, the authors challenge this assumption. These East Asian economies achieved rapid economic growth in the last three decades, a remarkably long period for such growth to persist with low and apparently even decreasing levels of income inequality. In fact, their experiences suggest that polices aimed at reducing poverty and income inequality actually stimulate growth, and low-income inequality may independently contribute to rapid growth.

Education and Growth

The workings of two "virtuous circles" are apparent in the East Asian economies. In the first, education contributes to economic growth, which in turn stimulates further investment in education. In the second, which is discussed in the following section, education contributes to low levels of income inequality, which also stimulates additional investment in education.

Although the correlation of human-capital accumulation (i.e., education) with economic growth has long been apparent, the direction of causality has remained unclear until recently. However, both human-capital theory and endogenous growth theory predict that educational investments will enhance growth by increasing the productivity of labor and an economy's ability to produce or adapt new ideas. Microeconomic analyses confirm this conclusion. Recent work by Robert Barro using cross-economy regressions to test whether characteristics of economies several decades ago can predict later growth rates supports this causal relation.[1]

It is also evident that education best enhances economic growth when it occurs in conjunction with an increasing demand for skilled labor. Education levels alone will overpredict rates of growth in countries with a weak demand for educated labor, such as Egypt, the Philippines and Sri Lanka, and these countries may experience diminishing returns to investment in human capital. In East Asia, on the other hand, policies such as an orientation toward manufactured exports helped maintain high levels of demand for skilled workers, resulting in constant or even increasing returns to educational investments, even at higher overall levels of supply. It was therefore the combination of increasing supply of and demand for skilled labor that generated faster economic growth in East Asia than in other developing regions.

The other half of this virtuous circle connects rapid economic growth to increasing investments in education both at the household and the national level. This is not due to greater government commitment to education—public expenditure on education as a percentage of GNP is roughly the same in East Asia as in other developing regions. Rather, the combination of rapid economic growth and declining fertility allowed for the expansion of the education system, increased enrollment rates, and greater expenditure per student (increasing education and decreasing fertility also form a virtuous circle).

Education and Inequality

Evidence from more than 80 countries shows a clear correlation between high enrollment rates in basic education and low levels of income inequality. Additionally, causality appears to run in both directions. In other words, increasing education is both a cause and an effect of lower inequality—the second virtuous circle. Educational expansion can tend to increase inequality as the number of workers holding high-wage jobs increases (*the composition effect*), but this effect can be offset by the decreasing scarcity rents that educated workers will earn as the pool of skilled laborers expands (*the compression effect*). For example, as education levels rose in Korea, a worker with a high school education earned 47 percent more than a primary school graduate in 1976, but by 1986 this premium had eroded to just 30 percent. In Brazil, on the other hand, where enrollment in higher education increased much more slowly, the premium for higher education levels barely changed. In Brazil the composition effect dominated and inequality increased, while in Korea the compression effect was dominant, leading to overall decreases in inequality.

The tendency of lower income inequality to increase the demand for education comes from both the demand and supply sides. On the demand side, it is readily apparent that if two countries have similar levels of average per-capita income, then the country with lower income inequality will have a higher demand for education because the poor will face less of a liquidity constraint. Conversely, the country with higher inequality will have more households that are too poor to invest in education even if its returns are high. Governments are also better able to supply widespread educational opportunities when inequality is low because the tax burden to support such programs can be spread across a broad sector of the population. In a highly unequal society, the rich would have to be taxed heavily to support the provision of education for the poor, a burden that they are likely to resist, for example, by trying to channel spending on education into subsidies for university students where the children of the rich can capture the benefits. While East Asian and Latin American countries each devote a roughly similar proportion of GNP to education, the share of this spending allocated to primary and secondary education rather than to higher levels is consistently higher in the Asian countries.

Low Inequality and Growth

Can low inequality stimulate economic growth independently of its effects on education? Results of cross-economy studies find that there is in fact an inverse correlation between growth and income inequality, but due to the weaknesses of cross-economy analyses, this result can only be viewed as suggestive. Nevertheless, the effect of reducing inequality may be substantial. Simulations suggest that if Korea had had Brazil's level of inequality in 1960, its GDP per capita in 1985 would have been 15 percent lower than the level actually realized, and that is without including the negative effects of higher income inequality on demand for education.

There are four reasons why policies that reduce income inequality (by increasing the productivity and earning power of the poor rather than via income transfers) might enhance economic growth. First, they may result in increases in savings and investment by the poor. Capital market imperfections often prevent the poor from borrowing to finance investment in human capital, even when returns are high. As a result, a larger proportion of additional income earned by the poor is likely to be invested in health, education, and nutrition, resulting in higher-than-proportionate increases in productivity, and hence in economic growth. Even if the increased savings and investment generated among the poor are offset by decreases among the more wealthy, the efficiency and marginal returns on such investments by the poor are likely to be relatively high compared to those on other savings and investment opportunities.

Secondly, low inequality is likely to enhance political and macroeconomic stability as it reduces the incentives for inefficient fiscal and economic policies that radically shift between those serving the interests of a narrow economic elite (such as high subsidization of higher education) and equally damaging populist measures (e.g., the creation of large numbers of unproductive government jobs). Low inequality can also help governments avoid damaging policies, such as exchange rate overvaluation, which favors consumption of imports by elites at the cost of jobs and foreign-exchange earnings in agriculture and other export-oriented sectors. Governments may also find themselves with enhanced policy flexibility in responding to unanticipated negative shocks, since the benefits of growth will be more widely shared, and the absolute incomes of the poor are likely to be more secure, with only rates of income growth substantially affected. Finally, declining inequality is likely to contribute directly to political stability by legitimizing the government in the eyes of the public.

Third, decreasing inequality may also have an important effect by improving the opportunities available to the poor, thus increasing their incentive to work hard. Barriers to upward mobility or an inability to realize a substantial proportion of the rewards from increased labor productivity can discourage the extra work effort that is important for economic growth. In fact, the work ethic associated with students and laborers in East Asia may not be an exogenous cultural trait, as is often assumed, so much as an endogenous response to the incentives and opportunities that reward extra effort in these economies. Land reform in Korea and Taiwan is a clear example of a policy that both reduced inequality and increased productivity.

Finally, lower levels of income inequality mean higher incomes for rural agricultural households, which in turn are likely to lead to better agricultural policies that contribute to agriculture sector growth rather than undermine it. In addition, higher rural incomes stimulate demand for both agricultural inputs and manufactured outputs, enhancing growth in these sectors as well—the multiplier effects of agricultural growth on other sectors can be quite substantial. The tendency for the share of agricultural GDP to decline in these economies occurs not because of agricultural stagnation, but because manufacturing and other sectors, boosted by agricultural growth, grow even faster than the agriculture sector.

Conclusion

Investment in education stands out as the most effective policy for both enhancing economic growth and reducing income inequality, and, via two virtuous circles, growth and declining inequality will further increase the demand for and supply of education. However, education alone cannot explain the rapid growth and low inequality experienced in East Asia. Policies that promoted a dynamic agriculture sector, and the pursuit of labor-demanding, export-oriented growth, also contributed. In addition, low inequality itself may have directly contributed to growth.

Thus, the conventional wisdom that countries must necessarily choose between growth and equality is called into question. The solution is not to be found in income transfers to the poor, but rather for policies that reduce inequality by eliminating consumption subsidies for the wealthy and that increase the productivity of the poor. East Asian leaders, whether by design or by luck, have successfully implemented such policies, and other regions now have the opportunity to benefit from this lesson.

Note

1. Robert J. Barro, "Economic Growth in a Cross-Section of Countries," *Quarterly Journal of Economics* 106 (May 1991), 407–443.

Summary of

Economic Theory and the Welfare State: A Survey and Interpretation

by Nicholas Barr

[Published in *Journal of Economic Literature* 30, June 1992, 741–803.]

This article surveys the literature on the welfare state in economic theory, presents data on the nature and extent of the welfare state in ten developed countries, and analyzes two areas in detail—cash payments to individuals and financing systems for health care. This summary emphasizes the author's discussion of economic theory, with only brief treatment of the more empirical and detailed sections.

Definition and Goals of the Welfare State

The term "welfare state" is used as a shorthand for the state's activities in providing cash benefits, health care, education, food, housing, and other welfare services. Such activities grew rapidly in the 1960s and 1970s, and by 1980 accounted for 12 percent to 28 percent of GDP in many developed countries. There are many institutional and political variations in the nature of the welfare state from one country to another; one of the most important is the distinction between residual and universal welfare states. A residual welfare state provides means-tested "safety net" programs for the poor, as in the U.S.; a universal welfare state provides services for all socioeconomic groups, as in Germany.

Academic and political discussion of the welfare state mentions a broad range of objectives, including economic efficiency, poverty relief, reduction in inequality, promotion of dignity and social solidarity, and administrative efficiency. Some of these are hard to define; some are inherently in conflict with each other, raising fundamental normative choices.

Market Failures and Social Insurance

Public intervention in a market economy is often justified as a response to market failure. Traditional categories of market failure are only slightly relevant to the welfare state. Income externalities can provide a basis for intervention; if the rich have a preference for redistribution to the poor, then voluntary transfers may be less efficient than government programs when the numbers of individuals are large. Merit goods that are believed to involve important positive externalities, such as education or sanitation, may be most efficiently provided by the public sector. Such arguments, however, justify at most a residual welfare state with a handful of universal services and infrastructure programs. They do not explain why so many countries have gone much farther.

More important is a newer category of market failures, typically due to information problems faced by both consumers and insurers. Consumers may have imperfect information about the quality of the product or about its price; the information problems are severe in health care, sharply reducing the efficiency of the market. Even if consumers are well informed, they may not be able to buy what they want in the area of social services and insurance; three additional problems limit the ability of the private sector to provide the insurance coverage that consumers want.

The first is adverse selection: if an insurer cannot distinguish low and high risk customers, it will offer pooled insurance rates based on the average risk. However, if individuals know their own level of risk, low-risk groups can opt out and find cheaper alternative coverage or self-insurance, leaving the original insurer with a riskier-than-average population. An analogous problem arises in other cases of asymmetric information, such as used car markets, and limits the extent and efficiency of transactions in those markets.

The second insurance problem is moral hazard: if individuals know they are insured, they take too few precautions, and, when making claims, they will use resources inefficiently. As an example of the latter problem, if medical care is fully insured, neither doctors nor patients have any incentive to avoid excessive consumption.

A final insurance problem concerns unpredictable probabilities, such as the likelihood of inflation eroding the value of pensions, or probabilities that approach certainty, such as the need for treatment of the chronically or congenitally ill. While most people would like to insure themselves against such events, private insurance is clearly impossible.

Social insurance schemes, with compulsory, universal membership, can overcome some of these problems. Adverse selection does not arise if everyone is compelled to have the same public-sector insurance. The social contract, which is less specific than a private one, can provide some protection (perhaps changing over time) against such diverse risks as future inflation or congenital illness. Universal benefits, unrelated to any insurance premiums—such as family benefits in many countries and Canadian, Swedish, and British health care—perform a similar function to universal insurance coverage.

Cash Benefits

Unemployment compensation faces many of the insurance problems mentioned above. Adverse selection can arise, since workers can sometimes conceal their likelihood of voluntary future unemployment. Moral hazard exists because any compensation makes unemployment less unattractive. Probabilities of unemployment, for many groups of workers, are unpredictable and/or quite high at times. Thus private-sector unemployment insurance is essentially unknown, aside from specialized programs for low-risk groups (e.g., mortgage-protection policies, and keeping up homeowners' monthly payments in case of unemployment).

Retirement pensions are offered by the private sector, but they are unable to insure against the important risk of unanticipated inflation after retirement. No one knows the probability distribution of future inflation rates, and if a high rate occurs, it affects everyone at once; both these factors make it impossible to sell inflation insurance. Only the public sector can provide this much-desired form of insurance. Large and growing expenditures are required, particularly in view of the aging of the population of developed countries.

There is a longstanding debate over the merits of full funding of pension liabilities, versus pay-as-you-go systems, such as social security in the U.S. Which makes it easier to pay pensions in the future? The empirical evidence is inconclusive: countries like Sweden and Japan, with funded public pensions, have often put the resulting capital funds in relatively low-yield investments, losing much of the expected benefits of their cautious approach. Even in theory, it is not clear that pay-as-you-go pensions reduce a society's total savings; the greater pension contributions required for full funding may cause offsetting reductions in nonpension private savings.

The distributional impact of cash benefits varies widely across countries. One measure of this impact is the percentage of families who would otherwise have been poor (below 50 percent of median income), who were moved out of poverty by government programs. In the mid-1980s, this percentage ranged from 82 percent in Sweden to less than 23 percent in the U.S. Sweden's welfare state transferred 10 percent of GDP to the poorest 20 percent of its population; in the U.S., the transfer to the poorest fifth was 5 percent of GDP.

Medical Care

Private markets are inefficient in health care for all the reasons discussed above. The information needed for rational decision making is technical and often inaccessible. Adverse selection—low-risk individuals opting out of broad insurance pools, leaving a higher-risk population behind—is a chronic problem. Moral hazard—overuse of medical care because it is free or subsidized—is inescapable, though it is reduced by copayments and deductibles. People want coverage for pre-existing and congenital problems, which are uninsurable for a private insurer. The inefficiencies of the market, as predicted by theory, can be seen in the U.S., which relies most on the private market for health care: the problems of high and rising costs, gaps in coverage, and unequal access are all worse in the U.S. than in other developed countries.

> A hypothetical pure private market for medical care and medical insurance would be highly inefficient and also inequitable. That view is hardly controversial; what is less clear is the specification of the least bad alternative. [781]

Rapidly rising costs have affected virtually all health care systems, leading to interest in incentives for cost containment. Prospective payment systems provide payment *ex ante*, imposing all risk of cost increases on the medical supplier. Prospective budgets for hospitals (fixed sums per inpatient case) are now widespread in Europe. Diagnosis related groups, a more refined form of prospective payments, are used by U.S. Medicare, paying a fixed price for each of almost 500 diagnoses. Health maintenance organizations (HMOs), a rapidly growing institution in the U.S., receive a fixed annual payment from each member and agree to provide all medical care needed by the members. All of these prospective payment systems, however, create unfortunate incentives for the providers to lower the quality and/or quantity of care supplied; and they do not address the problem of uninsurable risks.

An alternative regulatory approach sets annual national, regional, or local budgets for medical care, with payments to doctors and hospitals at fixed fees per service subject to the budget limits. Several European countries, as well as Canada and New Zealand, employ variants of this approach. Funding can be centrally administered, as in Canada, or decentralized to numerous sick funds, subject to government approval, as in Germany. The critical point is that "budget constraints of this sort control physician *incomes* not physician *actions*, leaving doctors largely autonomous in treating their patients" [787], unlike the U.S. experience with managed care.

There is a continuing need for reform of health care provision, both to increase the flow of information and to improve the structure of incentives for providers and patients. Several European countries are considering experiments with competition, less as cost containing devices than as ways to make providers more responsive to consumers.

Conclusion

> Many parts of the welfare state are a response to pervasive market failure, and therefore serve not only distributional and other objectives . . . but also efficiency objectives such as income smoothing and the protection of accustomed living standards in the face of uninsurable risks and capital market imperfections. [757]

The market failures that lead to welfare state measures require a two-part intervention strategy: social insurance, which makes universal coverage possible, must be combined with a regulatory regime that includes stringent financial control. While there are no perfect solutions, the search for better institutions inevitably continues.

Social insurance, unlike private insurance, charges premiums that need not be directly tied to individual risk; is such a system still insurance? The social insurance systems of the welfare state can be viewed as a contract entered voluntarily by risk-averse individuals behind John Rawls's veil of ignorance; behind the veil of ignorance, individual levels of risk are unknown. Universal benefits and assistance programs can also be seen as a form of insurance. "By offering cover prior to birth, the welfare state is acting like ex ante actuarial insurance with a long time horizon. . . . From this perspective the nature of the welfare state is determined in part by the choice of time horizon." [795]

Summary of

Welfare

by Robert Kuttner

[Chapter 6 in *The Economic Illusion* (Boston: Houghton Mifflin Company, 1984 and Philadelphia: University of Pennsylvania Press, 1987).]

An ongoing conflict between two incompatible criteria for distributing income—need and the market—continues to shape the evolution of the welfare states of Europe and North America. The widely varied systems of social services exhibited by these states reflect uneasy compromises between market criteria for distribution and state efforts to temper market extremes, compromises that are partly shaped by ideological foundations, implications and impacts of welfare, the role and capabilities of governments, and individualist versus communal values. The conservative view is that social welfare is "associated with wasteful aid for the (undeserving) poor" and creates a drag on economic efficiency. This view is dominant in some countries, particularly the United States. [238] However, the universalism of a social service provision, exhibited mostly in the Northern European social democratic states, is not only apt to be more equitable, but also more efficient, especially when the tendency of these systems toward fiscal excess is contained.

Welfare and Efficiency

The acceptance of a role for the state in supporting needy citizens who have failed to thrive in the market system goes back at least as far as the Elizabethan poor laws. While this role has increased over time, it has remained dependent on the market as the engine of growth that generates the revenue supporting the benefit programs. Welfare states therefore have several key concerns regarding the social and efficiency impacts of social programs. One issue is how special needs can be provided for without isolating or stigmatizing the needy; poor laws stigmatized those who required assistance, relegating them to an inferior class of citizenship with fewer rights than others. In theory, modern welfare states have created social safety nets that are a right of full citizenship. However, in some states, while the legal rights of recipients may no longer be curtailed, isolation and stigmatization are still major problems.

Two other concerns arise with respect to efficiency and economic health. Conservatives argue that social welfare systems are economically destructive for two reasons. First, in assuring freedom from want the state may also encourage freedom from work and breed improvidence; second, politicians pandering to the electorate will seek to expand the welfare state until it overburdens the private market economy. There is little practical support for the first claim. Evidence suggests that publicly provided social services are not necessarily squandered, and in fact may be used more efficiently than those that are privately provided. Moreover, there is little to prove that improvidence and worklessness by choice increased after the establishment of major welfare state institutions. Private wealth and income still largely determine an individual's place in society and welfare systems still only provide for minimal subsistence.

On the other hand, fiscal excess has become a very real concern for welfare states as expenditures increased during the postwar period. This danger is particularly acute in systems that provide universal benefits, although it is not inevitable even in these cases. Some states allocate as much as 60 percent of national income to welfare programs—an unmanageable burden during periods of reduced economic growth and higher unemployment. This often results in an intensification of social bargaining and political conflict. In fact, welfare states appear to reach a natural limit when public spending reaches around 50 percent of GNP.

Models of Welfare Provision

There are several different possible ways of providing particular social services. Means-tested programs are most closely related to the original poor laws. However, while targeting aid to the "truly" needy may sometimes be the most efficient solution, there are serious drawbacks to this approach. It tends to stigmatize and isolate the poor in separate programs and does not build a broad-based political constituency in support of equality or the welfare state itself.

Another alternative is the social-insurance approach. Otto von Bismarck was one of the leading architects of this welfare provision method that was further developed by Sir William Beveridge in the 1940s. While the motivations were in part charitable, this system also provided a strategy for competing with socialism and winning worker allegiance to the state. However, the theory of social insurance does not propose a public direct-assistance program for the poorest, but rather a system of earned benefits that depends on the premiums that an individual has paid into the insurance fund. The system therefore reflects, rather than alters, market outcomes, redistributing market-determined income over time to provide for calamities or old age; it does little to encourage income redistribution among members of society to alter wage-based inequalities. Thus, the poor may still be forced to depend on the modern equivalent of poor relief. The approach is more consistent with market capitalism and is therefore preferred by conservatives.

Citizen or universal entitlements go a crucial step beyond other alternatives by shifting from the market to need as the criterion of distribution. Benefits are offered to citizens as a matter of right, regardless of their private means and without a specific contribution requirement. Rather than creating a dual society divided between poor recipients of assistance and the rich, universal entitlement systems foster and reinforce a sense of community and solidarity. They also build a strong, broadly-based political constituency in support of the social-benefits system. However, in addition to the high and potentially spiraling costs of these systems, which can undermine the strong market economic system that they require to function, they may also be forced to become less redistributive as they become more universal. Beyond a certain point, universalism based on citizenship and redistribution based on need are conflicting principles. Furthermore, universalism may conflict with the principle of adequacy, as universal benefits may have to be distributed so thinly that they cannot meet the needs of all;

the wealthy, however, remain unaffected since they can use their own resources to purchase better quality benefits in the private market.

Models of the Welfare State

These models of benefit distribution represent ideal types, but because of practical and ideological reasons, most states exhibit some mixture of the three. For example, a society with a system of thinly distributed universal benefits may have to provide supplemental means-tested benefits to meet the needs of its poorest members. In a highly individualistic, anti-welfare society such as the U.S., the contribution-for-benefit aspects of social-insurance systems may be emphasized as a politically useful myth, while underplaying the fact that these systems may actually be designed to have substantial redistributive effects (e.g., through payment of pension benefits to the retired poor that exceed their contributions). In addition, social benefits are typically provided in a number of different sectors and many states utilize different benefit systems in different sectors. This is in part because it is easier to achieve universalism in the provision of social services such as health than in income support programs. In general, North American and European states can be categorized along a spectrum indicating the most and least universalistic states with respect to welfare provision for their citizens: at one extreme is the U.S. and at the other are the social democratic states of Northern Europe.

The U.S. model of the welfare state is less universalistic in two main respects. First, it spends less on social aid—12 percent of GNP as compared to 20 percent in Northern Europe. Second, the U.S. system is fragmented in nature and tends to rely more heavily on means-tested poor relief type benefits rather than on universal provision. The result is an adversarial and isolating system of poor-relief that destroys the ideal of social citizenship and that claims only a weak constituency among the middle class.

On the other hand, there is great variability across sectors of assistance in the U.S. system. For example, free universal education is provided up to the college level—a universal benefit often largely ignored in debates on these issues because it so clearly contradicts the country's individualistic and market-oriented norms. However, the U.S. is virtually the only industrialized country that does not guarantee equal access to health care as a basic citizenship right. The separate, means-tested Medicaid system provides clearly inferior service to that purchased privately or with insurance by the wealthier members of society. This dualism is typical of many components of the U.S. system: the state provides equality of treatment among the poor, but at a very low standard, while the rest of society is either self-provisioning or participates in social-insurance systems. The better-off can obtain direct state benefits only if they first undergo pauperization to qualify. However, at the same time, the middle class and wealthy realize substantial indirect benefits from subsidization via tax relief for much of the family's private welfare spending. For example, middle-class tax relief for mortgage interest payments far outweighs government support for housing for the poor, but these essentially invisible components of the tax welfare state are often overlooked.

Many Northern European states provide their citizens with a wide range of universal income-support and social-service benefits, and, at least until the economic slump of the 1970s, only a few of their citizens were forced to rely on the means-tested supplemental systems. In the mid-1970s, means-tested benefits accounted for less than 5 percent of social spending in most of these states, compared to more than 26 percent in the U.S. The universal benefits provided include family allowances (flat cash payments to all families regardless of status) and cash-housing allowances. An unemployed single parent in France receives family and housing allowances equal to about 79 percent of the average wage, while in Sweden the rate is 94 percent.

Nevertheless, these systems of universal provision of benefits are highly dependent on very high or full employment levels, both to reduce the need for state assistance (especially the means-tested supplemental benefits) and to generate the tax revenues needed to pay for the benefits. The higher rates of long-term unemployment that have persisted in much of Europe since the mid-1970s have therefore severely strained these systems. As tax rates on the employed are raised to support benefits for the unemployed, the coalition of support for the universal welfare state has weakened. Nevertheless, these states have done a far better job of maintaining a unified system with a minimum of indignity for the poor than the U.S. and Britain. Their more equitable systems have also achieved greater efficiency than those of the minimalist welfare states that so imperfectly utilize private markets for social purposes.

Summary of

What Is Distinctive About Swedish Social Democratic Ideology?

by Timothy Tilton

[Published in *The Political Theory of Swedish Social Democracy: Through the Welfare State to Socialism* (Oxford: Clarendon Press, 1990), 248–280.]

This article identifies five themes that embody the enduring values of Swedish social democratic ideology. Together they create a distinctive whole that has shaped both the unique Swedish model of economic and social policy and the evolution of the movement's critique of a liberal capitalist society under changing economic and political conditions. While it may be difficult for other countries to adopt the particular institutions and policies of the Swedish system, the core values of equality, democracy, freedom, solidarity, efficiency, work, and security that shape the system may be more readily transferable.

Dominant Interpretations of Swedish Democratic Ideology

To date, three alternative interpretations have dominated the understanding of Swedish social democratic ideology. All have weaknesses, but the new analysis presented here arises from a synthesis of these views. The first comes from the work of Herbert Tingsten, who emphasized the change in the party's ideology from its origins in Marxist socialism to its support of welfare statism. Tingsten argues that there were inherent tensions between the essentially Marxist doctrine first adopted by the Swedes and the current realities of parliamentary politics and tardy capitalist development. This inevitably led to the steady decline of unrealistic and unachievable Marxist elements, leaving a watered-down ideology that promoted gradual reforms for the public interest rather than increasing class conflict. However, while this account of the development of social democracy has been very influential and has useful elements, it contains some serious analytical flaws. In particular, Tingsten fails to show that Swedish social democracy ever adhered as closely as he claims to broad Marxist perspectives. Alternative analyses must therefore be considered.

A second approach was developed by Leif Lewin who focuses his analysis of Swedish ideology on the "socialist conception of freedom," which is distinctly different from that of the liberals. Rather than regarding the state as a threat to freedom as liberals do, social democrats view it as an instrument that can potentially free people from the domination of capital and poverty. Moreover, while liberals believe that equality is incompatible with freedom and economic growth, social democrats argue that these are complementary values. Lewin's thesis is powerful and well-documented. However, it is important to note that freedom is not the central social democratic value; rather, Swedish social democrats place at least equal importance on several other mutually reinforcing values, such as equality, solidarity, and democracy.

The third important interpretation of social democracy denies any ideological motivations, characterizing it instead as a fundamentally pragmatic system. The key problem with this interpretation is that it assumes that "ideological" is equivalent to "unrealistic," and thus the opposite of "pragmatic." This need not be the case if ideology avoids irrational interpretations and takes practical concerns into account. Moreover, it is not reasonable to expect ideology to offer a specific policy blueprint as some pragmatists demand; instead, it provides a core set of values that shapes the policy-making process and serves as a basis for a decent society. "Politics regularly requires improvisation and muddling through, but far from obviating the importance of ideology, such episodes allow one to see which values and predispositions shape the new policy." [257]

An Alternative View: Five Central Themes

Five central themes or values characterize the core of Swedish social democratic ideology. Together they form an integrated, coherent whole that shapes and drives national social policy. The first is the idea of *integrative democracy* as the standard of legitimacy. This entails a belief in democracy and full participation not only in the political arena but also in the economic and social realms. The starting point of the social democratic ideal is the deproletarianization of the working classes, which is achieved by overcoming the political, economic, and material disadvantages that rendered them passive. The goal is integration into the economic life of society as an equal partner, not domination over other classes. The system thus aims for "the rule of all," preferably on the basis of consensus. [259]

The second key theme is the concept of *society and state as the people's home* (the *folkhemmet*), a home characterized by solidarity, cooperation, and equality where no one is privileged or unappreciated. This concept replaces the patriarchal and class-stratified social welfare system that first arose in the early days of Sweden's industrial development with an ideal based on equal rights and universal access to services controlled not by aristocratic beneficence, but by democratic decision making.

The third theme argues for the *compatibility,* even *complementarity,* of socioeconomic equality and economic efficiency. While social science has not resolved the debate about whether or not there are trade-offs between the two, Swedish social democrats have consistently sought to maximize the development of society's human resources, arguing that generating the economic growth needed to support higher standards of living depends on a political compact with labor that creates an atmosphere of cooperation rather than antagonism. In addition to offering full employment and a larger worker role in management, egalitarian wage structures are promoted on the basis of equity and efficiency. In a system of equal pay for equal work, profits should actually reflect a firm's efficiency, rather than its bargaining power with respect to workers. Some social democrats go still further, arguing that efficiency should be restructured to emphasize employee welfare rather than profits as the key indicator.

A preference for a *socially controlled market economy* is the fourth theme, implying public control, but not necessarily public ownership, of productive enterprises; nationalization is one possible means for doing this, but not generally the preferred one. There are four strategies of social control. Rather than advocating heavy market regulation, the first focuses on restructuring and equalizing the background conditions that determine what resources individuals bring to the market and how markets operate. Framework legislation, the second strategy, targets markets directly with the intention of making them more nearly perfect in the liberal sense, for example by improving the supply and exchange of employment information, subsidizing labor mobility, establishing production standards, and providing special incentives to some industries. The third strategy reflects a particularly Swedish approach that advocates neither a fully market nor fully planned economy, but rather a planned market, i.e., a system that recognizes producers and consumers as independent economic agents and regulates the framework within which they interact. The fourth strategy comes from the view that property is a bundle of divisible rights that can be placed in a number of different hands, rather than a block that must always be transferred as a whole. Thus, instead of outright nationalization of industries, private enterprises are gradually surrounded and infiltrated by measures that increasingly direct their efforts toward public objectives.

The fifth theme makes explicit a perception that is implicit in many of the others, that is, the conception that rather than necessarily threatening individual liberties, *proper expansion of the public sector can extend freedom of choice.* Health insurance, pensions, and full employment policies can provide increased security, freedom from anxiety and poverty, and greater choice and opportunity. This principle in turn rests on two others—(1) government is democratic and effectively represents society's wishes; and (2) taxes are not an abuse of citizen's freedoms or a form of coercion but rather a means of allowing people to pay for desired public services.

The Critique of Capitalist Society

While the core values of Sweden's Social Democracy have remained relatively constant, its critique of liberal capitalist society has evolved with changing political and economic circumstances. The movement has generally avoided utopianism and has instead focused on identifying and remedying the abuses of liberal capitalism. Thus, rather than seeking to replace capitalism with socialism, the goal has been to reshape the market system in such as way as to ensure that all individuals possess the capacities and the resources to function effectively within it. In so doing, the movement has succeeded in broadening its basis of support from blue-collar workers to members of the poorer rural strata, the new middle class, and employees at large.

The social democratic critique began with a focus on the proletarianization and exploitation of workers who were prevented from achieving material well-being, security, and power. It sometimes advocated the socialization of ownership, among other measures, to remedy the situation. However, even then socialization and planning were seen only as the means (and only one of several possible means), and not the ends of social democracy. At the same time, there was growing recognition that poverty was less tolerable to people than exploitation, and that socialization would not be accepted if it threatened economic growth. This led to a decreasing emphasis on formal ownership of the means of production and advocacy of socialization, and an increasing acceptance of the attitude that the government's role was to adjust markets and their impacts, but not substitute for them, i.e., that Swedes should "[l]et private industry under society's control take care of what it can. Society should not intervene unless it is necessary."[1] This attitude is the foundation of the "historic compromise" between labor and ownership, whereby cooperation in industrial restructuring was exchanged for better wages, guarantees of full employment, and other social benefits.

The position of Swedish workers has steadily improved, and the economy has in fact been gradually but increasingly socialized and subjected to greater control by labor and government. Yet Swedish social democracy is still characterized by two general tendencies—the dominant one sees private enterprise as a key way of increasing productivity that should be accepted within the framework of the welfare state, while the second is wary of increasing the concentration of capitalist wealth and power. Both the Swedish set of institutions and social democratic ideology should therefore be regarded as evolving, rather than as finished products, each of which is subject to the influence of pragmatic judgments about how best to achieve social democratic goals. "Social Democrats make their own ideology, but not just as they please; they make it within a tradition of the values of equality, freedom, democracy, solidarity, security, work, and economic efficiency." [276]

How Ideology Shapes Policy

It is frequently argued that ideology is of minor importance in shaping policy, which instead is said to be driven by necessary functional adaptations to modern industrial society, the power of the labor movement, or state capacity. However, these factors alone cannot adequately explain the significant variations in national policies with respect to the structure, coverage, financing, and benefits of social programs. In fact, the influence of social democratic ideology is apparent in the formation of a number of distinctive elements of Swedish social and economic policy, such as the promotion of full employment, the universalism of social policy, and the adoption of an unusually comprehensive form of industrial democracy that includes solidaristic wage policy, active labor-market policy, collective capital formation, policies that support women and families, and a host of others. This ideology's greatest achievement, however, has been its ability to persuade opponents and create a general consensus in support of these policies.

Note

1. Tage Erlander, Valfrichetens Samhalle (Stockholm: Tidenforlag, 1973), 281.

Summary of

The Three Political Economies of the Welfare State

by Gøsta Esping-Andersen

[Published in *International Journal of Sociology* 20 (Fall 1990), 92–12.]

A sound analysis and comparison of welfare states require a clear understanding of both the origins and characteristics of a welfare state. However, the two dominant approaches for explaining these origins are inadequate; a third attempt, based on the class-mobilization theory, is also unsatisfactory. In addition, the practice of defining welfare states solely based on their level of social expenditures is misdirected. By shifting the focus from expenditures to social citizenship, and by modifying the class-mobilization approach to account for coalition structures and institutional legacies, a more interactive and accurate model of welfare states can be formed. This model allows welfare states to be viewed not as linearly distributed systems (advocating more or less welfare spending) but rather as consisting of specific regime type clusters.

Dominant Explanations of the Welfare State

Although their answers differ, political economists since the 19th century have sought to identify the sources of welfare-state development and the division of responsibilities between the market and the state for achieving social welfare. Classical liberals distrusted the state, arguing that the market is the best means for reducing inequality and class divisions. They feared that democracy, in the form of universal suffrage, might politicize divisions, contradict markets, create inefficiencies, and eventually lead to socialism. Nineteenth-century conservatives (for example the German historical school) favored patriarchal neoabsolutism, rather than an unfettered market, as the best means to promote capitalism while containing class struggles. Marxists trusted neither the market nor the state to guarantee equality.

Two types of models have come to dominate explanations of why welfare states came into being. Systemic or structuralist theory focuses on functional requirements for the reproduction of society and the economy as the source of the welfare state. For example, the theory's "logic of industrialism" variant argues that industrialization makes the development of social policy both *neces-*

sary—to replace collapsing pre-industrial modes of social reproduction (a function that the market cannot adequately perform alone, because not everyone is able to participate in it)—and *possible*, due to the accompanying growth of a rational and efficient bureaucracy. However, this thesis does not adequately explain why social policy only emerged long after traditional communities were mostly destroyed. It can only provide an essentially liberal response, arguing that a certain level of development and surplus had to be achieved before social policy could be adopted, otherwise such policies would have been a drag on the economy.

The institutional alignment theory arose in response to the classical liberals' promotion of a laissez-faire state based on separating the economy from social and political institutions. Karl Polanyi and others argue that this separation would destroy human society and that the economy must instead be embedded in social communities. Social policy is thus essential for the survival of society. The democratic-institutionalist approach argues more specifically that democratic institutions are necessary for the welfare state to emerge and that in such a system majority groups—whether farmers, capitalists, or wage earners—will pursue socially managed distribution to compensate for market weaknesses and inequality. The problem with this argument is that the actual development of welfare states has not been as closely linked to democracy as the theory suggests. In some states social policies were actually implemented in an effort to suppress demands for democratization (for example France under Napoleon II and Germany under Bismarck), while welfare state development was slowest in states where democracy arrived early (for example the United States, Australia, and Switzerland).

The class-mobilization thesis offers an alternative explanation for the welfare state that is based on the social-democratic political economy. It emphasizes the role of social classes as the main agents of change via parliamentarism and the balance of class power as the key determinant of outcomes. This theory argues that the social policies of the welfare state do more than just alleviate the current ills of the economic system. By providing social rights, income security, and other benefits, these states create a social wage that becomes a source of power. This frees wage earners from the competition and stratification inherent in the market system that limit their capacity for collective mobilization, thus shifting the balance of power between classes.

This social-democratic model of parliamentary class mobilization as a means for creating equality and justice has become a leading hypothesis in the current debate about the foundations of the welfare state. However, this thesis also faces several objections, the most important of which concerns its "linear view of power," i.e., the implication that "a numerical increase in votes, unionization, or parliamentary seats will translate into more welfare statism." [101] Socialist parties rarely, if ever, achieve an outright parliamentary majority. Additionally, the role and size of the working classes began to decline exactly at the historical moment in which modern welfare states were consolidated, so mobilization of these groups cannot independently explain the origins of welfarist social policies.

Overcoming these weaknesses of the class-mobilization thesis requires shifting from a monocausal to a multicausal model of welfare-state development. The most promising approach still begins with class mobilization but also looks at class-political coalition structures and at the institutional legacy of past regimes. The origins of the welfare-state edifice can then be found not only in the working-class movement but also in its success in forming alliances with farmers' organizations; social democracy in the long-run is often sustained by new alliances between workers and white-collar strata. Other aspects of the past institutional legacy that may be important include the prevalence of political or denominational fragmentation in unions, the nature of the rural economy, and the strength of conservative forces, including their ability to capture rural classes and prevent rural class alliances with working classes. In addition to overcoming the working-class minority problem, the coalitions thesis helps to explain why countries with similar levels of labor mobilization can still produce very different policy outcomes.

A Respecification of the Welfare State

In addition to reassessing the origins of the welfare state, it is also necessary to reevaluate its definition. The standard assumption that a state's commitment to welfare is adequately reflected by its level of social expenditure is at best misleading. This linear approach implies that all spending counts equally and that more spending generates more welfare; this ignores nonlinear interactions between power, democracy, and welfare. For instance, when a state such as Austria directs a large share of its welfare expenditures toward benefits for privileged civil servants, or when states support tax privileges for middle classes, the impacts and implications of these welfare measures are clearly different than those for comparable expenditures aimed at maintaining full employment or assisting the poor and working classes.

A more nuanced definition of the welfare state begins with T. H. Marshall's proposition that the core idea centers on social citizenship, the key principles of which are: (1) a set of social rights that decommodifies the status of individuals with respect to the market; and (2) a system of social stratification in which the status of individuals as citizens competes with or replaces class status.

Decommodification of an individual means granting him or her means of welfare other than those provided by the market. It can be measured by the degree to which distribution is independent of market mechanisms. The minimalist definition of a decommodifying welfare state is one in which citizens can

freely opt out of work for reasons such as health, education, or family obligations when "they deem it necessary for participating adequately in the social
community." [107]

Not all forms of social assistance or insurance, including many means-tested
programs and those requiring long worker-contribution periods for eligibility,
necessarily bring about decommodification. Social assistance that focuses on
minimal, needs-tested benefits has minor decommodifying effects and may in
fact strengthen the market. Compulsory state social-insurance systems may
offer much greater entitlements, but here again decommodification may not be
substantial since eligibility is often based on prior contributions. Even those
states offering basic, equal benefits to everyone may not be as decommodifying
as they appear since they usually cannot provide benefits at a sufficient level to
provide a real alternative to work.

Neither can it be assumed that welfare states automatically create more egalitarian societies or enhance social mobility; each state creates its own system of
stratification. Means-tested social-assistance systems are specifically designed to
stigmatize assistance and sharply separate the "poor" from wage earners. Social
insurance models explicitly reflect a form of status politics, by creating different
benefit programs for different class and status groups. Even universalistic benefits arrangements, which initially promote status equality, can eventually disin-
tegrate into dualistic systems as growing working-class prosperity and a rising
new middle class lead to increasing numbers of better-off individuals who supplement low levels of universal benefits with privately purchased services.

Regime Clusters

These different approaches to rights and stratification reflect qualitatively different relations among the market, the family, and the state and can be clustered
into regime types that run contrary to the more common assumption of linear
distribution of states (with respect to power distribution, level of welfare, etc.).
One cluster encompasses "liberal" welfare states—especially the United States,
Canada, and Australia—that focus on means-tested assistance and modest universal transfers or social-insurance plans. In this cluster overall social reform is
severely limited, receipt of benefits is stigmatized, decommodification is minimal, and a dualistic stratification system is generated in which there is relative
equality among poor recipients of state benefits and market-determined welfare
among the better-off.

The second cluster includes states such as Austria, France, Germany, and Italy
in which the acceptance of social rights prevails over the liberal obsession with
market mechanisms. However, these rights remain tied to class and status in a
corporativist welfare system of social insurance, yielding negligible redistributive effects. Also, these states frequently displace the market as a welfare pro-

vider and reduce private insurance and job-related benefits to a minimum. Since they are often committed to the preservation of traditional family values, family support services, such as day care, may be underdeveloped.

The third and smallest cluster includes the highly decommodifying social democratic states in which the principle of universalism, rather than dualism or corporativism, dominates. Norway and Sweden are the most notable examples. Equality at a high standard for all is promoted, rather than minimal standards of equality for the poor as espoused by other states. This generates essentially universal solidarity in support of the state. These states are grounded in the guarantee of the right to work and the right to income protection both as a matter of principle and because full employment is essential for ensuring the universal provision of benefits. They typically provide more benefits to families, and do so preemptively, rather than waiting until the family's capacity for self-provision is completely exhausted.

Of course, none of these states is a pure example of its cluster type. The U.S. social security system is compulsory and has significant redistributive effects, the Swedish unemployment insurance is essentially voluntarist, and European corporativist regimes have been influenced by both liberalism and social democratic ideas. However, classification by regime types still reveals much more about welfare states than does the traditional linear approach.

PART IX

Critiques of National Income Accounting and GNP

Overview Essay

by Jonathan M. Harris

It is often said (generally by economists) that economics is a cumulative science. Economic practitioners of today, in this view, select the best of all previous economic thought, build on what is most valuable, and discard what has been found wanting. As we have seen in earlier sections, many of the complex issues of what truly constitutes human welfare have fallen by the wayside in modern economics. The field of welfare economics itself has all but disappeared. Dollar valuation has become the single criterion for inclusion of any aspect of human experience into economic analysis.

Most of the arcane theoretical issues involved in this evolution of economic thought are, of course, unknown to the general public, as well as to researchers in other academic fields. But everyone is familiar with Gross National Product (GNP). Both to professional economists and to laypersons, GNP and its variant, Gross Domestic Product,[1] represent the most readily available index of how "well" the economy is doing. Expressed as GNP per capita, it tells us how "well" the average citizen is doing—a higher per capita GNP is the prime measure used to distinguish a rich economy from a poor one. To judge by the widespread success of the GNP measure, it has become the single criterion that replaces all that obsolete theorizing about how to measure welfare.

Clearly, the implications of this widespread acceptance of GNP as "the" measure of economic success are profound. A few may protest that GNP is really a measure of production, not of welfare. But lacking any other comprehensive measure of welfare, GNP fills this role by default. It therefore governs not only the thinking of economists and of the general public in this area but also the shaping of economic policy on a variety of levels.

In addition to the absolute level of GNP, the rate of change in GNP over time is a crucial economic indicator. In the short term, the rate of change in GNP is carefully monitored as a guide to macroeconomic policy. In the United States, if GNP declines for two successive quarters, the economy is considered to be in recession. Despite the preachments of monetarist and New Classical economists to the effect that government policy is ineffective, we typically see a rapid response on the part of the Federal Reserve Bank, and sometimes a more delayed response by fiscal authorities, to such a "slowdown" in the economy. On the other hand, if GNP grows too rapidly, the Federal Reserve Bank will be quick to apply the monetary brakes to avert the risk of inflation. Thus we have come to accept the principle that GNP should be not just at a high level but should also be growing continually at a steady rate to maintain economic welfare.

Long-term growth is of even greater importance to economists than short-term macroeconomic fluctuations. Modern economic growth theories stress that the determinants of long-term growth, such as savings and investment rates, technological diffusion, and investment in human capital, are the most fundamental factors in the welfare of nations. GNP is the universally accepted measure of long-term growth. The idea that a nation with a lower per capita GNP might be better off—perhaps due to greater equity, an unspoiled environment, or more leisure time—is completely foreign to theories of economic growth. This perspective, of course, powerfully determines the actual policies followed by the world's developing nations, under the guiding hand of such transnational financial institutions as the World Bank and the International Monetary Fund.

What Does GNP Measure?

Despite its widespread acceptance, and despite the perception that we all "know" what GNP is, the definition and measurement of GNP have been rife with ambiguities and paradoxes since its beginnings. One of the originators of GNP accounts, Simon Kuznets, was well aware of the problems in calculating a single measurement of national product. In a classic article summarized here, Kuznets points out that the very definition of GNP is based on ambiguous concepts whose interpretation requires significant value judgments. One of these terms is the word "value" itself. When we say something has value, we do not necessarily imply that it has a price, or if it does that its price fully captures its value. But for purposes of aggregation, all elements of GNP must be expressed in money value.

This forces us to take one of two approaches. We can decide to include in GNP only those things that are traded in markets, at their market value. Or we can attempt to assign values to nontraded good and services. Either approach represents a value judgment. If we choose the former, we are implying that anything that does not have an explicit money price has no value, at least in economics. If we choose the latter, we will have to decide which nontraded goods and services are worthy of being included in our calculation and find some way of assigning them an appropriate money value.

In practice, GNP calculation embodies numerous judgments of this type. For example, the value of nontraded government services (such as national defense) are estimated at their cost of production. But the value of housework is not estimated or included in GNP. Many such decisions as to what has or does not have "value" are involved in the calculation of what we have come to regard as an objective measure of national economic activity.

Thus even in what appears to be merely an accounting exercise—the summing up of all economic activity in the nation—we are compelled to confront the same knotty questions that have driven economists to abandon the field of welfare economics as hopelessly unscientific. Does the high monetary value placed on advertising, tobacco, liquor, gambling, or pornographic entertainment imply that these economic activities have true value? If an individual spends money in these areas, does this contribute to his/her welfare? To the national welfare? If a parent spends more time taking care of children, and less time earning money, does s/he thereby lower national economic welfare? If the government orders expanded production of nerve gas, does this increase national welfare? There is no single obvious answer to questions such as these. Nonetheless, our judgment on all of these questions will be reflected in the techniques which we choose for calculating national income.[2]

These many problems and paradoxes have led to an expanding critical literature on the calculation of GNP statistics and their use in policy formulation. Critics have approached the issue from several perspectives. One approach analyzes methodological weaknesses in the formal structure of GNP accounts. A feminist critique emphasizes the omission or undervaluation of women's work in standard GNP. An ecological critique deals with the omission or distortion of the environmental and resource impacts of economic activity. Yet another group of critics has concentrated on the implications of GNP analysis for development, arguing that a focus on GNP often leads to inequitable or destructive development policies. The articles summarized in this section offer a selection of analyses from these different, though overlapping, critiques.

Unresolved Issues: Equity, Investment, and Well-Being

The articles by Fred Block and Robert Eisner make the case that GNP accounts are in many respects inconsistent, misleading, and inadequate as a measure both of production and of national well-being. GNP accounts include no measure of equity and implicitly validate the pricing structures associated with a particular, perhaps highly inequitable, distribution of income. Goods that are demanded by high-income individuals (e.g., mansions, luxury cars) automatically become "valuable," while goods that are needed by low-income individuals (e.g., affordable housing, mass transit) are not so "valuable" and may not be produced at all if there is not sufficient "effective demand" (buying power) to make their production profitable. GNP also fails to measure volunteer work, household work, leisure time, and nonpecuniary rewards of work.

Major problems also arise in the treatment of investment, both private and public. More efficient forms of capital, achieving the same output with less investment, show up as decreases in GNP (i.e., investment in energy efficiency). Government purchases are all treated as consumption, although spending on education and infrastructure is clearly investment. Investment by consumers in education and training is also considered consumption. This gives a narrow and distorted picture in which business spending on physical capital (buildings and machinery) is the only economic activity considered to be productive investment.

Eisner, echoing Tjalling Koopmans's warning about "measurement without theory," argues that the feckless adding machine of GNP accounts seriously misstates investment levels and thus leads to erroneous policy prescriptions. An example is overgenerous depreciation allowances that encourage excessive investment in physical capital, to the detriment of research and development, education, training, and health. A myopic focus on government budget-balancing is another negative consequence of simple-minded GNP accounts that fail to distinguish productive public investment from wasteful consumption.

What Happened to Women?

Marilyn Waring argues that GNP systematically excludes or undervalues women's contributions to the economy. Household work, whose value may be as much as 50 percent of standard GNP according to studies cited by Ann Chadeau, is not included in official statistics. It should also be noted that patterns of sex discrimination reduce the wage, and therefore the GNP contribution, of women's work in traditionally female sectors of the economy, such as nursing and paid childcare. Waring points out that the importance of this omission can be even greater in developing countries where so much of the traditional economy is based on women's work. Much of this remains invisible to development economists, who accordingly emphasize urban, industrial, and cash crop production, which are more easily measurable in GNP.

The implication of this critique is not simply that GNP is male-biased and unfair to women (although this is certainly true). Since so much of women's work (even when it is occasionally performed by men) involves the caregiving, community-building aspects of life, we can see that the view of well-being that we get from standard national income accounts systematically devalues community and family in favor of market production. The policy implications of this are sweeping. Taken in conjunction with Eisner's points about public investment, it suggests that public support for childcare, education, and investment in community facilities all suffer from their relative "invisibility" in GNP.

Accounting techniques, as we are beginning to understand, are inextricably tied to our value judgments and policy decisions. Under the guise of neutral authoritativeness, GNP embodies numerous biases, notably regarding gender. (A feminist critique would no doubt recognize this as a familiar feature of many male-dominated institutions.)

Accounting for the Environment

The articles by Peskin and Meyer offer an overview of the area of natural resource and environmental accounting, which has expanded exponentially in recent years. Peskin's 1981 article is remarkably prescient; his work prefigures the explosion of interest in the topic that has swept through even such unlikely venues as the World Bank during the last decade. Meyer provides a more recent snapshot of this work-in-progress, showing how independent research groups such as the World Resources Institute, national statistical agencies, and transnational institutions, including the United Nations and the World Bank, have struggled to keep up with the many data-gathering and analytical issues involved in integrating environmental and economic accounting.

The starting point of this line of thought, like those of other GNP critiques, is an internal inconsistency in national income accounts. Net National Product (NNP) is calculated by subtracting depreciation from GNP, thereby adjusting GNP's sum of economic value added to take account also of value lost when capital wears out or is used up. But this adjustment is made only for manufactured capital, not for "natural capital," which includes the asset value of natural resources. Changes in the value of other kinds of environmental assets, such as the absorptive capacity of air and water, are also unaccounted for. Thus if a nation chops down its forests, depletes its soils, and exhausts its mineral resources, the standard measure of NNP will show only gain as these resources are transformed into saleable goods. Clearly, consistent treatment of capital assets would require a depreciation adjustment for natural capital as well as for manufactured capital.

When such an adjustment is calculated for resource-dependent developing nations, there is typically a significant effect on NNP, and an even more dramatic impact on net investment. In some cases, what previously appeared to be a substantial net investment actually becomes negative after adjusting for natural capital depreciation. Traditional accounting would send exactly the wrong message in such a case—a country whose economic position is actually worsening over time would appear to be becoming wealthier due to the omission of resource depletion and environmental degradation from its national accounts.

At first glance, it appears that the simple adjustment of including natural capital depreciation will correct this problem, but in practice the issue is much more complex. The valuation of natural capital depreciation is no simple task, involving both value judgments and methodological problems. An important issue is the choice of discount rate for estimating environmental damages that cumulate over time, such as soil erosion. Taking the broader view that Peskin espouses, we must also estimate a value for environmental services, such as pollution absorption, and environmental damages, such as loss of biodiversity. It proves easier to show the existence of a major problem with standard NNP measures than to prescribe a solution—although much effort has gone into the attempt to construct consistent environmental and economic accounts.

Implications for Development Theory

If, as the articles we have discussed have argued, standard national income analysis offers a biased view (ignoring issues of equity, misstating the value of investment) omitting much of women's contribution, and failing to reflect environmental degradation, it can hardly be a good guide for policy. But as Hazel Henderson argues, it is precisely this narrow measure of GNP or NNP that is used by multinational development agencies and national governments to determine the goals and policies of developing economies. Policies that are destructive to community and to the environment, or that increase inequity and the exploitation of women, can thus be endorsed as successful in raising GNP. Without better indicators, damaging policies are likely to continue. Can we do better? Henderson suggests that no single index can capture the multiple goals of development and proposes the use of a range of social and economic indicators.[3]

The next section of this volume reviews the work that has been done in developing some of these alternative indicators. Before moving to the area of new indicators, however, it is worth considering the common threads among the different lines of criticism of GNP that we have reviewed. The sources of these critiques are varied: economists concerned about inconsistent methodology, feminists arguing for a fairer evaluation of women's work, and ecological economists attempting to elevate natural capital to a more prominent position in economic theory. But all imply a different approach both to the measurement of national income and to the formulation of development policies. In particular, they suggest a different kind of analysis and policy in the area of social investment.

The main component of standard GNP is consumption; standard economic analysis sees investment as a means to greater future consumption. In GNP accounts, investment is defined exclusively as private business investment in the production of goods and services. As we have seen, government spending is considered as consumption rather than investment, as is individual spending on human capital (education and training). Investment in social capital—the community-strengthening institutions that provide the backdrop for all economic activity—generally cannot be measured in national income accounts. Nor can environmental conservation and investment in natural capital (such as agricultural soil rotation practices) be easily measured. Yet all these forms of investment are crucial to a healthy economy and society. Standard national income analysis encourages us to neglect these types of investment in favor of a single, narrowly defined concept of investment in manufactured capital to facilitate increased consumption. As Marilyn Waring points out in her article summarized here, there are vast public policy implications that arise from a more appropriate valuation of productive services now invisible to GNP accounting.

The abandonment of the broader issues that in the past have been the subject of normative economics has led modern economic theorists to rely excessively on a narrow measure of human welfare; this in turn has led to erroneous prescriptions of how society should invest to increase welfare. Insofar as increased consumption promotes well-being, policies promoting economic growth in accordance with standard measures of national income will be successful. But in considering the many dimensions of well-being that these measures fail to capture, standard economic theory, as embodied in GNP accounts, will prove a poor guide to use of human and natural resources in economic development.

Notes

1. The difference between GNP and GDP is whether or not the foreign earnings of individuals and corporations are included in the total. U.S. GNP, for example, includes the foreign earnings of U.S. residents and corporations but excludes the earnings of foreign individuals and corporations from activities in the U.S. U.S. GDP includes all income earned within the U.S., regardless of the nationality or residence of the recipient, but excludes earnings of U.S. residents and corporations from foreign sources.

2. An overview of the problems and paradoxes involved in using GNP/GDP as a measure of national welfare is provided by Clifford Cobb, Ted Halstead, and Jonathan Rowe in "If the GDP Is Up, Why Is America Down?" *Atlantic Monthly* (October 1995), 59–78.

3. Hazel Henderson, "What's Next in the Great Debate About Measuring Wealth and Progress?" *Challenge* November–December 1996. In this article, Henderson updates her review of multiple development indicators. Despite recent work by both public and private institutions on developing indices that take into account social and economic factors, she favors "unbundled quality-of-life indicators" over the use of any single index.

Summary of

The Concept of National Income

by Simon Kuznets

[Published in *National Income and Its Composition*, 1919–1938
(New York: National Bureau of Economic Research, 1941), 3–60.]

For those not intimately acquainted with this type of work it is difficult to realize the degree to which estimates of national income have been and must be
affected by implicit or explicit value judgments. [5]

[National income] is essentially an appraisal of the final net product of the
business and public economies of the country, two of the three important social institutions that contribute to the production of economic goods; and excludes completely the product of the third—the family. [10]

[The use of market criteria] swells national income with items that represent
what many citizens condemn as a misuse of energy and the inadequacies of the
existing social structure. It includes dreadnoughts, bombing planes, poison
gas, and patent medicines because they are rated economic goods in our country today. [20]

Calculation of national income has never been a matter of objective observation
alone but has always involved observation embedded in a matrix of theoretical
analysis, value judgments, and ultimately somewhat arbitrary definitions, often
driven by expediency and data availability. In this classic work, Kuznets presents
the first systematic definition and calculation of U.S. national income and discusses the countless ambiguities and judgments (many more than appear in this
summary) that arise in the process.

"National income may be defined as the net value of all economic goods produced by the nation." [3] This definition involves four ambiguous terms: "net
value," "economic goods," "produced," and "nation." While there are core
areas of agreement on the meaning of each term, there are also peripheral areas
of disagreement, where subjective elements inevitably enter the definition of
what is to be measured. Thus national income is necessarily an appraisal of the
economic system, not a colorless statement of fact. Denial of any role for judgment would turn national income accounting into a useless summary of all
transactions, many of them obviously unproductive or involving double-counting of productive activity.

Economic Goods

All economic goods may be sources of satisfaction; but the converse is not true,
since many satisfactions come from personal activities that are conventionally

excluded from economic analysis. No definition of the boundary between economic and noneconomic activities can be applicable to all times and places, but for "mature economies" in the 20th century we may define economic goods as those that "usually appear on the market." [7] However, even this is not free of ambiguity because of the treatment of goods that are usually, but not always, marketed.

Several different detailed definitions are possible; the one adopted for national income calculations includes all goods sold by private enterprises or public agencies, plus barter (such as payment in kind), products retained by producers for their own consumption (especially important on farms), and the services provided by residential real estate that is owned and occupied by consumers. The definition excludes all other household services and nonmarket production and free services of public capital (such as roads). The exclusion of household services is compelled both by convention and by lack of data but is nonetheless arbitrary: unemployed people may perform many varieties of household labor outside the market, while employed people often hire others to perform some of the same tasks.

Nonproductive transactions, which add nothing to the available flow of goods, include gifts and other transfers, gambling, receipt of capital gains, and theft. Neither private charity nor public relief payments add anything directly to the nation's supply of goods, though the recipients may later spend the money in ways that stimulate production. Capital gains are in part the result of gambling on other people's changes in tastes, and in part the result of real investments that change the value of enterprises and properties. In the latter case, the investments are included in national income directly, so inclusion of the resulting capital gains would be double-counting. However, despite these exclusions, enterprises or agencies that facilitate charity, relief, gambling, or the receipt of capital gains are providing real services and should be counted. That is, employment in charities and casinos adds to national income, even though receipt of charity payments or gambling winnings does not.

What about the treatment of goods that some consider desirable and others undesirable? Such goods add less to the satisfaction of society as a whole than to their individual purchasers. A number of theoretically appropriate schemes could be suggested to address this problem, but none appear to be possible to carry out. Practicality dictates reliance on the law to express society's judgment: only illegal activities are excluded.

Economic Value

A common yardstick of economic value is needed to measure the disparate goods and services that make up national income. Market price is the obvious candidate; identification of economic value with market price solves many problems. Three categories of problems, though, are not resolved; these involve goods that do not appear on the market, "peculiarities of the market mechanism," [24] and the valuation of government services.

Goods that are not marketed are often valued at the price of comparable marketed goods. The comparability may be limited, however, precisely because of the institutional difference between market and nonmarket provision. Payment in kind gives an employee much less choice in consumption than the equivalent payment in cash.

A different problem of goods that are not (yet) marketed occurs when production is in progress, but incomplete by the end of the reporting period. In this case, there is no alternative to valuing goods at the cost of production, essentially using past market prices for the inputs rather than current market prices for the outputs.

There are limits to the validity of market price as a measure of value, even for marketed goods. The value of goods ultimately results from the satisfaction they are capable of yielding, but

> market demand reflects human needs only so far as they are backed by purchasing power. No one supposes that the distribution of income parallels the distribution of wants or satisfactions . . . . Therefore we cannot claim that our estimates of national income, based as they must be upon market valuations, evaluate goods as means of satisfying directly or indirectly the present or future needs of the population. [24–25][1]

Yet once we accept society's judgment as to what is productive, there is no alternative to reliance on market prices as a measure of value.

In economic theory, it is only the price in a competitive market that can be identified with the social value of a product. Many markets are of course monopolized to varying degrees, allowing prices to be set above the competitive level. It would be essentially impossible to correct for this problem, and one could argue that society has accepted existing, imperfect market structures and the prices they imply.

The use of money in transactions may itself introduce problems of valuation, for the value of money can fluctuate even if the supply of goods remains constant. Inflation and deflation do not affect all goods equally, making the process of adjustment for price changes a difficult one. The most common method of adjustment is to construct price indexes for the same goods at different times, a process that entails a set of technical difficulties of its own. One important problem arises when the goods on the market change in composition or quality. When entirely new goods appear, or old ones undergo substantial changes in quality, any price index becomes an uncertain guide to the value of money.

How should government services be valued? There are two leading alternatives. One is to measure the value of government by the amounts paid to it by enterprises and households, in the form of taxes, fees, etc. This would assume that, for society as a whole if not for each individual, what we pay is a measure of the value of what we get. The other is to measure the cost, in labor and materials, of providing government services.

Distinction between Net and Gross

National income is the *net* value of goods produced during a given time period. If the material inputs into production of a good have already been counted, it would not do to count them again; only the value added to previously counted inputs should be included. Alternatively, we could count only the value of final consumption, not that of the intermediate consumption of inputs into further production processes.

But what counts as a production process? Individual wage earners could view themselves as enterprises engaged in producing labor services, and deduct the cost of food, clothing, and other necessary inputs. By convention, we do not make this calculation. Economic goods are assumed to exist for human beings, rather than human beings existing for the production of goods; this gives a privileged status to final consumption by households, as usually defined. The result is that national income includes labor income on a gross basis, and enterprises on a net basis. For self-employed individuals, only those costs that they identify as business expenses are deducted.

Even within enterprises, there are complex issues related to the distinction between gross and net product. The calculation is straightforward when intermediate goods are fully used up within the reporting period. But when durable capital goods are only partially consumed, how should they be counted? An estimate is needed of the fraction of the total value of the goods that are consumed in each period. In essence this involves forecasting the useful life of the equipment, a process that is surrounded by uncertainty. There is no practical alternative to using the estimates made by business enterprises. However, it is clear that current, or replacement, values should be used, while businesses typically use book value, or historical cost. National income figures need to be adjusted to reflect current market values.

The Meaning of "Produced"

There are several points in the flow of goods, and payment for them, at which national income could be evaluated. We could calculate either the net value of goods produced, or total factor payments by producers to individuals, or total expenditure on final goods, or total value of final goods consumed. For any reasonably short period, no two of these measures will be the same. The value of goods produced is preferred because production is the source of payments and consumption, and because it is generally the largest of the measures, making it more likely that the other income concepts can be calculated as components of it.

When should a good be considered to be "produced"? It would simplify calculation to consider a good as produced only when it is actually sold on the market. However, the disadvantage of this approach is that many production processes occur over long periods of time; calculation of work in progress is needed for accurate short-term measures of economic activity. The alternative adopted for national income accounting, as previously mentioned, is to count only the portion of the production process that occurs within each reporting period. Price changes during the production process can therefore lead to complications in accounting.

National Economy as Object of Measurement

Calculation of *national* income incorporates the results of the historical accidents that led to today's boundaries; often nations are not self-contained or natural economic units. Totals for industries, occupations, enterprises, or regions might be more meaningful. Some of these can be assessed by dividing national totals into meaningful subtotals.

Still, national totals are undeniably needed. Several definitions of the "nation" could be adopted, depending on whether productive activity occurs inside or outside of the country, whether it is owned by citizens or noncitizens, and whether it is owned by residents or nonresidents. Different definitions are useful for different purposes. In order "to reflect the kind of international relations that prevailed during most of the nineteenth and into the twentieth century," [54] the appropriate definition includes activities owned or performed by residents of the country, regardless of citizenship or of the location of the activity.[2]

Summary

In defining national income the fundamental distinctions . . . imply fundamental notions concerning the meaning of economic productivity—notions that represent a social philosophy. . . . In formulating these notions we attempted in general to hold consistently to two theses. The first is that needs of ultimate consumers provide the touchstone by which the results of economic activity are to be judged . . . The second thesis is that in judging relevance to needs, the overt expression of social judgment, the standards followed by society in its economic institutions are to be accepted as a guide. For this reason we excluded only such activities as are considered harmful or not productive by society, and adopted the market price basis of valuation. [57–58]

Notes

1. Kuznets argues for the first approach, while contemporary national income accounting uses the second.

2. This definition is used in GNP, the preferred measure until the 1990s. Recent discussion more often uses GDP, including all activities located within the country, regardless of ownership or citizenship.

Summary of

Output

by Fred Block

[Published in *Post-Industrial Possibilities* (Berkeley: University of California Press, 1990), 155–188.]

Over the past half century, the focus of national politics has been narrowed from the classic issue of well-being to that of changes in individual and family real income. This shift closely relates to changes in the way people think about output. The development of national income accounting in the 1930s and 1940s has meant that output is no longer a vague concept; it can be precisely calculated and provide us with a seemingly clear indication of how well the economy is doing.

Despite these advances, this article contends that Gross National Product (GNP) is becoming "an increasingly problematic measure of economic output." [155] This is due to three factors: (1) there are many dimensions of well-being excluded from this measure; (2) there are methodological and theoretical inconsistencies in GNP construction; and (3) there is a growing discrepancy between popular perceptions of well-being and measured changes in GNP.

What GNP Measures

GNP is not, nor does it claim to be, a measure of public welfare. Because it lacks a distributive dimension, it cannot distinguish between an egalitarian and an inegalitarian distribution of wealth. Nor does it measure other important elements of welfare, such as environmental quality and life expectancy. GNP does purport to be the best measure of economic growth. Nevertheless, critics assert that it cannot even perform this task adequately given the confines of its current methodology.

GNP measures the value of final goods sold on the market. There are evident problems with this approach. Some goods, such as radio broadcasts, do not have market prices. The creators of GNP accounting thus decided that these outputs would be labeled intermediate goods, e.g., radio programming was considered part of the total advertising expenditures of the sponsors. Goods and services provided by the public sector and nonprofit organizations that had no final market price experience similar fates; their outputs are determined by summing the market prices of their inputs—labor, materials, and interest payments. This has the effect of presenting nonmarket production as inherently inefficient. A more efficient use of labor in these sectors is calculated as a loss of output, and a less efficient use as an increase in output.

Several other categories of production are excluded from GNP accounts because they fail to meet the criterion of market pricing. Some of these are not even considered intermediate goods. One such category, estimated at 20 to 40 percent of GNP, is household work. This includes activities ranging from child care, meal preparation, and cleaning to maintaining and improving housing and consumer durables. The same holds true for volunteer activities performed outside of the home. The exclusion of these activities gives way to certain anomalies, such as Pigou's case of a man who marries his housekeeper and diminishes total GNP. During the last 30 years, the increasing number of married women in the workforce has shifted much of this formerly uncounted output to the marketplace. The resulting measured increase in GNP does not necessarily correspond to any increase in utility.

Economic theory tells us that labor is a disutility, which is why we are paid for it. By the same token, leisure provides utility, but it is unaccounted for in GNP because it has no market price. This means that two societies could have the same GNP, but the average worker in one might have half the work week of the other. Many problems arise when trying to put a dollar value on leisure: the value will differ between people depending on the utility they derive from it, and one must separate voluntary leisure from involuntary leisure. Nevertheless, the total value of leisure would certainly be substantial. In fact, one study determined that in 1965, the dollar value of leisure was actually greater than GNP.[1]

While economists generally regard work as a disutility, many people derive nonpecuniary rewards from work, such as companionship, a sense of meaning, intellectual challenges, and social status. It would certainly be difficult to calculate these benefits, but extensive research findings indicate that they are of great importance in determining individual well-being.[2] As with leisure, two countries may have the same levels of GNP, but the labor force in one might be engaged in repetitious, boring work, while employees in the other enjoy stimulating, challenging work.

GNP also fails to account for the indirect effects of production on various aspects of human existence. Innumerable problems arise in calculating these externalities. An obvious example is environmental degradation: how does one calculate the depreciation of environmental assets when the resiliency of the Earth to human actions is unknown; what levels of strain will lead to cumulative failures that affect human life? Environmental impacts are also closely linked to health; the repercussions on the productive capacities of the workforce should not be ignored. Some consequences include poor health and increased health care costs, more sick days, and shorter life expectancies.

With the exclusion of so many important elements of output, it is easy to see why studies fail to correlate improvements in well-being with increases in GNP. GNP measures only a fraction of the utility produced by economic activity. The dilemma of changing GNP to include well-being is that although the emphasis on market prices in GNP accounting provides a truncated view of economic output, adding a whole series of complex imputations to GNP accounting can potentially deprive the national income accounting system of the appearance of objectivity. When efforts are made to estimate some of these values the problem of "utility for whom" is raised. Within the marginalist framework, individuals have different preferences that reflect the utility of the product to them. When expressed in the market, the sum of these preferences produces a seemingly objective measure of aggregate utility. The objectivity of this approach is compromised, however, when economists substitute their own valuations for those of economic factors.

Measurement Problems in GNP Data

Even within the narrow scope of activities that national income accounts attempt to encompass, a number of measurement problems arise. One such case occurs with the purchase of capital goods. Since these purchases are counted in GNP, technical advances that reduce capital expenditures have the effect of decreasing the contribution of the capital goods sector to GNP. Another problem arises from the difficulty in separating quality changes from simple price increases. These accounting problems are particularly pervasive in the growing service industry where costless quality changes and continuous innovation are common. Lack of standardization in other industries, such as the construction sector, also poses problems when trying to calculate constant dollar outputs.

Another measurement problem relates to the balance between "productive consumption" and "consumptive production." Productive consumption increases human capacity; for example, education provides a consumer good and simultaneously enhances an individual's productive capacity. Medical care, social services, and vacations fall under the same category. Nonpecuniary rewards of work would fall under the category of consumptive production, because there is consumption of status and intellectual challenges at the same time that goods and services are being produced. This meshing of consumption and production is a major problem in a methodology that requires an activity to be either investment or consumption, but not both. This is a serious problem in economic accounting since, with the blurring of the two, one can consume more today and still have more for tomorrow.

GNP and Problems in GNP Data

The previous discussion shows that many increases in utility, such as improvements in quality and the growth of productive consumption, are understated in GNP figures. Yet, it would certainly belie popular sentiment to say that people are much better off than GNP figures indicate. Rather, there is a current of dissatisfaction and disgruntlement running through America today that runs counter to the country's GNP record.

Part of the reason for this dilemma lies in the fact that people's ideas about how well they are doing are largely affected by expectations. For instance, it has been found that people were not able to adequately account for inflation in the 1970s and thus had distorted perceptions of their real income. Perceptions of other people's well-being also play a role. As incomes rise, so does spending on positional goods, i.e., status goods that cannot keep up with demand. Examples include rare paintings, 50-yard-line football tickets, and apartments in Manhattan. Once the exclusive domain of the upper economic echelons, demand for the acquisition of these goods has trickled down to a large segment of the middle class. Since there will always be positional goods that are even more exclusive and valuable, they will continue to play a significant role in people's perceptions of well-being.

Positional goods and the illusion of wealth do not explain all of the perceived loss of utility. It may also be partially attributable to the increasing participation of married women in the labor force. While some of the utility previously produced by unpaid family members has moved into the marketplace, some utility is no longer produced at all, or only produced at the cost of great family stress. For example, community organizations that were comprised mostly of housewives may still have the same number of volunteers, but their members may now only be able to contribute half the amount of time. These activities often contribute significantly to quality of life. At the same time, balancing work and volunteer activities also places considerable stress on those who try to do both.

Another cause of utility loss may be due to the mismatch between production and demand. In the market economic model, needs almost automatically turn into demand, which is quickly satisfied by entrepreneurs. In reality, there are many factors that can interfere with this process. In the 1970s and 1980s, such a mismatch occurred in low- and moderate-priced housing, leading to a rise in homelessness. Also, public concern for environmental quality and occupational health and safety are rarely met with swift response due to the slow nature of the political process. In sum, both the case of positional goods and the examples of mismatch reinforce the insight that institutional variables intervene between economic growth and improvements or deterioration in the utility people receive.

Ultimately, GNP growth rates have very little to do with whether or not people are better off. In fact, it is not at all difficult to imagine zero GNP growth in a highly dynamic economy that is producing progressively higher levels of human satisfaction.

Notes

1. William Nordhaus and James Tobin, "Is Growth Obsolete?" in Stanley Moss, ed. *Measurement of Economic and Social Performance*, 509–532.
2. See Christopher Jencks et al., "What is a Good Job? A New Measure of Labor Market Success," *American Journal of Sociology* 93 (6) (May 1988) and F. Thomas Juster, "Preferences for Work and Leisure," in *Time, Goods, and Well-Being*, eds. Juster and Stafford.

Summary of

Divergences of Measurement and Theory and Some Implications for Economic Policy

by Robert Eisner

[Published in *American Economic Review* 79 (March 1989), 1–13.]

Macroeconomic analysis has been beset by a "failure to match theoretical constructs with appropriate empirical counterparts," [11] leading to inordinate confusion in public discourse and policy making. Particular problems arise from relying on current and past values of critical variables as proxies for the future expectations on which outcomes actually depend, employing measures of income and production that are too narrowly defined, and weaknesses in the conventional measures of saving, investment, and capital. We should heed Tjalling Koopmans's warning about the dangers of "measurement without theory" and seek to better reconcile the two.

Current versus Expected Values

Critical problems arise in the estimation of major macroeconomic values because key arguments in the estimation functions are expected values. For example, response to an increase in the money supply will depend on *unobservable* expectations about both the likelihood of increasing inflation and the duration of the change, so we are often reduced to estimation based on current and past variables for which data are available. However, if future values will be based on expectations about certain variables, then we must first ask whether the effects of existing data on expectations were considered when generating the estimation functions, and then whether we can assume that the same expectational relations will apply in the future. The most critical problem arises with regard to investment, because it is entirely forward looking. In theory, investment behavior depends primarily on the expected future values of variables such as output, profit, and interest rates, and very little on their current or past values, yet the latter are used as arguments in investment functions.

Measures of Income and Product

Income is theoretically defined as what we can consume while maintaining our level of real wealth, but there are many discrepancies between this definition and measurement of income in practice. For example, capital depreciation allowances have been steadily increasing and may be overstated, resulting in underestimation of national and individual income, and net savings as well. The calculation of capital gains and interest earnings also falls short. *Real* capital gains—i.e., the nominal gain less the increase necessary to compensate for inflation—should be included in income, but capital gains are left out of income accounting entirely. On the other hand, nominal interest earnings are fully included in income, but again, it is only real interest earnings that should be counted.

The failure of national income statistics to include imputations for some important nonmarket outputs is also a concern. We do impute values for some items, especially net rent of owner-occupied housing. But the same is not done for other durable goods such as automobiles; car rental is included in national income, but the use of our own cars is not. Housework is another well-known example of this problem. Ignoring it results in overestimation of growth rates of total output as women increasingly move from uncounted work in the home to paid, counted jobs in the market and in miscalculations of total productivity changes as well.

Problems also arise from counting the same expenditures differently if they are made by a firm, by its employees, or by the government. In particular, the practice of including all of government output in GNP, even though much of it is really intermediate output, overestimates GNP. For example, a firm's employment of security guards is counted as intermediate input, but when the government hires more police officers—or invests large amounts in national defense—national income, as presently calculated, increases.

Deficits and National Saving and Investment

While the differences between theoretical and measured values of income are substantial, they are actually quite small compared to the discrepancies in saving and investment measures. First, because investment can be defined as the acquisition or production of capital that will contribute to current and future output, production of durable goods like automobiles, research and development expenditures, and education costs should all be included. Yet all of these are treated as consumption expenditures. Government expenditure on education is thus pejoratively labeled as government spending, rather than as investment, which is viewed more favorably.

Gross saving consists of personal and corporate saving plus government saving (i.e., budget surplus). We are frequently bombarded with dire warnings that national saving is too low and the government budget deficit too high, but two adjustments can nearly wipe out this deficit. First, the government, like private firms, should only count real depreciation charges on capital in current outlays, rather than current capital expenditures. Second, only real interest payments on the national debt should be charged to current outlays, rather than nominal payments.

Serious discrepancies between theoretical constructs of net foreign investment and official measures occur because much of overseas investments of U.S. firms and foreign investment in the U.S. are counted at their original costs. They should instead be adjusted for changes in their value either in the local currency and in changing exchange rates in dollars. Measuring these values in real, current market terms would virtually wipe out the calamitous "debtor nation" image of the U.S. (in 1988), because U.S. foreign investments have appreciated much more (in the currencies of the countries of investment) than have foreign investments in the U.S. (in dollars), and the falling value of the dollar has further increased the relative value of U.S. overseas investments.

The differences between conventional measures and indices that better reflect theoretical constructs may be substantial. The author's "total incomes system of accounts" (TISA) produces estimates of net national product that are 30 percent greater than standard measures and estimates of real gross private domestic investment four times those measured by conventional indices. Research and development, education and training, and health investments—all left out of current capital stock measures—account for fully 48 percent of the TISA measure.

New Behavioral Relations, Theory, and Policy

Changing the value of a few variables cannot remedy these problems; adjustment must include rethinking fundamental economic relations. For example, standard production functions such as Cobb-Douglas only include arguments for labor and capital, but a strong case can be made for adding variables for government infrastructure capital, research and development, and human capital. Preliminary testing of the latter two suggests that they could both have significantly positive coefficients. We should thus be taking a much broader view of capital than advocates of tax credits and other incentives for standard business investment would propose.

Investment functions should also be respecified to include more in capital than just business plant and equipment. This might help to overcome some of the empirical weaknesses of investment theory that relates a firm's capital expenditures to the ratio between its market value and its capital replacement costs. Because firms' investments in the experience, skills, and dedication of their employees affect market values, but are not yet included in the assessment of capital replacement costs, investment theory has proven largely irrelevant as it is currently used.

Similar problems arise when economists derive monetary and fiscal policy prescriptions based on inadequate and often irrelevant indices, at times resulting in a serious misdirection of macroeconomic policy. For example, when real government budget surpluses were miscalculated as deficits in the late 1970s (due to a failure to distinguish between real and monetary values of government debt at a time of high inflation), a great deal of confusion arose because, contrary to prevailing theories, unemployment was also increasing. This misunderstanding led to policies that probably made matters worse.

Provision for the Future: The Case of Social Security

Social security accounts are an area of particular concern, in part because of the dire warnings about our budget deficits. One proposal for dealing with this is to incorporate all "contingent liabilities"—the present value of expected future payouts less expected contributions—into the general federal accounting framework. In principle this is not a bad idea, but given the current problems with mis-measurement it would actually only compound the problem. The alternative proposal that we place social security trust funds in entirely separate budgets is even worse. We may face problems with social security accounts in the future as aging baby boomers will have to be supported by relatively fewer workers. The best solution to this problem is to raise the productivity of the work force, and the best way to do this is by increasing investment in public, social infrastructure, in research and development, and in human capital (including education, training, and health care). This is how the government should use the current surpluses in the Social Security system, but because of the present misinterpretations of macroeconomic variables, this is politically difficult.

If, on the other hand

> ... we had federal budget and national accounting measures that properly classified all of this vital capital accumulation, the choice of wise public policy, and the economic analysis on which it would build, might be much easier. [10]

Summary of

Selections from Counting for Nothing: What Men Value and What Women Are Worth

by Marilyn J. Waring

[Wellington, New Zealand: Bridget William Books, 1987.]

This book, by a prominent feminist from New Zealand, critiques the exclusion of women's unpaid labor from the United Nations System of National Accounts (a system quite similar to U.S. national income accounts) and suggests revisions of the accounts that would allow a more adequate treatment of women's work. This summary covers portions of Chapters 2, 3, 9, and 11 of the book.

Warfare and Women's Work

Although there were earlier attempts to measure a nation's entire output, national income accounting is largely a product of the 20th century. It assumed its current form in studies performed in the U.S. and Britain at the start of World War II to calculate the potential resources that could be mobilized for the war effort.

The focus at that time was on measurement of the resources that could be mobilized for war. Therefore, national income was defined to include only marketed output, or activities that were easily convertible into marketed output. Household labor was generally excluded, except when a family farm or other enterprise produced marketable goods. Yet this wartime categorization has lived on for decades beyond World War II and has the effect of rendering much of women's labor invisible to economists.

Ignoring Household Labor

Despite token acknowledgments of women's vital economic role, most statistical agencies persist in ignoring the importance of unpaid household labor. In developed countries it is sometimes claimed that labor-saving devices have reduced the burden of maintaining a home. However, from 1920 to 1960 there was an increase in average household labor time for American women who were not employed outside the home, despite urbanization and the spread of labor-saving devices. Women still feed, clothe, and nurse their families, involving substantial labor in such activities as cooking, cleaning, driving, and shopping, even if new devices have reduced the required physical effort. Women continue to perform the majority of household tasks even when they work outside the home.

In rural areas, particularly in developing countries, the range of women's work is even larger. Women in rural Africa do more than half of the hoeing, weeding, harvesting, transporting, processing, and marketing of crops, and almost all carry water and fuel and feed and care for family members. Of these activities, only marketing of crops was traditionally reflected in national income. After many years of discussion, the United Nations now recommends that all household production of marketable products should be counted, whether or not the products are actually marketed. However, implementation of this recommendation differs widely from one country to another. Some major categories of African women's work, notably carrying fuel and water and feeding and caring for family members, are still excluded from the U.N.'s recommended accounting procedures.

Surveys in many countries show that housewives frequently have exhausting, lengthy work weeks. Yet they are routinely classified as "unproductive" or "unoccupied" in official statistics. Biased images of the division of labor can interfere with economic development efforts, as when aid agencies have mistakenly assumed that they should teach better farming practices to rural African men and home economics to women, missing the fact that women make most of the decisions about farming.

Subsistence Agriculture, Urbanization, and Nutrition

Around the world, rural poverty is leading to urban migration in search of paid work. While earned incomes are higher in the towns and cities, the volume of goods and services that a family can afford may be smaller because many subsistence activities are no longer possible. Even if subsistence agriculture and other rural household productive activities are correctly valued at local, rural prices, they generally cost less than the equivalent urban goods and services. Thus urban migration creates a spurious appearance of economic growth, as more people obtain basic necessities through higher-priced delivery systems.

Urban migration also affects nutrition, as household production of traditional foods gives way to the purchase of unfamiliar, often imported and/or processed foods, which are accompanied, in many cases, by a range of new nutritional deficiencies and diseases. Nonetheless, buying higher-priced foods adds more to national income, seemingly creating more welfare than traditional agriculture. This statistical illusion contributes to the frequent bias of aid agencies in favor of new cash crops (often assumed to be raised by men) rather than well-established basic food crops (more often raised by women).

Imputing a Value to Women's Work

In 1970 the Chase Manhattan Bank carried out an informal survey to determine the amount of work done by a U.S. housewife and the cost of hiring people to perform the same services. The estimated 99.6 hour work week included 44.5 hours as a nursemaid, 17.5 hours as a housekeeper, 13.1 hours as a cook, and an assortment of smaller tasks. The total cost of hiring these services, extrapolated to the entire country on an annual basis, exceeds half of that year's reported GNP, or twice the government budget. Such enormous numbers are not an artifact of a single study; many researchers have estimated that the household sector's contribution is worth 25 to 40 percent or more of GNP in industrialized countries.

Any of several methods could be used to impute a value to unpaid household labor (just as national income accounts now do, for example, for owner-occupied housing). Household tasks could be valued at the cost of hiring household help, or the cost of commercial services that perform equivalent functions (as in the Chase Manhattan survey), or the wages of similarly skilled workers, or the wages foregone in the market by those working at home (the "opportunity cost" of household labor), or the average wages of market workers, or the value of noncash benefits received (housing, food, clothing, medical care, etc.).

The household contribution to national income varies a great deal, depending on which of these approaches is chosen. Estimates in a Canadian study ranged from 34 percent to 53 percent of GNP, using varying methods of imputation. The cost of household help, or equivalent commercial services, is lowered by existing patterns of sex segregation in employment—as is any estimate that relies on women's rather than men's wages. Opportunity cost calculations depend on the alternatives assumed to be available to homemakers; the World War II experience showed that many could move quickly into traditionally male, skilled industrial pursuits when necessary, suggesting a rationale for a high opportunity cost. When, as usually occurs, household work extends past 40 hours per week, should higher pay be imputed for overtime?

Conclusion

The public policy implications of imputing women's work into the national accounts are vast. First, per capita GDP would change markedly. A more reliable indicator of the well-being of the community would be available, because all caring services, subsistence production, and that vast range of life-enhancing work would be visible and counted. And priorities would change. . . . The needs for training and retraining the unpaid work force would receive attention as a policy priority. Unpaid workers could make a realistic claim on the public purse as opposed to being condemned to "welfare." *Every decision made* by a government would be influenced in a profound way. [284–285]

Yet even a system that imputed the value of women's household labor would be imperfect, in the sense that GDP would not provide an adequate measure of welfare. Women's essential role in reproduction—a subject that defies any attempt at imputation of monetary values—is not recognized. Nor would other important values, particularly in the area of the environment, be automatically included. Still, imputing a value for women's work in national income accounts is a crucial step toward overcoming patriarchal conceptions of economic theory, public policy, and development strategies.

Summary of

Measuring Household Activities: Some International Comparisons

by Ann Chadeau

[Published in *The Review of Income and Wealth* 31 (September 1985), 237–253.]

The unpaid (nonmarket) labor performed in households by and for the benefit of their members goes uncounted in most standard economic measures, which focus only on market transactions. Yet its importance as a source of economic value and as an essential condition for social reproduction is unassailable. This paper reviews several macroeconomic approaches to measuring this labor or the associated household production, discussing the aims pursued, the activities measured, the methodologies used, and the availability of statistical data. The results of a number of major macroeconomic studies all clearly indicate that the value of household labor as a percentage of GNP is significant. Data availability remains the greatest constraint to furthering our understanding of relations between the household and market sectors.

Aims Pursued

Efforts to measure the nonmarket work or production of households usually pursue one of two main goals. The first is improving national accounts. It has long been recognized that in principle, measures of national income should include nonmarket production if they are to be an accurate reflection of total economic activity or total welfare. Exclusion of nonmarket production also leads to an overestimation of the rate of growth of national income. For example, as women increasingly shift from household work, where their production goes uncounted, to the market labor force, the real change in their total labor or production may be small, but the effect on measures such as GNP is substantial.

The second aim is comparison of productive activities in the household and market sectors, which can be done on either a monetary or nonmonetary basis. Nonmonetary measurement allows direct comparison of the number of hours of work in the market and nonmarket sectors, usually based on time use surveys. These studies are especially useful for comparison of the amount of household work done by women who do and those who do not participate in the market labor force, as well as for evaluation of how household work varies with other factors, such as the age and gender structure of the household.

Monetary comparisons require imputing money values to various types of housework, a complex methodological issue. Because the results are so sensitive to the method selected, analysts do not advise simply adding monetary estimates of the value of household labor or production to national income figures. This can, however, be a useful and illuminating basis for comparison and does at least suggest an order of magnitude for the value of household contributions.

Activities Covered

Neither "work" nor "production" encompasses all of the activities performed within a household, but either of these concepts can be used as the basis for selecting which activities matter. That is, we can consider either "unpaid household labor" or "production for own account," each of which yields slightly different results. One common approach to defining work in the household is the "third person" criterion: "housework is restricted to those activities performed within the household by one of its members for the others producing indirect utility and which could be done for pay by someone not belonging to the household." [240–241] This definition thus separates work from leisure, meeting biological needs and market work.

The production approach takes a somewhat broader view of relevant household activities: "a productive act is one which can be performed by a unit distinct from the one who consumes the end result" [241], although for the production under consideration here the producing and consuming units—the household—are in fact the same. Implementation of this approach is more difficult than the work-based approach due to lack of data on the nature and quantity of household output, especially with respect to services, since most household surveys have focused only on time use. Quality differentiation is also problematic, as is accounting for the psychological value of production by household members for themselves, which has no market substitute.

Methodologies

At present, the main methodological issue is how to confer a money value on unpaid household labor. There are two general approaches. The first entails estimating the cost of hiring someone else to do the work, i.e., the *foregone expense*. The wage rate used may either be that of a single housekeeper performing all functions in the household or a number of task-specific rates can be used (e.g., cook, nanny, etc.). Alternatively, the value of all household production can be estimated based on the prices of equivalent goods and services in the market. The household is then treated as a self-contained producing unit, and intermediate consumption and capital expenses such as food and housing are subtracted from the total value of production. The net value added by household members can then be used to impute an income for this unpaid work.

The *foregone wage* approach entails estimating the money income that each individual in a household would have earned if he or she had been employed for the same amount of time at a market wage rather than doing unpaid household work. The wage rate used may be either that of a domestic household worker or the wage that the individual could expect in the market given his or her qualifications (i.e., the opportunity cost or potential earnings approach).

There are a number of limitations to the estimates of the value of household labor or production generated by these methods. First of all, they can be quite unrealistic from a macroeconomic standpoint. For example, shifting all household work to the market would have profound impacts on prices and wages for the equivalent goods and services in the market, and it is simply implausible in any event. The potential earnings method, meanwhile, is based on the weak assumption that individuals are free to participate in the labor force at will and that they can always find jobs suited to their qualifications. It also creates the paradox that housework done by a person with high qualifications is more valuable than the same work done by a low-skilled individual.

Additional problems arise when making international comparisons, since each method is based on price systems, standards of production, and levels of social protection that vary from country to country. For example, a country's wage rates will depend on the degree to which it is socialized. Differences in tax rates or social security contributions can also complicate the comparison.

Results and Conclusions

The results of a number of major macroeconomic studies that evaluate the value of unpaid household labor as a percentage of GNP indicate that although the precise values estimated must be treated cautiously, the order of magnitude of this figure is unquestionably significant. The lowest estimate (which only takes married women into account) was one-fifth of GNP, while the highest (which takes all men and women into account) was fully half of GNP.

Each method of analysis produced remarkably consistent results, although there was considerable variation in the estimates among the different methods. The potential earnings approach produced the highest estimates, while methods that based wage calculations on global substitutes (e.g., an all purpose domestic worker) produced the lowest values. This is because the wage rates of domestic servants in industrialized countries are well below average.

The results of the studies are inconclusive with respect to whether the trend in the relative magnitude of household work is increasing or decreasing. Factors such as declining family size, improved household equipment, and the move of women into the market labor force would suggest a declining trend, but changing standards of home size, comfort and cleanliness, decreasing average work hours in the market sector, earlier retirements, and other factors may contribute to the opposite trend. However, total time inputs in both the market and household sectors may not have changed significantly over time. Differences in the level of productivity in each of these sectors also remains a controversial issue.

Increasing the availability of statistical data is essential to further work in this field. Time use studies are useful sources of information, but more data on household production of goods and services would be especially valuable, because comparisons of production rather than work better represent interactions between the market and household sectors. This is especially true in developing countries, where nonmarket subsistence production is still so important, and where imputing money values for time is both more difficult and less realistic. In industrialized countries, recognizing and studying *both* the producing and the consuming functions of households would yield a clearer definition and understanding of the boundary between the market and the household and of how and why it shifts over time. Gathering data on the nature and volume of household output should be a priority of future studies.

Summary of

National Income Accounts and the Environment

by Henry M. Peskin

[Published in *Natural Resources Journal* 21 (July 1981), 511–537.]

The debate about how accurately GNP indicates what people really care about continues, especially with respect to the effects of environmental regulation on GNP and on well-being. "The issue is whether the gains to society expected from the regulation—gains which generally do not show up in GNP—are being more than offset by losses in GNP precipitated by the regulations." (511) This paper considers how well present GNP accounts measure changes in environmental quality and proposes modifications that more accurately account for these changes.

Present GNP Accounting of Environmental Changes

Changes in both the physical environment and in environmental policies affect investment, consumption, and government activity and should be reflected by changes in GNP, but the size and direction of the changes to be expected may not be obvious. Industrialization and rising GNP have historically been associated with environmental degradation, but this may not always be the case. We need to examine the composition of goods and services produced, the pollutants generated, and the impacts on labor and capital productivity, before drawing conclusions about what changes to expect. For example, if rising GNP is propelled by an expanding service sector, additional degradation may be minor, while increases in one type of pollution or degradation may be more than offset by decreases in another. In addition, declining air and water quality may inhibit the ability to produce certain goods, thus decreasing GNP. There is therefore no straightforward relationship between GNP and environmental quality.

The situation is complicated still further when environmental policies aimed at reducing pollution are factored into the equation. Expenditures arising from environmental regulation have different impacts on GNP depending on whether they are made by businesses, government or consumers, and on whether they are spent on investment goods, labor, or other goods and services. Business expenditures on pollution control equipment count as intermediate costs, showing up as reductions in GNP. "In effect, these expenditures divert labor and material away from items counted in the GNP and toward the production of a cleaner environment, which is not counted in GNP." [513] Government and consumer expenditures on such equipment, however, show up as changes in the composition, but not necessarily the level, of GNP. Meanwhile, any environmental expenditures that increase employment may yield short-run increases in GNP, while the long-term effects may be in the opposite direction. Clearly the present GNP accounts do not adequately reflect the effects of environmental changes on GNP or on social well-being.

Several modifications of the GNP have been proposed to make it a better measure of production and/or social well-being and to account more adequately for environmental changes. One alternative is the measure of economic welfare (MEW), which basically rearranges the items presently included in the national accounts and adds imputed values for several items not included in the conventional measure, including household work, leisure, and the services of durable goods, such as cars. Environmental impacts are included in a correction for the "disamenities of urbanization," but this variable includes more than just the effects of pollution, so it does not help much in accounting for environmental changes.

Another alternative is the net national welfare (NNW) measure developed in Japan, which treats the environment separately via an "environmental maintenance cost" and a variable that accounts for remaining uncontrolled pollution. However, the direction of change of the NNW in response to environmental changes can still be ambiguous, so it is not a satisfactory alternative. The environmental adjustment calculated by the NNW is, however, fairly substantial, in contrast to the relatively small value calculated for urban disamenity by the MEW model.

A Modified Accounting Structure

The concept of environmental capital as a depreciable stock that contributes to income generation provides a framework for more effective modifications of GNP accounts. "This framework is based on the view that the environment, like the capital embodied in ordinary plant and equipment, generates useful services." [517] Clean air, for example, supports life, provides oxygen for combustion, and absorbs waste products—services that are just as necessary to business as those of labor and ordinary capital. Environmental capital, like ordinary capital, has a finite supply and hence a scarcity value, but the services it provides are not exchanged in markets, so scarcity values are difficult to observe and must be imputed. Some object to this approach on the grounds that access to clean air is a right, not a good to be bought and sold, but it is essential to impute some price to implement the alternative accounting system.

Incorporating the services of environmental capital into the national accounting structures requires the addition of three accounting entries. The first is the value of productive services provided by the environment to businesses and other consumers, entered on the input side of the accounts. On the output side, the second entry values the resulting environmental damages caused by use of these services. In addition, since these two entries usually are not equal, a balancing entry, "net environmental benefit," equal to environmental services less environmental damages will also appear on the input side of the accounts. These entries are not captured in the present accounts because they are not priced. Policy changes, such as imposition of effluent charges that would cause the value of environmental services to appear in firms' ordinary accounts, could rectify this without adding new entries and would also promote efficient allocations, but no full coverage schemes of this type currently exist.

The modified accounts are quite similar to those in the existing accounting structure, except that the accounts for industry, government, and households each include these three new entries. In addition, the most significant difference is the addition of a new account for the environment as a producing sector that provides environmental services and consumes environmental damages. These four sector accounts are consolidated to produce the modified GNP account, which in this form will equal conventional GNP less environmental damage. We could, however, rearrange the placement of the new entries in the input and output accounts to generate other versions of modified GNP, since the particular accounting arrangements are arbitrary. Modified GNP can therefore equal conventional GNP: (1) less environmental damage; (2) plus environmental services; or (3) plus net environmental benefit.

There are advantages and disadvantages associated with each of these modifications. The first modification performs much better as an indicator of well-being than conventional GNP and moves in the correct direction in response to environmental changes. The second does take direct account of environmental services, but it may be prone to double counting, since some of the value of these services may already be reflected in firm profits. It also has the disadvantage that it always declines with increasing pollution control expenditures. The third modification only moves in the "correct" direction (increasing environmental services and decreasing environmental damage both increase GNP) if there is technological change. Otherwise, decreasing environmental damage must always be accompanied by equivalent decreases in the use of environmental services, and the GNP measure remains unchanged, making this variation an ineffective indicator of well-being.

Implementation of the Modified Accounts

Preliminary efforts to implement this modified framework have been undertaken. These efforts relied on existing data and could at best make only crude estimates of environmental services and damage, and many categories of environmental services (e.g., recreational and aesthetic services) could not be included at all. The estimates of environmental services proved to be relatively small compared to other major components of GNP, so the differences between conventional and modified GNP were not substantial. While this may reflect the relative scale of the "environmental problem," more comprehensive estimates of environmental services might have produced much different results.

One advantage of the modified accounts is that they do not destroy the existing accounts system, which has been used for many years and usefully serves certain analytical and policy purposes. However, gathering the data to produce better estimates within the modified system would entail diverting substantial resources, and we must ask whether this investment is worth the benefits. Some argue that conventional accounts are effective as they are and that efforts to collect and use additional data should be carried out independently. However, this assumes that only serving traditional economic concerns within the existing system is adequate, even as we are becoming increasingly aware of new economic concerns that are only imperfectly revealed in markets. In addition, independent efforts might have difficulty drawing attention away from familiar—and official—GNP accounts. It is therefore better to expand the existing national accounting system than to try to create an independent system, but we should aim to do this without weakening the current system and draw as much as possible on the vast array of existing data sources that are already available.

Summary of

Environmental and Natural Resource Accounting: Where to Begin?

by Carrie A. Meyer

[Published in *Issues in Development* (Washington, DC: World Resources Institute, 1993), 1–20.]

Accurate measurement of sustainable income is impossible without taking into account environmental factors, since the depletion and degradation of natural resources and the environment threaten future production and consumption. Policy makers therefore need indicators that incorporate environmental assets and services to guide the allocation of resources for sustainable development. This article sorts through some of the confusion and controversy that surrounds environmental and natural resource accounting, analyzes some of the attempts to provide such indicators, and offers suggestions on how to adopt these new methodologies.

Issues in Environmental Accounting

The most glaring omission in national accounts is that of natural capital depreciation. Net Domestic Product (NDP) adjusts for manmade capital depreciation, but not natural capital depreciation. When natural assets are depleted, both the activity of extracting the resources and the value of these assets enter positively into GNP. Natural resource accounting attempts to fill this gap, while environmental accounting encompasses a broader range of issues and more complex problems. Natural resource accounting takes the market value of the expended resource into account, while environmental accounting attempts to incorporate all of the nonmarketed services and benefits provided by the environment.

The practical difficulties of this task are enormous and the potential pitfalls many. For instance, the popular technique of contingent valuation (CV) has been criticized for being difficult to execute, expensive, and prone to exaggerated and unrealistic estimates. Thus, consensus seems to be that pure valuation methodologies, such as CV, should be avoided if there is more readily available and reliable data. Valuation techniques aside, there exists the fundamental problem of delineating the boundary of "natural productive capital." Most would agree that timber and mineral resources should be included, but there remains uncertainty over whether to include the depreciation of air, soil, and water resources. "As the line between resource depletion and changes in nonmarketed environmental services begins to blur, the controversy increases." [4]

Another conceptual problem that arises when trying to create a true measure of sustainable income is that physical depreciation of natural capital does not necessarily imply an economic depreciation or vice versa. Natural capital revenues can be invested in manmade capital or human capital. In this case, we would have physical depreciation, but not economic depreciation. However, natural and human capital are not substitutable forever. At some point environmental degradation threatens our very survival.

Revising Existing Systems of National Accounts

The United Nations System of National Accounts (UNSNA) provides a standard to which most countries adhere closely. While this approach includes a system of balance sheets to calculate the total assets of a country, the core income and product accounts do not treat natural capital as an asset. The absence of natural capital in these figures may be attributed to the relative abundance of natural resources as compared to population size and the types of economic activities that existed 50 years ago, when national income accounts were first established.

The United Nations has been actively seeking alternatives to the current system. One effort resulted in the *Handbook of Integrated Environmental and Economic Accounting*,[1] which provides guidelines for satellite-integrated environmental and economic accounts. These satellite accounts are fully compatible with core accounts. Adjustments to core accounts have been made with an eye toward the eventual incorporation of environmental accounting. Nevertheless, the Handbook falls short of advocating a standard model for environmental accounting, leaving countries to decide which approach, if any, to adopt until international consensus is reached.

Accounting methods offered by the United Nations and some others, such as the system developed by Henry Peskin,[2] aim to develop comprehensive approaches for full environmental accounting. If successful, full environmental accounting would greatly increase the information available to policy makers.

While some countries have made small adjustments to their national accounts, no country has yet overhauled its system to make it entirely environmentally inclusive. This is understandable when considering the enormous technical and political undertaking involved. Furthermore, no country would want to make radical changes in its system without the endorsement of the UNSNA, since such an act would be contrary to the intent of a unified system.

Natural Resource Accounting Case Studies

A number of pioneering empirical studies have provided guidance and set precedents for environmental accounting. Rather than attempting to construct complete environmental accounts, these case studies have generally focused more specifically on measurement of natural resource depletion. Natural resource accounting case studies of Indonesia and Costa Rica by researchers working with the World Resources Institute, using methodology consistent with the U.N. guidelines, have concentrated on a few principal natural assets—forests, soils, significant minerals, water, and fisheries—to calculate a measure of NDP adjusted for natural resource depletion.[3] The results for both countries showed that the depreciation of natural capital was quite large, resulting in significant alterations to estimated growth rates and investment levels.

Case studies of Mexico and Papua New Guinea have been prepared under U.N. auspices, using the proposed U.N. framework for integrated environmental and economic accounting.[4] In contrast to the WRI studies, which use resource depletion estimates to adjust NDP, the U.N. work emphasizes the expansions of existing national accounts to include environmental information. This included estimates of the value of environmental services as well as assets. They calculated two adjusted NDP values, one accounting for resource depletion only (EDP_1) and a second including both resource depletion and resource degradation (EDP_2). The results for Mexico in 1985 showed a divergence of 13.3 percent from standard GDP for EDP1 and 17.7 percent for EDP_2. The results for investment estimates are even more striking: net investment is cut by 50 percent in EDP_1, and by more than 100 percent in EDP_2 (i.e. net investment becomes negative when resource depletion and degradation are taken into account). For Papua New Guinea over the period 1985–1990, EDP_1 varied from 1 percent to 8 percent below standard GDP, while EDP_2 was from 3 percent to 10 percent below standard GDP.

The Future of Environmental Accounting

Given the many conceptual problems of developing an indicator that accurately reflects sustainable income, is it even worthwhile to start making such adjustments? Some caution that environmental accounts may run the risk of encouraging a false sense of policy security, especially when using methods that only account for resource depletion. Others claim that such approaches will have little significance in industrialized countries where environmental problems are focused on pollution, and resource depletion is overwhelmed by production in various economic sectors.

Given the huge costs of overhauling an entire accounting system, is this comprehensive approach the most cost-effective way to improve environmental management? "Without doubt, even back-of-the-envelope calculations of natural resource depletion help to put resource use in perspective, and when major increases in GDP reflect nothing more than the consumption of natural capital, policy makers should know." [2] Sectoral approaches that are certainly less data intensive may also be more cost effective in the long run.

Where to Begin

Efforts to change accounting structures should be driven by the information needs of policy makers. They are only useful to the extent that they can improve economic and environmental policy, and their implementation depends on their acceptance into the political system. Good communication about the policy utility of environmental and resource accounting is vital to this acceptance, as is the credibility of the proposed methodology.

> There is no single recipe for how to establish credibility and achieve consensus. Beginnings can be made by bringing people together from different institutions; obtaining the UN *Handbook of Integrated Environmental and Economic Accounting*; establishing international links with organizations, individuals, and governments developing environmental and resource accounts; focusing first on resource depletion (especially in developing countries); initiating case study research efforts; or gathering data. [15]
>
> Altering the world's accounting systems to account for the depreciation of our natural assets and to better reflect sustainable income will take considerable time, effort, and money. It won't happen overnight. But, by taking deliberate steps from many angles toward that end, we can begin to bring the costs and benefits of changes in the environment to the attention of policy makers and to improve our ability to plan for a more sustainable future. [17]

Notes

1. United Nations Department for Economic and Social Information and Policy Analysis, Statistical Division, *Integrated Environmental and Economic Accounting* (New York, 1993: United Nations, Handbook of National Accounting, Series F, No. 61).

2. Henry M. Peskin, "Alternative Environmental and Resource Accounting Approaches," in Robert Costanza, ed. *Ecological Economics: The Science and Management*

of Sustainability (New York: Columbia University Press, 1991), 176–193; also Henry M. Peskin, "A National Accounting Framework for Environmental Assets," *Journal of Environmental Economics and Management* 2 (1976), 255–262.

3. Robert Repetto et al., *Wasting Assets: Natural Resources in the National Income Accounts* (Washington, DC: World Resources Institute, 1989); Tropical Science Center and World Resources Institute, *Accounts Overdue: Natural Resource Depreciation in Costa Rica* (Washington, DC: World Resources Institute, 1991).

4. Jan van Tongeren et al., "Integrated Environmental and Economic Accounting: A Case Study for Mexico," and Peter Bartelmus et al., "Integrated Environmental and Economic Accounting: A Case Study for Papua New Guinea," in Ernst Lutz, ed. *Toward Improved Accounting for the Environment: An UNSTAT–World Bank Symposium* (Washington, DC: World Bank, 1993).

Summary of

The Indicators Crisis

by Hazel Henderson

[Published in *Paradigms in Progress: Life Beyond Economics* (San Francisco: Berrett-Koehler Publishers, 1992), 149–191.]

GNP is not only a domestic indicator of economic growth, it is also a performance measure used by multinational funding agencies to assess the economic progress of developing countries. As such, GNP is an economic instrument that has been exported from the North to the South.

This article suggests that GNP is an inappropriate measure of true progress even in the Northern countries for which it was developed and is especially damaging when used as an indicator of develop national progress. A range of alternative social development indicators is suggested, drawing on extensive literature, including critiques and modifications of GNP as well as complementary social and environmental indicators.

Reexamining Old Indicators

Most global crises today are symptomatic of deeper changes in human perception. Such paradigm shifts occur with great regularity throughout human history. Key elements of such shifts are changing beliefs about what is important, what is valuable, what goals should be pursued, and what ways to measure collective progress toward these goals. "The old slogans of economic progress, industrial modernization, and a growing GNP now compete with the emerging slogans of the new paradigm: quality of life, human potential, and the search for ecological balance, social justice and global citizenship on our small, fragile Planet Earth." [147]

Modern economics, which developed along with the Industrial Revolution, has failed to keep pace with changing patterns of industrialization. As such, the field has mostly focused on describing change rather than monitoring and forecasting emerging trends. "As technological change accelerates, economics is now merely backing us into the future looking through the rearview mirror." [148]

In the past, economists of all ideological stripes, from Marxists to supply-siders, agreed that the goal was to expand production. Disagreement rested on the means of achieving this goal and the societal landscape that would accompany it. However, as social goals changed, so did the emphasis on productivity as an indicator of progress. The debate in economics today asks to what extent should we seek productivity, rather than merely how we should measure it.

GNP has thus come under attack as a measure of national progress. Simon Kuznets, GNP's American originator, never intended GNP to be used as an overall measure of progress. However, economists have failed to clarify its limitations or warn the public against its use as an indicator of human improvement. As a result, most countries today use GNP or GDP as their principal measure of progress.

Recently, new indicators have emerged to challenge GNP. The proliferation of these indicators has occurred against the wishes of most economists who have illiquid intellectual investments in GNP accounting, such as textbooks, data series, and computer models. Initial attempts were directed at adjusting GNP to account for the "bads" as well as the "goods" of industrialization by subtracting from gross GNP some of the social costs of urbanization, congestion, crime, etc. Advances have also been made in the formulation of social indicators that capture societal values ignored by GNP. These efforts have been largely inspired by the belief that GNP, and its "materialistic view of 'progress' cannot guide humanity beyond consumerism toward moral growth and sustainable development." [150]

Politicians share the blame for the perpetuation of indicators such as GNP, unemployment, inflation, and trade deficits. These often misunderstood instruments of economic policy are used by politicians to disguise the economic reality of the day, to mystify, and to manipulate voters. As a result, people have come to see economics as politics in disguise. The demand for quality of life indicators is partly born out of the desire to see real results for which politicians can be held accountable.

The Problem with GNP

While international organizations have helped to develop alternative indicators, such as the Human Development Index (HDI), mainstream indicators are still commonly used by these agencies to set goals and assess progress in the developing world. The United Nations still includes GNP as an indicator in its conditional loan applications and requires countries applying for loans to set up a system of national accounts. Politicians in less developed countries note the perverse no-win effects of trying to please international donor agencies by boosting GNP growth. Indeed, rising GNP often reflects increasing natural resource exploitation, worsening unemployment rates, and greater inequalities in income distribution.

GNP provides a narrow, and often ethnocentric view of wealth and progress, while ignoring diverse visions of development. For example, an in-house audit of 1,000 World Bank projects found that not one had met its project goals. This suggests that donor agencies must do more to decode the cultural characteristics of a country and work harder to identify what values and goals the country seeks to promote before deciding on international loan and assistance packages.

In 1991, the World Bank conceded that income growth indicators may mask real changes in welfare for large parts of the poor population. The Bank also redefined economic development to include sustainability and environmental protection, but this highly political redefinition fails to confront the need to alter all the Bank's statistical methods of measuring progress. While the development debate has now shifted toward more realistic and results-oriented indicators of progress, the Bank and other international donors have yet to institutionalize this paradigm shift.

The fundamental problem with GNP is that it equates real wealth—natural resources, skills, specific cultural assets, and human ingenuity—with mere money. Obviously, much is lost in the process and developing countries are subsequently left with a generic shell as their measurement of true wealth. This reliance on money-denominated per capita incomes is also subject to serious distortions in an era of wildly fluctuating currencies. Accordingly, indicators such as HDI, which use the purchasing power parity framework, offer far more useful and reliable measures, since they quantify the number of work hours needed to purchase a pound of rice, rather than simply indicating market value.

Moving Toward Improved Social Indicators

While GNP was never intended as a measure of total welfare, the power of statistics is that numbers attract attention and, when widely disseminated over the mass media, they can distort perceptions of well-being. Accordingly, there needs to be a range of social indicators that is disseminated on the same scale and with the same regularity as GNP. These indicators should be country-specific and incorporate specific national goals for development. Furthermore, human imagination and creativity should be considered unlimited resources in new equations.

No single correct method will emerge. Rather, new indicators will allow for the disaggregation and illumination of overlooked detail, both locally and sectorally. Indeed, it would be counterproductive if these new indicators were aggregated, "leading to more fetishizing of one single index." [176] Accordingly, local indicators are a good way to safeguard against this tendency toward overaggregation. These new indicators will spark debate about relevant regional and national issues, replacing the arcane indicators that have lost their meaning due to overaggregation and misuse by spin doctors who obscure economic realities.

Many barriers still exist to the adoption of more realistic measures of human progress. Among them: (1) economic theories are still grounded in static notions of equilibrium that cannot embrace change; (2) many governments do not want to be held accountable to their citizens for their performance; and (3) academic conventions change slowly and statisticians are more comfortable measuring quantities than deciding what ought to be measured.

PART X

Alternatives to Gross National Product: A Critical Survey

Essay
by Richard W. England

Introduction: Issues in GNP Accounting

Efforts to measure a nation's aggregate income date back to the 17th century, when Sir William Petty devised one of the first national income estimates. During the three centuries that followed, the national income concept slowly evolved as economists developed their understanding of how economic systems operate and as the key economic issues faced by society changed. However, the major thrust for the creation of modern national income accounting came with the economic crisis of the Great Depression, the political and military conflict of World War II, and the emergence of Keynesian macroeconomic theory. [Carson 1975, Ruggles 1993]

As Robert Eisner has observed, "The national income and product accounts . . . have been among the major contributions to economic knowledge over the past half century." [1989:1] Since 1945, national income statistics have found a variety of practical uses. For instance, they help to inform the design of government fiscal and monetary policies, influence corporate investment plans, and are commonly used to assess economic development strategies in less developed nations. From their inception, however, the national income and product accounts have also been used to make international comparisons of well-being and to track changes in a country's level of welfare.

Simon Kuznets, one of the architects of national accounts, indicated that the connection between production and welfare is implicit in national income accounting:

> National income may be defined as the net value of all economic goods produced by the nation. . . . Any claim to significance such a total would have would lie in its presumptive usefulness as an appraisal of the contribution of economic activity to the welfare of the country's inhabitants, present and future.

Kuznets makes clear that the construction of national income accounts includes normative judgments:

> An investigator can decide intelligently what items to include and how to treat each only by formulating criteria of productivity and the principles of valuation to be applied. . . . For those not intimately acquainted with this type of work it is difficult to realize the degree to which estimates of national income have been and must be affected by implicit or explicit value judgments. [1941:3–4]

As the previous chapter has shown, GNP and allied accounting concepts such as GDP[1] have been sharply criticized during the past quarter century by a wide array of commentators. Many of those critics have questioned whether national income data adequately measure the state of or changes in economic well-being. A typical defense of GNP and its conceptual siblings has been to deny that they serve as measures of economic welfare.[2] This defense is too facile, however. Leading economic historians and macroeconomists readily cite data on real per capita GDP *as though* they can provide insights into standards of living and economic progress. In their influential text on economic growth, for example, Barro and Sala-i-Martin observe that real per capita GDP in the United States grew by a factor of 8.1 from 1870 to 1990. [1995:1, 4] They then conclude, "Even small differences in . . . [annual GDP] growth rates, when cumulated over a generation or more, have much greater consequences for standards of living than . . . short-term business fluctuations. . . ."[3] Because of welfare-tinged interpretations of GDP data by many economists and politicians, the critics of GDP deserve a serious hearing, especially by those who seek to understand the sources of human well-being.

This essay critically surveys a number of quantitative measures that have been proposed either as complements to or substitutes for GNP/GDP. These alternatives typically raise some combination of the following needs:

- to specify the distinction between intermediate and final output
- to distinguish between "goods" and "bads"
- to account for asset depreciation in a comprehensive manner, including both manufactured and natural assets
- to divide net output between consumption and capital accumulation on a reasonable basis
- to take account of nonmarketed goods and services
- to take account of the welfare implications of various forms of social inequality.[4]

Part I of this essay reviews efforts to develop adjustments or complements to existing GNP accounts. Some of these efforts are clearly relevant to the fundamental question of how GNP/GDP relate to human well-being. Other efforts appear more technical but often have implications both in terms of the choice of what to measure and the formulation of options by policy makers.

Part II surveys some more comprehensive efforts to develop alternative measures. We have chosen to focus on those which seem to come closest to achieving the objectives either of improving or replacing GNP accounts; other contributions to the development of this field of analysis are mentioned (and footnoted) but are less fully explicated here.

Part I: Complements and Adjustments to GNP

What Should Be Included? — Intermediate versus Final Goods

From the earliest days of modern national income accounting, deciding what products of human activity belong in GNP has been a contentious issue. Kuznets argued for inclusion of goods that are scarce and alienable sources of satisfaction to their users and that are legally exchanged in the marketplace.[5] [1941:6–8] He acknowledged that this accounting criterion was an arbitrary one and that many sources of human satisfaction would remain undetected and unmeasured by national income accountants if his criterion were officially adopted.[6]

At the same time, Kuznets also noted that not all commodities currently produced, exchanged, and consumed are a source of final satisfaction to their users. [1941:36–40] Rather, they are intermediate inputs required to produce other useful goods. Thus, one of the authors of national income accounting reluctantly conceded that work clothing and commuting expenses should probably be treated as intermediate expenses of production and not as final consumption yielding subjective utility to employees.

In his assessment of national income accounting, Juster took this argument a step further:

> At present we classify everything purchased by households as final consumption . . . and most of the things purchased by business enterprise as intermediate products. . . . [However,] most of what we now call final product is really intermediate in the more fundamental sense. [1973:72–74]

What exactly is the fundamental distinction between intermediate and final output? Juster argued that all products used to maintain the flow of services from existing assets be excluded from final output and that products be included in final output only to the degree that they increase the flow of services from tangible and intangible assets via net investment. In practical terms, this would mean that all production that goes to support human labor (e.g., food and clothing) should be considered intermediate, rather than final production. Application of this criterion would sharply reduce empirical measures of a nation's net final output, a consequence that Kuznets anticipated and opposed.[7] However, Juster was correct when he concluded,

> [W]e can provide a better set of distinctions between intermediate and final product than the ones now embedded in . . . our existing accounts. . . . Converting some but not all of our present final outputs to intermediate outputs should represent an improvement in what we now measure as net output . . . . [1973:76]

More recently, Christian Leipert has tried to adjust GNP data to account more reasonably for intermediate costs of production. He proposes that we measure "defensive expenditures . . . made to eliminate, mitigate, neutralize, or anticipate and avoid damages and deterioration that industrial society's process of growth has caused to living, working, and environmental conditions." [Leipert 1989:28] These defensive outlays should then be eliminated from measures of aggregate final output.

Leipert identifies six spheres in which major defensive costs occur: the environment, transport, housing, personal security, health, and the workplace. This implies that national income should exclude environmental protection expenses, security services, prisons, and many health costs, as well as some legal costs. Outlays for auto repairs and medical treatment resulting from road accidents, for example, should not be treated as final consumption but rather should be seen as unfortunate intermediate costs associated with provision of transportation services. Even outlays on extending metropolitan highway networks do not "increase the quality of life, but rather . . . can be regarded as a cost factor stemming from a specific type of development in the transport system and regional structure." [Leipert 1989:35–36]

Although one might quibble with the details of his estimates, Leipert has given a plausible demonstration that intermediate expenses for defensive purposes comprise a substantial portion of GNP as currently measured. In his esti-

Table 1. Defensive Expenditures as Percent of GNP, Federal Republic of Germany, 1985

Environmental protection services of industry and government ·	1.33%
Environmental damages	0.80
Costs of road accidents	1.1
Costs of extended travel routes	2.2
Higher housing costs due to urban agglomeration	0.75
Costs of personal security	1.26
Defensive health care costs	2.6
TOTAL	10.24

Source: Leipert (1989:41).

mates for West Germany, he found that defensive expenditures exceeded 10 percent of GNP, "only the tip of the iceberg" in Leipert's view. (See Table 1.) It would seem, then, that GNP figures typically overestimate the aggregate value of final output currently available to satisfy present wants (via consumption) or future wants (via asset accumulation).[8]

What Should Be Deducted?—Depreciation of Manufactured and Natural Capital Assets

Economists have long accepted that for many purposes the concept of Net National Product (NNP) or Net Domestic Product (NDP) is a better measure of true economic production than the corresponding GNP or GDP figures. Capital goods are produced in any given year and measured as gross investment in GDP; but capital goods also wear out or depreciate during the same year. We must therefore subtract depreciation from gross investment and from GDP to obtain a true picture of the nation's production during the year. In other words, final output net of asset depreciation is a better measure of society's capacity to service the present and future needs of its members.

In standard national income accounting, however, the depreciation adjustment is applied only to *manufactured capital*, such as buildings and machinery. The depreciation of *natural capital* such as forests, fisheries, and soils is unaccounted for. In recent years, various adjustments to national income accounts have been proposed so that asset depreciation would be measured more comprehensively, thereby allowing a more realistic estimate of the net output available for current consumption and asset accumulation.

Robert Repetto and his associates at the World Resources Institute (WRI) have proposed a depreciation adjustment to take account of various forms of natural resource depletion. As they have noted,

> [T]here is a dangerous asymmetry today in the way we measure . . . the value of natural resources. Man-made assets . . . are valued as productive capital, and are written off against the value of production as they depreciate. . . . Natural resource assets are not so valued, and their loss entails no debit charge against current income that would account for the decrease in potential future production. (Repetto et al. 1989:2]

Particularly in developing nations dependent on natural resource production and exports, this exclusion of resource depletion from their national income accounts results in exaggerated numbers for both net output and also capital formation.

In a widely cited case study of Indonesia, the WRI found that accounting for soil erosion, deforestation, and petroleum extraction lowered estimates of Indonesian domestic output quite significantly from its official level. In 1984, for example, the Indonesian government reported the nation's GDP to be 13.5

trillion rupiah (deflated to 1973). After taking into account the market value of net changes in the physical stocks of forest, soil, and petroleum resources, the WRI researchers estimated that the official data ignored 2.3 trillion rupiah of natural resource depletion, a sum equal to 17.3 percent of GDP. During the period from 1971 through 1984, the annual WRI adjustment for these three forms of resource depletion averaged 9 percent of GDP. [Repetto et al. 1989:6]

The methodology employed by WRI to derive these estimates has been criticized, however. Salah El Serafy questions the use of annual changes in the market value of proven reserves of natural resources as an adjustment to GDP: "Since the resource stocks are normally much larger than annual extraction, re-estimation of their [physical] size, as well as incorporation of changes in their value . . . following price fluctuations, can dwarf the adjustment specifically due to extraction." [1993:14] As El Serafy points out, discovery of new physical reserves in excess of the current extraction rate results in a positive adjustment to GDP.[9] El Serafy considers the resulting measure "erratic and economically meaningless." [El Serafy, 1993:22] From the perspective of long-run sustainability, discovery of large reserves of an exhaustible resource constitutes questionable progress if previously discovered reserves are currently being consumed at a rapid pace.

In an effort to improve the accounting reform pioneered by Repetto, El Serafy has proposed that the *user cost* of natural resource depletion be used to adjust GDP. [1993, 1996] User cost is that portion of the receipts from selling a nonrenewable resource, net of extraction costs, that must be reinvested in other assets to maintain a flow of future income after the resource stock has been completely depleted. El Serafy demonstrates that user cost as a fraction of net receipts equals $1/(1 + r)^{n+1}$, where r is the interest rate for investment purposes and n the remaining life of the resource stock at the current extraction rate. In general, this leads to a smaller negative adjustment for resource depletion, since part of the income from sales of natural resources is considered "true" income to be included in GDP. However, El Serafy's method also greatly reduces the positive adjustments to GDP resulting from discoveries of new resources.[10] (See Table 2 for an application of the user cost approach to the WRI data on Indonesia.)

This user cost methodology suggests that nations whose GDP growth rates depend heavily on natural resource exploitation suffer from a variety of illusions. Net product and net capital formation are overestimated. Fiscal deficits of central governments that own natural resource enterprises are underestimated. Current account deficits in a nation's balance of payments may be masked by unsustainable sales of natural assets. These statistical distortions encourage a policy of excessive reliance on short-term natural asset depreciation, with serious consequences for future environmental sustainability.[11] Clearly, economic development policies require less narrowly focused accounting measures. This

Table 2. Adjustments by El Serafy for Natural Resource Depletion, Indonesia, 1971–1984

	Deforestation	Soil Erosion	Petroleum User Cost	Total
		Percent of Official GDP		
1975	−3.3	−1.1	−5.6	−10.1
1979	−9.3	−0.7	−9.8	−19.8
1971–1984	−6.8	−6.8	−7.8	−14.6
(ann. avg.)	(combined deforestation and soil erosion)			

Note: The years 1975 and 1979 are chosen as examples because 1975 represents the smallest total adjustment and 1979 the largest during the period 1971–1984.
Sources: Repetto et al. (1989:6), El Serafy (1993:24).

observation also raises other issues in addition to the question of natural capital depreciation—issues that, as we will see, have not gone unremarked by development economists.

What Else Is Important?—Basic Development Indicators

In a effort to provide aggregate data relevant to less developed nations, the World Bank has issued its World Development Report annually since 1978. The intellectual and political thrust of the reports was clearly started in the inaugural issue by the Bank's president, Robert S. McNamara: "The past quarter century has been a period of unprecedented change . . . in the developing world. And yet despite this impressive record, some 800 million individuals continue to be trapped in . . . absolute poverty. . . . The twin objectives of development, then, are to accelerate economic growth and to reduce poverty." [World Bank 1978:iii]

The premise that economic growth and poverty reduction are "inextricably linked," although not logically equivalent, led the World Bank to propose a set of basic development indicators, only one of which is GNP per capita.[12] Initially, the Bank's list of basic indicators included energy consumption per head and food production per capita. By the early 1980s, however, the list had evolved to a different set of six variables: a country's population, area, per capita GNP, life expectancy, adult illiteracy rate, and inflation rate.

The notions that economic development is a multidimensional process that cannot be measured by per capita income alone, and that poverty's impact is reflected in literacy and longevity statistics, are very reasonable claims. Furthermore, by publishing a diverse set of basic development indicators, the World Bank invites us to ask how people in nations with similar average incomes can face highly dissimilar life experiences. As Table 3 shows, the average citizen of

Table 3. World Bank Basic Indicators, Selected Low-Income Nations, Early 1990s

Nation	GNP Per Capita (official exchange rates) ($)	Life Expectancy (years)	Adult Illiteracy Rate (%)
India	310	61	52
Kenya	310	59	31
Mali	310	48	68
Nicaragua	340	67	35
Nigeria	320	52	49

Source: World Bank (1994:162).

India or Nicaragua is more likely to read and write and will probably live longer than his or her counterpart in Mali despite nearly identical levels of per capita GNP. Clearly, there are other dimensions to human welfare than that measured by GNP.

However, we should not overestimate the World Bank's commitment to a multidimensional view of economic development. Although the authors of the 1994 World Development Report warn us (in a technical footnote) that "GNP per capita does not, by itself, constitute or measure welfare or success in development," they also state (in the main text) that "the main criterion used to classify economies and broadly distinguish different stages of economic development is GNP per capita." [World Bank 1994:157, 230] Thus, in the view of the World Bank, a nation can achieve a higher "level of economic development" simply by increasing its GNP per capita. Fundamentally, then, the World Bank has not yet incorporated the various criticisms of national income accounting into its framework of analysis.[13] While other indicators are acknowledged, GNP remains the Bank's prime measure of development.

While the World Bank, like most of the economics profession, continues to rely primarily on GNP or GDP, other analysts have taken on the task of developing alternative measures. Different approaches to modifying national income analysis have been proposed by scholars, including Robert Eisner, Herman Daly, and John Cobb, as well as by national and transnational institutions, including the U.S. Commerce Department's Bureau of Economic Analysis, the United Nations' Department for Economic and Social Information and Policy Analysis, and the United Nations' Development Programme (UNDP). Part II reviews four major proposals for new systems of national income accounting. Each of these four emphasizes different basic issues relating to the treatment of social and environmental factors in national income accounting. None has yet gained general acceptance; but each introduces important new perspectives on measuring national production and well-being.

Part II: Alternative Measures of Income and Well-Being

The contributions reviewed thus far clearly indicate the shortcomings of standard GNP/GDP analysis in capturing social and environmental factors and suggest various ways of modifying or supplementing standard accounts in response to these problems. They also raise the question of whether a more thorough-going revision of national income accounting methodology could create a better measure of production and/or well-being. The prospect is tantalizing—can we arrive at a new measure that is free of the distortions, omissions, and biases inherent in standard GDP? There have been several notable efforts to construct alternative measures or accounting systems. This section reviews four of the most comprehensive—though very different—proposals for GDP alternatives.

Eisner's Total Incomes System of Accounts

For two decades, Robert Eisner (1978, 1985, 1989) has championed major reform of our system of national income accounting. In his view, we need to develop "better measures of economic activity contributing to social welfare[,] . . . measures which capture as fully and distinctly as possible both the flow of current consumption and the accumulation of capital contributing to future welfare." [Eisner 1989:2, 7]

Eisner's total incomes system of accounts (TISA) aims to extend and revise the official national income accounts in a variety of ways. First, he questions the practice of treating government and household purchases as expenditures on final output and business purchases on current account as intermediate outlays.[14] He argues that a large portion of government purchases (on roads, police, the military, and the courts) is intermediate in nature and should be excluded from GDP. [Eisner 1989:9] Furthermore, work-related spending by households, e.g., commuting expenses, is an intermediate cost of production and not a source of consumer satisfaction. Finally, TISA shifts some consumption services provided by businesses to their employees and clients from the intermediate to final output category.

Another area of accounting reform addressed by TISA is the need to acknowledge that some products make a contribution to social well-being and deserve to be counted as final output but are presently excluded from GDP because they are not exchanged in the marketplace. These nonmarket outputs, many of which are produced within the household sector, include meal preparation, house cleaning and painting, care of the young and elderly, and services of household durables.[15] If one makes imputations for these various forms of production within the home, the household sector's share of GNP exceeds one third. [Eisner 1989:36]

A third issue raised by TISA is the need to assign net output between current consumption and capital accumulation on a reasonable basis. At present, the national accounts assume that private businesses undertake all of society's investment activity and that capital accumulation consists of building up business holdings of plant, equipment, and inventories. This highly skewed perspective on social investment ignores all acquisitions of tangible assets by government and households, with the exception of new home purchases. It also excludes investments in intangible assets, such as new technologies and literacy skills. If one attempts to measure accumulation of both tangible and intangible assets by all sectors of society, not just business investment in physical assets, one arrives at a much larger estimate of social investment. Eisner found, for example, that the Commerce Department's gross private domestic investment figure for 1981 included only 26 percent of his extended estimate of total gross investment in the United States for that year. [1989:49] Hence, claims in the business press that the U.S. invests too little in its economy should be treated with considerable skepticism. Furthermore, indiscriminate cuts in federal spending to eliminate the budget deficit could reduce public investments in transportation, education, new technologies, and the like.

Eisner's TISA proposal is a wide ranging and impressive one. It invites us to shed several misleading fictions embedded in the national income and product accounts. One is that business enterprises exist only to produce and invest on behalf of ultimate consumers. Another is that households are unproductive and exist merely to enjoy commodities purchased from the business sector. Still another is that government property is unproductive and that government purchases make no contribution to the nation's wealth.

Despite these strengths, however, the TISA framework has several limitations, especially if the goal is to trace all of the links between economic activity and social well-being. As Ruggles has noted, Eisner declines to include the value of leisure time in his estimate of nonmarket output. [1991:455–456] In addition, TISA ignores issues associated with employment (both the personal satisfaction of being productive and also dissatisfaction with poor working conditions) and eschews analysis of income distribution issues. Finally, TISA does not address Repetto's concerns about depreciation of natural capital assets, including soil erosion, fossil fuel depletion, and depletion of forests and fisheries.

Integrated Economic and Environmental Satellite Accounts

During recent years both the United Nations and the U.S. Department of Commerce have launched significant revisions of their national income accounting systems. These reforms incorporate some of the earlier suggestions of scholarly critics[16] and focus on linking (1) asset accumulation and depreciation to current income accounts and (2) economic activity to availability of natural and environmental resources. The proposed revisions do not alter the fundamental structure of standard GNP/GDP accounting. Rather, they provide additional or "satellite" accounts dealing with the impacts of economic activity on natural resources and the environment. Satellite accounts, while separate from standard GNP accounts, are sector-specific and so can readily be integrated with the standard accounts for purposes of analysis. The United Nations has produced a handbook that provides extensive sector-by-sector guidelines for integrated environmental and economic accounting.[17] National resource and environmental accounting frameworks have also been developed to varying degrees by Norway, France, the Netherlands, and Japan.

In a critique of its own accounting practices, the Commerce Department's Bureau of Economic Analysis (BEA) points to several "points of asymmetry" between its traditional treatments of natural resources and of structures and equipment. In particular, depreciation of business fixed assets has been subtracted from GDP to estimate NDP, but depreciation of government fixed assets and natural resources has not. Also, additions to the stocks of plant, equipment, and inventories owned by businesses count as capital formation, whereas new government buildings and equipment or additions to proven mineral reserves do not. [BEA 1994:39] [18]

To remedy these problems, the BEA proposes to shift from current practices to a system of integrated economic and environmental satellite accounts (IEESA). The proposed IEESA asset and production accounts have two prominent features: (1) treatment of natural and environmental assets as a part of the nation's wealth, and (2) disaggregation of accounting categories to highlight interactions between the economy and its natural environment. As Table 4 details, the asset account tracks opening and closing stocks of various nonfinancial assets and assigns changes in the value of those stocks to (1) depreciation, depletion, and degradation of assets, (2) domestic capital formation, and (3) market revaluations of stocks.[19] This asset account is linked to the current production account (Table 5) by data on gross investment in various forms of assets and on current rates of depreciation, depletion, and degradation of those assets.

The IEESA asset table aims to account comprehensively for all of the (non-human) assets contributing to the nation's productivity and well-being. Made assets include all artifacts produced by human effort, without regard for who owns those assets. For example, business computers, family homes, and public airports all fall into this category. Developed natural assets are gifts of nature that have been transformed to some degree by human effort. These include livestock, crop fields, and known reserves of petroleum. Nonproduced environmental assets have economic significance but have not (yet) been molded by human activity. These include wildlife, old growth forests, and undiscovered mineral deposits.

Table 4. IEESA Asset Account (billions of dollars)

Asset Category	Opening Stocks	Depreciation, Depletion, and Degradation (−)	Capital Formation (+)	Revaluations (+, −)	Closing Stocks
•Public and private made assets					
1. Structures and equipment					
a. Pollution abatement and control	—	—	—	—	—
b. Other	—	—	—	—	—
2. Inventories	—	—	—	—	—
•Developed natural assets					
1. Cultivated biological resources	—	—	—	—	—
2. Proved subsoil assets	—	—	—	—	—
3. Developed land	—	—	—	—	—
•Nonproduced environmental assets					
1. Uncultivated biological resources	—	—	—	—	—
2. Unproved subsoil assets	—	—	—	—	—
3. Undeveloped land	—	—	—	—	—
4. Air and water	—	—	—	—	—

Source: BEA (1994:41).
Note: Only categories are shown; data not yet available.

Although the BEA does not yet collect data for most of the cells in Table 4, some estimates are available. At the end of 1987, for example, total made assets in the United States exceeded $12.2 trillion. Of that total, assets devoted to pollution abatement and control equalled $277 billion. In the developed natural asset category, the value of agricultural land came to $486 billion. Estimates such as these inform us about the links between the nation's wealth and the natural context for human activity.

The IEESA production account (Table 5) calls for expanded measurements of gross and net domestic product. On the one hand, capital formation in the form of natural assets (I_c) is now included in gross domestic investment. This includes expansion of livestock herds, restoration of eroded agricultural lands, and discovery of natural gas fields. GDP from the perspective of final uses thus equals $(I_a + I_b + I_c) + (W_4 + N_4) + (W_5 + N_5) - (W_6 + N_6)$. Intermediate inputs used to produce this aggregate final output consist of $(W_1 + W_2 + W_3) + (N_1 + N_2 + N_3)$.

Alternatively, one can measure GDP via the value added approach. In any particular industry, intermediate inputs from other industries are used. Taking the example of agriculture, these intermediate inputs are $(W_1 + N_1)$. Capital and labor are put to work within agriculture itself, and they generate a value in addition to that of the raw materials consumed during production. For agriculture, the value added is $V_1 = (L_1 + P_1 + T_1 + D_1 + S_1)$. In contrast with the traditional BEA approach, note that IEESA value added includes depletion and degradation of natural assets. For the economy as a whole, then, GDP equals $(V_1 + V_2 + V_3)$. Measurement of net domestic product also requires adjustment if one adopts the IEESA scheme. In addition to subtracting $(D_1 + D_2 + D_3)$ from GDP to arrive at NDP, one also needs to deduct $(S_1 + S_2 + S_3)$, the depletion and degradation of natural assets.

Full implementation of the IEESA reforms would provide us with several important kinds of information not currently available. Imports of waste disposal services (W_6), for example, would measure the degree to which the U.S. economy exports its own waste disposal problems to maintain environmental quality at home. (Anecdotal evidence suggests that disposal of U.S. wastes in developing nations is occurring on a significant scale.) Assignment of the use of waste disposal services to specific industries and to consumption activities $(W_1, W_2, W_3,$ and $W_4)$ would provide an indicator of which sectors of the macroeconomy place the greatest stress on the natural environment.

As the BEA has noted, the net impact of its IEESA adjustments on net domestic product is not obvious in advance:

> [T]here is an expectation that such accounts will show that U.S. economic growth as currently measured is not sustainable. . . . This expectation may well stem from focusing on depletion and degradation to the exclusion of additions

Table 5. IEESA Production Account (billions of dollars)

Goods and Services	Industries			Final Uses				Total Output
	Agriculture	Mining	Others	Consumption	Gross Investment	Exports	Import	
Pollution abatement and control assets	—	—	—	—	I_a	—	—	Q_a
Other made assets	—	—	—	—	I_b	—	—	Q_b
Natural assets	—	—	—	—	I_c	—	—	Q_c
Waste disposal services	W_1	W_2	W_3	W_4	—	W_5	W_6	W
Other nondurable commodities	N_1	N_2	N_3	N_4	—	N_5	N_6	N
Factors of production								
Labor income	L_1	L_2	L_3					
Property income	P_1	P_2	P_3					
Indirect business taxes	T_1	T_2	T_3					
Depreciation of fixed made assets	D_1	D_2	D_3					
Depletion and degradation of natural assets	S_1	S_2	S_3					
Gross value added	V_1	V_2	V_3					

Source: BEA (1994:47).

[to resource stocks]. . . . Because of . . . offsetting changes, it is conceivable that . . . IEESA NDP differs little from traditional NDP. [1994:48]

This claim is misleading, however. Even if new petroleum reserves are discovered within the U.S., thereby reducing national dependence on energy imports for a number of decades, those newly proved reserves have not increased the physical quantity of fossil hydrocarbons underneath the country. On the contrary, that quantity decreases monotonically as domestic production and consumption of oil takes place. The IEESA accounting system is also vulnerable to El Serafy's criticism, which was discussed earlier, since it uses total economic value of reserves rather than the user cost method. While providing valuable information, the IEESA framework thus does not offer a complete basis for the analysis of long-term sustainability. Lange and Duchin (1993) have suggested that the main function of this type of accounting is national or sector-specific natural resource and environmental monitoring and policy analysis.

Unfortunately, since the publication of BEA (1994), the U.S. Commerce Department has not proceeded with refinement of the IEESA approach, mainly because of Congressional budget cuts. A review of the IEESA methodology by a study panel of the National Academy of Sciences is planned. It is to be hoped that this important initiative will soon move forward again.

Social Issues and the Human Development Index

The revised and alternative national income accounting measures discussed so far have concentrated on identifying final uses of gross output and on proper measurement of asset depreciation and depletion. Although that discussion is highly relevant to human well-being, we have not yet faced the question of who benefits from the use of net output. As we shall see, raising the question of who benefits immediately leads us to issues of poverty and inequity.

An eminent economist who has persistently addressed the issue of social inequality and its implications for human welfare is Amartya Sen (1981, 1992). As Sen [1993:40] has posed the issue,

Economics is not solely concerned with income and wealth but also with using those resources as means to significant ends, including the promotion and enjoyment of long and worthwhile lives. If . . . the economic success of a nation is judged only by income . . . , as it so often is, the important goal of well-being is missed.

Mortality data, which are simple to use and readily accessible, are valuable indicators of how a nation's net output has been used. Sri Lanka, for example, promoted mass literacy early in this century. Its government expanded medical care in the 1940s and also began to distribute rice to the hungry. In 1940 the Sri Lankan death rate was 20.6 per 1,000; by 1960 it had fallen to 8.6 per

1,000. Similar changes took place in the Indian state of Kerala. Despite a per capita GNP considerably lower than the Indian average, life expectancy in Kerala now exceeds 70 years. [Sen 1993:45] The lesson is clear: society's level of well-being depends not only on the level of net income per capita but also on how that income is distributed and utilized.

Several efforts to capture this important lesson in a single numerical index have been undertaken within the past 20 years. Early social indicators included the Physical Quality of Life Index (PQLI) and the International Human Suffering Index (HSI). These can be considered as forerunners to the most intensively researched and best-known social indicator to date, the United Nations Development Program's Human Development Index (HDI).

Published for the Overseas Development Council, the PQLI combines three basic indicators of well-being: infant mortality, life expectancy at age one, and basic literacy. For each indicator, a nation's performance is placed on a scale from 0 (worst possible performance) to 100 (best possible performance).[20] A simple average of the three scaled values serves as a country's PQLI.

Does the PQLI indicate anything about a nation not already revealed by its per capita GNP? Perhaps not for the higher-income countries.[21] For low- and middle-income nations, however, there is substantial variation in PQLI scores among nations at comparable levels of per capita GNP. [Morris 1979:53] For example, during the early 1970s, the PQLI of Sri Lanka, a low-income nation, exceeded the average PQLI of 32 upper middle-income countries, an outstanding accomplishment. [Morris 1979: Appendix A] By studying such outliers in detail, we can discover what factors favor human well-being even at low income levels.

A more ambitious, but less compelling, effort to measure well-being is represented by the Human Suffering Index. Originally published by the Population Crisis Committee in 1987, the HSI uses a set of ten indicators to measure dimensions of social well-being. (See Table 6 for a list of these component indicators.) For any nation, each indicator value is scaled from 0 (most favorable) to 10 (least favorable). The ten scaled values are then simply added to obtain the country's HSI.

This deceptively simple procedure masks a host of conceptual problems. First, the ten component indicators were selected without any (reported) theoretical rationale.[22] Clean drinking water, for example, promotes good health whereas high life expectancy is a consequence of good·health. Second, the political freedom and civil rights measures utilized to construct the HSI are of dubious quality. Third, the welfare significance of a country's inflation rate is far from obvious. If an unanticipated inflation redistributes real wealth from wealthy lenders to poor peasants, is that redistribution desirable or not? Finally, the scaling of some component indicators is inexplicable and arbitrary. Why does a nation with an inflation rate less than 4 percent per year receive a perfect

Table 6. Component Indicators of Human Suffering Index

- Life expectancy (years)
- Daily calorie supply (per capita)
- Access to clean drinking water (%)
- Infant immunization (%)
- Secondary school enrollment (%)
- GNP per capita ($)
- Inflation rate (% per year)
- Telephones per capita
- Political freedom (0–10)
- Civil rights (0–10)

Source: Population Crisis Committee (1992).

score of 0 for that indicator whereas a nation with an annual inflation rate of 4.1 percent receives a score of 1?[23] The primary lesson that we can learn from the HSI is that moving from GDP to a richer, multidimensional measure of well-being requires serious conceptual groundwork.

The Human Development Index (HDI) reflects just such a concern for conceptual foundations. Created by the United Nations Development Program (UNDP),[24] the HDI builds on the following premise:

> People are the real wealth of a nation. The basic objective of development is to create an enabling environment for people to enjoy long, healthy, and creative lives. . . . Human development is a process of enlarging people's choices. . . . [A]t all levels of development, the three essential ones are for people to lead a long and healthy life, to acquire knowledge and to have access to resources needed for a decent standard of living. [UN 1990:9–10]

Thus, the HDI "emphasizes sufficiency rather than satiety" [UN 1994:91] and views the expansion of output and wealth as a means to promoting human development, not an end in itself. [UN 1990:10] Human development, in turn, has two sides: "the formation of human capabilities—such as improved health, knowledge and skills—and the use people make of their acquired capabilities—for leisure, productive purposes or being active in cultural, social and political affairs." [Ibid.]

Since income is necessary but not sufficient to achieve human development, the UNDP uses real per capita GDP, expressed in purchasing-power-parity dollars, as one component of its Human Development Index.[25] Recognizing that low incomes typically satisfy basic needs whereas high incomes are spent in part on luxuries, the U.N. transforms per capita GDP to take account of the declining contribution of a higher average income level to human development.[26]

The formula used for this transform accords very little weight to increases in GDP above the world median per capita GDP ($5,120 in 1995). The claim implied by this specification is that continued economic growth above the basic needs level contributes little to the human development of its citizens.

If the welfare contribution of extra GDP is subject to rapidly diminishing returns, what other factors encourage "a process of enlarging people's choices"? The HDI focuses on longevity and access to education.[27] For each of the three component indicators of the HDI (transformed income, life expectancy at birth, and educational access), a country is given a percentile score ranging from a fixed minimum to a fixed maximum[28] (Table 7). The Human Development Index is then computed as a weighted average of the three percentile scores.

How useful is the HDI as a measure of well-being? If one's goal is to detect differences among the developed nations, it is not a discriminating tool, despite the U.N. claim that it "applies equally to less developed and highly developed countries." [UN 1990:2] As Table 8 demonstrates, the HDI scores of the top ten nations scarcely differ from one another. Further inspection reveals why: All enjoy nearly universal adult literacy, and the transformation procedure for income levels essentially equalizes their adjusted per capita GDP data. Only the combined school enrollment ratios of the top ten countries differ to a significant degree. We doubt, however, that a set of nations including the U.S., Japan, Spain, and Sweden is as homogeneous as the HDI scores suggest.[29]

Despite the UNDP claim of universal applicability, we believe that the HDI is best used as a measure of the welfare effects of economic development strategies in the less affluent nations of the world. The stark differences among developing nations are suggested by Table 9. Brazil, Costa Rica, and Turkey are at similar stages of economic development as measured by (unadjusted) per capita GDP. However, Costa Rica receives a substantially higher human development rating because its average citizen will live a decade longer and is far more likely to be literate. Among even poorer nations, similar differences are revealed by

Table 7. Maximum and Minimum Value for Component Indicators of HDI

Indicator	Maximum Value	Minimum Value
Educational access		
Adult literacy (⅔ weight)	100%	0%
Combined enrollment ratio (⅓ weight)	100%	0%
Life expectancy at birth	85 years	25 years
Transformed per capita GDP	$5,488	$200

Source: UN (1995:134).

the HDI methodology. Sri Lanka, Congo, and Pakistan have similar average incomes, but Sri Lanka clearly outranks the other two in longevity and schooling.

Of course, these HDI data provide only fragmentary evidence about the
extent and sources of well-being within particular nations. They do, however,
invite political debate on national development strategy as well as international
dialogue on development assistance policy [UN 1994:101]. Furthermore,

Table 8. Top Ten HDI Scores, 1992

Nation	Life Expectancy (Years)	Adult Literacy (%)	School Enrollment Ratio (%)	Transformed Per Capita GDP ($)	HDI Score
Canada	77.4	99	100	5,359	0.950
USA	76.0	99	95	5,374	0.937
Japan	79.5	99	77	5,359	0.937
Netherlands	77.4	99	88	5,343	0.936
Finland	75.7	99	96	5,337	0.934
Iceland	78.2	99	81	5,343	0.933
Norway	76.9	99	88	5,345	0.932
France	76.9	99	86	5,347	0.930
Spain	77.6	98	86	5,307	0.930
Sweden	78.2	99	78	5,344	0.929

Source: UN (1995:155).

Table 9. HDI Score, Selected Developing Nations, 1992

Nation	Life Expectancy (Years)	Adult Literacy (%)	School Enrollment Ratio (%)	Unadjusted Per Capita GDP ($)	HDI Score
Costa Rica	76.3	94.3	66	5,480	0.883
Brazil	66.3	81.9	70	5,240	0.804
Turkey	66.5	80.5	61	5,230	0.792
Sri Lanka	71.9	89.3	66	2,850	0.704
Congo	51.3	70.7	56	2,870	0.538
Pakistan	61.5	35.7	25	2,890	0.483

Source: UN (1995:156–157).

HDI-based research reveals "large disparities within developing countries—between urban and rural areas, between men and women, between rich and poor." [UN 1990:2] These social and economic disparities are concealed within national averages and can depress the well-being of a substantial portion of a nation's population. In U.N. 1992 report, the UNDP introduced a gender-sensitive version of the HDI. Taking account of gender differences in life expectancy, schooling, wages, and labor force participation lowers the HDI ranks of the U.S. and Canada but raises the Scandinavian countries to the top of the list. The 1992 report also introduced the use of Gini coefficients to calculate income distribution-adjusted HDI scores.

The HDI has been the subject of several critical reviews. [Kelley 1991, Srinivasan 1994] The critics have questioned whether HDI provides significant information beyond what is already available from separate indicators including GDP per capita. Goulet [1992] has suggested that the use of multiple indicators is essential to capture social, political, cultural, and ecological aspects of development.

Clearly, some important information is lost in the construction of the index. Income above basic needs levels counts for very little; specific health and nutrition data are not reflected except insofar as they affect life expectancy. Issues of political freedom and human rights are not included. Gender issues were not dealt with until 1995, when the Human Development Report offered a Gender-Related Development Index similar to HDI but adjusted for the disparities between men and women.

Despite these shortcomings, we believe that the perspectives on development revealed by the HDI, together with others offered by the ongoing series of Human Development Reports, constitute a useful contribution to the measurement of well-being and the identification of its sources. The HDI has stimulated, and will continue to stimulate, a welcome reorientation in development theory away from a narrow focus on GDP growth.

"Green National Product": The Index of Sustainable Economic Welfare

Our survey of alternatives to GDP has touched on a diverse set of issues so far. Various authors have advocated taking account of intermediate and defensive costs of production, accumulation and depreciation of both natural and also government capital, and social issues, such as poverty and discrimination. Only recently, however, have we witnessed an effort to integrate all of these issues into a single accounting scheme and to measure the welfare effects of macroeconomic activity and social inequality in a comprehensive manner. That ambitious project has been led by Herman Daly and John Cobb. [Daly and Cobb 1989, 1994]

This effort involves an interesting partnership between an economist (Daly) and a theologian (Cobb), both of whom care deeply about environmental sustainability and social justice. They acknowledge their intellectual debt to the pioneering work of Nordhaus and Tobin, who first calculated a Measure of Economic Welfare in 1972, taking account of such factors as unpaid household labor and "urban disamenities." Daly and Cobb have named their proposed substitute for GDP the Index of Sustainable Economic Welfare (ISEW). The ISEW was first calculated in 1989 for the United States over the period 1950–1986. [Daly and Cobb 1989] It has since been updated to 1990 and revised by Clifford and John Cobb in response to an extensive collection of critical responses. [Cobb and Cobb, 1994]

Daly and Cobb begin the difficult task of constructing an aggregate welfare measure by arguing that it is the current flow of services to humanity from all sources, not the current output of marketable commodities, that is relevant to economic welfare. Hence, Daly and Cobb start with the U.S. Bureau of Economic Analysis' personal consumption expenditure and then perform a lengthy series of adjustments to officially measured consumption in order to estimate the sustainable flow of useful services. (See Table 10.)

The first adjustment, one for income distribution, recognizes "that an additional thousand dollars in income adds more to the welfare of a poor family than it does to a rich family." [Daly and Cobb 1994:445] This is generally con-

Table 10. Index of Sustainable Economic Welfare, U.S., 1990 (1972 $, billions)

BEA personal consumption	$1266
Personal consumption adjusted for income distribution	$1164
+Services of household labor	+$520
+Services of consumer durables	+$225
+Services of highways and streets	+$18
+Consumption portion of public spending on health and education	+$45
−Spending on consumer durables	−$235
−Defensive private spending on health and education	−$63
−Cost of commuting and auto accidents	−$67
−Cost of personal pollution control	−$5
−Cost of air, water, and noise pollution	−$39
−Loss of wetlands and farmland	−$58
−Depletion of nonrenewable resources	−$313
−Long-term damages from nuclear wastes, greenhouse gases, and ozone depletion	−$371
+Net capital growth	+$29
+Change in net international investment position	−$34
Index of Sustainable Economic Welfare	$818

Source: Daly and Cobb (1994: Table A.1).
Note: Total differs from sum of items due to rounding.

sistent with the principle of diminishing marginal utility of income but differs sharply from the neoclassical practice of accepting unadjusted dollar incomes as proxies for utility or well-being.[30] Thus, the greater the degree of income inequality, the lower the flow of economic welfare associated with a particular aggregate flow of consumption services.[31]

After adjusting BEA consumption expenditure for income inequality, Daly and Cobb take account of four service flows currently omitted from that official consumption measure: those derived from household labor, from the existing consumer durable stock, from public streets and highways, and from public spending on health and education. The authors admit, and rightly so, that their imputation for household labor is too low since each hour is valued at the wage rate of paid domestic workers (and hence no value is placed on managerial functions within the home). In our opinion, Daly and Cobb also underestimate the services of government programs since they claim that "government expenditures . . . are largely defensive in nature . . . [and do] not so much add to net welfare as prevent the deterioration of well-being by maintaining security, environmental health, and the capacity to continue commerce." [1994:467]

This claim that government programs are largely defensive even extends to public (and, for that matter, private) education. Despite decades of scholarly research on the economics of education, the authors contend that schooling mainly serves to ration job vacancies by making credentials scarce and hence qualifies as neither consumption nor capital formation. Not surprisingly, Eisner has identified "the almost complete exclusion of human capital" as the most serious defect of the ISEW accounting framework. [1994:99]

Daly and Cobb continue their journey from personal consumption expenditure to sustainable economic welfare by deducting current spending on consumer durables. Since it is the entire stock of consumer durables that provides services, not newly purchased durables, this is an appropriate adjustment. (As Table 10 shows, however, imputed services of the consumer durable stock and spending on new household durables roughly cancel one another.) The authors also try to account for personal spending of a defensive or intermediate, not welfare-producing, nature by deducting household costs of commuting, auto accidents, and pollution control. Personal expenditures on education and medical care are also assumed to be in large measure defensive and not a net contributor to human well-being.

Still another deduction from personal consumption is an estimate of the current cost of air, water, and noise pollution. For 1990, this amount equalled $39 billion (in 1972 dollars), a surprisingly low figure. Daly and Cobb mention several reasons for believing that their estimate of current pollution damages is too low. [1994:471–477] One is that their water pollution estimate includes the effects of siltation and point discharges into waterways but not the impact of nonpoint emissions. Another is that their estimate of air pollution cost includes damages to crops, forests, and durable equipment but excludes human health effects.[32]

The depletion of natural assets is another set of concerns addressed by Daly and Cobb. Following the example of Repetto et al. (1989), they estimate and then deduct the annual loss of productive services associated with the past and present conversion of wetlands and farmland to urban uses. A marsh area converted to an airport runway, for example, no longer provides present and future benefits of flood protection, groundwater purification and storage, wildlife preservation, and scenic vistas. The loss of high-quality farmland to suburban development or soil erosion requires that crops be grown on less fertile fields with heavier doses of chemical fertilizers. Because Daly and Cobb assume that land development is irreversible, that substitutes for the services of wetlands and farmland are not readily available, and that the marginal annual loss of benefits rises with cumulative land conversion, their accounting methodology ensures escalating aggregate costs of land development as time unfolds.[33]

Extraction of nonrenewable energy in the forms of oil, coal, natural gas, and nuclear fuel is another category of natural capital depletion incorporated in ISEW. As Daly and Cobb correctly observe, "depletion of nonrenewable resources . . . [is] a cost borne by future generations that should be subtracted from (debited to) the capital account of the present generation." [1994:482]

But what economic value should be placed on this debit entry in society's ledger? Although the architects of ISEW express qualified appreciation for the user-cost approach of El Serafy (1993), they opt instead for valuing the annual depletion of nonrenewable energy reserves at the hypothetical marginal cost of a renewable substitute, ethanol.[34] Because they assume that the real marginal cost of producing ethanol rises 3 percent annually, their estimate of the aggregate value of energy depletion escalates rapidly even if the physical flow of nonrenewable energy extraction stagnates. (See Table 11 for their U.S. estimate.)

Table 11. ISEW Estimate of U.S. Nonrenewable Energy Depletion

Year	Actual U.S. Nonrenewable Energy Output (billions of barrels)	Assumed Marginal Cost of Ethanol (1972 $ per barrel)	Estimated Nonrenewable Energy Depletion (billions of 1972 $)
1950	5.6	$8.3	$46.8
1970	10.2	$15.3	$157.0
1990	11.1	$28.1	$312.6

Source: Daly and Cobb (1994:501).
Note: The BTU content of coal, ethanol, natural gas, and nuclear fuel has been converted to an equivalent number of barrels of petroleum.

Having deducted various forms of natural capital depletion from society's current flow of consumption services, Daly and Cobb next try to account for the environmental damages imposed on future generations because of past economic activity. [1994:487–491] In particular, the ISEW methodology acknowledges that fossil fuel combustion, nuclear energy production, and chlorofluorcarbon (CFC) use result in the accumulation of stocks of persistent pollutants within the global environment. These stocks include atmospheric methane and carbon dioxide, stratospheric chlorine, and spent nuclear fuel.

Although Daly and Cobb are correct that transferring expanding stocks of hazardous materials to future generations is inconsistent with sustainable development, their method for estimating these long-term environmental damages is incomplete at best. In the case of greenhouse gases and nuclear wastes, they assume that the long-term environmental damages resulting from nonrenewable energy use and suffered by U.S. citizens are proportional to the *cumulative* consumption of fossil fuels and nuclear power within the U.S. since 1900.[35]

This methodology has several serious flaws. First, it assumes that there is a fixed proportion between current nonrenewable energy use and current emissions of persistent pollutants even if the mixture of nonrenewable fuels evolves over time.[36] Second, it assumes that energy-related pollutants persist indefinitely once emitted into the environment. This premise ignores the finite, though lengthy, half lives of many environmental pollutants. Finally, since greenhouse gases circulate throughout the atmosphere regardless of their country of origin, the long-term damages from fossil fuel consumption suffered by U.S. citizens depend upon past trends in global energy consumption, not just those in the U.S.

When they account for the long-term damages to stratospheric ozone resulting from CFC production and use, Daly and Cobb employ a somewhat different methodology: ISEW assigns an environmental cost of $5 per year to each kilogram of cumulative world production of CFC-11 and CFC-12. The use of global output is entirely appropriate since the welfare loss from ozone depletion suffered by U.S. residents is indifferent to the country of origin of CFC molecules. As with fossil fuels and nuclear energy, however, ISEW ignores the eventual depreciation of a persistent pollutant, in this case the stratospheric chlorine associated with CFC use. Furthermore, the ISEW estimate ignores the lengthy time lags from CFC production to CFC discharge into the troposphere to CFC arrival in the stratosphere. These lags are important determinants of the time pattern of damages associated with CFC production.

We mention these criticisms not in an effort to discredit the ISEW methodology but rather to alert the reader to a crucial point. Daly and Cobb have transformed BEA consumption into ISEW via a sequence of 20 specific adjustments. In the end, however, most of those adjustments are too small to explain the growing divergence between per capita GNP and per capita ISEW that seems to have occurred since 1970. (See Figure 1.)

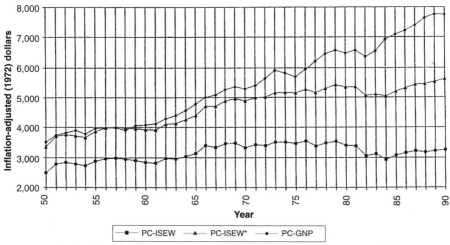

PC-GNP is per capita GNP.
PC-ISEW is per capita Index of Sustainable Economic Welfare.
PC-ISEW* is per capita ISEW excluding adjustments for depletion of natural
resources and long-term environmental damage.

Figure 1. Alternative Measures of Economic Welfare.
Source: Cobb and Cobb (1994: Figure C-1).

As Table 12 shows, personal consumption expenditure in the U.S. grew by
$928 billion between 1950 and 1990. During that same period, ISEW grew by
only $438 billion. Hence, the total adjustments to BEA consumption shifted in
a negative direction by $490 billion between 1950 and 1990, thereby ensuring
divergent time paths for the measures of official consumption and sustainable
welfare. Over 58 percent of that change in total adjustments to personal consumption—more than $285 billion—is accounted for by the estimated long-
term damages from nonrenewable energy and CFC use. For various reasons already noted, however, the ISEW estimates of those damages are highly
speculative and very preliminary. Hence, the growing gap between GNP and
ISEW could be an artifact of the ISEW methodology and not an accurate measure of empirical trends.[37]

Daly and Cobb complete their computation of ISEW by taking account of
changes in the domestic and international capital position of the U.S. economy.
They argue, quite properly, that the current level of economic well-being can be
sustained only if growth in the domestic capital stock matches population
growth, thereby equipping workers with the same amount of capital per head in
the future as in the past. Their measure of net capital growth is far too narrow,
however, since it focuses on business investments in tangible plant and equipment and ignores social investments in human skills, scientific knowledge, and
ecological restoration. Their final adjustment, for changes in the net interna-

Table 12. Components of the Gap between Official Consumption and ISEW (billions of 1972 $)

Year	BEA Consumption (1)	Total Adjustments to Consumption (2)	ISEW (1) + (2)	Long-Term Environmental Damages
1950	337.3	+42.9	380.2	−85.1
1990	1,265.6	−447.4	818.2	−370.6
Change, 1950–1990	+928.3	−490.3	+438.0	−285.5

Source: Daly and Cobb (1994: Table A.1).

tional investment position of a nation's economy, is a compelling one. No country, not even the United States, can indefinitely sustain a particular level of domestic economic welfare by selling its physical assets to foreigners and by accumulating financial liabilities abroad.

In sum, Daly and Cobb have successfully synthesized many of the criticisms of national income accounting within a single welfare-oriented framework. The revised version of the ISEW presented by Cobb and Cobb also takes into account criticisms raised by a number of highly qualified commentators. [Cobb and Cobb, 1994] As the authors readily admit, however, many of their numerical estimates are still preliminary and based on highly speculative assumptions. Hence, ISEW should be seen as a springboard for future research on national accounting and not as a completed framework filled with accurate data.

Conclusion

By this point it should be clear that the quest for an alternative—or alternatives—to GNP/GDP is far from over. None of the efforts we have cited has managed to solve all of the conceptual and data-gathering problems.

It is of great importance that understanding human well-being, and the components that go into it, should continue to improve; for this, continued work on a variety of indicators is critical. Among the large, public efforts that have been described here, we feel that continued support is especially merited for the satellite accounts being developed by the U.N., by the U.S. Department of Commerce, as well as by Norway, France, the Netherlands, and Japan. The Human Development Index of the UN Development Programme is the leading international social indicator and should be widely used and further developed. Among private efforts, we have paid the most attention to the ambitious scope and careful, though unfinished, work of ISEW. It continues to be refined through the work of the organizations Redefining Progress and the Human Economy Center.

This survey has shown the necessity to reject the temptation, often unconscious, to use gross national or domestic product as a measure of social well-being and overall economic progress. We have seen that GNP/GDP as an accounting device is vulnerable to a number of criticisms. These may seem technical to those not immersed in the arcana of accounting, but the human meaning of the technical issues is that faulty policy may result from misuse of these tools. As Simon Kuznets emphasized in the early days of GNP accounting, the technical issues reflect value judgments, and these value judgments will in turn be reflected in policy formulation.

While noting several efforts that are eminently worthy of public and private support, we caution that it may not only be the indicators that must change: the users must also adjust to some new ideas. Perhaps chief among these is the idea that there is no single indicator that will do all that we want. One indicator may be most appropriate for one purpose and a different one for a different purpose. The most important use of all is the attempt to answer the frequently posed questions: How are we doing? Are things getting better or worse? How can we judge the success of our major policies? For this purpose—the broad assessment of human welfare—we may need to accustom ourselves to the idea of using several different indices. (See the Henderson summary, in the previous section and work by Dennis Goulet referred to earlier.)

This suggests an important role for education, in helping policy makers as well as the public to achieve more tolerance for complexity—for the realization that important issues cannot generally be well represented in a single, simple bottom line. We conclude this essay then, with a challenge to us all: to continue developing, and supporting the development of, better indicators and to temper our hopes and wishes, so as to see in any indicator only what it can show and not what it cannot show.

Notes

1. For the formal distinction between GNP and GDP, see footnote 1 in Part IX's Overview Essay.

2. Juster (1973:26), for example, observes that "[E]conomists generally have no desire to turn the accounts into some sort of happiness index. . . . [There] may well be more important considerations than mere material goods and services, but they are not within the purview of the economist or the social accountant."

3. In a similar vein, see Maddison (1991:5–8).

4. For earlier discussions of this set of issues, see Kuznets (1941) and Juster (1973).

5. He did, however, weaken this criterion by including foodstuffs consumed on the farm and services of owner-occupied housing (Kuznets 1941:9).

6. Kuznets mentioned, as other sources of satisfaction excluded from GDP, services

produced within the household that could have been purchased in the marketplace (clothes washing, shaving, etc.), but one might also add conversations with one's friends and viewing a beautiful sunset.

7. His reluctance seems rooted in a commitment to some combination of humanist philosophy and neoclassical economics: "[Widening] the scope of intermediate consumption . . . reduces the net national product . . . to that exceedingly minor magnitude that may be considered as not involved in the replacement of all goods, human capacity included, consumed in the process of economic production. No purely analytical or empirical consideration can invalidate this extension. . . . [However, we] do not look upon human beings . . . as units for the production of other goods; consequently, we do not view the raising and education of the younger generation or the sustenance of the working population as intermediate consumption destined to produce or sustain so many [human] machines . . . It is this idea of economic goods existing for men, rather than men for economic goods, that gives point to the concept of ultimate consumption. . . ." (Kuznets 1941:37–38).

8. Repetto et al. point out, however, that the "notion of 'defensive' expenditures is elusive, since spending on food can be considered a defense against hunger, clothing a defense against cold, and religion a defense against sin." (1989:17)

9. In the WRI study of Indonesia, domestic output adjusted for resource depletion exceeded official GDP in 1974 by 35.7 percent because of significant discoveries of new oil reserves (Repetto et al. 1989:4, 39).

10. In the user cost method, the discovery of new reserves is not directly included in GDP, but will somewhat reduce the user cost deduction, because it extends the expected lifetime n of the reserve and thus reduces the fraction $1/(1+r)^{n+1}$.

11. El Serafy (1993) discusses these and other policy distortions resulting from use of the standard GDP measure.

12. A similar set of indicators can be found in the World Bank's Social Indicators of Development annuals.

13. To be fair to the World Bank staff, we need to point out that they are fully aware of these criticisms. See, for example, World Bank (1994:230–234).

14. The official accounting scheme does count business purchases to accumulate inventories as spending on final output (inventory investment).

15. The U.S. Commerce Department accounts do include an imputation for the market value of services produced by owner-occupied housing units. Otherwise, the household sector is assumed to consume, not produce, final goods and services.

16. In particular, the approach taken by the U.N. and the U.S. Commerce Department's Bureau of Economic Analysis has much in common with the proposals by Henry Peskin (1981, 1991) for a sector-specific valuation of environmental services and environmental damages. Peskin notes this similarity in a recent paper (1996) but also notes that his approach is driven more by economic theory, while the UN/BEA approaches are driven more by a need for consistency with existing GNP/GDP accounts.

17. For a brief description of the U.N. accounting reforms, see Bartelmus (1992). This system of environmental and economic accounting, SEEA for short, is discussed in detail in the 1993 U.N. report.

18. Interestingly, in the early days of U.S. national income accounting, "depletion

[of natural resources] was treated symmetrically with depreciation [of plant and equipment], but no entry was made for additions to the stock of mineral resources parallel to the treatment of investments in structures and equipment. As a result of dissatisfaction with this asymmetric treatment, the entry for depletion was removed . . . in 1947" (BEA 1994:36).

19. The two exceptions are business inventories, which are assumed to not depreciate and environmental stocks of air and water. In the latter case, it is hard to imagine how one would estimate the total value of the world's atmosphere and waters so the BEA proposes measuring only the monetary value of changes in air and water quality (BEA 1994:46).

20. The literacy scale ranges from 0 to 100 percent of the population 15 years and older who are literate. The infant mortality scale ranges from 229 deaths (0 percent) to 7 deaths (100 percent) per 1,000 live births. The life expectancy scale extends from 38 years (0 percent) to 77 years (100 percent). These ranges were chosen to allow improved future performance even by those countries with the best current score for each indicator (Morris 1979:41–44).

21. Excluding oil-exporting nations, the correlation between PQLI score and per capita GNP is very high for affluent nations.

22. The Population Crisis Committee (1992) reports that unemployment, external debt, child labor, extent of urban slums and other indicators were also considered, but the criterion used to pick the indicators in Table 7 is unclear.

23. One might also question the use of telephones per capita to measure access to "communications technology." In some nations, the postal service provides phone access to its customers. Hence, personal phone ownership is not essential in those countries.

24. A panel of outside consultants, including Gustav Ranis, A. K. Sen, Keith Griffin, Meghnad Desai, and Paul Streeten, assisted the UNDP (UN 1990:iv).

25. Purchasing-power-parity dollars compare incomes across countries in terms of ability to purchase goods, rather than by using currency exchange rates. This avoids the distortion introduced by unrealistic or volatile exchange rates.

26. In the original 1990 U.N. report, the transformed income figure was the log of real per capita GDP levels up to $4,861 (the average official poverty line for 9 industrial nations). Above $4,861, it was assumed that extra per capita real GDP yielded no additional human development. This stringent assumption was relaxed in later reports, probably in reaction to criticism. For a survey of criticisms of the original HDI specification, see UN (1991:88–91).

27. The original HDI used adult literacy to measure educational access (UN 1990). From 1991–1994, the UNDP reports used a weighted average of adult literacy and mean years of schooling. Since 1995, the combined enrollment ratio for primary, secondary, and tertiary education has replaced mean years of schooling (UN 1995).

28. Until its 1994 report, the UNDP used the actual maximum and minimum values for each indicator within the sample of nations surveyed during a year. That practice led to a "moving goalpost" problem. Revised scores are now available for 1960–1992 using "fixed goalposts" in UN (1994:105). The maximum real GDP per capita is now set at $40,000, corresponding to a transformed income of $5,448 for 1995.

29. One fact revealed by the HDI methodology is the poor life expectancy of the average U.S. citizen compared to the average Canadian, Japanese, or European. That difference reflects, in large measure, the poor life prospects of Afro-Americans (Sen 1993:44–45). Thus, despite having a higher unadjusted average income, the U.S. ranks below Canada in HDI score.

30. In one of the critical responses collected by Clifford and John Cobb in their volume on The Green National Product, Eisner (1994:100) does not object to Daly and Cobb's declining-marginal-utility-of-income assumption but argues that their adjustment for income inequality should take place after all other adjustments to BEA consumption have occurred. In the second edition of For the Common Good, Daly and Cobb note, but fail to pursue, the self-criticism that "our calculus of economic well-being has failed to take in account . . . that happiness is apparently correlated with relative rather than absolute levels of wealth or consumption" (Daly and Cobb 1994: 460). Recall the arguments of Duesenberry (1949).

31. The authors considered several indexes of distributional inequality (harmonic means of quintiles, Gini coefficient, etc.) but chose an index based on the share of income accruing to the lowest quintile of households. This approach, they argue, "gives special weight to the plight of the poorest members of society, which fits well with the theory of justice propounded by John Rawls" (Daly and Cobb 1994:465).

32. The authors also acknowledge that their time-series estimates of annual changes in pollution costs are highly unreliable.

33. An alternative approach to the valuation of environmental losses has been suggested by Roefie Hueting (1991). He suggests the establishment of a standard for environmental sustainability (e.g., maintenance of soil fertility). An estimate of the costs of meeting this standard (e.g., through soil conservation measures) would then be the figure used to correct national income to account for unsustainable use of natural resources.

34. This is consistent with Hueting (1991), who also suggests using the costs of an alternative, renewable technology to evaluate the depreciation of nonrenewable resources.

35. The factor of proportionality assumed is $0.50 of future annual damages per barrel-equivalent of nonrenewable energy consumption, in 1972 real dollars.

36. During the 20th century, petroleum and natural gas have substituted for coal in many nations. Since coal is a dirtier fuel, that substitution has lowered the emissions propensity of nonrenewable energy use.

37. Manfred Max-Neef (1995) presents data suggesting declining sustainable welfare in several industrial countries, using an ISEW index for the United Kingdom, Germany, Austria, and the Netherlands. However, this hypothesis may simply reflect repeated application of the same imperfect methodology, not empirical evidence that economic growth lowers the quality of life.

References

Barro, Robert J., and Xavier Sala-i-Martin. 1995. *Economic Growth*. New York: Mc-Graw-Hill.

Bartelmus, Peter. 1992. "Accounting for Sustainable Growth and Development." *Structural Change and Economic Dynamics*. 3(2): December. 241–260.

Bureau of Economic Analysis. 1994. "Integrated Economic and Environmental Satellite Accounts." *Survey of Current Business*. 74(4): April. 33–49.

Carson, Carol S. 1975. "The History of the United States National Income and Product Accounts: The Development of an Analytical Tool." *Review of Income and Wealth*. 21(2): June. 153–181.

Cobb, Clifford W. and John B. Cobb. 1994. *The Green National Product: A Proposed Index of Sustainable Economic Welfare*. Lanham, Maryland: University Press of America.

Daly, Herman E., and John B. Cobb. [1989] 1994. *For the Common Good:Redirecting the Economy Toward Community, the Environment, and a Sustainable Future*. Boston: Beacon.

Duesenbury, James B. 1949. *Income, Saving, and the Theory of Consumer Behavior*. Cambridge, MA: Harvard University Press.

Eisner, Robert. 1978. "Total Incomes in the United States, 1959 and 1969." *Review of Income and Wealth*. 24(1): March. 41–70.

———. 1985. "The Total Incomes System of Accounts." *Survey of Current Business*. 65(1). 24–48.

———. 1989. *The Total Incomes System of Accounts*. Chicago: University of Chicago Press.

———. 1994. "The Index of Sustainable Welfare: Comment." In Clifford Cobb and John Cobb, eds., *The Green National Product*. Lanham: University Press of America. 97–110.

El Serafy, Salah. 1993. "Country Macroeconomic Work and Natural Resources." *Environment Working Paper No. 58*. Washington, DC: The World Bank.

———. 1996. "Weak and Strong Sustainability: Natural Resources and National Accounting." *Environmental Taxation and Accounting*. 1(1): May. 27–48.

Goulet, Denis. 1992. "Development Indicators: A Research Problem, A Policy Problem," *Journal of Socio-Economics*. 21(3). 245–260.

Hueting, Roefie. 1991. "Correcting National Income for Environmental Losses: A Practical Solution for a Theoretical Dilemma." In Robert Costanza, ed., *Ecological Economics: The Science and Management of Sustainability*. New York: Columbia University Press.

Juster, F. Thomas. 1973. "A Framework for the Measurement of Economic and Social Performance." In Milton Moss, ed., *The Measurement of Economic and Social Performance*. New York: Columbia University Press.

Kelley, Allen C. 1991. "The Human Development Index: 'Handle with Care.'" *Population and Development Review* 17(2): June. 315–324.

Kuznets, Simon. 1941. *National Income and Its Composition, 1919–1938.* New York: National Bureau of Economic Research.

Lange, Glenn-Marie, and Faye Duchin. 1993. "Integrated Environmental-Economic Accounting, Natural Resource Accounts, and Natural Resource Management in Africa." Prepared as Technical Report No. 13 of Winrock International for USAID Bureau for Africa. Summarized in Rajaram Krishnan, Jonathan M. Harris, and Neva R. Goodwin, eds., *A Survey of Ecological Economics.* Washington, DC: Island Press.

Leipert, Christian. 1989. "Social Costs of the Economic Process and National Accounts: The Example of Defensive Expenditures." *Journal of Interdisciplinary Economics* 3(2): 27–46.

Maddison, Angus. 1991. *Dynamic Forces in Capitalist Development.* Oxford: Oxford University Press.

Max-Neef, Manfred. 1995. "Economic Growth and Quality of Life: A Threshold Hypothesis." *Ecological Economics.* 15(2): November. 115–118.

Morris, David. 1979. *Measuring the Condition of the World's Poor: The Physical Quality of Life Index.* New York: Pergamon.

Nordhaus, William, and James Tobin. 1972. "Is Growth Obsolete?" *In National Bureau of Economic Research, Economic Growth. Research General Series, No. 96E.* New York: Columbia University Press.

Peskin, Henry M. 1981. "National Income Accounts and the Environment." *Natural Resources Journal.* 21: July. 511–537.

———. 1991. "Alternative Environmental and Resource Accounting Approaches." In Robert Costanza, ed., *Ecological Economics: The Science and Management of Sustainability.* New York: Columbia University Press.

———. 1996. "Alternative Resource and Environmental Accounting Approaches and Their Contribution to Policy." Italy: Fondazione Eni Enrico Mattei Noti Di Lavoro (Working Papers Series) 77.96.

Population Crisis Committee. 1992. *The International Human Suffering Index.* Washington: Population Crisis Committee.

Repetto, Robert et al. 1989. *Wasting Assets: Natural Resources in the National Income Accounts.* Washington, DC: World Resources Institute.

Ruggles, Richard. 1991. "Review of The Total Incomes, System of Accounts by Robert Eisner." *Review of Income and Wealth.* 37(4): December. 455–460.

———. 1993. "National Income Accounting: Concepts and Measurement. Economic Theory and Practice." *Economic Notes by Monte dei Pashi di Siena.* 22(2). 235–264.

Sen, A. K. 1981. *Poverty and Famines.* Oxford: Oxford University Press.

———. 1992. *Inequality Reexamined.* Cambridge, MA: Harvard University Press.

———. 1993. "The Economics of Life and Death." *Scientific American.* 268(5): May. 40–47.

Srinivasan, T. N. 1994. "Human Development: A New Paradigm or Reinvention of the Wheel?" *American Economic Review*. 84(2): May. 238–243.

United Nations Department for Economic and Social Information and Policy Analysis, Statistical Division. 1993. *Integrated Environmental and Economic Accounting*. New York: United Nations.

United Nations Development Program. 1990–1996. *Human Development Report*. Oxford: Oxford University Press.

World Bank. 1978. *World Development Report, 1978*. Washington, DC: The World Bank.

———. 1994. *World Development Report, 1994*. Oxford: Oxford University Press.

———. 1995. *Social Indicators of Development*. Baltimore: Johns Hopkins University Press.

Subject Index

Fable of the Bees: or, Private Vices, Publick Benefits (Mandeville), 7, 17–18
Factor-selective egalitarianism, 264–66
Fairness:
  and equality, 269
  justice as, 276–79
  opportunity, equality of, 240
  perceptions of, 105
  policy, development/economic, 270
  theory of, 254–55
False consciousness, 12
Family life, 30, 32
Federal Reserve Bank, 336
Feminists, 228
First Principles (Spencer), 75
Food distribution, egalitarian, 28
Forgone wage, 360
For the Common Good: Redirecting the Economy Toward Community, the Environment, and a Sustainable Future (Daly and Cobb, Jr.), 29
Fortitude, 16
Framing effects, 167, 178
France, 50–52, 64, 98, 324, 332, 398
Freedom and the market, relationship between, 34–35, 39–40, 293, 298, 299, 306–7
Frontier Issues in Economic Thought series, xvii–xvix
Fully Sustainable Development, xxvii
Functionings/capabilities, development ethic based on, 284–85, 304–6
Future events and Keynes's philosophy, 98

Game theory, 89, 112, 114
Gang behavior, 221
GDP (gross domestic product), xxvi, xxxi, 7, 11, 33, 282, 377–78, 389–90
  see also Accounting, national income
Gender inequalities, 285, 309, 392
General Theory of Interest, Employment, and Money (Keynes), 84
Genetics and subjective well-being, 8
Germany, 332, 376–77
Gift exchange norms, 39
Global Development and Environment Institute (G-DAE), ii, xxiii, xxiv
GNP (gross national product), xxvi, xxxi, 7, 282
  alternative measures of income and well-being, 381–98

defending, 374
depreciation of manufactured/natural capital assets, 377–81
equity/investment and well-being, 337–38
household contribution to, 357
implications of widespread acceptance of, 335
improved social indicators, 371–72
intermediate *vs.* final goods, 375–77
means-ends confusion, 310
output, problematic measure of economic, 347–51
problem with, the, 370–71
reexamining old indicators, 369–70
what does it measure, 336–37
women, exclusion/undervaluation of, 338–39
  see also Accounting, national income
God and property rights, 50
Good, the, 85, 245, 273–75, 305–6
Good life, the, 247–48, 284
Goods:
  collective, 19–20
  demerit, 20
  dominant, monopolistic control of, 257
  environmental, 137–38, 159–60
  ethical limitations of the market, 37–38
  external, 16
  final, 375–77
  intermediate, 375–77
  merit, 20
  national income, 342–44
  negative-rights, 298
  political, 39
  positional, 217, 350
  positive-rights, 284, 300–301
  preference satisfaction, 170
  public, 19–20, 215–16
  shared, 39–40
  social, 5–7, 24–25
  social meanings of, 256–57
  of the soul, 16
Government:
  aggregate individual preferences/design policies, 102
  art sponsored by, 38
  Bentham, Jeremy, 63
  Burke, Edmund, 98
  censorship, 38

criminal behavior, 222
freedom and the market, relationship
  between, 307
Keynes, John M., 100
lump-sum transfers, 105
market approach to government
  funding, 38
Mill, John S., 67
neoclassical economic model, 135
Nozick, Robert, 241
people's capitalism, 254
Pigou and Coase, theories of, 134
property rights, 137
regulation, 132–33
Veblen, Thorstein, 79
Greatest happiness principle, 62–63, 74
Green national product, 392–98
Green taxes, 122, 127
Gross and net, distinction between, 345
Group differences, 230

*Handbook of Game Theory with Economic
  Applications* (Aumann and Hart), 113
*Handbook of Integrated Environmental
  and Economic Accounting,* 366, 368
Happiness and satisfaction with life, 29,
  62–63, 74
  Aristotelian approach, 16
  Bentham, Jeremy, 61, 63
  declining well-being, indicators and
    causes of, 30
  egalitarian individualism, 52
  historical turning point?, 32–33
  interpersonal comparisons, 114
  labor market externalities, 31–32
  material well-being, 26–27
  money, 30–31
  moral values, 24
  myths, 174–75
  psychological realism and economic
    assumptions, 166–67
  social values, 6
  socioeconomic outputs, 6
  theory of happiness, 176–77
  traits shared by happy people, 175–76
Harmony of interests in the marketplace,
  78
Harvard Law Review, 141, 149
Health and material well-being, 27–28
Health maintenance organizations
  (HMOs), 319

Hedonistic theories, 51, 75, 148, 191–92,
  194–95
History of economic thought, 49
  Aristotelian approach, 16–17
  *Fable of the Bees: or, Private Vices,
    Publick Benefits,* 17–18
  founding fathers (Smith and Bentham),
    50–52
  mid-century changes (Mill, Bastiat, and
    Marx), 52–53
  modern view, 18
  neoclassical economic model, 53–57
  overview, 15–16
  Reformation, the, 17
*History of Economic Thought: A Critical
  Perspective,* 64, 77
Holistic approach to valuation, 139
Honesty, acquisition of a reputation for,
  232–33
Household labor, 355–61
Human Development Index (HDI),
  282–83, 292–93, 370, 371, 389–92,
  398
Human existence *vs.* essence, 68
Human nature, 75, 105
Human Suffering Index (HSI),
  388–89
Human transactionism, 15
Hypothetical valuation, 139, 140

Idealism, philosophical, 74
Ideal markets, 9, 86
Ideology that prevails in the economic
  society, 25
Imperfect information, 102, 104–5
Imperfect markets, 118–19
Imperfect rights, 58, 59
Imperialist expansion, 79
Impersonal market norms, 37
Impossibility of a Paretian Liberal (Sen),
  245
Incentive issues, 105–6, 206
Income:
  distribution, 20
  inequality, 217–18, 284
  marginal utility of, 96
  nation's per capita, 281
  security, 32
  well-being and poverty, 295
  see also Accounting, national income
Incomplete markets, 102, 104–5

Name Index

423